Experiential Learning
and Change

Experiential Learning and Change

THEORY DESIGN AND PRACTICE

GORDON A. WALTER

Associate Professor of Organizational Behavior
and Industrial Relations
Faculty of Commerce and Business Administration
The University of British Columbia

STEPHEN E. MARKS

Associate Professor of Counseling Psychology
Faculty of Education
The University of British Columbia

A Wiley-Interscience Publication

JOHN WILEY & SONS, New York · Chichester · Brisbane · Toronto

Library of Congress Cataloging in Publication Data:

Walter, Gordon A 1943–
   Experiential learning and change.

   "A Wiley-Interscience publication."

   Includes bibliographical references and index.

   1. Learning, Psychology of. 2. Change (Psychology)
3. Social psychology. I. Marks, Stephen E., 1942–
joint author.

LB1051.W235   370.15′23   81–330
ISBN 0-471-08355-0   AACR1

Printed in the United States of America

10 9 8 7 6 5 4 3 2 1

To
our mothers
Florence Walter and Anita Marks
and in memory of
our fathers
Charles Walter and Joseph Marks
and
also in memory of
Charles Monroe Walter

Preface

The purpose of this book is to provide unity to a field that is currently fragmented. Experiential learning is often seen as a technique, a gimmick, an illustration, or something appended to other fields. Competing approaches, disciplines, and schools of thought devote more time to trying to prove that their view is the best one rather than learning from adherents of different approaches. In contrast, this book does not take sides, nor does it advocate one school of thought. More important, experiential learning is seen as a *field in and of itself* and not symbiotic with a single therapy, technique, theory, or methodology. In short, the book strives for systematization and integration of the diverse, exciting, and growing new field of experiential learning and change.

The book is arranged in two parts, each of which addresses broad issues common to a variety of experiential approaches. Following the general Introduction, Part 1 examines the foundations for experiental learning. Chapter 1 describes seven model types of human functioning that organize a wide variety of different theoretical explanations of human behavior. The rest of Part 1 consists of a typology of underlying change processes affecting human behavior. Part 1 addresses the question of *how and why* individuals learn and change. Part 2 emphasizes applications. Sixteen common methods of instruction are analyzed using the concepts presented in Part 1, and a comprehensive and concrete approach to conducting and designing experiential learning activities is offered. It gives our view of *what to do*. Part 1 is a foundation or analytical basis for the actual pragmatics of designing and conducting learning experiences discussed in Part 2. Individuals mostly interested in theory and research relating to individual change could concentrate on Part 1, while those interested in applications could concentrate on Part 2.

The book avoids the excessive detail characteristic of treatments of specific aspects of learning processes and the narrowness of books written for specific settings or specific types of activities. It can be read at many levels so that both beginning and advanced practitioners in the field of conducting learning experiences will find material of value in it.

Contributions to and responsibility for various aspects of the book are detailed as follows: Part 1 is primarily researched and written by Gordon Walter. In Part 2, the description portions of the methods chapters are primarily researched and written by Stephen Marks, who also conceived the set of dimensions in Chapter 11. The phases of learning schema of Chapter 7 originally appeared in brief form in an article coauthored by Marks and William L. Davis. The remainder of Part 2 and the introduction essentially were written jointly, and the entire work benefits from extensive mutual editing, criticism, and rewriting by both authors.

We have received guidance, reference leads, feedback, expert judgments, material from private libraries, opinions, and encouragement from a large number of friends and colleagues. In particular, we thank Merle Ace, Peter Frost, Ralph Loffmark, Vance Mitchell, Larry Moore, and Craig Pinder in the Faculty of Commerce and Business Administration, Marshall Arlin, Vince D'Oyley, Les Greenberg, Sharon Kahn, and especially Steve Foster in the Faculty of Education, and Ken Craig in the Department of Psychology, all at The University of British Columbia. From other universities, we are indebted to Larry Cummings, Tom Cummings, Gerald Leinwand, Craig Lundberg, Sandy Martin, and Raymond Miles, and outside the university to Mal Weinstein of the City of Vancouver Health Department and our close friend Michael McDowell. We would also like to thank the many students who assisted us with the project: Ian Forsythe, Marian Fraser, Brian Harper, Derek Nordin, and especially Toni Demers, and Betty Andersen, and Marie Long, Betty Reid, Nancy Schell, and Lucy Westaway, who helped with the typing of some of the manuscript; we thank Cam MacDonald, whose word processing expertise and commitment to our task was indispensable in assembling the manuscript. Dean Peter Lusztig provided very useful support, aid, and advice throughout the project. Grant number W76-0827 of the H.S.S.R.C. (formerly the Canada Council) was of critical value to the scope and depth attained in this work. Finally, our loving appreciation is extended to Dorothy Walter and Donna Meadwell for their understanding and support throughout the project. Without all these people, completing the task would not have been possible. Thank you.

GORDON A. WALTER
STEPHEN E. MARKS

Vancouver, British Columbia
February 1981

Contents

Experiential Learning and Change

Experiential Learning and Change

Introduction

I never teach my pupils;
I only attempt to provide
the conditions in which
they can learn.

Albert Einstein

For the purpose of this book, experiential learning is defined as a sequence of events with one or more identified learning objectives, requiring active involvement by participants at one or more points in the sequence. That is, lessons are presented, illustrated, highlighted, and supported through the involvement of the participants. The central tenet of experiential learning is that one learns best by doing.

Experiential learning has evolved from being an exploratory, experimental technique in the 1950s and 1960s in growth centers such as the National Training Laboratories and the Esalen Institute, to being common practice currently wherever learning is pursued. Its principles and techniques are derived from modern theories of effective learning, as documented by Cantor, 1946, 1953; Knowles, 1970, 1975; Postman and Weingartner, 1969; Rogers, 1969; and others. In 1953, for example, Nathaniel Cantor, in *The Teaching—Learning Process* (1953, pp. 286–312), outlines the following nine propositions for modern learning:

1 The pupil learns only what he is interested in learning.
2 It is important that the pupil share in the development and management of the curriculum.
3 Learning is integral; genuine learning is not an additive experience but a remaking of experience.
4 Learning depends on wanting to learn.
5 An individual learns best when he is free to create his own responses in a situation.

1

6 Learning depends on not knowing the answers.
7 Every pupil learns in his own way.
8 Learning is largely an emotional experience.
9 To learn is to change.

Cantor's nine points about effective learning also can be applied to the general qualities of experiential learning, wherein the emphasis is placed on engaging the individual in the experience of learning. In contrast, we can examine the traditional instructional technique of the lecture, known to be used as early as the fifth century B.C., and established as the common method in university teaching in medieval times when manuscripts were rare and costly (McLeish, 1976). The lecture approach to learning is based on an entirely different set of assumptions; Cantor described orthodox teaching, of which the lecture is symbolic, as follows (1953, pp. 59–72):

1 It is assumed that the teacher's responsibility is to set out what is to be learned and that the student's job is to learn it.
2 It is assumed that knowledge taken on authority is education in itself.
3 It is assumed that education can be obtained through disconnected subjects.
4 It is assumed that the subject matter is the same to the learner as to the teacher.
5 It is assumed that education prepares the student for later life rather than that it is a living experience.
6 It is assumed that the teacher is responsible for the pupil's acquiring of knowledge.
7 It is assumed that pupils must be coerced into working on some tasks.
8 It is assumed that knowledge is more important than learning.
9 It is assumed that education is primarily an intellectual process.

In short, participation is limited to listening, reading, writing, and possibly speaking. Little or no effort is made to integrate thought and action by linking concepts to behavior. In contrast to experiential learning, an intellectual learning experience fails to address the pupil as a total person.

The Characteristics of Experiential Learning

Experiential learning is operative when participants are fully involved, when the lessons are clearly relevant to the participants, when individuals develop a sense of responsibility for their own learning, and when the learning environment is flexible, responsive to the participants' immediate needs.

Involvement results from engaging in an activity. To learn how to drive a car, people do not register for a course consisting solely of lectures and assigned readings on driving. They do read about, listen to, and think about the basic rules of driving, but the integration of this material only begins to occur through riding in a car and then actually "taking the wheel." Similarly, when traveling on a commercial airline, people are comforted to know that the pilot has logged hundreds of hours on flight simulation training equipment and has years of flying experience as well as the appropriate book learning.

Involvement affects attitude change and growth as well as skill development. The armed services use experience-based training to prepare people for the discomfort, depersonalization, and emotional stress encountered in combat. The Outward Bound wilderness programs use direct involvement for building self-confidence, coping skills, and independence. Individuals have a need for some degree of mastery over their environment, and can satisfy that need to a greater degree when directly involved in their learning (Erikson, 1950). Active learning can be motivating and self-reinforcing.

The *relevance* of a particular topic is readily demonstrated through the use of experiential techniques, since information is linked to behavior and practical applications can be considered. Insights are also gained from the interpersonal exchange involved in addressing a topic since relationships are a central component in everyone's life. Participants consistently report an appreciation of the personal significance of this component of their learning.

Experiential learning promotes participant *responsibility* in a number of ways. Participants have to choose the amount of energy to invest and how to respond in the activities. Their responses in the learning situation can then be related directly to their choices. If they desire different outcomes, they must behave differently to achieve them. The responsibility for managing this change is solely in their hands. Second, most experiential activities provide opportunities for participant involvement in determining the goals of the learning experience. Consequently, participants become committed and gain a real sense of responsibility for the success of the learning experience.

Experiential learning is *flexible* in its uses, which can be discussed under three major headings: settings, participants, and types of learning experiences, including their purposes and objectives. The settings for experiential learning include: educational institutions from preschools to graduate programs in universities, government agencies, business and industry, health and community service agencies, churches, and other groups are currently using experiential techniques to some degree.

Within these settings, it follows that experiential approaches can be used with participants of widely differing needs. For people with very little life experience, the techniques can concentrate on expanding their experience base; for university students, the techniques can concentrate on linking intellectually relevant experiences and personal development with theory and empirical research. For experienced and older individuals from many groups, the techniques can concentrate on bringing order, comprehension, and new skills to their life experiences. The scope of the activities can range from simply sharing information or learning very specific skills to developing new approaches for coping with much larger and pervasive issues such as changing careers or adjusting to the loss of a spouse.

It is useful to classify learning into five broad types of experiences. *Education* is primarily information assimilation or cognitive development. *Training* implies a skill focus or behavioral practice and generally features high levels of physical involvement. Most parents accept the need for sex education for their teenaged and preteenaged children, but few would approve of sex training. In *professional development* the material which is assimilated is broad, complex, and related more to the total nature of the participant than to a specific skill. Counselor development or leadership development is more abstract than training directed at operating a lathe or even an airplane.

Personal growth refers to the expansion of awareness about the self and change of cognitive, affective, and behavioral patterns associated with coping. Thus "sensitivity training" is not really training but personal growth; in fact, it was through this misleading label that much of the past controversy about the technique was generated. Many people went for training but found that no skill was taught and so became confused and at times overwhelmed by their expanded awareness (Campbell & Dunnette, 1968). *Therapy* refers to efforts to aid individuals in overcoming specific psychological problems. Like personal growth, increased awareness is valued, but it requires a deeper, more focused effort by a skilled therapist to alter cognitive, affective, and behavioral patterns in a systematic way for each unique case. A more complete discussion of these matters is presented in Chapter 11 under the heading "Types, Purposes, and Objectives."

Force Field Analysis

One useful way to view individual change is the force field analysis (Lewin, 1951). Rather than thinking of an individual as assimilating learning, in this view the individual is subjected to a variety of facilitating and restraining forces. The net balance of these forces is critical to whether the individual changes or not. The individual is a "black box" in a sea of forces; these are (a) forces internal to the participant, (b) forces generated by the leader, (c) the interpersonal effects of other participants, (d) the forces resulting from the physical setting, (e) the forces created by the structure of the activity, and finally (f) the forces generated by the climate or tone of the total experience. Each of these forces and its impact on learning are discussed below.

Forces *internal* to the individual can both restrain and facilitate change. These are the conditions that each participant brings to the learning experience. Restraining factors include habits and expectations of passivity in learning. For many, past disappointments and frustrations have resulted in disinterest in and possible withdrawal from all formal learning activities. Limited visibility reduces the odds of being called on and is expected to reduce the risk of being criticized, intimidated, or embarrassed. Many people are complacent about their lives and are unaware of, or feel no need to explore, any relationship between their behavior and what happens in a learning context. People are also anxious or fearful about expressing themselves, of being forced to do something they do not want to do, or of losing control. Many people are shy and reluctant to meet and interact with strangers; such interaction is often central to experiential learning activities. Participants' feelings about and past experiences with authority figures can be counterproductive. Fear, anger, resentment, jealousy, envy, and vulnerability can be destructive.

Facilitating forces within the individual include the desire to grow, change, or improve. Similarly, the social nature of people makes participation in group activities satisfying and therefore motivating, since the social context provides the potential for a wide variety of interaction and stimulation to occur. Also the natural tendency to be curious is often evoked by the experience.

The term "leader" is used to represent the person or persons responsible for conducting the activity, and is interchangeable with trainer, instructor, facilitator, and teacher. Leader-centered forces that inhibit growth include lack of technical and interpersonal competence, inappropriate pacing, counterproductive personal needs of the leader, destructive or impotent styles (Lieberman, Yalom, & Miles, 1973), untrustworthiness, and issues surrounding status differences. For example, the overly nondirective leader creates confusion in participants by not providing adequate guidelines for the proceedings. Insensitivity can result in leader resistance to change in the learning context. Dogmatic adherence to a starting time or refusal to entertain participant suggestions may diminish participants' feelings of involvement and control, and may divert their energy away from the learning objectives. Finally, status differences, which in most situations are inevitable, contribute to the distance between leader and group; this is exacerbated by leaders who attempt to increase their influence through status appeals for credibility. Leaders preoccupied with their status or their own needs introduce unproductive stimuli.

Technical competence is facilitating, and is indicated by an awareness of leader and participant needs and capacities, an ability to generate a learning design compatible with participants, time constraints, and facilities, and skills and knowledge to put the design into action. Proper preparation results in a sense of order, direction, security, and responsiveness for the participants and comfort and confidence for the leader.

Leader openness stimulates openness in participants. An engaging, personable, energetic leader stimulates those qualities in participants, thus increasing their willingness to become involved. Commitment to the task and the people, demonstrated through involvement, enjoyment, and a clear focus on the task, underscores relevance and also supports the participants in their efforts to become involved.

Ultimately the leader must blend these capacities into an overall style. To be maximally effective, this style integrates competencies with needs and matches them to the changing requirements of the instructional situation. The effective leader is able to influence participants in many ways. Herbert Kelman's (1958) system of compliance, identification, and internalization describes three useful style considerations. Participants comply with the leader out of a belief that they will be rewarded and their needs will be met. The identification process stems from a desire to respond to and please the leader. The internalization process depends on participants' clear appreciation of the relationship between what is requested of them and their existing values.

Fellow *participants* in an experiential learning situation can also restrain or facilitate change. Highly aggressive or dominant members reduce the active involvement of others by intimidating and inhibiting them while simultaneously monopolizing time or by generating distracting conflict. In addition, since opportunities to receive attention and recognition are seen as limited, participants may feel the need to compete for them. Or there is the "bad example" (Redl, 1942), one who arouses the destructiveness or uncooperativeness in others. Finally, participants can thwart each other's growth through personal insensitivity and unfamiliarity with experiential learning processes.

Conversely, participants facilitate each other's learning through the security and support resulting from membership in the group. The group also enables responsibility for learning to be shared and provides a framework for the satisfaction of social needs. Both of these processes can build mutual commitment and thus are motivational. Participants can serve as social models for each other; once a few participants commit themselves enthusiastically to the learning, others inevitably are pulled along. Excitement and enthusiasm once generated can spread to others in the group.

The importance of the *physical setting* for the learning experience is very often ignored or underestimated. A physical environment influences activities conducted within it and people are very sensitive to this. If participants' basic needs for comfort are not met by the setting, they will be distracted from the learning goals. A facility that is too small or too large, lack of privacy, insufficient or uncomfortable seating, inadequate or excessive light, heat, or ventilation, odors, inaccessible washroom facilities, and cold, drab, decor are all negative influences on the learning process. In addition, fixed seating and furniture, or inappropriate or inadequate furniture or other resources, create blocks to the success of an experiential learning activity. In contrast, comfortable lighting and temperature, a bright, warm decor, and privacy are generally facilitating. Another important quality of the physical space is its flexibility, that is, its potential for accommodating groups of various sizes and a variety of activities without inconvenience.

The *structure* refers to facets of the design of the learning experience and the instructional methods and materials used. Learning is facilitated when the structure of the activities matches the learning objectives and the level of understanding and sophistication of the participants. More on this topic is discussed in the second half of the book.

Climate is defined as the atmosphere or the general tone of the learning experience. The climate is in many respects the aggregation of the preceding forces, but as in group dynamics, the whole is more than the sum of the parts and is a force unto itself. Jack Gibb's (1961) treatment of defensive and supportive communication climates in small groups suggests a useful way of considering this matter. His defensive climate clearly inhibits learning; its six elements are evaluation, control, strategy, neutrality, superiority, and certainty. An emphasis on evaluation, control, and the assertion of superiority tends to evoke anxiety and competitive feelings in participants. Strategy breeds suspicion and fear of unfairness; certainty denies individuals the opportunity to participate in the determination of events and devalues their perceptions. Neutrality implies minimized mutual commitment among individuals.

The spirit of competition is pervasive in our culture and inevitably enters the learning context. The one-upmanship that goes along with competition is part of the superiority climate and can limit certain learning dependent on personal exploration. Further, since reward limitations both stimulate competition and are emphasized in competitive relations, Gibb's strategy factor is also involved.

The treatment of power, including domination by the leader, can profoundly affect the learning climate. A power climate exists when competition emphasizes up–down relationships, when organization emphasizes status differentials, and when the interaction between the participants and the leader is laden with sarcasm, anxiety-evoking demands, and control. The point to be emphasized about a power climate is that it activates participants in ways that often are highly inconsistent with the pursuits of the learning objectives. Participants may retreat from involvement and its associated vulnerability and concentrate on measures to assert self-control and maintain their self-respect.

Gibb (1961) describes supportive climates as the antithesis of defensive climates. In supportive climates, description, problem orientation, spontaneity, empathy, equality, and provisionalism replace evaluation, control, strategy, neutrality, superiority, and certainty respectively. Many advocates of supportive climates in a variety of contexts have argued for their facility. Rensis Likert (1967), for example, talks about the principle of supportive relations and group development as the central concept in his approach to organizations. His ideal organization does not merely use people; it develops them. Mutual acceptance between leader and participant is an essential ingredient of support, as is ease and openness with feelings. A friendly climate also provides a kind of support, because interpersonal warmth, regard, and closeness are intrinsically supportive. An achievement climate is also of great benefit to experiential learning. The enormous importance of support in learning, organizational, and therapeutic contexts has been documented, underscoring its significance in experiential learning.

To understand the individual in the learning situation better and more deeply, Part 1 offers a description of models for human functioning (Chapter 1), and an explanation of how these general forces are actually experienced in individual change (Chapters 2–6). Following this treatment, Part 2 presents applications, which elaborate for the reader just how the forces combine for a given instructional method, and how they can be organized, monitored, and used to facilitate learning.

PART ONE

Individuals and Individual Change

*If you want to know how
something works, try
changing it.*

Kurt Lewin

Change is ubiquitous. It is a central concern of all the behavioral sciences, each discipline scrutinizing different sources or phenomena associated with change. Various change processes typically are described from a specific perspective based on one model of human functioning, one discipline, or one methodological orientation, but these statements are not readily translated across a broad range of situations. For example, in a therapy setting, a psychoanalytic orientation might explain an individual's behavior very well, but in an organizational setting it would probably be less adequate in accounting for or explaining the dynamics of the situation. The opposite is true for these same contexts when interpretation is from a social psychological or sociological perspective. A straightforward yet multidisciplinary and comprehensive description of how change occurs or how it can be orchestrated is needed to aid understanding and managing experiential learning activities.

To meet this need seven models of human functioning and twelve change processes are explored in this section. The models of human functioning provide a broad theoretical base for the understanding of the change processes and their implementation in experiential learning. They are: conflict, fulfillment, consistency, cognitive/perceptual, contextual, learning, and life sciences. In terms of the change processes, the first and most straightforward is feedback, which refers to information being made available to individuals concerning the consequences of their behavior. The second, conditioning, refers to the presence or absence of pleasurable or aversive consequences that influence behavior. The third, coercion, implies punishment or potential punishment along with the deliberate evoking of fear and consequently coercion is distinguished from conditioning. The fourth, identification, refers to the process of acquiring new behavior through the observation of others. The fifth, persuasion, is the planned presentation of information evoking emotions and thoughts in convincing patterns. The sixth change process, support, is argued to enable change rather than induce it. The seventh and eighth change processes, restructuring and channeling, pertain to physical, legislative, and other environmental changes and associated social and interactional dynamics affecting individuals.

The ninth change process is quite different. The term re-cognition is introduced here and used to categorize approaches and mechanisms for changing the way an individual thinks. For example, internalized problem solving sequences, altered mental verbalizations and imagery, altered constructs for organizing, and even hypothesis formulation are included in this discussion. The tenth process, activation, refers to the energizing consequences of stimulation in providing the impetus for change. The eleventh, commitment, includes consideration of the role of "will" in change and the way in which the will is mobilized. Finally, action refers to the variety of overt ways in which the individual can be engaged in the learning experience. These are exploration, experimentation, practice, and performance. They serve as vehicles for the other change processes while at the same time providing linkages among them.

These twelve change processes broadly span the territory of individual change and are similar in that they are descriptive of general mechanisms by which change in individuals can be induced. However, the processes are not entirely parallel nor are they necessarily mutually exclusive. Taxonomy builders may be somewhat uncomfortable with the fact that feedback is a more generalized phenomenon than some of the other processes and that feedback relates to and is inherent in the dynamics of some processes such as channeling. In fact, feedback, conditioning, activation, channeling, and re-cognition are each present, in some form, in all the other processes while support and coercion are not present in any of them. This overlapping thus leads to a somewhat hierarchical descriptive system of individual change in contrast to a purely taxonomic one. What is important, however, is that all elements discussed in this section are well documented processes associated with individual change. By contrast, virtually all other treatments of change currently available tend to mix processes (e.g., conditioning) with theories (e.g., social learning) and techniques (e.g., family therapy) (see Burton, 1976). In short, no broad overarching system for exploring individual change has yet been generated. The one developed in the following section is built up from well known and documented but heretofore fragmented change dynamics.

The detailed discussion that follows considers each process from three perspectives: individual, interactional, and social. The individual perspective is concerned primarily with the behavior of a single person; the disciplines of counseling and psychotherapy are representative of this perspective. The interactional perspective is concerned with the dynamics of groups. The uniqueness of the individual, while central to the first perspective, is not the main focus here. Social psychology epitomizes this perspective. The social perspective is concerned with the impact of even broader forces and dynamics such as mass media and culture. Sociology and anthropology address these issues. The discussion is *not* intended to be *exhaustive* but *representative,* to capture the general nature of each process. As the perspective shifts, the processes display a range of differences from subtle to dramatic, depending on how they are translated into individual change. This treatment provides a richer appreciation of how the processes work. For example, from the individual perspective, support is discussed in terms of empathy and caring, which are central to change in a therapeutic context. From the interactional perspective in an organizational setting, support is viewed in terms of the leader's attitudes and behavior towards employees. From the social perspective, support for the individual is provided by laws, and institutions such as the church. The effective use of a given process depends on its influence potential across perspectives.

In the detailed descriptions that follow, each process is first defined in general terms and its principal features are described. Then it is examined from one or more of the three perspectives. Finally, selective comparisons are made across processes and perspectives. The order in which the processes are considered is based on whether a process or grouping of processes can be conveniently discussed without reference to other processes. Some of the processes like feedback, and, to a large extent, conditioning, can be treated without reliance on descriptions of any of the others. However, a process like activation incorporates aspects of some of those preceding its description. The closing existential processes, commitment and action, are in many ways defined in terms of the other processes and consequently must be treated last. The sequencing and grouping of specific processes into five chapter themes make the discussion of the labyrinthine subject matter less difficult. No ranking is implied in terms of the complexity of the processes in promoting change nor in terms of their relative importance, desirability, or effectiveness in changing behavior. However, before beginning this in-depth treatment, it is necessary to develop a comprehensive base of knowledge about individual behavior. The models of human functioning serve this purpose.

CHAPTER ONE

Models of Human Functioning

*Paradigms provide scientists not
only with a map but also with some
of the directions essential for
map-making. In learning a paradigm
the scientist acquires theory,
methods and standards together,
usually in an inextricable
mixture . . . That is the reason why
schools guided by different
paradigms are always slightly at
cross purposes.*

Thomas S. Kuhn

The manner in which leaders choose to understand or to interpret participant behavior is crucial to the entire learning endeavor. Leaders in experiential settings always take action with some model of human functioning
in mind, even though that model might be outside their level of awareness. The challenge confronted in this chapter is to organize the concepts
related to models of human functioning in a way that leaders can begin
to identify the salient characteristics of their own approaches. This problem is addressed through the identification of major themes around which
specific theoretical interpretations or alternatives can be clustered.

Seven different kinds of models of human functioning have been identified:

Conflict
These models focus on the resolution of the conflict within an individual's
complex aggregation of likes and dislikes, hopes and fears, pleasant and

unpleasant memories. The key elements of the conflict models are opposing mental forces.

Fulfillment
The individual is viewed in the fulfillment models as possessing capacities,
as being in lifelong pursuit of the development or realization of these
capacities, and as wishing to deal with life as effectively as possible. The
key element in these models is growth—its stimuli, its directions, and its
benefits.

Consistency
In the consistency models, individuals are seen as desiring control over
their lives and a sense of reality based on and compatible with past experiences. The key elements are stimulation, activation, responses to contingencies, and mental adjustment.

Cognitive/Perceptual
These models consist of mental representations of the world and one's self
in it. The constructs have a "self fulfilling" quality in that those used by
individuals affect their perceptions of the world, their actions, and their
interpretations of the environment's responses. The key element in these
models is mental organization for explaining, simplifying, dealing with,
and adjusting to the world.

Contextual
These models emphasize the individual's relationship with the social system, stressing the importance of the characteristics of the social situation
in determining behavior. Social roles predominate over individual differences. The key elements in these models are parameters for social structure and dynamics such as roles and norms.

Learning
According to the learning models, the individual attempts to acquire behavior that results in certain desired outcomes. The key elements are
reinforcement and modeling.

Life Sciences
These models depict individuals as having enormous mental and behavioral capabilities for complexity and flexibility which are applied in meeting a wide variety of physical and symbolic needs. Physical realities of both
the present and the past are used to articulate parameters which in turn
enable individuals to be seen in broad perspective. Key elements in these
models are physical survival in the dim past, adaptation, reproduction, and
comparisons over time and across species.

All seven kinds of models offer sound explanations of behavior, and each model has its special validity. However, when using any single model to describe all behavior, the applicability of the theories varies. For example, the conflict model provides a valuable explanation of an individual in a therapeutic context, but is less helpful in describing or accounting for an individual's behavior in an organizational context. Consequently, no single kind of model alone can offer as rich or as comprehensive an explanation of any given situation as the seven kinds of models considered together. By developing and maintaining an appreciation of all seven model kinds, the leader of an experiential learning activity can avoid the pitfall of being too highly committed to a single theoretical orientation.

The treatment of the material in this chapter is both comprehensive and selective. It is comprehensive in that a broad range of positions is included in the description of the seven model kinds. But, for several reasons, it is also selective and limited. First, the coverage of specific positions, though representative, is in no way exhaustive; many positions seen as tangential or repetitive were omitted. Second, no position or relationships among positions are considered in detail, the objective being rather to capture general qualities and themes and to compare them across the seven model kinds. Figure 1.1 provides a summary of the models and a guide to theorists associated with each. It is hoped that leaders can use the integration of this material to examine their particular theoretical orientation and to establish a base for analysing the dynamics of change in experiential learning.

Conflict Models

In the conflict model, it is assumed that the person is continuously and inevitably in the grips of the clash between two great, opposing, unchangeable forces. Life, according to this model, is necessarily a compromise, which at best involves a dynamic balance of the two forces, and at worst involves a foredoomed attempt to deny the existence of one of them. [Balancing and controlling the opposing forces creates anxiety for the individual.] There are two versions of the conflict model. In the psychosocial version, the source of one great force is in the person as an individual, and the source of the other great force is in groups or societies. In the intrapsychic version, both great forces arise from within the person, regardless of whether he or she is regarded as an individual or as a social entity. (Maddi, 1976, p. 20)

Psychosocial

Sigmund Freud's work (1925, 1927, 1930, 1933) represents the major contribution to the psychosocial view of human conflict. From his perspective, the individual is seen as wishing to gratify self-preservation, sexual, and death instincts (id), but is restrained from doing so by the

Model	Representative Theorists
Conflict	
Psychosocial	Freud, Murray, Horney, Erikson, Rapaport
Intrapsychic	Rank, Jung
Fulfillment	
Natural actualization	Rogers, Maslow, Allport, Fromm
Developed actualization	Adler, White
Competence and effectiveness	May, Frankl
Existentialism	Binswanger
Consistency	
Cognitive dissonance/balance	Festinger, Newcomb, Heider
Cognitive control	Kelly
Challenge	McClelland
Activation	Fiske and Maddi
Cognitive/perceptual	
Personal construct theory	Kelly, Bieri
Belief systems	Rokeach
Expectancies	Rotter
Developmental adaption	Piaget
Informational	Galanter, Miller, Pribram, Newell, Simon, Raphael
Contextual	
Field theory	Lewin
Symbolic interactionism	Mead
Interpersonal psychology	Sullivan
Communications	Bateson, Jackson
Costs and benefits	Thibaut and Kelley, Homans
Sociology–anthropology	Blumer, Garfinkel, Merton, Parsons
Learning	
Moderate behaviorism	Pavlov, Thorndike, Hull, Guthrie, Tolman
Radical behaviorism	Skinner
Social learning	Bandura, Walters
Cognitive behaviorism	Mahoney, Meichenbaum
Life sciences	
Ethology	Lorenz, Tinbergen, Harlow, Bowlby
Sociobiology	Wilson, Barash
Neuroscience	Watts

Figure 1.1 Models of human functioning.

requirements of the society (superego). The family is viewed as the central social unit for the individual as a child, and libidinal drive is the central instinctual force. The primary conflicts arise between the individual and the same sex parent. The child wishes to possess his mother or her father and monopolize attention and affection, but risks retaliation from the parent of the same sex for even experiencing these thoughts, not to mention acting on them. The consequences of the retaliation could be fatal and thus are the source of fear. The direction provided by the superego enables the individual to avoid actual interpersonal conflict, but the conflict is internalized and violations of the superego result in guilt. Tension is generated when coping with conflicts between drive gratification and the superego, because of the risks, losses, and frustrations involved. There is great potential for individual differences in coping with conflict.

Neo-Freudians such as Horney (1937, 1950) and Murray (1938), expanded the scope and complexity of Freud's basic position. Murray broadened the concept of the id, ego, and superego by postulating the possibility that not all impulses are socially undesirable. He maintained that nondefensive processes, such as rational thought and accurate perception of reality, play an important role in shaping behavior. He also proposed that acquiring standards for behavior need not be linked to childhood. Horney stressed the importance of culturally induced conflict. She argued that unfavorable home circumstances create anxiety, which in turn causes a defensive behavioral strategy and the distortion of a person's self-image. The ideal self-image, defined in terms of the "tyrannical shoulds" of the culture, alienates the individual from his or her real self. When the ideal self-image becomes dominant and ego functioning is reduced, developmental attempts are misguided. Tension is a destructive by-product of conflict.

Other major expansions of Freud's basic theory were made by the ego psychologists such as Erikson (1950) and Rapaport (1958). They considered individuals to have instincts for mastery as well as the instincts that had been emphasized by Freud. They saw the ego as having its own instinctual basis; Freud postulated that the instinctual basis of the ego was derived from the id, in response to conflicts with the superego. Erikson saw the individual going through or becoming fixated at stages of development from infancy to adulthood, rather than during the first few years of life only, as Freud had argued. He saw behavior as an active search for autonomy rather than as a defensive adaptation to conflict with society. Freud emphasized selected aspects of society (such as sexual taboos) and maintained that conflict for the individual was unavoidable; Erikson and Horney considered broad social issues and environmental factors, and saw much of society's pressure as archaic, unnecessary, and essentially neurotic. All the psychosocial models of conflict describe the individual as responding to specific pressures with expedient measures, which become habitual over time and lead to some degree of tension or self-alienation.

Intrapsychic

The second set of conflict models describes intrapsychic conflict. Otto Rank (1929, 1945), for example, describes tension as the result of two fears, the fear of separation (self-seeking and autonomy) and the fear of moving toward union (closeness and harmony with the world). He called these the fear of life and the fear of death respectively and it is through "will" that the individual balances the fears. Will is something more than ego; it develops through the process of saying "no" to external demands and "no" to impulses. Other similar conceptions of intrapsychic conflict take a still more positive view of the individual. Angyal (1951, 1965) and Bakan (1966, 1968, 1971) see the individual as attempting to maximize personal autonomy or agency and simultaneously experiencing a sense of communion with and surrender to a particular group. Again, conflict increases tension.

For Jung (1953), the central goal of life is the attainment of selfhood, through the integration of the individual unconscious, the collective unconscious, and the conscious:

> The ego (or conscious, individualistic mind), which is in conflict with the personal unconscious (formed of socially unacceptable mental content that was once conscious but has been forced out of awareness by defenses), and the collective unconscious (a communal, species memory, never achieving consciousness, representing the accumulated experiences of mankind and possibly even subhuman life). The collective unconscious is comprised of archetypes, or essences (universal forms) that predispose toward characteristically human thoughts and feelings. Although these thoughts and feelings can become conscious, the underlying archetypes cannot. Major archetypes are the shadow (the animalistic possibilities of man), the anima (the feminine possibility in men), the animus (the masculine possibility in women), the persona (the conventional mask adoped by persons in the face of social pressures), and the self (a conglomerate of all the opposing forces in a person). (Maddi, 1976, p. 656)

Here the future is in conflict with the past, and various elements from the past are in conflict with each other. The future serves as a place for potential partial resolution, and the mind or spirit channels and sculpts the past into a coherent future.

Both the psychosocial and intrapsychic models of conflict emphasize the continuing nature of instinctual impulses and the tendencies to act on them. During development, socially acceptable outlets for some of these impulses may be found, but not all impulses are easily managed.

Summary

The central concern of the conflict models is the generation and management of tension. Because of the complexity of the human experience, a wide variety of recurrent conflicts are possible, and some, such as fear of life versus fear of death, can never be resolved. Other conflicts, such as anima versus animus, allow for some resolution and take different forms and meaning at different times in an individual's life (Erikson, 1950; Levinson, Darrow, Klein, Levinson, & McKee, 1978).

Action, the essence of life, inevitably has pleasurable and painful consequences; simple, unbridled pursuit of pleasure is not realistic. Problems may arise from virtually any resolution or action, and therefore the fundamental challenge of a full life is the satisfactory management of personal conflict.

Fulfillment Models

The fulfillment model assumes only one great force, and localizes it in the person. This model construes life as the progressively greater expression of this force. Although conflict is a possible occurrence in the fulfillment model, it is neither necessary nor continuous. Indeed, when it occurs, it represents an unfortunate failure in living, rather than something unavoidable. (Maddi, 1976, p. 20)

The patterns of growth and development pervasive in nature symbolize the fulfillment models of human functioning. These models depict individuals as one of the following:

1 Growing and developing according to their inner beings (natural actualization).
2 Developing in a manner to achieve a true total selfhood (developed actualization).
3 Developing so as to act on and control their worlds (competence and effectiveness).
4 Growing toward completeness and authenticity rather than settling into a stunted relationship with the self or others (existentialism).

In all four views the individual is seen as growing and adapting with some source of internal guidance shaping that growth. Representatives of each of these alternative views are considered below.

Natural Actualization

Carl Rogers (1951, 1959, 1963) differed considerably from the conflict theorists in his use of the idea of organismic urges. The tendency for the individual to act out and develop as a result of these urges is the actualizing tendency. In addition there is a "self-actualizing" tendency which grows out of some of these forces. Self-actualization is a function of the combination of the personal experience of one's world and the formation of a self-concept; it is defined as "the inherent tendency of the organism to develop all its capacities in ways which maintain or enhance the organism" (Rogers, 1959, p. 161). Complications arise because the individual needs positive regard from others and because perceived status of self, associated with positive regard, becomes an experienced set of conditions of worth. Eventually, organismic urges not contributing to conditions of worth get labeled "bad" in the mind of the person, and incongruities develop. The consequence here is that:

> Experiences which are in accord with his conditions of worth are perceived and symbolized accurately in awareness. Experiences which run contrary to the conditions of worth are perceived selectively and distortedly as if in accord with the conditions of worth or in part or whole, denied to awareness. (Rogers, 1959, p. 226)

When the actualizing tendency is incompatible with conditions of self-worth, anxiety and tension result. Tension is avoided by limiting actualization. Unconditional positive regard opens the door to full actualization and allows the individual to work through tensions to a fuller being. Maddi summarizes the Rogerian view of both the fully functioning person and the maladjusted person as follows:

> The Fully Functioning Person (or ideal person) has received unconditional positive regard. Hence, he has no conditions of worth, no defensiveness, and there is congruence between self and potentialities. He is characterized by openness to experience (emotional depth and reflectiveness), existential living (flexibility, adaptability, spontaneity, and inductive thinking), organismic trusting (intuitive living, self-reliance, confidence), experiential freedom (subjective sense of free will), and creativity (penchant for producing new and effective ideas and things). The Maladjusted Person has received conditional positive regard. Therefore he has conditions of worth, incongruence between self and potentialities, and defensiveness. Also, he lives according to a preconceived plan rather than existentially, disregards his organism rather than trusting it, feels manipulated rather than free, and is common and conforming rather than creative. (Maddi, 1976, p. 658)

Like Rogers, Abraham Maslow (1962, 1967, 1969) used the concept of actualization, but he suggested that survival needs have first priority over the tendency to actualize. Maslow's list of survival needs includes physiological and safety needs, esteem, social, and love needs. Survival needs are aroused by deprivation and directed at experienced imbalances. Growth needs are more psychologically oriented; they are similar to Rogers' conditions for self-regard. Once survival needs are adequately met, growth motivation predominates and leads to actualization. Overall, the two views of self-actualization are similar except that unconditionality is not necessary in Maslow's scheme to reach full actualization. Further, Maslow sets cognitive understanding at the pinnacle of actualization. This was not emphasized by Rogers but seems reasonable given the uniqueness of human cognitive capacities.

Developed Actualization

The second fulfillment view of human functioning emphasizes "becoming" what is humanly possible in contrast to expressing what is biologically inherent. Gordon Allport and Erich Fromm offer examples of this view in which an "ideal" orients growth. Allport (1955, 1961) described two modes of functioning—propriate and opportunistic. The propriate mode implies striving toward an expression of the ideal self (proprium) and the opportunistic mode implies satisfying fundamental needs. In terms of motivation, this view is similar to Maslow's growth and deprivation concepts, but it differs in that individuals are seen as "pulling" themselves toward psychological maturity, rather than being "pushed" biologically to actualize. Growth and life are conscious rather than instinctive. Maturity, the outcome of growth, includes (Maddi, 1976, p. 119):

1 specific, enduring extensions of the self,
2 dependable techniques for warm relating to others (such as tolerance),
3 stable emotional security or self acceptance,
4 habits of realistic perception,
5 skills and problem centeredness,
6 established self-objectification in the form of insight and humor,
7 a unifying philosophy of life including particular value orientation, differentiated religious sentiment, and a personalized conscience.

The proprium, developed early in life, includes self-identity, sense of body, self-esteem, and rational coping (Allport, 1961). Propriate striving is pro-active because it anticipates the future; opportunistic functioning is reactive because it responds to ongoing stimuli.

Fromm's view is similar to Allport's. He sees as central the tendency to express one's "human" nature, not one's animal or opportunistic nature. Conflict is considered less important than the fulfillment of one's human nature (Fromm, 1941, 1947, 1955, 1956). In this model, a person strives to articulate an individual identity while developing and maintaining close relationships with something more than the self, such as the family. Therefore, the individual tends to cope with the world in a cognitively guided manner. The most desirable manner in which individuals can meet all their own needs, according to Fromm, is to maintain a productive orientation. Here the individual is active, trusting, open-minded, experimental, and modest. Other less desirable orientations include receptive (passive-submissive), exploitative (aggressive-conceited), hoarding (stingy-stubborn-suspicious), and marketing (opportunistic-unprincipled-wasteful). The productive ideal implies the need for a consistent, sane society in which all behave maturely. Thus, in the abstract, psychosocial conflict is minimized.

Competence and Effectiveness

The third version of the fulfillment model is more explicitly directed at ideals and less tightly associated with the notion of actualization. Adler and White offer examples of this approach. Adler (1927, 1930, 1931, 1964) argued that an individual strives for perfection (superiority) with the goal of a full life. Respect and encouragement in youth aid in the development of an active approach to life's limitations. Feelings of inferiority as well as actual physical inferiority lead to compensatory efforts. Adler's view, in contrast to the natural actualization view, explains why an asthmatic might become a great runner. Because of feelings of inferiority, an individual strives for superiority; the desired perfection is relative to the perceived inadequacy. "Fictional finalisms" are images or ideals of perfect living serving as targets for compensatory efforts; for example, a child thinks of becoming President of the United States. An active, constructive life style is considered best, because ambition is coupled with a service fictional finalism. In contrast, an individual of the passive constructive type tries to be attractive and charming rather than useful. The most undesirable types are the active destructive, which is rebellious, and the passive destructive, which is despairing.

R.W. White's view (1959, 1960, 1963) is similar to Adler's in its recognition of upward fulfillment motivation but different in other significant ways. For White the tendency early in life is to act in order to produce effects. Later, the ability or capacity to realize intended, specific objectives replaces the desire simply to produce effects. Competence can be directed toward ideals and can be pursued while comparisons with a performance standard are made. In contrast to Adler, White suggests that competence is most likely to be pursued in areas of natural strengths rather than in areas of weakness. In contrast to the natural actualization theorists, White argues that considerable competence in a few areas is pursued over limited competence in many areas. The "Jack-of-all-trades but master of none" is not White's ideal, although to be a master in many areas would be highly desirable. In pursuit of this goal, states of high tension would be expected, but, according to White's view, this is desirable. In contrast to the conflict models, tension generation rather than tension avoidance is expected.

Existentialism

The existential psychologists provide the fourth kind of fulfillment model (Binswanger, 1963; Boss, 1963; Frankl, 1960; Maddi, 1967; May, 1958; Tillich, 1952). Here the object in life is to achieve authentic being, that is, to be honest with one's self, to accept wholly one's self as what one is, to accept the world as one experiences it. It is a phenomenological model. Ideally, the individual is continuously "in touch" with being in the world (biological experience or *Umwelt*), being with others (social experience or *Mitwelt*), and being with one's self (personal experience or *Eigenwelt*). Further, the individual is constantly making decisions about life as it is experienced and acting on those decisions with intention. The result of being confronted with decisions is a constant choice between ontological anxiety (fear of doing something with unknown outcomes) and ontological guilt (realization that not acting is tantamount to giving up passively one's birthright). Ontological anxiety is stressful; ontological guilt is corrosive. These are similar to Rank's fear of life and fear of death. The most dynamic approach to life is to persist in acting and to accept the inevitable ontological anxiety.

For Rogers, the individual seeks fulfillment by expanding out from what is; for Adler, by compensating for what is lacking. But for the existentialists, individuals seek their unique meaning in the quality of existence. Consequently, for the existentialists, the thrust in life is neither outward nor upward but rather forward, especially in time. To live life fully is to experience continuously existence on the "cutting edge of time" (Pirsig, 1974).

The existential notions of *Umwelt, Mitwelt,* and *Eigenwelt* correspond roughly to Maslow's biological, social, and psychological needs, but no hierarchy is implied. Nevertheless, the psychological needs of symbolization, imagination, and judgment are unique to humans and central to the model. Because *Homo sapiens* alone among the animals can question the meaning of existence, they must use these capacities to do so. Thus Frankl (1960) speaks of "will to meaning" through which individuals determine for themselves the guiding purpose for life in the journey through time.

Persisting in the face of ontological anxiety requires courage, but the reward of courageous search is freedom. Courage is necessary to overcome the four fears of living. These are fear of meeting one's inevitable death, fear of the necessity of action in the absence of knowledge of outcomes, fear of meaninglessness, and fear of isolation. Through their symbolizing, imagining, and judging capacities, individuals assess, create, and consider alternatives for addressing these fears at any moment in time and thereby construct their own existence. The consequence of courage and persistence in addressing these fears is increased psychological complexity; this results in a richer experiencing of all aspects of life and an improved capacity to make the next set of decisions. While some limits are inevitable in this decision making, there are far fewer limitations than one would typically believe. "Life is best led by preparation for and commitment to the decisions that must be faced" (Maddi, 1976, p. 135). To take the apparently safe path of allowing others to make one's own decisions leads not only to banality and massive ontological guilt but also to a sense of powerlessness and "quiet desperation." For the existentialist, since ontological guilt is seen as highly corrosive and a greater burden than ontological anxiety, there is "no exit" from the challenge of life.

Summary

The four approaches to the fulfillment model of human functioning have significant similarities and differences. All consider the individual as unique and engaged in a process of what might be called genetic destiny. Growth may be outward in all directions, upward in a specific direction, or forward in time toward a more enriched experience. Each expansion is seen as central to fulfillment of one's potential. Tension is seen as necessary and even desirable in fulfillment models. This is in direct contrast to its unwholesome significance in conflict models. For example, conflict between fear of life and fear of death is resolved by growth, since the choice is not whether to confront the fear of life, but rather how to maximize relevant growth given the costs of confrontation. Impulses service the growth tendency; awareness may or may not guide development. A need for integration exists but is easily accomplished in normal conscious activity. Individuals are considered the masters of their fates, not servants to their competing subconscious urges. Inconsistencies and incompatibilities are relatively minor or naturally overcome as growth is pursued and therefore not the main focus of life. In some fulfillment theories, however, their resolution is a clear incentive for growth and development. Finally, the images of perfection pursued in the Adlerian or existential models are the product of the individual, in contrast to the externally induced ideals, like the superego, in Freud's and Horney's models.

Consistency Models

A consistency model

> emphasizes the importance of the information or emotional experience the person gets out of interacting with the external world. The model assumes

that there is a particular kind of information or emotional experience that
is best for the person, and hence, that he will develop a personality which
increases the likelihood that he will interact with the world such as to get
this kind of information or emotional experience. The personality is determined much more by the feedback from interaction with the world than it
is by inherent attributes of the human. (Maddi, 1976, p. 141)

No individual's life experience can be totally consistent over time but
a number of theorists argue that people actively seek some consistency.
The nature of this consistency can vary, depending on the particular
orientation, and could include minimizing cognitive dissonance, keeping
relationships in balance, moderating challenge, and pacing stimulation
for comfort. Some of these views of human functioning are compatible
with aspects of the conflict and fulfillment models, but others contradict
them, just as the fulfillment models at times seem to contradict the
conflict models. A brief consideration of compatibilities among these
views is summarized after the following descriptions of a number of
approaches.

Cognitive Dissonance and Balance Theory

These two positions are included because they represent two important
ways of conceptualizing consistency and have been the focus of considerable research. However, they are treated briefly because they describe
behavior rather than explain internal functioning. Cognitive dissonance
and balance theory have the same relationship to the consistency position
as defense mechanisms have to the conflict position. Just as the latter offer
an incomplete and peripheral explanation of how the conflict model functions, the former have comparable shortcomings in not describing the
central thrust of the consistency model, that is, how and why people try
to create consistency for themselves.

Cognitive dissonance theory is at once the most intuitively appealing
and yet one of the least documentable phenomena in psychology. Leon
Festinger's (1957) central idea is simple. Individuals experience various
conflicts before making choices, but after making these choices they experience a different discomfort, termed dissonance. More dissonance is experienced when the outcomes of alternative choices are relatively equally
valued. The tendency of individuals to distort reality in order to avoid
experiencing dissonance is central to the consistency notion. For example,
a group believing that extraterrestial beings would destroy the world on
a given date react to the absence of destruction by adopting the supple-
mental belief that their faith in the beings actually prevented the destruction. The more plausible explanation, that their original belief was inaccurate, is rejected and thus dissonance over the earlier choice is avoided.
There is a hint of fear of life as well as ontological anxiety in this conception

but the discomfort is experienced after, rather than before, a choice is made.

Balance theory (Heider, 1958; Newcomb, 1961) argues that individuals attempt to establish consistent affective patterns in their relations with others. For example, if person A likes person B and person C but persons B and C do not like each other, an imbalance is experienced. In this situation, person A will tend to prefer liking people who like each other. Both dissonance-reduction and balance-seeking tendencies appear to be neither universal nor continuous; in spite of their intuitive appeal as explanations, they predict less human behavior than other theories (Maddi, 1976).

Consistency/Cognitive Control

G.A. Kelly (1955) views the individual as a scientist searching for the truth. The purpose of this search is increased prediction and control of events, yielding a type of consistency to life. His is the final position discussed that treats inconsistency as undesirable and to be avoided. The individual's search for control recalls White's idea of striving for competence, and, for Kelly, the competence issue is fundamental. For White, competence is a continuing, driving force; for Kelly, a good cognitive map means cognitive competence. Cognitive development builds expectations and prescribes desired acts. In a sense Kelly describes the ideal intellectual ego; this ego totally controls both id and superego while maximizing its own efficiency in interfacing with the outside world.

According to Kelly, conflict between the expected and the realized could result in anxiety, hostility, or guilt. Revision of constructs is the response to anxiety. Hostility signals an attempt to bend the world to fit one's preconceptions, and guilt signals a sense of failure to predict and control. Defensive distortions of one's thoughts, as described in cognitive dissonance theory, are not probable according to Kelly, because reality dominates. Lack of balance can be corrected by developing increasingly differentiated cognitive structures, rather than simply by accepting dichotomous choices as implied in the balance and dissonance theories. Kelly does acknowledge, however, that some individuals would resolve such dilemmas in a manner predicted by balance theory.

Consistency/Challenge

David McClelland (1951; McClelland, Atkinson, Clark, & Lowell, 1953) offers an alternative approach to the consistency view. Here the individual tolerates, and even seeks, small degrees of inconsistency in life. McClelland argues that total lack of discrepancy yields one of the most uncomfortable states for humans—boredom. Consequently, a moderate degree of uncertainty and inconsistency in life is pleasureable and will be sought out. The manner and degree to which the individual seeks out inconsistency in the domains of affiliation, power, and achievement is a function of early life experiences. Rapid resolution of inconsistency facilitates understanding and increases the tendency to respond to cues. McClelland distinguishes the motive to approach something (success) from the motive to avoid another thing (failure), and argues that approach is learned when inconsistencies are small, and avoidance when inconsistencies are large. When a child can stack three blocks, encouragement from a parent to pursue a goal of stacking five blocks yields an anticipation of the pleasure of achieving a new success and perhaps receiving new rewards. In contrast, an overly high goal such as twenty blocks evokes the fear of the pain of failure and is thus associated with avoidance. For McClelland, needs are learned orientations based on anticipations of probable pleasurable or painful outcomes. Pleasure is the reduction of tensions; a person eats to reduce hunger.

McClelland also argues that the degree of need fulfillment depends on individual habits or *traits*. Cognition for McClelland is important, since ideas and values (called *schemata)* form bases for perceiving and interpreting cues as well as for imagining possible outcomes. While Kelly sees ideas as a way to eliminate inconsistencies, McClelland argues for their usefulness in seeking out mild inconsistency which can be capitalized on for pleasure. That is, modest challenges can be surmounted and yield success, but without challenge, and thus inconsistency, there can be no gratification. The degree of pleasure derived is a function of the relevance and effectiveness of habits evoked in a given situation, not on cognitive control *per se.*

Consistency/Activation

Fiske and Maddi (1961) argue that individuals do not seek consistency on a moment to moment basis. Instead, a consistency with early life experiences is sought. This consistency is not in the type of experience but in the activation level. Activation is arousal and energization of the organism. Individuals try to control their world to ensure that they experience a pattern of activation similar to the pattern they experienced in early life. For example, "morning people" are used to high activation bustle early in the day while "evening people" are used to high activation late in the day. Activation results directly from the impact of stimulation on the central nervous system, especially through the reticular formation (RF). The impact is a function of the variety, intensity, and meaningfulness of the stimulation. Variety is a function of novelty, change, and unexpectedness. Intensity refers to the strength of the stimulus; meaningfulness is the degree to which the stimulus is important or related to significant aspects of the person's world or his or her conception of it. Stimulation on sense organs can be externally induced, internally induced, or internally induced within the brain via the cortex. Thoughts are key sources of meaningfulness, stimulating and moderating other stimuli.

As the individual moves through life some stimuli will have decreasing activation consequences. The individual will be troubled by boredom. But in the normal course of development, cognitions become increasingly differentiated and thus the activation properties of a stimulus source can be heightened. In contrast, cognitive development by integration helps moderate the impact of stimuli. In short, the more detail one can discriminate, the more activation one experiences and the more detail is "put in perspective," the less it activates. Thus, through personal development, control of self, and structuring of the environment, the individual can keep activation levels from becoming too low or too high. The individual thus maintains a pattern of activation consistent with that experienced as a child. The object of life here is not control, growth, conflict minimization, or inconsistency minimization; it is maintaining a familiar pattern of stimulation and activation. Some people seek high activation and others low activation. Fiske and Maddi label behavioral manifestations of approach (attraction) as the active trait and avoidance (fear) as the passive trait. They also distinguish between types of people oriented to internal stimulation and those oriented to external stimulation.

Two ideal personality prototypes are active with high activation and have either external or internal traits. The external type, for example,

> will be a "go-getter," seeking out challenges to meet in the physical and social environment. He will be energetic and voracious in his appetites. Interested in a wide range of concrete, tangible events and things, he will be a hard man to keep up with. Although he will not be especially hampered by pressures toward conformity, he will tend to be a man of facts, not fancies. He will not spend much time in rumination or daydreaming. He will be straightforward and not complex and subtle so much as extensively committed and enthusiastic. He will want to encounter people and things rather continuously. If he also has a high need for meaningfulness, he will be a pursuer of causes and problems, a statesman, businessman, or journalist, rather than a scholar. But if he has a high need for intensity, he may pursue action and tumult *per se*, being an athlete or soldier or bon vivant. And if he has a high need for variety, he will show curiosity about causes and mechanisms governing men and things, being adventurer, explorer, or world traveler. (Maddi, 1976, pp. 367–368)

Summary

It is clear that an active, high-activation person is likely to grow and actualize; we recall the Rogerian insight that unconditional positive regard prerequisite to an individual becoming a fully functioning person.

Without such secure positive regard in youth, fears lead to increased passivity. Similarly, the active person would likely confront the ontological anxiety noted by the existentialists and thus avoid the corrosive aspects of the fear of life. In terms of the conflict models of human functioning, the active person of high activation would have relatively high tolerance for and comfort with conflict and, over time, would develop an exceedingly competent ego. In fact, with the exception of cognitive dissonance and balance theory, all the models considered to this point can be used to increase appreciation of the broad explanatory powers of activation models. Perhaps Zorba the Greek was right when he said, "Life is trouble, only death is not. To be alive is to undo your belt and look for trouble" (Kazantzakes, 1972).

Cognitive/Perceptual Models

In a cognitive/perceptual model

> the person is conceived of as an information processing system that is understandable in terms of the characteristics and content of this system. Behavior is not considered a direct function of external events but of the person's interpretation of those events. Stability and change in behavior, both between and within person variation, are viewed as reflections of stability and change in perception and cognition and of individual differences in the processes and capacities involved in them. External reality is not denied in this conception of personality, but it is seen as entering into the causation of behavior primarily through its transformation by the person. Without taking into account the nature of this transformation it is difficult, if not impossible, to predict or understand human behavior, according to this view. (Levy, 1970, pp. 250–251)

Cognitive/perceptual models of human functioning depict the manner in which thought processes control life experiences. Previously discussed consistency theories acknowledge cognitive processes, and conflict theories acknowledge ego functioning, but these models explore how thinking occurs. Kelly's theory of personal constructs is considered first. His approach has already been introduced in the discussion on consistency because of his emphasis on prediction and control. In general the models focus on how thought patterns are established, how they are changed, how they affect the individual's experiencing of the world, and how the individual acts on the world.

Personal Construct Theory

In George Kelly's model, experienced inconsistencies initiate thinking which in turn is directed toward gaining control. Kelly explicitly argues that life experiences are encoded into the brain via conceptualizations and that these conceptualizations become organized into a personal construct system. The individual's system of constructs affects what is perceived as well as how it is valued and contains superordinate constructs as well as hierarchically organized subordinate constructs. Thus a superordinate construct of "equality" is associated with chauvinism or racism, and such behavior yields a strong reaction for individuals with equality as a central construct. A construct that is superior for one person could be subordinate for another and vice versa.

According to Kelly, the personal constructs come into play in a three-part thought process of circumspection, preemption, and control. Circumspection refers to thinking about phenomena of significance, interest, or concern; alternative constructs are applied to the "problem" in light of past experience and in anticipation of possible outcomes. Preemption refers to choosing the primary construct for attacking the problem. Control includes acting upon conclusions derived from previous phases and evaluating the outcomes for accuracy of predictions and effectiveness of previous preemption and control efforts.

Construct systems affect the manner in which the individual experiences life in a number of ways. First, stimuli are coded as they impinge on the individual; for example, the subtly sarcastic comment of an acquaintance could be coded as either friendly or competitive. Second, individuals with a relatively large number of constructs with permeable boundaries among them would be likely to revise initial control measures because of their relatively high cognitive complexity and flexibility. According to Bieri (1961), and Bieri, Atkins, Briar, Leaman, Miller, and Tripodi (1966), cognitive complexity is a function of the number of different constructs plus the number of categories used for sorting. When complexity and flexibility are low, there is greater chance of misinterpreting outcomes. Anxiety generated by errors creates additional perceptual distortions in an individual and, since change is difficult for that person, life becomes threatening. The ideal mental state appears to be one of optimal cognitive complexity for a given environmental complexity. That is, one should be sufficiently cognitively complex to perceive one's environment accurately but not so complex that unnecessary effort is invested in managing the internal complexity or in overresponding to trivial factors in the environment.

Belief Systems

The Rokeach (1960) model of belief systems closely parallels the latter points noted in Kelly's model. Belief systems are divided into beliefs and disbeliefs organized at three levels: central (primitive), intermediate (how to make one's way in the world), and peripheral (attitudinal). Rokeach also uses the conception of time perspective, past, present, and future. The degree to which considerations are made broadly, involving much of the belief system, or narrowly, involving a single item, is of importance. For example, the mature person is able to delay immediate gratification in order to attain more highly valued long-term goals. This focus is obviously quite different from the central concerns in conflict models.

Open-mindedness is a function of the degree of differentiation in the disbelief system and the amount of communication possible between beliefs and disbeliefs. The flexibility inherent in open-mindedness is reminiscent of Bruner's (1957) idea of perceptual readiness. That is, open-mindedness is precognitive in nature. Anxiety is correlated with closed-mindedness or dogmatism and is probably both a cause and effect of inadequate coping.

Beliefs about the self and body image are also important to the overall Rokeach model. Those beliefs can be divided into attributions about the self on the one hand and action readiness or organization on the other. If attributions emphasize one's limitations, action is highly anxiety provoking. Therefore, it is difficult to act to create the conditions leading to positive self-esteem. A self-limiting cycle grows out of these attributions. Beliefs about body image are both the source and the result of attributions. Body image is of critical importance because it is vivid and at the nexus of intention and action. Body image mediates between the individual's beliefs about the world and the world as it is experienced.

Expectancies

Rotter's model (1954, 1966) emphasizes expectations concerning the capacity to act in the service of needs. He defines needs as McClelland does; needs are learned as a consequence of reinforcement contingencies in youth. His needs are (Rotter, 1954, p. 132):

1 Recognition-status: The need to be considered competent or good in a social, occupational, or play activity.

2 Protection-dependency: The need to have another person or group of people prevent frustration or punishment and to provide for the satisfaction of other needs.

3 Dominance: The need to direct or control the actions of other people, including members of family and friends.

4 Independence: The need to make one's own decisions, to rely on one's self, together with the need to develop skills for obtaining satisfactions directly, without mediation of other people.

5 Love and affection: The need for acceptance and indication of liking by other individuals.

6 Physical comfort: The learned need for physical satisfaction that has become associated with gaining security.

Rotter uses the concept of freedom of movement to identify the general expectation level of achieving positive need satisfaction. That is, need satisfaction generally is concluded to be attainable or unattainable depending on one's experiences. This is conceptualized in terms of personal action. Need value refers to reinforcement preferences; need potential refers to the probability that a number of relevant behaviors will occur. Thus, through development, the individual acquires needs and expectations of need gratification. The ideal person is able to forego immediate gratifications, sustain effort, and trust others because of a generalized expectancy of success. "Although the means by which this is accomplished will vary from one child to another, in general, Rotter's theory suggests the importance of the child being surrounded by adults who are trustworthy and of realistic demands and goals being set for him in terms of his ability to achieve them" (Levy, 1970, p. 423).

The notion of external versus internal locus of control of reinforcements is closely linked to generalized expectancies regarding success. Bartel (1968) found middle class children more internally oriented than lower class children, and attributed this to their relatively greater success in early life. It is also possible that limited educational advantages for lower class children restrict cognitive development and thus contribute to an inability to perceive opportunities for freedom of movement.

Internal locus of control is positively correlated not only with need satisfaction but also with self-esteem. The similarities between internal locus of control and the existential ideal of making decisions and acting emphasize the wisdom of that existential ideal. Further, if the ideal person has an internal locus of control, the ideal environment encourages self-reliance.

Developmental Adaptation

Piaget formulated a stopped or staged cognitive development model for children. The development trend is toward increasingly objective thinking, which is decreasingly superficial and magical. Thus at a particular age the concept of conservation of matter is understood (about seven or eight years of age). According to Piaget, progressing through thinking stages involves a change in the actual structure of thought since structure and function are highly interdependent. Further, Piaget emphasizes the notion that thought directs perception, so that reality is a function of one's cognitive construction of it (Wiggins, Renner, Clore, & Rose, 1976, p. 410). Rokeach supports this contention in that the closed mind not only is less permeable to information than the open mind but also deals differently with information.

Cybernetic Analogues

The final model offered is perhaps best typified by Miller, Galanter, and Pribram (1960) who, with Newell and Simon (1972) and Raphael (1976), emphasize the decision-making process. The individual is thought of as a servomechanism engaged in a feedback loop in which each unit of behavior is of a Test-Operate-Test (TOTE) character. If a test indicates incongruity between what is wanted and what exists, an operation is directed. If congruity exists, the person can move on to the next problem. Each act is the consequence of intention or will; intention is based upon the "plan" which is "any hierarchical process in the organism that can control the order in which a sequence of operations is to be performed" (Miller et al., 1960, p. 16). The plan is part of the "image" which is "all the accumulated, organized knowledge that the organism has about itself and the world" (Miller et al., 1960, p. 17). Plans are constructed from the image and pursued to the degree that outcomes are valued. Highly valued outcomes can be deferred ·for great lengths of time. Since the plan is hierarchical, some recurrent, short-term portions will come and go. Conflict may exist between plans, causing frustration and pain, but instinctual impulses are integrated into the plan and become an inherent part of it. Completion of a plan reduces tension and produces pleasure in attaining valued outcomes. Conversely, incomplete units of action (TOTE units) generate tension and increase perceptual sensitivity. Thus, before mailing an important letter one may notice every post box that is passed, but after mailing the letter one ceases to notice them.

Parts of the plan or the plan itself can be given up if the pain is too great and an alternative plan is available. Hypnotism and brainwashing are two alternative ways in which a plan can be abandonded. If habits or tactics remain and the plan is simply lost, a sense of compulsiveness is expected, but when the reverse occurs the syndrome would be labeled schizophrenia. The centrality of the plan in processing information and directing behavior is emphasized by Newell and Simon (1967). They define cognitive complexity not only in terms of the number of dimensions, but also in terms of the integrating rules and the complexity and flexibility of their use. The plan at once organizes life and makes manifest its inherent existential meaning.

Summary

All of the cognitive/perceptual models discussed have mutual consistencies. Conceptions of self and the world are organized in some highly complex and individualized cognitive manner. Thereby they affect perceptions of the world, response tendencies, and adaptation capacities. The object of life is to reach gratification and avoid particular levels or types of pain, frustration, or deprivation. Just as Tolman's rat, which was allowed to view a maze from above, subsequently performed necessary tasks better in search of reinforcements, humans use concepts to comprehend, anticipate, plan, and behave in order to reach desired outcomes. Discomfort is tolerated when necessary, especially in the short run, because it is balanced against potential gratifications. Conceptions about the self are central, and the existentialists' notions of continuous choice and the need for meaning in life are easily integrated into cognitive models. The problem central to the conflict models' view of competing desires and unacceptable impulses is addressed in the ego structures developed in the cognitive/perceptual models. The solution is one of mental mastery through cognitive complexity and flexibility.

Contextual Models

In contextual models, social dynamics and other ongoing external realities are more important than idiosyncracies of personality. Levy captures this position graphically.

> John Donne once observed that no man is an island . . . It is possible to argue, however, that just as an island's topography and other characteristics cannot be explained without recourse to the climate, surrounding ocean currents, and geological processes and structures of which it is a part, so the personality of an individual cannot be understood apart from the context in which he is found. (Levy, 1970, p. 307)

The fields of social psychology, sociology, and anthropology explore the interaction of the individual with the context, and from these fields some useful, fundamental conceptions of the individual have emerged. Lewin's work (1935, 1951) provides the starting point for this discussion, which proceeds from the more psychological to the more sociological view of the individual in the context.

Field Theory

Lewin's work provides a bridge between cognitive/perceptual models and contextual models of human functioning. Lewin emerged from the tradition of Gestalt psychology in which perception, and especially perception of the whole rather than independent parts, was emphasized. Perception of the self, the context, and most importantly, the self in the context was the key to the gestaltists' view; Lewin developed field theory to facilitate simultaneous consideration of this perceptual whole. According to field theory, behavior is a function of the individual's psychological field rather than a function of physical realities, but "the dynamics of the processes is always derived from the relation of the concrete individual to the concrete situation" (Lewin, 1935, p. 41).

According to Lewin, the psychological field has a complex construction. The personality has two regions: the outer, motoric region and the inner, personal region. Perception, cognition, and physical action take place in the outer region, and it is here that the "life space" representation of the individual's environment is experienced. Needs and tensions reside in the inner region, in a number of somewhat independent systems. Needs and tensions in one system can affect other systems and communication among systems is assumed. Needs are seen as basic; unfulfilled needs create tension. There is a tendency for the system as a whole to reach an equilibrium, but this does not imply a lack of tension in the whole system or in any individual system. *Tensions and needs* of the inner system *energize action* and the field forces of the outer system direct behavior. Tension is natural and, at normal levels, constructive.

Individuals move through their life spaces attempting to attain or maintain equilibrium. Objects in the life space are seen as having forces affecting the individual. Thus, attractive objects in the field are said to have positive valence and repulsive objects, negative valence. Distances, vectors, and barriers are used graphically to illustrate the dynamics of personality. The force field analysis of experiential learning in the Introduction of this book illustrates the value, simplicity, and intuitive clarity of the Lewinian approach to understanding human functioning.

Development or maturation, from this perspective, involves increasing the differentiation of the life space and the number of specialized functions and structures within it that are available to the person. Witkin (1965) added that maturity implies increasing the separation of feeling from perception, thinking from acting, and self from nonself. This implies that one's life space more closely approximates physical reality as one matures. Increased integration follows increased differentiation so that the individual can maintain a level of efficiency in coping with the world. The notion of cognitive complexity is obviously similar to differentiation of life space, but it is important to note that the life space involves the psychological experiencing of the self and the world rather than merely conceptions about the self and the world. A person with high cognitive complexity could exist in a relatively simple life space as, for example, a dedicated, single astrophysicist who lives alone in an observatory on top of a mountain. Development according to Lewin is continuous rather than epochal as asserted by Freud, Erikson, and many others. Further, development can be reversed; that is, structures can be eliminated.

Symbolic Interactionism

George H. Mead (1943) also saw individuals conceptualizing themselves in terms of interactions with the environment. He originally called himself a social behaviorist but current personality experts consider him a symbolic interactionist. The following captures the essence of Mead's view.

> In the course of learning to play games children develop the capacity to anticipate the responses of others and to put themselves in the position of others, to assume their attitudes. In this way they become able to participate in games, and, more generally, to take the role of the generalized other—they learn to respond symbolically to their own behavior as others would so that they can anticipate how others will respond to their behavior. (Levy, 1970, p. 310)

Language provides the means and internalization is the process by which the "generalized other" is experienced. Although this is obviously a highly cognitive model, Mead emphasizes that conceptions of the generalized other and the self in relation to others is the consequence of social interaction, especially early in life. Further, he builds on the more fundamental view that the person accepts the need to control hostile impulses in order to receive the benefits of organized society, especially protection from the hostile impulses of others. This acceptance can be overt or implicit; it assumes the existence of a society structured to define goals and to control the behavior of its members so that those goals are pursued. The establishment of a sense of self occurs early in life and is the behavioristic consequence of social reinforcements. Once established, the self is a rather stable entity.

Inte personal Psychology

Harry S. Sullivan (1947, 1953) blended Mead's approach with psychoanalysis. Through interpersonal relationships, the individual attempts to maximize satisfaction of fundamental needs while minimizing anxiety. The central strategy for accomplishing this is by seeking the approval of "significant" others in the family and among peers. Reality is constructed through communication with others and attributions and reactions of others, all of which create a sense of self. Subsequent interactions with others become somewhat self fulfilling prophecies. The family is central in determining the self-dynamism of the individual. That is, if the family of a child is chiefly derogatory, so will the child's self-dynamism be; it "will facilitate disparaging and hostile appraisals of itself" (Sullivan, 1947, p. 22). Similarly, parental permissiveness generates spontaneity and encourages independence, resulting in achievement. Ultimately, the sense of self is shaped by wider circles of people, groups, communities, and larger segments of society such as classes. Although development is seen to occur in stages similar to Freud's, the critical issues according to Sullivan are the social dynamics in each phase, not the psychosexual issues. These vary from trying to communicate in preverbal periods to attempting to meet sexual needs in puberty while coping with cultural norms, social forces, and family expectations.

Communication

As an extension of Mead's and Sullivan's ideas, the notion of communication has been proposed as a perspective for understanding human functioning (Bateson, Jackson, Haley, & Weakland, 1956; Jackson, 1968a, 1968b; Watzlawick, Beavin, & Jackson, 1967; Watzlawick, Weakland, & Fisch, 1974). From this perspective, the inevitability of one's interactions with the environment is the essence of being human; the structure of these interactions can be used as a basis for understanding behavior. The approach stresses the importance of relationships and feedback (in the sense of systems theory) in describing the communication process.

Much of the work conducted from this perspective has focused on schizophrenic behavior as explained by the double bind theory. The double bind requires ongoing or repeated interactions in a relationship. These interactions have three qualities: a primary negative injunction in the form, "you must or must not do this or I will punish you"; a secondary negative injunction, usually communicated nonverbally, contradicting the first; and a tertiary negative injunction preventing the individual from avoiding the first two (Watzlawick, 1968, pp. 63–65). Within the family, for example, a child absorbs conflicting messages from parents and significant others, and is also the object of their attributions. From this situation, the child makes inferences which affect later behavior. This is defined in transactional analysis as the scripting process (Berne, 1972; Steiner, 1974). Eventually, the individual can lose the ability to think rationally about certain aspects of life.

Intrapersonal and Interpersonal Costs and Benefits

John W. Thibaut and Harold H. Kelley (1959), George Homans (1950), and many other social psychologists view the individual as experiencing a set of relationships whereby costs and benefits are incurred. Costs include anxiety, pain, subservience, and effort expended to receive benefits. Benefits include drive gratification and the pleasure of need reduction. Most significantly, the individual must develop and maintain interpersonal relationships in which reciprocal benefits play a key role. Any individual is dependent on others for gratifications; if gratifications achieve or surpass some internally held standard, called a comparison level (CL), outcomes are considered satisfactory. Relationships are maintained if experienced or anticipated gratifications are equal to or greater than what could be achieved by changing. This standard is called the comparison level for alternatives (CL alt). The individual makes an ongoing cost and benefit analysis of relationships, based on both internal goals and market realities, much as a business person ideally makes economic calculations to optimize on investments. Additional constraints, however, limit choice; for example, a child cannot easily choose to terminate a relationship with its parents. Dilemmas arise either when the individual is dissatisfied and cannot find a superior alternative or when the individual experiences adequate gratification but new alternatives hold the possibility of higher satisfaction levels. In these circumstances, decision making is ruled by outcomes rather than by self-image or other facets of the individual's internal psychosocial world. Thinking serves gratification in a relatively uncluttered or unconflicted way.

Thibaut and Kelley's view in some respects is consistent with conflict, existential, cognitive, and other contextual models, but it is inconsistent with Rogers' or Maslow's view of self-actualization. Growth and development are sought not for their own sake but for self-improvement and better decision-making ability. These increased capacities can generate more alternatives from which to choose and thus raise the comparison level. Self-actualization is viewed as work and is ideally minimized since intrinsic gratification is not part of this model. The benefits of self-actualization relate to progress toward a state in which other extrinsic benefits will accrue. In fact, since self-actualizing increases potential for social gratification by making the individual a more desirable member of relationships, one can view self-actualization as a cost.

Sociology/Anthropology

Some model of human functioning is always present in the macro social sciences, but it is not always consistently or clearly articulated. Overt considerations of how individuals adapt to society can be organized into two general models, the structural functional model and the definitionist model.

Structural functionalism, like other contextual theories, emphasizes the "facts" of social organization. These include roles, norms, status, and the necessity of shaping individuals to fulfill positions within the society via rewards, punishments, and, most important, social acceptance. In the extreme view (Parsons, 1951), the individual is programmed early to behave in prescribed ways and to respond to social directives and pressures in a conforming manner. People do what is required to get what they want. Thought is directed primarily at the challenge of picking up clues and choosing appropriate behaviors. According to Merton (1957), it is important that all individuals share an understanding of their society's status system so that common expectancies and evaluations of outcomes will occur. Comprehension is likely to be precognitive as well as cognitive; one can react to a stimulus without conceptualizing it, although a sense of understanding usually contributes to efficient coping with the structure.

Role conflict and ambiguity constitute the chief sources of anxiety for the individual. Competing demands and unclear expectations increase the subjective quality of social behavioral processes. Most members of society carry a moderate amount of this burden and use recreation, intoxicants, television, and other diversions to escape from it. When the burden is great, individuals try to change the situation or themselves. It is a straightforward question of costs, benefits, and opportunities for change.

The definitionists see people controlling their environment, not serving it. Blumer (1969), for example, echoes and extends Mead's symbolic interactionism by placing the individual center stage in the role construction process. The sense of self affects the role an individual will take and how that role will be constructed (Turner & Shosid, 1976). The sense of self and attendant expectations for the self can easily be at odds with the expectations of society. Such conflicts result in negotiation between the individual and society to establish mutually acceptable arrangements. According to definitionists, perhaps as little as ten percent of individual behavior is structurally programmed.

Ethnomethodologists extend the definitionist position beyond the symbolic interactionists' conception (Garfinkel, 1967). Their position emphasizes a view of human functioning in which people think in complex linguistically determined ways. The goal is to make sense out of existence. Social rules are sufficiently ambiguous that a personal meaning is always available to the individual. It is at this level that sanctions, expectations, and negotiations take place. As with the existentialists, meaning may predominate over pleasure, and, consistent with Allport's thoughts on fulfillment, active coping with the world is seen as preferable to passive acceptance of and conformity to demands from the world.

Summary

The contextual models almost ignore the conflict and the actualizing models of human functioning. Anxiety is tolerated as part of the social condition and escaped when possible. Satisfaction and gratification are pursued; work and discomfort are avoided; social acceptance is needed. Thought is relatively simple and directed toward evaluation of social demands and possibilities. If self-actualization is to occur, it must be of two varieties. The first is creative fulfillment of a role and the second is through negotiating with the environment to construct roles. The contextual model graphically portrays how society and its regulations can result in a pattern of stimulation and guidance. Consequently, consistency models probably fit the more sociological type of contextual models.

Learning Theories Models

Resurging interest in behaviorism during the early 1970s was at least partially a reaction to overly enthusiastic emphasis on cognitive and actualizing models during the 1950s and 1960s. Most of the central notions of the behavioristic position were articulated by the late 1940s. For this discussion, "learning theories" is a preferred term to behaviorism since more recent social learning theories and the subfield of cognitive behaviorism are easily included within the former title but have broader implications than behaviorism alone.

> Personality formulations based on learning are characteristically historical in perspective, draw upon principles that are not considered species-specific or limited to personality, are not concerned with the specific content of behavior, and avoid postulating any kind of active agent, intrapsychic entity, or process. In addition, in accounting for behavioral acquisition and change these formulations give no special conceptual status to development and explicitly avoid the use of physiological, neurological, or genetic constructs. Thus, the personality theorist guided by a learning conception of personality restricts his domain of study to learned behavior and his explanatory constructs to those that can be anchored in the individual's interaction with his environment. (Levy, 1970, p. 436)

The discussion of learning theories first treats moderate behaviorism; second, radical behaviorism; third, social learning theory; and fourth, cognitive behaviorism. Although learning or change is the focus of these models, a clear conception of human functioning is emphasized.

Moderate Behaviorism

Moderate behaviorism refers to a broad set of models and insights regarding the reactions of individuals or the organism (O) to stimuli (S) and to reinforcement (R). The organism has drives for such things as sex, food, water, and air. The individual attempts to reduce drive tension through behavior. The process of conditioning refers to behavioral responses elicited by a new or conditioned stimulus; drives are the internal mechanism fueling the behavior. Thus the classical conditioning of Pavlov's dogs (1927) demonstrated that the unconditioned stimulus of food, presented simultaneously with a bell, resulted in the dog salivating at the sound of the bell, just as it had in response to the presentation of food. A secondary stimulus was substituted for the primary one. Thorndike (1898, 1911) showed that a third stimulus could be substituted for the secondary stimulus (that is, a light substituted for a bell). The key issue is evoking the drive that ultimately results in the behavior. In instrumental conditioning the second stimulus is presented after the behavior is elicited, not simultaneously with the primary stimulus. It is a reinforcement of the response and the response is instrumental in getting the stimulus. Thus stimuli can result in drive reduction as well as drive activation, and thereby can result in increased probability of the occurrence of the desired behavior.

Guthrie (1935) demonstrated that more contiguous (close in time) presentations of two stimuli resulted in faster classical conditioning. Hull (1943) showed that reinforcements could be presented simultaneously with generated behavior if connected to the activating stimulus. Thus, the model implies that connections made by individuals are rather mindless, conceptualizations have little value, and extinction or cessation of behavior occurs in the absence of continued positive reinforcement. Behavior reinforced over a long period of time may become habituated, that is, it will persist even in the absence of reinforcement. When reinforcements are intermittent rather than consistent, behaviors are extinguished more slowly. This outcome is not predicted by cognitive theorists, who suggest that expectations and probability estimates affect behavior in a different, more logical manner. George Kelly does not allow for habits except those of thinking in ways to gain control of life. Fulfillment and conflict models generally ignore the importance of behavioristic habits. Contextual models for the most part are behavioristic, even though they allow for some mediating thought. For example, although one tends to respond behavioristically to reinforcements, one can choose the stimulus and reinforcement environment.

Radical Behaviorism

Radical behaviorism, usually associated with J.B. Watson (1924) and B.F. Skinner (1938, 1953, 1969, 1971), allows for habits but ignores drives and drive activation. Here, the individual acts in a variety of ways, and when one of these actions is followed by positive reinforcement the behavior is more likely to occur again. This process is called operant conditioning. Reinforcements can be almost anything at a particular point in time; there is no assumption that they reduce drives. Superstitious behavior is behavior repeated in spite of very few reinforcements. This occurs when the behavior or the reinforcement at one point had special salience or value to the individual. The closest thing to actualization in this perspective is the spontaneous and somewhat random generation of new behaviors in the absence of sufficiently rewarded old behaviors. The more cognitive models of human functioning have little consistency with or relevance to the radical behavioristic position.

Social Learning

The social learning model views reinforcement as a determinate of behavior, but holds cognition as central to how the individual functions. Bandura and Walters (1963) reason that if life were only a trial and error process, few would ever reach adulthood. Necessary skills such as driving a car would be impossible to acquire through reinforcement alone. Our saving capacity is that of observation. By watching others act and by carefully noting action and vicariously experiencing the reinforcement, learning can proceed without direct involvement. According to Bandura and Walters, "the acquisition of imitative responses results primarily from the contiguity of sensory events, whereas response consequences to the model or to the observer have a major influence only on the performance of imitatively learned responses" (1963, p. 57). Thus vicarious reinforcement, in addition to actual reinforcement, can affect individual behavior. What the individual sees in a particular situation and what can be abstracted from it depend on cognitive differentiation and other mental capacities. Identification with the individual performing the modeling can be the result of some particularly attractive aspect of that person or of the relationship with the person. In a sense, the primary reinforcement in the process of identification is the inherent relationship with the object of observation, and the secondary reinforcement in the process is the reinforcement received personally by the model.

In social learning theory, it is assumed that the individual stores data about past reinforcements seen and experienced and that expectations are thus generated. Rotter's internal versus external locus of control is an example of this type of expectation. The basic drives discussed in behaviorism are organized into need categories such as recognition, dominance, independence, affection, and comfort; the individual is seen to be increasingly more thoughtful and more likely to make and implement plans as maturity is gained. This clearly is not pure behaviorism.

The social learning perspective emphasizes a more limited thought process than do the cognitive/perceptual models, but allows more for the construction of one's own world than does the contextual model. Conflict and fulfillment models have little relevance, with the exception that life is directed toward increased capacity to find gratification and to create alternatives where multiple needs and drives can be satisfied simultaneously. Although individuals are considered reinforcement-oriented, they are seen as more able to affect contingencies in this view than in the radical or moderate behaviorist's view.

Cognitive Behaviorism

Cognitive behaviorism is an extension of normal "mindless" behaviorism up to and beyond the points discussed under social learning. It also is somewhat of a hybridization of the cognitive/perceptual model of human functioning. In cognitive behaviorism, the individual does not respond to an objective and real environment but to a perceived environment. In other words, there are mediating factors in the reinforcement process. N. Miller (1935) noted the importance of perceptiostimulus in behaviorism and Lloyd Homme (1965) encouraged study on these "coverants" or covert operants of the mind. Bandura (1969) documented (behavioristic) clinical evidence of cognitive-symbolic mediation, and set the stage for "mental" expansion of the behavioristic paradigm. This expansion, however, does not extend so far as to negate totally Watson's aversion to representations of the mind as a spirit. No mind–body duality is implied in cognitive behaviorism. Instead, methodological leeway is allowed for inference beyond the strictly observable behavioral data, but the linkage to observation remains a tight one.

Mahoney (1974) offers three mediational models for cognitive behavior modification: covert conditioning, information processing, and cognitive learning. Covert conditioning has a number of facets. First it is acknowledged that the behavioristic stimulus can have a covert (inner) response that could eventually constitute a covert stimulus. Mental imagery, for example, is cited as mediating the effects of punishment (Mahoney, Thoresen, & Danaher, 1972), and is considered separable from behavioral response. Furthermore, recall is moderated by simultaneous use of imagery. According to Mahoney, the covert agent can be effectively thought of as (1) antecedent, (2) behavior, or (3) consequence. One, two, or all three of these events can be covert for a given situation and each covert element can interact functionally with overt elements or with each other (Thoresen & Mahoney, 1974). Individuals experience some "coverants" as "voices in the head" according to Meichenbaum (1973, 1974), Meichenbaum and Cameron (1973a, 1973b), and others who recently have moved aggressively to link this reality to the powerful change forces of traditional behaviorism. Based on these relatively modest extensions of the behavioristic paradigm, new therapies such as thought stopping, covert sensitization and desensitization, counterconditioning, covert control, and other self-instructional methods have been developed (Mahoney, 1974; Meichenbaum, 1975).

The information-processing mediational model borrows heavily from information-centered cognitive/perceptual models of human functioning. Issues of special interest to cognitive behaviorists (Mahoney, 1974, pp. 125–143) include:

1 Attention (recognition of effects, pattern matching, feature detection, etc.).

2 Encoding and short-term memory (e.g., mediating effects of duration of stimulus, repetition with related recall, *primacy-recency,* "chunking" of data bits (small groupings).

3 Retention, retrieval and long-term memory (the effects of visual versus verbal imagery on recall, recognition capacity, and consolidation).

The linkage to behavioral consequences is tighter in this model than in the cognitive/perceptual models, which pursue a more philosophical explanation.

The third mediational model is "cognitive learning." It builds on the views of Kelly, Rotter, and other cognitive/perceptual predecessors, and is based on the idea that people are both controlled and controlling, both the product and the producers of their experiences (Kanfer & Karoly, 1972). People are seen as highly conceptualy complex, not as the *tabulae rasae* of strict behaviorism. According to this model (Mahoney, 1974, p. 146), memory and thinking:

1 Mediate temporal intervals.
2 Impose regularities on experience.
3 Anticipate the consequences of actions.
4 Economize our problem solving efforts.

Attentional and relational factors are emphasized in this view. Distractions mediate pain. Thought control can aid in deferral of gratifications, but poor attentional tendencies can result in misperception and mislabeling, inattention or its opposite, maladaptive focusing or even maladaptive self-arousal. Since individuals "squeeze reality into organized perceptions" (Mahoney, 1974, p. 153), they can easily overattend or underattend to any given facet of reality.

Relational processes refer to transformations of information after encoding. These include classifying, comparing, evaluating, coding (through summary labels or imagery), inferring implications from the information, and calculating possibilities.

Summary

For the learning theorists, the organism first and foremost wants gratification and does what is necessary to receive positive reinforcements and avoid punishment. A world in which positive reinforcements exist simultaneously with punishments is not necessary and may not even be likely. Actualization would be a waste of energy if not connected with positive reinforcements. Similarly, pleasure is the reason for cognitive functioning and its proper focus. Consistency theories are applicable to the degree that a given tendency to respond to a stimulus such as challenge is habituated. More complex conceptual and contextual approaches go far beyond learning theories. These approaches assume much of what learning theory has demonstrated or is concerned with. However, they also go beyond the simpler view of the world implied in behaviorism models.

Clearly the informational and cognitive learning models dramatically expand the role of thought in cognitive behaviorism since thought is no longer conceived of in stimulus-reinforcement terms. But important learning theory perspective remains; teleology is still minimized, the mind does not have its own intentions, the purpose of life is simple. Thinking is directed toward the issues of discomfort and pleasure.

Life Sciences Models

> The brain developed first to be of service to the gut, not to enable us to
> develop art and philosophy and thought. (Bailey, 1960)

Many of the theories of human functioning discussed assume or imply a
biological core for humans. However, surprisingly little documentation
from the life sciences is used in creating these positions. This is unfortunate because the life sciences offer much important information about the
nature of human functioning. It is significant that social scientists have
now begun the task of incorporating this information into their paradigms
(Campbell, 1975). Life sciences considered in this discussion include
ethology, the study of animal behavior; sociobiology, the "systematic study
of the biological basis of all social behavior" (Wilson, 1975, p. 4); and
neuroscience, the study of the actual physical characteristics of the human
brain. Other significant life sciences are cellular biology, physiological
psychology, behavioral ecology, endocrinology, and biology. In addition,
both sociobiology and human ethology use anthropology for orientation.
Any comprehensive treatment of the life sciences within the context of
this book would be overwhelming and distracting to the reader, but a brief
consideration of the salient aspects of this approach is essential to an
understanding of human functioning.

Generally, the life sciences seek to describe those aspects of human
functioning that have physical and instinctual sources. Neurophysiology or
neuroscience scrutinizes chemical, electrolytic, and cybernetic aspects of
brain functioning, as well as the actual physical constitution of the brain.
Ethologists until recently restricted their attention to primates, using
naturalistic observation strategies and field experimentation to draw conclusions about instinctual and learned patterns of adaptive behavior. At
present, ethology is more broadly used in two different approaches. The
first draws analogies between humans and one or more other species.
Nobel prize winner Konrad Lorenz (1952, 1970, 1971) is perhaps the best
known of these ethologists, but one could also include popular writers such
as Ardrey (1966, 1970), Goodall (1965), Morris (1967), and Tiger and Fox
(1971). The second approach, advocated by Tinbergen (1951, 1968, 1972,
1973) and pursued by Bowlby (1973), is the application of ethological
methods to the study of human behavior, rather than the attempted application to *Homo sapiens* of ethological findings in other species. Both uses
of ethology are synthesized and extended in sociobiology.

Critics of the use of the life sciences to explain human behavior have
emphasized the enormous gap between instinct and behavior in humans
as evidenced by dramatic variations in behavioral patterns across cultures.
While social scientists focus on observables and manipulables, ethologists
or sociobiologists can only speculate, interpolate, and infer. For the most
part, however, the social scientist concentrates on exploring phenotypes

or phenomena while the sociobiologist attempts to understand genotypes or the principles or structures underlying the phenomena. Barash (1977) offers the following rhetorical argument for the sociobiological approach:

> Sufis are an ancient sect of Moslem mystics who have been particularly adept at highlighting the human penchant for self-delusion. When Nasrudin, the idiot-savant of Sufi literature was grovelling in the dusty street, a friend asked what the problem was. Nasrudin explained that he had lost his house key and was searching for it. The friend offered to help and after a long, unsuccessful search he asked whether Nasrudin was certain that the key was dropped in that spot. "Oh, no," replied Nasrudin, "I dropped it near my house," a full block away. Seeing his friend's perplexity, Nasrudin explained, "But the light is so much better here!" (Barash, 1977, p. 5–6)

There may well be a lesson in this: If psychology and the other behavioral sciences truly wish to find a key, they may have to look where it is a bit darker.

Ethology

Konrad Lorenz (1966, 1970) was the first to argue that much could be learned about human functioning through the systematic study of other species. Generally, ethologists study the way in which sustenance, social organization, mating, procreation, and rearing of offspring are accomplished in different species, and how the instincts that meet these fundamental requirements affect the destiny of the human species. Lorenz emphasized the study of aggression, a virtually universal propensity among vertebrates and an issue of great interest following World War II.

Instincts associated with aggression were found to be linked in complex ways to behavior such as attack. For example, a male stickleback is more ferocious within its own well-defined territory than when outside it. Internal states such as hormonal balance also affect behavior. For example, the mating season of the stickleback correlates with the hormonal levels associated with aggression. Finally, specific cues, called innate releasing mechanisms, trigger instinctual responses. The male stickleback displays an inflated red belly in season to attract females, but when this visual cue is presented by a possible intruder, it triggers attack. Attack against intruders even occurs when an appropriately marked dummy, with no other resemblance to a fish, is used. Innate releasing mechanisms, environment, hormonal state, and territory are all central in explaining aggression in animals. Other mechanisms, such as mental "imprinting" of a mother's image on baby birds during a critical youthful period, are used to explain other adaptive tendencies.

The first and simplest application of ethology to human functioning emphasizes the comparisons between human behavior and that of other species. For example, Tinbergen (1968) noted that aggression in species other than human beings seldom leads to murder and never to genocide. This is because other species have developed submission signals and have evolved mechanisms for tests of strength resulting in minimizing risks of fatality. The reason for the difference is that in the genetically brief period of 4000 years (and especially during the last 100 years) instruments for killing humans have short-circuited "normal" instinctual controls on fatal outcomes. To kill each other, people no longer have to engage in hand-to-hand combat, or even to see each other. The human propensity for social organization and intergroup aggression further separates the individual aggressor from the victim. Social mechanisms such as dehumanizing the enemy also contribute to this process, but ethologists tend not to speculate in this area.

The second ethological approach is the application of the ethological method to the human species. Tinbergen summarizes:

> The potential usefulness of ethology lies in the fact that, unlike other sciences of behavior, ethology applies the method or "approach" of biology to the phenomena behavior. It has developed a set of concepts and terms that allow us to ask:
>
> 1 In what ways does this phenomenon (behavior) influence the survival, the success of the animal?
> 2 What makes behavior happen at any given moment? How does its "machinery" work?
> 3 How does the behavior machinery develop as the individual grows up?
> 4 How have the behavior systems of each species evolved until they became what they are now?
>
> The first question, that of survival value, has to do with the effects of behavior; the other three are, each on a different time scale, concerned with its causes. (Tinbergen, 1968, pp. 141–142)

Tinbergen's observations of human tendencies toward group aggression demonstrate this extension in reasoning. Another application of this second ethological approach is provided by Bowlby (1973), who documented a wide variety of naturalistic experiments exploring the significance and implications of attachment and loss in humans. He described the phenomena of separation of a human child from its mother, and built upon ethologist Harlow's (1966) findings that infant rhesus monkeys prefer a cloth dummy "mother" with no milk to a wire dummy "mother" with milk. According to his view, attachment to a mother figure is a primary instinctual response in humans; it is not a learned tendency related to feeding and comfort.

When fear is evoked in a child who is separated from its mother, the child's response is to get back to the mother. This is true even if taking the direct path to the mother actually increases the danger, such as when a child runs across a road in front of an oncoming vehicle. Key fear-evoking stimuli for children are noises, sudden changes in illumination, sudden movements, strange or unfamiliar people, animals, and darkness. Bowlby argues that fear of each of these stimuli, especially in the absence of the mother, undoubtedly contributed to the survival potential of a child in our evolutionary past. Thus fear and separation are related to instincts for survival. In contrast to conflict models of human functioning, this ethological model points out the positive value of fear and its survival function.

Bowlby even goes so far as to postulate that anxiety is closely related to these underlying dynamics of separation. Anxiety and loneliness are seen as important and deep-rooted instinctual bases for infant survival. Anxiety in a world with real dangers is natural according to this view, whereas conflict models assert that anxiety is the outcome of unresolved conflicts. Loneliness implies lack of attachment and support according to the ethological view rather than lack of romantic fulfillment. One possible implication is that even Maslow's higher needs are, in reality, complex cultural adaptations of basic survival instincts. The desire not to be frightened by the sudden or unexpected recalls the consistency theories. The idea that immediate environmental stimuli and specific sequences of events mediate the effects of a particular stimulus recalls the cognitive/perceptual and contextual models. However, the belief that adaptive behavior is learned through basic reinforcements, association, and generalization mechanisms is opposed by the *Homo sapiens* ethologists, for whom attachment is not learned but instinctual.

Sociobiology

Sociobiology has a totally evolutionary orientation. It echoes ethology in this regard but goes further by using population statistical analysis and other techniques to paint a more complete picture of the nature of human functioning. From this perspective, the core of existence is the passing on of the individual's genes through reproduction. The new sociobiology differs from the Darwinian notion of survival in that the latter stresses survival of the species while the former stresses survival of the individual's genes. "Fitness" is a key term describing the genotypical characteristics of an individual that contribute to successful genetic continuation. Barash states:

> Evolutionary theory suggests that living things should devote themselves totally to the production of offspring. And in a real sense they do. Thus, such maintenance activities as eating, defecating, resting, scratching, preening, or whatever, are ultimately of importance only as they translate to inclusive fitness. The same applies even more directly to social activities such as

fighting, courting, defending territories, and avoiding predators. In fact, true hedonism, like true altruism, probably has no place in the biological world. Insofar as animals do something because they enjoy it, that very enjoyment is interpretable as an evolutionary strategy inducing living things to function in a way that ultimately enhances their fitness. In other words, organisms are programmed to seek rest when they are weary or food when they are hungry or to scratch when they itch, because to some extent these satisfactions are adaptive. (Barash, 1977, p. 179)

A brief summary of the evolutionary background of *Homo sapiens* provides a starting point for the sociobiological perspective. Following this, some salient aspects of life such as aggression and territoriality, sex, mating and reproduction, altruism, competition, and social coordination can be considered.

Wilson (1975) summarized the accepted phylogeny of *Homo sapiens*. As a result of ecological change, about 14 million years ago our predominantly fruit-eating predecessors began to move from the jungle to the open woodlands, and, about 5 million years ago, to the savanna and grasslands. They began eating grain and competing with other animals for carrion. Group organization was necessary for survival, as was improved running, free use of the hands, and a stronger opposable thumb. Brain size increased rapidly: 400–500 cubic centimeters 3 million years ago, 1000 cubic centimeters 1 million years ago, 1400–1700 cubic centimeters for Neanderthal Man, and 1900–2000 cubic centimeters for *Homo sapiens.* The increased thinking ability that accompanied increased brain size led to improved social organization, resulting in domination by *Homo sapiens* of the environment. About 10,000 years ago, the advent of agriculture set the stage for man's final ascent. Biologically, however, our species has changed little in a brief 10,000 years, and sociobiologists argue that to understand the true nature of people today one must look at what must have occurred in the dim past. Herein lies the significance of the Sufi story offered earlier.

Barash (1977) speculated that sugar tastes sweet to humans because ripe fruit was more nourishing for our predecessors than green fruit. Similarly, sex has a number of important "fitness" implications. For *Homo sapiens,* estrus, or the period of female "heat," has been replaced by continuous sexual activity. This provides a critical and durable male–female bond for human marriage which in turn is necessary for the long child-rearing period in our species (Wilson, 1975, p. 554). The need for such an additional bond is easily assertable. Wilson emphasizes, however, that sex is an antisocial force for all species; at the very least it introduces genetic dissimilarities and inevitably correlative conflicts of interest. For example, in invertebrate societies of high social organization and high cooperation, whole generations of "sisters" are genetically identical and have no reproductive functions or capacities.

The object of mating is the transmittal of genes, and for sexual species both the male and female contribute half of the genes to each offspring. The individual purpose of life is to have successful offspring, that is, offspring that also reproduce. The reproductive instinct is strong because one would not exist unless one's parents and other ancestors had this instinct. In mating, the male tries to attract as many females as possible and mate with them all. The female selects the one male who is most "fit" and who also is likely to be the most responsible during the rearing of offspring. Thus both sexes attempt to maximize their genetic fitness through different instinctive reproductive strategies.

The human species is both the most widely distributed and broadly characterized on the planet because its intelligence has allowed both genetic and social variations. In his chapter on the four pinnacles of social evolution Wilson states:

> To visualize the main features of social behavior in all organisms at once, from colonial jellyfish to man, is to encounter a paradox. We should first note that social systems have originated repeatedly in one major group of organisms after another, achieving widely different degrees of specialization and complexity. Four groups occupy pinnacles high above the others; the colonial invertebrates, the social insects, the nonhuman mammals, and man. Each has basic qualities of social life unique to itself. Here, then, is the paradox. Although the sequence just given proceeds from unquestionably more primitive and older forms of life to more advanced and recent ones, the key properties of social existence, including cohesiveness, altruism, and cooperativeness, decline. It seems as through social evolution has slowed as the body plan of the individual organism became more elaborate. (Wilson, 1975, p. 379)

This supports the notion of self-actualization—each individual can pursue his or her genetic potential to its fullest since, ultimately, such pursuit increases the individual's probability of success. The very intelligence and dominance of *Homo sapiens* both generates and is the result of this genetic diversity. It also explains why a broad variety of social systems have worked for *Homo sapiens* (in contrast to other species, where there is little room for error) and why some social system or cultural organizing force is necessary. Almost anything will work, but something is necessary. Remember, 10,000 years is a very brief period of time in evolutionary terms.

Aggression is an issue of central interest to sociobiologists and it seems to occur primarily when contest competition (one wins and one loses) is central to fitness. By contrast, scramble competition (one wins and the other is unaffected) provides no incentive for aggression. Our predecessors formed tight groups to protect themselves from predators and to hunt (or scavenge) for food. Group aggression, therefore, is biologically predicted (Tinbergen, 1968). For mating activities, however, group cohesion is limited since individual males compete with each other for females, who attempt to select the best of the males. Money, status, and power, as well as physical attraction, are the means by which this competition takes place, and thus competition in the "man's world" is seen as natural by sociobiologists. Territorial defense occurs when individuals are engaged in contest competition and when the territory (job, house, country) is defendable. Finally, increases in one-to-one contact due to crowding increase the likelihood that contest encounters will occur and thus affect levels of aggression. The presence of male sexual hormones is correlated strikingly with aggression in both males and females in virtually all vertebrates.

Altruism is the antithesis of the type of selfishness just discussed. It involves risking or even sacrificing one's own fitness to increase another's fitness. Thus an individual prairie dog will sound an alarm when a predator comes near its "town" even though this action increases its own risk. Sociobiologists argue that this type of altruism is highly justifiable when parents attempt to save their offspring. It becomes less so with nephews, nieces, and so forth, depending on the degree to which genes are shared. Altruism is also justified in a community in which reciprocity is general. According to Barash (1977), group survival is a much less acceptable explanation of altruism than family, kin, and reciprocity factors. These factors are surprisingly well documented in explaining altruism in virtually all species. In short, "altruism" is pursued when there are selfish fitness implications. This is very similar to Thibaut and Kelley's model in which individuals weigh costs and benefits before acting, except here the "weighing" was done half a million years ago.

The human ability to communicate is as profound and unique as human intelligence when compared to other species. "The great dividing line in the evolution of communication lies between man and all of the remaining ten million or so species of organisms" (Wilson, 1975, p. 177) and "the development of human speech represents a quantum jump in evolution comparable to the assembly of the eucaryotic cell" (p. 556). The implications for the social behavior of humans are profound, especially since "social behavior comprises the set of phenotypes farthest removed from DNA. As such it is an evolutionarily very labile (unstable) phenomenon" (Wilson, 1975, p. 202).

Thus social behavior is the result of genotypical propensities such as mating, which are transformed through communication. And here humans have another unique capacity. Prestige, wealth, attractiveness, territory, and power are currencies by which men attract potential mates; communication is the process by which the attraction and its interpretation occur. It is through communication that culture is transmitted, so that "underprescribed" social behavioral tendencies in humans compared to other species can be prescribed in a different fashion.

Underprescription does not mean that culture has been freed from genes. What has evolved is the capacity for culture, indeed the overwhelming tendency to develop one culture or another. More ominously Wilson concludes: "Human beings are absurdly easy to indoctrinate—they seek it" (1975, p. 562). And in light of such events as the Jonestown mass suicide of 1978 this extreme assertion is highly credible.

The implication is that conformity and susceptibility to influence contribute to tribe effectiveness, and group effectiveness is central to the survival of a given group of genes. This is of such importance that Wilson states:

> If war requires spartan virtues and eliminates some of the warriors, victory can more than adequately compensate the survivors in land, power, and the opportunity to reproduce. The average individual will win the inclusive fitness game, making the gamble profitable, because the summed efforts of the participants give the average member a more than compensatory edge. (Wilson, 1975, p. 562)

This observation is consistent with Tinbergen's thesis that group aggression is more natural in humans than individual aggression. Also noteworthy is Wilson's assertion of the paramount importance of the spread of genes through warfare; in the old testament, for example, we read of the tendency of conquerors to kill male children and rape women to begin a new people. Perhaps the most disturbing aspect of this explanation of human warfare, and the role of sex and communication in war, is that the other models of human functioning are far less adequate in explaining such a historically ubiquitous and important phenomenon.

Returning to the issue of communication, it is emphasized that communication is the process by which humans' unique intelligence is used to create enduring social organization. The profundity of this assertion is that the other aspects of human nature, such as competition for mates, are merely the materials that communication fashions into a livable environment. A person, then, is most of all an influencer and an influencee, and the capacity to communicate serves this evolutionary purpose. Intercultural variation is enormous, but sex and communication are universal in all cultures. Psychologists might say that individuals use influence in order to get power, but it is also possible that individuals compete for power to get influence so that they can increase their long-term fitness both directly and indirectly. The implications here are highly complex and for this reason the notion of altruism becomes increasingly indistinguishable from that of selfishness in the human species.

Neuroscience

Neuroscience, the modern extension of neurophysiology, takes an even more fundamentally biological approach to human functioning. Here the physical portions of the brain as well as their functions and interrelationships are scrutinized. Chemical and electrical properties of function and dysfunction are studied in a variety of ways, from altering chemical states to electron microscopic examination of the morphology of a nerve cell. An example from Watts (1975) describing the electrochemical action of the neuron or nerve cell communicates the flavor of this model:

> The postsynaptic neuron is a biologic battery that attracts ions, discharges electricity and recharges itself chemically, using its own enzymes. The electrical discharge ordinarily is triggered by a chemical, but it can also be electrical. As the wave of depolarization speeds to the presynaptic membrane, the all-or-none conducting principle of the neuron makes it temporarily inactive as it recharges. This fact imparts to it a property similar to a switch that can be "on" (conducting) or "off" (nonconducting). (Watts, 1975, p. 23)

Clearly, the neurophysiological view of man parallels that of physiology. Fuel is taken in and processed by cells through complex chemical cycles (e.g., Krebbs) to yield energy. Energy then powers enzyme and chemical generation as well as ionization and other processes. These produce the potential for intercellular communication through electrochemical exchanges among neurons. The purpose of this intercellular communication is to coordinate activity in order to incorporate more chemicals for sustaining life. The reader is reminded of Bailey's (1960) quote at the beginning of this section: "The brain developed first to be of service to the gut, not to develop art, philosophy and theology." This remains so even though humans have uniquely large brains.

The brain is a metasystem with 122 regions and tracts organized into two distinct systems, the limbic and lateral. The limbic system controls basic body and brain functions and contains fifty-three regions linked by thirty-five tracts. This metasystem is somewhat analogous to fifty-three computers linked with cables containing thousands of wires. The lateral (corticerebellar) system contains nineteen regions and fifteen tracts and includes functions such as thinking and speech (Watts, 1975, p. 33). The relationships among these regions are complex. For example, interpersonal communication taps many regions and is the expression of need state, mood, and thought. In this case mood tends to overwhelm thought. Thus no simple "regional" description is now used to explain thought. Popular notions such as left brain versus right brain (rational versus emotional) have little support in modern neuroscience. An alternative view of regions and functions follows.

The limbic system is organized into four groups of regions, the forebrain, midbrain, thalamus, and hypothalamus. Of the five regions in the forebrain, one primarily affects pleasant moods, another violence and unpleasant moods, another mood integration, another immediate memory, and the fifth affects sense of time. The midbrain controls the forebrain, provides linkages to the lateral system through the reticular formation (RF) region, and integrates thalamus and hypothalamus activity.

In short, the midbrain is a central clearing house for moods, memory, time, and sensory data. The hypothalamus "controls specific expressions of hunger, thirst, sex" through the autonomic nervous system and "regulates vital functions of body temperature, breathing, circulation, and electrolyte balance" (Watts, 1975, p. 34). The linkages between the regions are complex and multifaceted with intermediary and coordinative roles played by the number of brain regions. Interestingly, the human limbic system contains five times as many linkages to coordinate the regions as its closest primate relative. This implies dramatically increased complexity of response to stimuli and greater internal coordination compared to any other species. Good feelings tell the brain that the system is working adequately, and bad feelings that it is not. The object of life is to coordinate the complex system so that it can live. Pleasure is an indication of success. It is not surprising that scientists in this field wax enthusiastic when they see "50 trillion cells work in harmony under efficient control by the CNS (central nervous system)" (Watts, 1975, p. 43). While the technical terminology is a bit ponderous, it makes the physical reality behind all the points discussed in this chapter meaningful and tangible. Furthermore, this approach stands as an important reminder that all the models in fact may be good expressions of the true nature of human functioning.

Thinking is known to be the function of the lateral system and a response to audiovisual or mood stimulation. Its prime purpose is to deal with uncertainties and with communication. Kelly's cognitive model and the cybernetic analogue models are close parallels to the manner in which thinking is viewed in neuroscience. The lateral system works in broad and complex coordination with the limbic system where short-term memory occurs, and where many stimuli are organized and integrated before transmittal. Thinking deals with uncertainties introduced by audiovisual stimuli, which are processed (analyzed) in the temporal and occipital areas to provide interpretation or comprehension of the messages. This function occurs in the secondary sensory analysis or neocortical areas. Somatic sensory data undergo similar processing in parietal areas, and the superior longitudinal fasciculus delivers choices from all three areas to the prefrontal areas (Watts, 1975, p. 278).

Mood can affect thinking which in and of itself tends to be slow, tedious, and boring, but thinking can also occur with or without mood and vice versa. An unpleasant uncertainty results in one region of the dorsal medial thalamic nucleus determining the balance of lateral and limbic system involvement needed. High stimulation leads directly to greater limbic involvement, and unpleasant stimuli of high intensity result in virtually instinctive responses. For a pleasant uncertainty, the lateral system works with the limbic system in a smooth but highly activated state, generally labeled excitement (Watts, 1975, p. 279). These latter points echo McClelland's observation that pursuing success is quite different and generally more effective in the long run than avoiding failure.

The phenomenon of long-term memory is also of importance in this approach to human functioning:

> Long term memory begins about the age of three, after short association fibers complete their connections in the lateral cerebral cortex. The connections are probably not changed significantly after the first three years of life. Memory capacity varies with the efficiency of memory circuits. A passive circuit does not explain the living, changing dynamic brain physiology. There is active, selective participation of neurons and *glial* cells. (Watts, 1975, p. 293)

The brain has many parallel circuits; if some are damaged, others nearby with similar destinations carry the signal. Many inputs travel to both hemispheres simultaneously, confirming the message. Memory storage probably takes place in both hemispheres simultaneously. In ninety-six percent of individuals the left cerebrum governs speech. The right cerebrum contains circuits that perform thinking before, during, and after speech.

> Long-term memory is stored in lateral neocortical areas, beside the areas that store recent memory in the five cerebral lobes. It is nonlimbic, somatic and intellectual, an acquired, conditioned memory. The left pulvinar controls the temporal, parietal and occipital areas for audiovisual speech. The right pulvinar controls the right lateral long-term cortical circuits for thinking memory storage. The four lateral cortical long-term storage areas joined by the occipitofrontal fasciculi and the arcuate fasciculus form a long-term memory circle with the pulvinar and dorsomedial nucleus at the centre. (Watts, 1975, p. 293)

The complexity of the processes is awesome, but some points are noteworthy. Repetition and intensity of input increase lasting power of memories. Chemically, memory is the result of specifically produced protein molecules deposited on a neuron. All mental activity is oriented to the problems of living. Of further interest here is the social learning insight regarding observational learning. Relationships and reinforcements affect the retention of visually acquired data.

In this model, the purpose of life and everything within it is to sustain itself; neurophysiology thus provides a simple solution to the dilemma posed by the existentialists. Pleasure is seen as preferable to pain, but, contrary to Thibaut and Kelley's comparison level of alternatives model, there is no need to maximize the pleasure/pain ratio. Instead, the more simple behavioristic assumption that pleasure is pursued and pain avoided seems justified. Activation theory is also consistent with neuroscience. For example, unusual activation patterns could indicate a problem requiring attention. Lewin's conception of metasystems, systems, and energizing processes is remarkably consistent with the current neurophysiological reality.

One way in which neurophysiology extends the notion of activation relates to the linkages between the limbic and lateral systems. When the limbic system is highly activated and "alive" it provides energy, stimulation, and a positive orientation for thinking. Since the limbic system is highly integrated with the physiological totality of the individual, this may well be taken to support the old saying: "Healthy body, healthy mind."

Conflict models of human functioning are also relevant here. The incredible complexity of the human brain makes problems of internal coordination and conflicts highly likely; Freud merely oversimplified. The dichotomy of pursuit of pleasure and avoidance of pain, for example, increases the chances of simultaneously incompatible mental processes. Furthermore, memory can be at odds with limbic response tendencies. This is especially true when the subtlety of the mood component is added to the complexity of thinking. It is also noteworthy that, in neuroscience, virtually every psychopathology has been associated with some inadequacy in organic functioning or chemical state. Finally, the complexity of the brain and its many linkages and transmittal alternatives lends support to fulfillment models which argue for activity leading to growth. In cognitive/perceptual, developmental terms, it is easy to see increased differentiation and integration combined with flexibility as growth ideals for the brain. Together these notions have dramatic "quality of life" implications for the total organism.

Summary

The life sciences serve as a capstone perspective to this chapter. Behavioral scientists since the nineteenth century have built on some conception of the physiological reality of humans. Since the 1940s much of this building has been less and less closely linked to the scientific advancements occurring simultaneously in the life sciences. Statistical and technological research capacities have in the last twenty years expanded the appreciation for the incredible complexity of evolutionary, instinctual, and neurophysiological aspects of life. The age-old debate of nature versus nurture is not rekindled by this acknowledgment because the current wisdom of the life sciences emphasizes above all a high degree of adaptability within humans, and complex and distant or "loose" linkages between instincts and outcomes. The more that is known about the physiological basis of behavior, the more profound the appreciation for the developmental possibilities and potential in the species.

Although this section does not provide enough life sciences material to give a true mapping of the physical reality of humans, it is adequate in emphasizing that caution should be exercised in making generalizations based on any oversimplified model of human functioning. For example, the current left brain–right brain dichotomy is a graphic illustration of taking a fragmentary and outdated finding of neuroscience and positing its importance to a wide variety of issues related to human functioning, including thinking and personality.

However, on the positive side, the life sciences provide a wholesome and refreshing perspective for understanding the purposes and meaning of life. For example, the fitness implications of instinct gratification put the pursuit of pleasure into perspective. Also, experienced threat and danger, labeled social needs by the contextual theorists, might very well have their genesis in the child's instinct for attachment to the mother. Or, as Barash asks, "Why is sugar sweet?"

Conclusion

Each of the models of human functioning has implications for experiental learning. However, when used in combination their explanatory power is increased—the whole is greater than the sum of the parts. In experiential learning, there is a great deal of potential for tension and conflict, yet the format provides people with the opportunity for self-direction and growth. The activities can be familiar or unfamiliar and be related to the participants' backgrounds and experiences in an infinite variety of ways. The leaders, participants, and the actual learning environment generate forces and provide reinforcements that influence learning. Any one model may explain some of these general conditions but probably would not explain them all equally well. The complexity of neurophysiology alone graphically illustrates the meaningfulness and importance of the position taken in this chapter. That position is simply that each of the models discussed does in fact explain some facet of human functioning.

Competition among alternative perspectives has energized research and provided valuable criticism, but a more important insight into human functioning has been deemphasized. All the models are valuable, but only for a given individual in a given situation at a given time would one model be more valuable than others in explaining behavior and providing guidelines for bringing about productive change. The tendency for leaders focusing on inducing change is to acquire a specific technique or set of techniques and to concentrate on their efficient and effective use. On the average, this is a reasonable and productive strategy. However, most models of change are based primarily on one given model of human functioning, and too often practitioners lose track of the importance of the connection between their change strategies and the implied model of human functioning. Consequently, many opportunities for learning are lost as a result of not considering a variety of models of human functioning. It is hoped that this chapter will aid leaders in transcending assumptions, overcoming myopia, and tapping more fully the rich potential for change offered by the various methods used in the experiential approach.

CHAPTER TWO

Outcome Centered
Change Processes

What is being abolished is
autonomous man.

B.F. Skinner

The change processes of feedback, conditioning, and coercion specifically emphasize outcomes or consequences. Feedback is the simplest of these processes and one of the most widely discussed elements of personal change in experiential learning. Its presentation here is intended to clarify some pivotal but often misused notions and then explore the ways that feedback can be used from individual, interactional, and social perspectives. The discussion of conditioning summarizes the significant, practical aspects of pleasurable and aversive consequences of participant actions. Finally, coercion is discussed to focus attention on this ubiquitous force and to distinguish clearly between coercion and punishment.

Feedback

Four aspects of feedback require consideration before a thorough exploration of its individual, interpersonal, and social ramifications. Feedback can be of a sensory or static (knowledge of results) character, intrinsic or extrinsic, positive or negative, and informational or confrontational. Smith and Smith (1966) question the tendency of using the terms feedback and knowledge of results (KR) almost interchangeably. They see the two processes as quite different, and distinguish between dynamic sensory feedback and static feedback (KR):

Dynamic sensory feedback refers to movement-generated stimuli that provide an intrinsic means of regulating motion in relation to the environment. Knowledge of results given after a response is a static after effect which may give information about accuracy but does not provide dynamic regulating stimuli. Dynamic feedback indication of error is more effective in performance and learning than static knowledge of results. (Smith & Smith, 1966, pp. 220–221)

Sensory feedback deprivation can result in halucinations and a variety of other dysfunctions while KR cannot.

Annett's (1969) distinction between intrinsic and extrinsic knowledge of results parallels this dynamic-static distinction. Briefly, intrinsic KR results as a natural consequence of performing many tasks. For example, a person driving an automobile is constantly getting musculature feedback as to where his or her foot is. We know where our limbs are not because we are consciously attending to that concern but because we are continually receiving feedback from our muscles, joints, and nerves. This process is referred to as proprioceptive feedback (Schmidt, 1971). Extrinsic KR refers to information provided to individuals from the external environment concerning the consequences of their actions. The automobile speedometer provides extrinsic KR which permits the driver to adjust the speed of the car by pushing or letting up on the accelerator. Generally, when individuals are provided with information about how they are performing a task and their relative success at it during the activity, they will learn the task more quickly and effectively than when the feedback is absent. Research by Annett (1969), Weber (1969), Walter and Miles (1974), Kim and Hamner (1976) and many others have documented the positive effect of giving performance feedback (KR) in conjunction with goal setting on productivity. Butler and Jaffee (1974) examined the impact of evaluative feedback on discussion group leaders' verbal behavior and showed that favorable feedback enhanced task orientation and unfavorable feedback increased negative social-emotional behavior (i.e., displays of tension, antagonism, and disagreeability).

Feedback can also be seen as *positive* or *negative*. Colloquially, saying favorable things to individuals is often incorrectly labeled positive feedback. The "systems" definition of feedback yields the opposite terminology by focusing on the impact of the feedback rather than its specific content.

When the signals are fed back over the feedback channel in such a manner that they increase the deviation of the output from a steady state, positive feedback exists. When the signals are reversed, so that they decrease the deviation of the output from a steady state, it is negative feedback. (Baker, 1973, p. 52)

Positive feedback loops are very often desirable when growth or expansion is needed (Odum, 1971). Examples are compound interest or an incentive program to promote sales. One of the most common unpleasant examples of positive feedback is the screech created when a microphone is placed too close to a speaker. Negative feedback, on the other hand, is a necessary prerequisite for all purposeful behavior (Rosenblueth, Wiener, & Bigelow, 1968). It aids in bringing the system to homeostasis or in guiding it to a specific goal. Virtually all attempts to assist individuals in achieving a goal or regulating behavior may be classified as negative feedback. Common examples of mechanisms based on a negative feedback principle are thermostats and elevators.

Finally, feedback can be either *informational* or *confrontational.* Informational feedback simply involves giving individuals information. Confrontational feedback also provides information but implies that more demands are placed on the recipient. This kind of feedback is directed toward lack of awareness about incongruities in one's behavior and matters having high personal meaning. For example, in a work setting, individuals might be unaware that their boisterousness distracts others, or they might profess to have a certain attitude or act in prescribed ways but actually behave in a contradictory manner. Generally, the more personal the content of the feedback and the more meaning this content has for the individual, the greater the likelihood that the feedback will be confrontational in nature. Delivery also can introduce a confrontational quality to feedback, as discussed more fully below.

Individual Perspective

The fields of counseling and psychotherapy, and the T-group, sensitivity group, and human potential movement have invested a great deal of energy in examining the role of feedback in changing individuals. The attention is focused on ways of understanding how feedback works, as well as on guidelines and techniques for providing effective feedback.

Schein and Bennis (1965) considered the effects of feedback in a T-group setting using Lewin's unfreezing, changing, and refreezing model of change. Unfreezing occurs when individuals receive information about themselves or their behavior that is inconsistent with their self-perceptions. Once unfreezing has occurred, individuals can begin to incorporate new information and change their behavior. These changes then stabilize as the individuals receive congruent feedback, or refreezing. The cognitive/perceptual and cognitively oriented contextual models of human functioning are central in this analysis of feedback. It is also important to note that confirming or congruent feedback is every bit as crucial as disconfirming or inconsistent feedback; the former enables individuals to get closure on old events and to open themselves to change in other areas.

Argyris' (1968) notion of feedback further expands the understanding of this process. He differentiates feedback for the acquisition of competence from feedback for therapy. In the competence mode the individual is seen as aware, open, and trusting of others. Feedback within this context should be clear, minimally evaluative, and directly verifiable. The receiver evaluates the "goodness" or "badness" of the content. Here the applications of the fulfillment, cognitive/perceptual, and conflict models of human functioning all seem relevant, with the fulfillment model predominating in the assumptions of many recent change theorists.

In the therapy model, the individual is seen as unaware, closed, defensive, and more concerned with survival than with learning or adaptation. In survival, internal processes dominate to such a degree that the individual is closed to competence-related change. Effective feedback within this context consists of information that is evaluative, interpretive, and subjective. Consequently, the type of information given has to be matched to the needs of the recipient in order to maximize the chances for success. This also serves as an important elaboration of the implied dynamics of Schein and Bennis' emphasis on unfreezing.

Argyris stresses that the individual giving feedback should have a clearly constructive intent, and that the individual receiving the feedback should have a desire to learn. It would seem difficult, in Argyris' system, to be both constructive and confronting.

For the less confrontational approach to interpersonal feedback, Anderson (1970, p. 344) stated that feedback should be:

1 Intended to help the recipient.
2 Given directly and with real feeling, and based on a foundation of trust between the giver and receiver.
3 Descriptive rather than evaluative.
4 Specific rather than general, with good, clear, and preferably recent examples.
5 Given at a time when the receiver appears to be in a condition of readiness to accept it.
6 Checked with others in the group to be sure they support its validity.
7 Inclusive of only those things that the receiver might be expected to do something about.
8 Not . . . more than (the receiver) can handle at any particular time.

Confrontation. Successful confrontation initiates self-examination, questioning, or change (Egan, 1970, p. 294). Therefore, life events as well as interpersonal feedback can serve as a confrontational stimulus to the individual and give the confrontee information he does not possess or is considered to possess in an inadequate way; interpretation of the confrontee's behavior; directly challenging the other's behavior; self-involvement of confronter with confrontee as a mode of confrontation; group situational variables that are considered confrontational—for example, group exercises, the contact itself in a contact group, being with strangers; "processing"—that is, group self-criticism; withdrawal of reinforcement; the use of videotape. (Egan, 1970, p. 295)

Information of greater meaning for the confrontee will have more confrontational impact. Interpretation of behavior rather than mere factual feedback generally contains more meaning and often can stimulate reconceptualization by the receiver about behavior or coping. Feedback can also challenge the confrontee to master the incongruity seen by the confronter.

Egan also emphasizes the need for a sense of safety in relationships and contexts when confrontation is attempted, thus acknowledging Argyris' and Anderson's concern for constructive feedback. This is treated more fully in our discussion of the support change process. Since confrontation implies emotional as well as factual aspects of feedback, Egan focuses on the need to deal constructively with aggression. Some guidelines for the confronter are (Egan, 1970, pp. 334–335):

1 Confront in order to manifest your concern for the other.
2 Make confrontation a way of becoming involved with the other.
3 Before confronting, become aware of your bias for or against the confrontee. Do not refrain from confrontation because you are against him.
4 Before confronting the other, try to understand the relationship that exists between you and him, and try to proportion your confrontation to what the relationship will bear.
5 Before confronting, try to take into consideration the possible punitive side effects of your confrontation.
6 Try to be sure that the strength or vehemence of your confrontation and the areas of sensitivity you deal with are proportioned to the needs, sensitivities and capabilities of the confrontee.
7 Confront behavior primarily; be slow to confront motivation.
8 Confront clearly; indicate what is fact, what is feeling, and what is hypothesis. Do not state interpretations as facts. Do not engage in constant or long-winded interpretations of the behavior of others.
9 Remember that much of your behavior in the group can have confrontational effects (e.g., not talking to others, your emotional attitudes, etc.)
10 Be willing to confront yourself honestly in the group. No set rules will provide assurance that confrontation will always be a growthful process

in the sensitivity-training group. But groups can learn much from both the use and abuse of confrontation.

It is noteworthy that in the domain of personal growth, interpersonal feedback is closely aligned with self-disclosure (Luft, 1970). Both individuals here in essence must experience some confrontation since prior to giving feedback they develop awarenesses in collecting and organizing their own reactions. Culbert (1970) argued further that mutuality and intimacy in the feedback relationship affect both self-disclosure and the receipt of feedback. It takes two to see one, because the individuals' self-image limits a simpler means of reality testing. Finally, broad areas of free self-disclosure increase the potential for self-acceptance and thus increase the individual's openness to feedback. Again, the cognitive/perceptual and contextual models of human functioning are central to seeing the effects of feedback in change.

Videotape Feedback. Another view of the interrelationship of self-image and feedback in individual change is provided by research on videotape feedback. The documented, powerful impact of videotape feedback is attributed by Hogan and Alger (1969) and Stoller (1968) to the vividness of the technique. Dramatic unfreezing can result (Danet, 1968), and confrontees can be overwhelmed by too much video feedback. A moment's reflection on the neurophysiological description of human functioning offers a reason for the power of this feedback mechanism. Memories about childhood are stored primarily in visual form and these are the raw material for one's self-image. Videotape feedback provides similarly vivid visual images of self that short-term memory and judgment must acknowledge as more accurate, objective, and real than images stored internally. Moreover, this comparison can be made directly, without words or confusing emotions or questions about the degree to which the source of feedback is merely meeting emotional needs. Match and mismatch is graphic and profound.

Some of the conflict models and the cognitive/perceptual and contextual models of human functioning imply or affirm the need for unfreezing in change (e.g., Freud, Rokeach, Sullivan). Other models deemphasize the desirability and the need for aggressive unfreezing in individual change (e.g., Kelly's theory and the fulfillment models). The encounter technique offers an interesting inconsistency in that it idealizes interpersonal confrontation yet articulates a fulfillment kind of philosophy. If fulfillment were truly the assumed model of human functioning, a feedback strategy such as that outlined by Argyris would be the most relevant in encounter. There should be no need to confront defenses and one should only need to provide neutral information and acceptance. On the other hand, it is perhaps the fulfillment model that is too limited.

Interactional Perspective

The feedback process has also received extensive consideration in terms of its role in groups. The concern here is not with the personal attributes of those involved but with the effects of the feedback on the tasks at hand or, more generally, the behavior of the individuals or groups under consideration.

Feedback procedures also have been widely used to promote change in the survey feedback approach (Bowers, 1976; Likert, 1967). Katz and Kahn (1966) discuss the value of gathering information on numerous organizational issues and then feeding it back to subgroups throughout an organization. The resulting discussions center on problems perceived as consequences of new information; explorations of possible change are based on an increased understanding of the underlying organizational processes. The cognitive/perceptual model is central to understanding why the survey feedback approach is effective.

Miles, Hornstein, Calder, Callahan, and Schiavo (1971) commented on the differences between survey feedback from this perspective and from the individual perspective:

> First, in psychotherapy and human relations training the process of feeding back subjective data is mediated by the therapist and/or other group members, respectively; in survey feedback however, the process is mediated by objective data which group members have planned, collected, analyzed, and interpreted. Second, in therapy and training the analysis of data occurs mostly at the intrapersonal, interpersonal or group level; survey feedback usually focuses more centrally on the role, inter-group, and organizational levels. (Miles et al., 1971, p. 310)

In addition they stress the value of the increased objectivity in feedback achieved through the survey approach and see its effects as follows:

> The data may corroborate the client's feelings ("Yes that is just how things are."); or the data may have a disconfirming effect if they contradict beliefs ("I never would have expected that people could see things that way."). In addition, the data have inquiry-encouraging effects; clients begin to wonder why people responded as they did, what the underlying causes were, and how they might be altered. (Miles et al., 1971, p. 310)

Survey feedback can also be classified as static feedback although the process by which it is gathered and presented is quite "dynamic."

Social Perspective

Feedback is an important process at a more general social level. As our social system becomes more complex, the need for information and feedback becomes increasingly important and harder to achieve. Singer vividly describes this dilemma:

> During a time of great change, as organizations proliferate and become more complex, linkages between individuals and organizations upon which they depend become vague, less discernable; and there develops a puzzling contradiction, for, as our society becomes more rationalized in a technological-economic and social sense, much more that is important to the individual attempting to cope becomes enmeshed in a grey, ambiguous, difficult to define panoply of channels and procedures; people become less sure about their rights, their legitimacy in seeking them, their way of communicating their feelings, opinions and needs to such institutions and, therefore, to their society. (Singer, 1973, p. 1)

From this perspective, feedback occurs through governing and political processes, news media, and less formalized procedures ranging from opinion polls, hot-line shows, letters to the editor, demonstrations, confrontations, and, ultimately, riots or other civil disruptions. These processes provide the means for a society to find out how its members feel about a given situation or event, the means for individuals to assess the relative effects of their attempts to influence events, and the means for establishing a common understanding of exactly what is happening in society, that is, a sense of social reality.

The concept of social reality is of particular value. Cartwright and Zander point out: "Often there are no bases in logic, objective reality, or evidence of the senses that enable a person to arrive at a judgment or opinion that is clearly correct. With respect to a matter where no direct evidence is available, the subjective validity of an opinion becomes established simply by the fact that members of the group agree" (1968, p. 142). The tendency for individuals to seek a common sense of reality emphasizes the intrinsic value of conformity in groups and explains its occurrence even in the absence of reinforcement contingencies. Rosenberg (1965) showed that uncertainty in one's self or associates was positively related to conformity; Hochbaum (1954) showed similar effects resulting from lack of self-confidence. The competence and control notions of White, Adler, and the cognitive/perceptual theorists are consistent with these observations on the tendency to search for social reality in which feedback is perhaps most identified with "consciousness."

In general, societal feedback seems associated less with attitudinal and behavioral change than with a focusing of attention and a raising of consciousness on specific issues. That is, a change in emphasis rather than in action.

Conditioning

Conditioning, like feedback, is a widespread process of change, present in some form in all the other processes discussed. There are two general types of conditioning, classical and operant. Pavlov (1927) was responsible for much of the early work in classical conditioning, and Thorndike (1898) and Skinner (1938) are the original investigators of the instrumental and operant conditioning models. Since Skinner's early work, operant conditioning has become both a major research focus (Honig & Staddon, 1977) and an applied clinical focus (Karoly, 1975; Krasner, 1971). Classical conditioning is "a process by which a response comes to be elicited by a stimulus, object, or situation other than that to which it is the natural or normal response . . . a reflex, normally following on a stimulus A, comes to be elicited by a stimulus B, through the constant association of B with A" (Drever, 1964, p. 48). Examples of this type of conditioning are pervasive. In public school, the bells or buzzers signifying class changes become associated over time with all the complex feelings related to the school experience. These feelings can be elicited years after graduation when the individual happens to be in a situation where a similar bell or buzzer sounds. Instrumental or operant conditioning is a process in which the stimulus following a given behavior is used to increase or decrease the probability of that behavior; that is, behavior is controlled by its consequences. A person steps in what appears to be a shallow puddle of water and gets wet up to the ankle, and is thus operantly "punished." Avoidance of puddles is the behavioral change. The Skinner quotation opening this chapter seems grandiosely out-of-touch with the limits of operant controls possible in this serendipitous world.

Several processes in addition to classical and operant conditioning are central to understanding how conditioning works:

Positive reinforcement—
 adding a pleasant consequence resulting in increased responding.
Negative reinforcement—
 taking away an unpleasant consequence resulting in increased responding.
Positive punishment—
 adding an unpleasant consequence resulting in decreased responding.
Extinction—
 time-out.
Negative punishment—
 removing a pleasant consequence resulting in decreased responding.

(1) Consequences can either be added or taken away, and
(2) both pleasant and unpleasant consequences can be used for the purpose of increasing behavior and for the purpose of decreasing behavior. (Karoly, 1975, p. 202)

Reinforcers are of two basic types, primary or secondary (conditioned). Primary reinforcers such as food, air, and water, possess a reinforcing quality because of their own characteristics and not because of any previous conditioned association, whereas secondary reinforcers gain their significance through association with primary reinforcers. Money is probably the most common example of a secondary reinforcer.

Schedules that describe the frequency and pattern of reinforcing or extinguishing stimuli are also important in changing behavior. These are:

Continuous schedule—
    rewards are given each time the desired behavior is exhibited.
Fixed interval schedule—
    rewards are given only after a specified amount of work, activity, or action has been completed.
Variable interval schedule—
    the time between the reinforcements is varied around some mean temporal value.
Variable ratio schedule—
    the number of responses per reinforcement is varied randomly around some mean frequency. (Bandura, 1969, pp. 27–29)

Schedules of reinforcement have a profound impact on the manner in which behavior is changed, and must always be considered along with the choice of reinforcer. Generally, reinforcement is more effective when "delivered contingently, consistently, and with minimal delay" (Bandura, 1969, p. 200; see also Guthrie's early, 1935, contiguity notions). In terms of schedules, variable interval and ratio formats produce the most enduring high rates of responding.

At this point it is important to consider some of the differences between reinforcement and feedback, for although they are often considered to be the same, they are not. Knowledge of results (KR) may have reinforcing qualities, but dynamic sensory feedback differs from reinforcement in a number of ways. Reinforcement does not rely heavily on perception and requires a motivation or need base. Feedback, however, is very dependent on perception and is also affected by the delay, intermittency, and extinction issues that are important for reinforcement. Delays in reinforcements reduce effects, but delayed sensory feedback disrupts the individual's behavior immediately and seriously. Intermittent reinforcement produces higher and more stable rates of response; intermittent feedback, on the other hand, does not increase the stability of the response, and can have a detrimental effect on performance. The withdrawal of reinforcements results in a gradual decrease of response frequency, or extinction; the withdrawal of sensory feedback causes immediate and severe deterioration of response (Smith & Smith, 1966, pp. 212–216). Since feedback and reinforcement are usually incorporated in the same behavior, it is very difficult to separate them in practice. Nevertheless, they are different. *Cybernetic Principles of Learning and Educational Design* (Smith & Smith, 1969) thoroughly explores these differences.

The pragmatics of conditioning are concerned with the specific procedures used for the conditioning process. From the individual perspective, there are many well defined and highly specific therapeutic procedures such as "systematic desensitization." From the interactional perspective, numerous social dynamics with conditioning implications have been studied in depth. For example, various social factors such as prestige have conditioning significance, and expectations about reinforcement contingencies can also affect change. Finally, characteristics of the larger social milieu, such as traffic regulations or tax law, have conditioning qualities.

Individual Perspective

Classical and operant conditioning methods have been extensively used in counseling and psychotherapy (Bergin & Garfield, 1971; Kanfer & Goldstein, 1975; Krumboltz & Thoresen, 1976; Wolpe 1976). The classical methods include systematic desensitization, aversion methods, and implosive therapy; the operant methods include positive and negative reinforcement, punishment, extinction, time out, and shaping (Karoly, 1975, pp. 205–222). It is also important to note that, although these methods emphasize conditioning, there are also re-cognition aspects to be discussed. These methods have been used to treat a broad range of problems ranging from phobias, sexual dysfunctions, and obesity to speech problems, study habits, and disruptive classroom behavior. They have been used successfully with groups of all ages and degrees of mental health. Some examples from the classical and operant methods are presented below to illustrate how conditioning procedures are actually used.

Systematic desensitization (Wolpe, 1976) is the most common application of classical conditioning principles. An undesirable response such as fear or anxiety is inhibited by substituting activities that are inconsistent with the unwanted response. States of relaxation and calmness developed prior to substitutions in this context help reduce anxiety and fear.

> For example, if a person has a fear of heights and feels very anxious and uncomfortable each time he has to go into a tall office building and take the elevator higher than the third floor, we would help him inhibit his anxiety in this situation by teaching him to relax and feel calm. Thus, we would desensitize him or counter-condition his fear of heights. (Morris, 1975, p. 230)

A hierarchy of anxiety-producing situations is established and the individual is trained to relax. The therapeutic interaction consists of presenting, during a state of relaxation, the anxiety-producing stimuli starting at the low end of the hierarchy. When the relaxation and not the anxiety comes to be associated with the stimuli, the process is repeated for the next step in the hierarchy. The treatment is completed when the situation or event at the top of the hierarchy no longer elicits any anxiety or fear. In the case of the individual who is afraid of heights, this might be looking down to the street from an open window from the fortieth floor of a building.

Classical conditioning principles have also been used to treat individuals with alcohol and drug problems. This process, called aversion therapy, pairs an unpleasant response such as illness and vomiting with the undesired drinking or smoking behavior. Over time, the undesired behavior becomes associated with the unpleasant response and thus the frequency of the behavior is reduced.

Operant methods have been used with considerable success in counseling and psychotherapeutic settings. The major categories under which these changes can be classified are building behavioral capabilities, increasing the likelihood of desired behavior, reducing the likelihood of excessive behavior, and maintaining behavioral progress (Karoly, 1975, pp. 206–226). Positive and negative reinforcement procedures can be used to increase the frequency or likelihood of desired behavior. Some guidelines for using positive reinforcement are (Karoly, 1975, p. 213):

1 Identify reinforcers by observing their functional effects on behavior rather than assuming that what is a reward for one individual will serve the same function for another.

2 Identify activity reinforcers after systematic observation of the individual across and within a variety of natural settings.

3 Deliver reinforcers immediately, contingently, and consistently to maximize reinforcement and minimize resistance.

4 Reinforce behavior often while bringing it to optimal frequency; then, "thin out" to reduce extinction.

5 Use a variety of reinforcers to minimize loss of potency due to repeated presentation of a single reinforcing stimulus or event.

6 Use social reinforcement (the verbal and nonverbal behavior of people) whenever feasible to permit the developing behavior to be maintained across settings. If necessary develop social reinforcer effectiveness by fading the use of primary reinforcers.

Taking away averse stimuli also can increase the frequency of a desired response. In a weight loss program, negative reinforcement was used as follows:

The dieter stored large pieces of pork fat in his refrigerator equal in amount to the excess weight to be lost. The investigators simply instructed their subjects to remove the bags of fat contingent upon proportional weight loss. This technique in combination with others seemed very effective. (Karoly, 1975, p. 214)

Punishment, extinction, and "time out" can be used to reduce the frequency of undesired behavior. A perhaps frightening example is the punishment of schizophrenic children's destructive behavior to reduce its frequency (Bucher & King, 1971). In extinction, the reinforcers that typically sustain certain behaviors are removed. A child ceased to throw her food on the floor after the rest of the family began ignoring her behavior (Miller & Miller, 1976). In "time out," a form of extinction, the individual with undesired behaviors is removed from the situation rather than removing or attempting to change the reinforcers supporting the behavior.

Generalization and expectations are two important considerations for this discussion. Generalization processes depend on simultaneity of events and connections made by the individual; it is important to realize that the conditioning process may involve not only generalized reinforcers (secondary versus primary) but also generalized stimuli and responses or behaviors. Stimulus generalization refers to the nonreinforcement side of the conditioning sequence. The sight of food "made" Pavlov's dogs salivate, and when the dogs were presented simultaneously with a bell the conditioned behavior was eventually sufficiently generalized that the bell alone would "stimulate" salivation. The term "response generalization" refers to generating or allowing other responses to a particular stimulus, rather than simply pairing a given stimulus with a given response.

The issue of expectations focuses on behavioristic versus cognitive and other models of human functioning. Do humans have teleological capacities? Strictly speaking, a discussion of expectations does not belong under the heading "conditioning," which is an anti-teleological, behavioristic notion. Nonetheless, the rise of cognitive behaviorism (Mahoney, 1974) legitimizes such a consideration. The point is simple but noteworthy. Expectations about probable reinforcements and punishments affect behavior and attitudes (Lawler, 1971). The manner in which this occurs and the degree to which it is controllable according to Lawler are quite different than for the view held by advocates of pure classical and operant conditioning.

In summary, conditioning approaches are direct extensions of the learning theory models of human functioning and have provided concrete, manageable strategies for behavior change. Compared to approaches based on other models, these procedures for helping people change can be described in detail and replicated with relative ease.

Interactional Perspective

The impact of conditioning processes has been examined under a variety of experimental conditions. Again, the emphasis is on understanding the process rather than the specific individual's behavior in those situations. In addition, within this perspective there is a shift in attention from how conditioning and reinforcement mechanisms affect change in individuals to how relationships provide reinforcers.

The *Handbook of Operant Behavior,* edited by W.K. Honig and J.E.R. Staddon (1977), provides a comprehensive overview of conditioning from an interactional point of view.

> Theoretical questions are asked of the manner in which different forms of operant behavior are generated and maintained. Yet this behavior is itself used in turn to obtain answers to theoretical questions of all kinds. (Honig & Staddon, 1977, p. 6)

The book considers issues such as shaping, conditions for stimulus control, measurement of sensory thresholds, and recovery. A knowledge of the existence of this information is important since specific parts of it can be selected and related to any given learning situation. However, this task is far beyond the scope of the present discussion.

A consideration of the ways in which relationships and interactions reinforce behavior is perhaps more readily applicable to most learning environments. For example, the phenomenon of uniformity is attributed to the tendency for individuals to seek a sense of "social reality," a state seen as inherently reinforcing if one assumes the perspective of the consistency and contextual models of human functioning. Further, an individual's conforming and nonconforming behaviors are rewarded and punished through other people's expressions of personal liking or disliking. Deviation from central norms begets aversive consequences (Festinger, Schachter, & Back, 1950, 1968; Schachter, 1968). Deviation is ignored at first and the individual may experience mild punishment through subtle feelings of rejection. If the deviance is continued, group members direct evaluative comments to the deviant; negative judgments, derision, and ridicule all serve as punishment. Extensive deviation or unresponsiveness to the second level of group reaction can lead to rejection by the group. At this third level, group reaction is more accurately labeled coercion. This qualitatively different process is discussed more fully in the following section of this chapter but it suffices to say here that its significance transcends mere punishment. Positive social reinforcements can be thought of generally as social need fulfillment (Maslow, 1955, 1962), but the life sciences model of human functioning supports the possibility that a survival instinct (Bowlby's concept of attachment) is a function of group membership. Consequently, punishment and coercion in groups can have great significance and enormous conditioning effects.

There are a number of other concepts that further describe the reinforcing aspects of social interaction. A wide variety of social scientists have explored the value of approval and attention as reinforcers. The prestige of the source of the approval and the attraction of the individual to the source both moderate the impact of a given interpersonal exchange; the significance of the exchange is moderated, therefore, in terms of its reinforcing value. Consequently, the attraction of individuals to a group increases the impact of the interpersonal reinforcers coming from group members.

Expectations of future rewards also can serve as an inducement for change. According to Blau (1967), an individual has power in a relationship when "one induces others to accede to his wishes by rewarding them for doing so" (p. 115). Therefore, the anticipation or expectation of positive reinforcement can also condition behavior. Many behaviorists avoid this teleological issue in reinforcement, but social scientists who focus on behavior from either the interactional or social perspective generally accept the role of expectations as outlined in the cognitive models of human functioning (Cummings & Schwab, 1973; Farden, 1973; Porter, Lawler, & Hackman, 1975). For Blau (1967), respect in relationships is the state in which one individual does not expect something for nothing.

Blau's social exchange theory formalizes his definition of respect and provides a bridge to the discussion of conditioning from the social perspective. He explores the use of reinforcements as a utilitarian social process and argues for the necessity of a norm of reciprocity. In the words of the eminent George Simmel, "all contracts among men rest on the schema of giving and returning the equivalence—If every grateful action, which lingers on from good turns in the past were suddenly eliminated, society (at least as we know it) would break apart" (Blau, 1967, p. 1). Thus the significance of conditioning here is its use in a social exchange process rather than as a behavioral control. The image is that of a huge marketplace in which independent individuals make mutually acceptable decisions from a universe of possibilities with the ultimate result that everyone, in the long run, gives and receives reinforcements or conditions one another's behavior.

Social Perspective

The division between the interactional and social perspectives in this discussion is certainly not a clear one. However, the object here is to build an overview of the approaches to conditioning, not to focus on the intricacies of any one interpretation. From this perspective, socialization and resocialization processes are examined in a variety of settings in terms of their conditioning qualities (Farden, 1973, pp. 91–114, 161–174).

The contextual and learning models of human functioning describe how conditioning processes using reinforcements and opinions from others, and especially from significant others, result in certain predispositions. These predispositions extend to acquiring certain roles prescribed by the society. The conditioning needed from the social system to keep the individual performing as desired is relatively small compared to the effort which initially directs behavior, attitude, and role acquisition. For the most part, individuals perform roles out of habit and because some natural conditioning occurs as a result of this performance. Alternative roles are seldom attempted, even experimentally, since the reinforcement contingencies of the "learning period" are less attractive than the reinforcement contingencies of continuation. Resocialization requires overcoming this resistance by dramatically altering the type and format of the conditioning process. Prisons, the military, and psychiatric hospitals all must first eliminate the existing patterns of reinforcements that maintain the "unresocialized" behavior. These "total institutions" (Farden, 1973, p. 169) have control of the individual's complete environment; they are able to change conditioning patterns and hence induce a member's acquisition of different roles, expectations, and behavior.

The modern work organization closely approximates these institutions in many ways (Whyte, 1956). This is especially true for members who are transferred a great deal and for those with aspirations for great organizational success. Complete involvement in a "total institution" implies that the organization's systematic distribution of rewards, and the meaning attached to given rewards, can have a maximal effect on an individual whose previous conditioning expectations have been eliminated or dramatically altered. To a great degree organizations are "Skinner boxes," although they are often not used "efficiently" as such.

Given this conditioning control capacity of many modern organizations, it is not surprising to find behaviorism emphasized in organizational human change strategies. The following description is offered to explain in more detail how conditioning has been applied within an organizational context, for understanding how organizations function is a critical component of understanding how individual behavior might be changed. Luthans and Kreitner (1975) for example, emphasize the importance of distinguishing between "(1) *behavior,* specific things people do in the course of working, (2) *performance,* behavior measured in terms of its contribution to organizational goal achievement, and (3) *effectiveness,* summary indices of organizational success" (p. 64). In so doing, valuable behaviors can be identified and either negatively or positively reinforced. Rewards are contingent on performance.

How reinforcement is assessed by the recipient, or what is perceived as a reward by a given individual, must be constantly evaluated. Small rewards for incremental behavior change is the strategy prescribed by these authors, who also hold to the Skinnerian view that positive reinforcements are preferable to punishment. Punishment leads to a plethora of undesirable dynamics including sabotage, behavioral inflexibility, and negative feelings toward its administerer (Luthans & Kreitner, 1975, pp. 120–123). Undesirable behavior should be allowed to become extinct and desirable behavior should be rewarded so that it displaces the undesirable behavior. Other organizational behaviorists (Cummings & Schwab, 1973) include the expectations of participants in their prescriptions for the use of reinforcements. It appears that clearly anticipated punishment has significant behavior control potential and fewer liabilities than actual punishment. For these and similar theorists, cognitive/perceptual models have equal status with learning models of human functioning.

Coercion

Because coercion is not an overt process in most learning situations, it is treated briefly here. Coercion as a change process goes beyond punishment:

> The idea of coercion creates symbols and images of fear and terror, arbitrary and irresponsible naked power, violence and the threat of physical brutality, the negation of freedom and individuality, or radical infringement of the rights of personality and the sacred domain of the human spirit. (Cook, 1972, p. 107)

The use of punishment can be seen by individuals as a legitimate use of power, and "legitimate power results in willing compliance" (Blau, 1967, p. 200). But coercion implies movement beyond the bounds of legitimacy (Simon, 1957; Walter & McDowell, 1975/1976) and beyond willing compliance. Because a sense of legitimacy ultimately resides within the individual, the boundary between aversive conditioning and coercion can never be clearly defined. Virtually all individuals are upset by a parking ticket although few question the legitimacy of the power exercised. But many individuals feel coerced if their car is towed away; both the punishment and incursion on one's property are considered beyond the bounds of legitimacy. Similarly, rejection from a group because of deviance is seldom seen as legitimate by the deviant and the threat of expulsion is also experienced as coercive. Coercion, moreover, often places the individual in a forced choice situation, and the choice is between two undesirable alternatives, conformity or group censure.

Ultimately, coercion depends on the capacity, will, and willingness to punish others beyond the bounds they consider legitimate. Thus the moral repugnance accorded law suits, strikes, war, torture, or the use of nuclear weapons implies a concern for the individuals against whom these tactics might be directed, or at least implies empathy with those individuals. For this reason, a moral justification for transgression would be necessary in order to define the bounds of legitimacy more broadly. The British in Nigeria, for example, militarily enforced a program designed to reduce the sleeping sickness affecting up to forty percent of the population in some villages. This was done even though the villagers felt enormous fear that the program of brush cutting would make certain local gods angry and vindictive. By British reasoning the program was for the villagers' own good, and legitimate because it saved lives, but the villagers were clearly coerced (Jones, 1972, p. 253; Zaltman, Kotler, & Kaufman, 1972).

Coercion has been examined predominantly from the social perspective (Pennock & Chapman, 1972) and for this reason, that perspective is considered first.

Social Perspective

Coercion as an instrument of war and political control has been commonplace throughout history. This type of control through fear is also prevalent in religion. There are many examples of threats of "hell, fire, and brimstone" by a vengeful God. For example:

> And I will heap evils upon them; against them, they shall be wasted with hunger, and devoured with burning heat and poisonous pestilence; and I will send the teeth of beasts against them, with venom of crawling things of the dust. (Deuteronomy 32: 23, 24)

> He has made my flesh and my skin waste away, and broken my bones; ... he has sated me with wormwood. He has made my teeth grind on gravel and made me cower in ashes. (Lamentations 3: 4, 16)

Total institutions such as mental hospitals and the military typically remove traditional reinforcements and support. In the extreme, this removal can also be coercive. Goffman (1961), for example, noted that in some organizations individuals go through a virtual "stripping" process, in which their sense of individuality is reduced. The haircuts and physical examinations of military induction both ritualistically and realistically perform this function. Similarly, Schein (1956) described the brainwashing of POWs by Chinese as both a physical and mental tearing-down process, facilitated by exhaustion, malnutrition, social disorganization, and alienation from one another and home ties. The coercion of beatings and torture was hardly necessary after this coercive removal of familiar reinforcements.

Interactional Perspective

A number of inquiries into coercion from the interactional perspective have been made, among which Stanley Milgram's is perhaps the most widely known and popularized (Milgram, 1963, 1965). He studied the willingness of individuals to follow orders to inflict pain on others through the use of electrical shocks. He found that, as the physical distance between the shocker and the "shockee" (an experimental confederate) was increased, the shocker could be encouraged to increase the shocks to virtually lethal proportions. Attachment provides a limit to the willingness to induce pain; formal directives to induce pain increases one's own willingness to do so.

The phenomena of scapegoating and deviant-directed hostility in groups point out similar dynamics. In the case of scapegoating (Coch & French, 1948), individuals are singled out and ridiculed by the group in order to keep them at the bottom of the group's hierarchy. They receive less empathy for pain experienced, much the same as for the receivers of shocks in Milgram's studies. Similarly, as was noted in the conditioning section, the deviant is first ignored (distancing) and then punished for transgressing group norms. At some point punishment is escalated and the deviant is rejected by the group. Punishment becomes coercion, and the group's willingness and capacity to coerce is dependent on the importance of the violated norm and on the cohesiveness of the group (Kelley, 1952).

One unintended effect of coercion is that coerced individuals reduce their evaluation of the coercer (Cartwright & Zander, 1968, pp. 139–164, 270–277, 485–502). Moreover, as Ring and Kelley reported in 1968, the coerced person becomes suspicious of the source of the punishment and questions that person's competence. This reaction is expected if one assumes a consistency or cognitive/perceptual model of human functioning. Anger and resentment are often directed by the coerced person toward the coercer. Therefore, the degree to which personal attraction is central to the relationship is key in determining the relative effectiveness of future coercive attempts. Given the above, it is interesting to note that threats and ultimatums are valued highly in an atmosphere of collective bargaining (Brown, 1965; Walton & McKersie, 1965). By contrast, in family or friendship relations, threats and ultimatums generally are labeled destructive and individuals are counseled to avoid such behavior (Steiner, 1974). The major effect of interpersonal coercion is alienation.

Coercion also fosters behavior change through fear. When coercion is significant, fear may predominate over alienation, resentment, and anger. Redl (1942) argues that fear not only leads to submission but also to *adoration,* since by accepting the standards, directives, and opinions of the coercer, the coercee avoids experiencing the emotion of fear. In Freudian terms, the fear inducing source is introjected into the personality of the individual. Thus, an instructor who aggressively induces fear and submission through daily performance pressure in the case method is more "respected" than hated. In other educational arrangements, examinations create the fear in a more detached manner and in a way that is less demanding on the instructor. According to this logic, admiration is inevitably given to the tough teacher who makes the threats of the situation credible. From the conflict models, then, fear can have "desirable" influence and emotional effects quite different from those emphasized by the contextual models, as illustrated by the discussion of scapegoating and similar group dynamics.

Individual Perspective

Coercion in the domain of counseling and therapy often is experienced and justified differently than in interactional and social perspectives. For example, mental institutions use aggressively confrontational videotape feedback to force patients to acknowledge their own suicidal propensities (Resnik, Davidson, Schuyler, & Christopher, 1973). The stripping process, which Goffman observed in therapeutic settings, also is obviously highly coercive and designed to unfreeze and challenge the individual's self perception. The use of drugs, electroshock, and other freedom reducing procedures are, no doubt, extremely coercive, as illustrated by modern dramatizations such as *One Flew Over the Cuckoo's Nest.* Yet their continued use implies their functional value. The Cathexis Institute claims a high cure rate for schizophrenics using a coercion technique consisting of interpersonal hostility and a Synanon type group aggression "game" in which the introjection of the therapist's superego becomes a replacement for the patient's superego. The fear-induced change is apparently an extreme version of that discussed by Redl. The dependency of the patient on the therapist can generate a strong fear that then can be used by the therapist. Many argue that such processes cannot create "mental health," no matter what outward signs of change are recorded.

Coercion, therefore, is qualitatively distinct from punishment. The key criteria appear to be a forced choice among undesirable alternatives, depersonalization, and the fearful and angry reactions of the individual who is coerced. When individuals feel the bounds of legitimacy have been transcended, they probably feel coerced. It is likely that half-hearted coercion is less effective than either simple punishment or extreme coercion, since here resentment and anger are marshalled in defense against efforts to bring about change.

Summary

Feedback and conditioning are central change processes in experiential learning. For this reason, leaders should be aware of their dynamics and try to take advantage of them. Conversely, coercion, under most circumstances, is undesirable and effort should be made not to generate this process, even inadvertently.

CHAPTER THREE

Leader Centered Change Processes

*The teacher if he is
indeed wise does not bid
you to enter the house of
his wisdom but leads you
to the threshold of your
own mind.*

Kahlil Gibran

This chapter considers three change processes, identification, persuasion, and support. These processes are grouped together, not because of their similarity, but because each places a strong emphasis on the personality of the leader and on participants' reactions to and relationships with that individual. Personal qualities and emotional reactions are central to all three. The identification process, for example, relies on participant pleasure derived from contact with the object of identification or "model." Persuasive ability depends on the leader's attractiveness and trustworthiness perceived by the participants, as well as a host of other factors. The third process, support, reverses the emphasis of the first two. Here the focus is the leader's capacity to be emotionally and practically constructive for the participants, and the vehicle is the leader's personal contact with the participants.

Identification

The identification change process is more complex than might at first be surmised. This is partially because conditioning processes are intimately bound up with the overall identification process through the relationship between the individual and the "model." It is not simply modeling based on attraction, although the model does demonstrate attitudes, behaviors, or skills that the individual may or may not attempt to emulate. The tendency to attempt matching is a function of the attractiveness of the model, the relationship between the model and the individual, and, in addition, the reinforcements that the individual perceives the model to receive as the result of the demonstrated action. Distinctions between identification and imitation have sparked debate in the past, as has the distinction between the acquisition and the performance of the modeled response. Observationally induced change resulting in behavior change is often labeled imitation; similarly induced attitude change is often labeled identification. Bandura, however, argues convincingly that

> if the diverse criteria . . . were seriously applied, either singly or in various combinations in categorizing modeling outcomes, most instances of matching behavior that have been traditionally labeled imitation would qualify as identification, and much of the naturalistic data cited as evidence of identificatory learning would be reclassified as imitation. (Bandura, 1969, p. 190)

Therefore, whether identificatory processes are called imitation, observation, or even osmosis, they should not impede an analysis of how such processes work, how they are combined with other change processes such as conditioning, and how change is induced through the total process.

The "social learning" approach to changing maladaptive behavior holds the identificatory change process as central. Social learning is perhaps best articulated by Bandura (1968, 1969, 1977), Bandura and Walters (1963), and Flanders (1968). Conditioning alone explains little according to social learning:

> In the social learning view, people are neither impelled by inner forces nor buffeted by environmental stimuli. Rather, psychological functioning is explained in terms of a continuous reciprocal influence between personal and environmental determinants. Within this approach, symbolic, vicarious, and self-regulatory processes assume a prominent role. (Bandura, 1977, p. 7)

Beyond the effects of vicarious reinforcement of observed behavior, "stimulus and symbolic processes" also occur (Bandura, 1969, p. 128). These are especially important for the *acquisition* of matching responses. But the *performance* of responses depends heavily on actual (or real) reinforcement. Furthermore, "the anticipation of positive reinforcement for matching responses by the observer may, therefore, indirectly influence the course of observational learning by enhancing and focusing observing responses" (1969, p. 130). The individual must perceive the correlation between events and anticipate outcomes (Rescorla, 1972). In this regard, certain visual stimuli focus attention by eliciting feelings or instincts such as aggression. For example, one individual who when young was beaten by a large person tended to become "violent at any slight provocation by a large sized person" (Bandura, 1977, p. 38; Berkowitz, 1973).

The attentional aspects of the modeling process are closely related to re-cognition, to be discussed later, but Bandura summarizes the characteristics of models that encourage high degrees of attention from observers.

Of much greater importance for social learning, however, is the acquired distinctiveness of model attributes (Miller & Dollard, 1941). By being repeatedly rewarded for imitating certain types of models and not rewarded for matching the behavior of models possessing different characteristics, persons eventually learn to discriminate between modeling cues that signify differential probabilities of reinforcement. Thus, models who have demonstrated high competence (Gelfand, 1962; Mausner, 1954a, 1954b; Mausner & Bloch, 1957; Rosenbaum & Tucker, 1962), who are purported experts (Mausner, 1953) or are celebrities (Hovland, Janis, & Kelley, 1953), and who possess status-conferring symbols (Lefkowitz, Blake, & Mouton, 1955) are likely to command more attention and to serve as more influential sources of social behavior than models who lack these qualities.

Other distinctive characteristics, such as age (Bandura & Kupers, 1964; Hicks, 1965; Jakubczak & Walters, 1959), and sex (Bandura, Ross, & Ross, 1963a; Maccoby & Wilson, 1957; Ofstad, 1967; Rosenblith, 1959, 1961), . . . which are correlated with differential probabilities of reinforcement likewise influence the degree to which models who possess these attributes will be selected for emulation.

The affective valence of models, as mediated through their attractiveness and other rewarding qualities, (Bandura & Huston, 1961; Grusec & Mischel, 1966), may augment observational learning by eliciting and maintaining strong attending behavior. (Bandura, 1969, pp. 136–137)

According to Bandura, cognition enters directly into the identification process in two major ways. The first cognitive factor involves individuals' views of themselves, the world, and themselves in the world. Interest in a particular model is partially a function of how realistic the model is as an ideal. Thus for most men Nicklaus is a more realistic model than Van Cliburn, simply because more men see themselves as potentially good golfers than as potentially good pianists. The second cognitive factor in identification is memory, or the actual retention of observed events. Overt rehearsal of modeled action and covert or symbolic rehearsal both strengthen retention. The corollary here is that retention is impaired by lengthy, uninterrupted model presentations (Bandura, 1969, p. 141). Clear implications for effective model presentations can easily be advanced. Models should be presented in small units and in spaced intervals.

They should be attractive in a variety of ways and should overtly demonstrate linkages between stimuli, emotions, actions, and outcomes.

Individual Perspective

Modeling procedures have been used successfully to change maladaptive behavior such as fears, anxieties, and behavioral excesses and to teach a broad range of new behaviors and skills such as decision making and assertiveness (Marlatt & Perry, 1975). One example from each of these categories is provided to illustrate how the procedures are used. For snake phobias, the client observes the therapist handle the snake and gradually comes to perform the same actions without any associated fear or anxiety (Bandura, Blanchard, & Ritter, 1969). This procedure is called participant modeling. For delinquency behavior, clients are exposed to examples of alternative ways of handling difficult situations when they are on parole. In one study the modeled dialogue depicts a parolee successfully declining peer group requests to go drinking (Sarason & Ganzer, 1971, 1973). The clients watch two models having the conversation and then practice the presented behavior in pairs or with a therapist. Variations of this same procedure are also used for many other types of assertiveness training.

In summary, modeling procedures can be used effectively to "transmit new patterns of behavior, to eliminate unwarranted fears and inhibitions, and to facilitate expression of preexisting modes of response" (Bandura, 1971, p. 703). Modeling enables individuals to acquire complex behaviors without relying on trial and error. It is also transportable to the individual's actual home or work environment. Finally, modeling can be provided by a wide variety of resources in the community. Used by itself or in conjunction with other methods this identificatory change process is effective in both clinical and nonclinical settings.

Interactional Perspective

The interactional level of analysis offers further insights into and applications of the identification process. Kelman (1958), for example, explored the effects of a highly attractive, charismatic leader on the attitude of college-bound students. In this conception, change is seen to result from the individual's creation of a satisfying and self-defining relationship with the model. According to Kelman, the key source of attraction is the model's perceived power, defined as a personal attribute such as attained success; Bandura, on the other hand, emphasizes direct control over reinforcements relevant to the individual. Kelman found that individuals demonstrate attitude change when the salience of their relationship to the model is high. Again unlike Bandura, he does not emphasize the individual's vicarious experience of the ongoing reinforcements received by the model. Instead, the reward for the individual is the sense of having a relationship with the highly valued and attractive model. There is no expectation that acquisition and performance of the modeled action will bring actual rewards other than a sense of closeness to the model. It is for these reasons that John F. Kennedy, for example, could change attitudes in a large number of individuals as long as their identity needs were being serviced through his continued presence or image and his overt displays of desirable characteristics.

Redl (1942) offers a two-sided view of group emotion and modeling that includes fear and love. He identifies three model types that induce change through identification: the leader, the patriarch, and the tyrant. The leader conception is similar to Kelman's; individuals are seen to be attracted to the model and to want love from or a reciprocal relationship with the model. In the absence of real consequences, imagined consequences may be adequate. The individuals incorporate the ideals of the model to attain the desired relationship. The patriarch's love is also desired but, in this case, rather than avoiding the unhappiness of withheld love, individuals try to avoid the fear of negative reactions from the admired and loved model. There is a subtle but important difference, emotionally and psychodynamically. The withdrawal of affection is assumed to be legitimate by individuals who incorporate the conscience of the model for fear reduction. Finally, the tyrant is coercive and perhaps sadistic. Individuals both fear and hate the model and are anxious about their aggressive reactions to the model. Paradoxically, they incorporate the entire superego of the model because they fear that their aggression might lead to their own destruction. In all three cases, powerful emotions toward the model create an issue in self-definition for which the model serves as a well-defined and satisfying resolution. Here, the conflict paradigm of human functioning is assumed, rather than the learning or contextual paradigms of Bandura and Kelman respectively.

Groups also can be a source of identification and in this discussion serve as a bridge between the interactional and social perspectives. Virtually all members of society belong to a number of reference groups; housewives, athletes, parents, and teachers exercise certain attitudes and actions affirming the self-definition of the individual. Sutherland and Cressey (1970) stated that criminals, for example, acquire complex attitudes and skills through membership in tight groups. Janis (1968) argued that external threat leads to reduced individuality and increased identification with the group. Schwitzgebel and Kolb (1974) validated the rationale of parents who remove a delinquent boy from a peer group having a bad influence by moving to a new neighbourhood where he might establish relationships with a better set of models. This parental act is called restructuring and will be discussed later.

Most sociologists (Winch & Gordon, 1974) accept the family as the prime socializing group. At one level, younger children learn behaviors and attitudes compatible with the views of parents and older siblings through feedback, conditioning, and coercion. Identification through love, fear, genetic inheritance, proximity, and extended contact are all present in the family context. Much of the deepest identity formation results from "symbiotic" relationships between the mother and individual children. The term symbiosis refers to neither person functioning as an independent individual. Parents experience their children's fun vicariously, and children depend on parental responsibility. The dependency yields high identification with the parents through both the fear and love mechanisms elaborated by Redl and perhaps others as well. Identification, in addition to conditioning, is a key to personality formation. As Kelman observed, imitation occurs only when the salience of the relationship is high; in the case of families, the acquired actions become very deeply ingrained before the relationship loses salience.

Social Perspective

From the social perspective, the attractiveness of the model can be considered primarily in terms of status. When the chief executive officer of a business organization begins wearing a company tie, his status conspires with the other sources of identification to encourage emulation. Dress and demeanor are minor changes symbolizing the greater act of conformity. The door is opened to more significant although less overt change through identification. Here the satisfactions derived from the individual will affect future identificatory acts.

Other procedures and activities operating at a social level are intimately related to identification. The advertising industry relies heavily on identification for the promotion and sales of anything one cares to mention. This process is actively pursued through all forms of mass media, especially television. Presentations of models on television increase the models' status, identificatory power, and subsequent ability to influence behavior (Gordon, 1971; Walter, 1978). For example, Walt Disney established a public image through his television programs and films. This image continues to serve as a source of influence over customers as well as employees. The remark, "Every time somebody makes a pornographic movie, I make more money," attributed to Disney, is still often repeated by employees who serve in minor organizational roles. They identify with the totality of the enterprise symbolized by Disney.

From a political perspective, identification is a powerful source of influence. Figures like Hitler, Churchill, Roosevelt, and most other popular leaders of their respective eras personally symbolized ideas, values, and expectations readily adopted by a large portion of the individuals in their societies. Conditioning and coercion alone cannot account for the influence enjoyed by this type of leader. Identification aids in the mobilization of energy and resources.

Summary

Identification is a powerful force in changing behavior. It is complexly derived from and related to a number of other processes, and encompasses feedback, conditioning, and even coercion. However, the points used to describe feedback and conditioning are inadequate to describe identification as a change process, since it is quite likely that identification is as much or more a function of the attributes and emotional displays of the models than of overt extrinsic reinforcement contingencies.

Persuasion

Persuasion changes behavior through the planned presentation of information. This discussion is divided into five sections. The first two, emotional impact and cognition, concentrate on how a persuasive stimulus actually affects the individual. The individual perspective is emphasized in both of these sections. The third and fourth sections, flow of presentation of events and source of information, expand the individual perspective and then concentrate on interactional aspects of persuasion. The fifth section examines additional phenomena associated with persuasion. All the sections systematically describe the manner in which persuasive events are experienced. In the summary, a four-stage process model of persuasion is presented to reorganize and summarize the material already discussed. The major emphasis throughout is on the affective aspects of persuasion based more on the form it takes, than on the content it contains. Here Freud is instructive when he asserts:

> Since men are so slightly amenable to reasonable arguments so completely are they ruled by instinctual wishes, why should one want to take away from them a means of satisfying their instincts and replace it with reasonable arguments. (Gordon, 1971, p. 365)

Emotional Impact

Any persuasive event creates or stimulates emotions in the individual. For example, The American Cancer Society tries to persuade people not to smoke by evoking fear through an advertisement in which one individual refuses an offered cigarette by saying "No thanks, I can live without it." A similar message is conveyed in a poster showing two hands loading cigarettes into the chamber of a large Smith and Wesson revolver. Hitler, in addition to fear, used extravaganzas that communicated a sense of enormous capacity for force. Mighty deeds were demonstrated to put force to strong words, evoking feelings of power and awe in the audience. Such appeals can have an impact on emotions ranging from fear to sex, and they implicitly offer tangible rewards. Postponing death and being power-

ful are the two rewards offered respectively by the Cancer Society advertisement and Hitler. The reward for buying a shiny new car pictured in
front of an elegant home is even more obvious. The strength of an emotional appeal can affect its impact, but no simple rule applies to mild or
extreme approaches (Karlins & Abelson, 1970, pp. 6–10).

There are two ways in which absence or reduction of emotional impact
affects persuasive ability. The first relates to the notion of cognitive dissonance and the second to the elimination of threats related to a persuasive
act. First, since individuals experience dissonance as emotionally discomforting, arguments providing dissonance-reducing interpretations of observed events are persuasive (Zimbardo & Ebbeson, 1969, p. 80). This
implies the dominance of the conflict, consistency, cognitive/perceptual,
and learning models of human functioning. People tend to believe that
which is not too discomforting, or that which actually aids in avoiding
discomfort. Second, for persuasion to be effective, existing blocks to the
message must be removed.

Confronting prejudice is a challenging persuasion circumstance because
of the discomfort caused by the inherent threat to the individual's current
view of the world. Frontal attacks on prejudice result in entrenchment
rather than change. The persuasive messages must be presented so that
they do not threaten the individual; conditions need to be established that
increase the individual's willingness to hear what is being said or to do
what is requested or suggested. For example, the old Red Cross approach
to blood donation through an appeal to patriotism did little to assuage
anxiety and fear surrounding the process. But the gift to donors of pins
representing white "drops of blood," a modest symbol of bravery, did have
marked positive effects on people's willingness to become donors. In general, the arousal of guilt or anxiety increases resistance to change. Correla-
tively, these feelings place a requirement for their own resolution within
the change itself. For a blood donor, receiving a pin for bravery counters
the resistant feelings and justifies the effort. The emotional impact of fear,
sex, love, and power are used daily to persuade individuals, communities,
and nations, by agents ranging from the "merchants of God" to political
demagogues (Gordon, 1971).

The issue of emotional arousal will come up again and again in the
following discussion, but before exploring persuasion events more deeply,
cognition must be considered. Few educators are as skilled as they might
be in their efforts to change individuals and, while many of the current
priorities are not condoned, it is acknowledged that the "popular" influence agents have much to teach academics about persuasion.

Cognition

The faculties of judgment and memory are central to a discussion of
cognition. The cognitive component of functioning, unlike the emotional

impact component, does not emphasize the instinctual aspects of the conflict model or the conditioning aspects of the learning model. Instead, researchers such as Bieri, Atkins, Briar, Leaman, Miller, and Tripodi (1966); Hovland, Janis, and Kelley (1953); and Sherif and Hovland (1961) have examined individuals' intellectual responses to a message in terms of judgment and other mental effects. The latter two works especially contribute to our understanding of the phenomenon of the anchoring of judgments and attributes through social stimuli.

The process of anchoring can be divided into "centering" and "distancing" aspects. Since individuals attempt to order and arrange stimuli into patterns, values ultimately must be applied when no explicit standards for grouping them exist. Individuals begin this process with specific reference points, or judgment anchors. One way anchors affect judgment is exemplified by Kiesler, Collins, and Miller (1969) in a discussion of contrast effects:

> The subject is asked to place one hand in a bucket of hot water and the other in a bucket of cold water. After a few minutes, both hands are simultaneously immersed in a third bucket with water of moderate temperature. The experience and judgment that the water in this third bucket is simultaneously hot and cold is ubiquitously compelling. The hand formerly in the hot water now feels cold, whereas the other hand, formerly in the cold water, now feels hot. (Kiesler, Collins, & Miller, 1969, p. 240)

Anchors also affect judgment through assimilation. When an individual is asked to make judgments about a set of stimuli such as blocks of identical size and shape but differing weights and is provided with an anchor at either end of the series, "the entire distribution of judgments is shifted toward the anchor" (Kiesler, Collins, & Miller, 1969, p. 242). On the other hand, if the anchor is extremely divergent from the stimuli the effect is reversed. That is, rather than judgments being pulled toward the anchor, the judgments are displaced even more from the anchor (Sherif, Taub, & Hovland, 1958). When judgments concern more abstract or ambiguous stimuli than the weight of blocks, additional factors modify these general tendencies. Intensely held attitudes and attitudes of key value to the individual's identity (Sherif & Cantril, 1947) increase the potency of anchoring. Ego involvement is the term used to describe this general state and is defined as "the arousal . . . of the individual's commitments or stands in the context of appropriate situations" (Sherif, Sherif, & Nebergall, 1965, p. 65). The latitude of an indiviual's acceptance, noncommitment, or rejection of an issue is closely aligned with the judgment process. The higher the individual's involvement the less divergence from a personal value can be included in the latitude of acceptance. The latitude of noncommitment also decreases as involvement increases. Together these concepts form a powerful complex process.

Mark Antony's funeral oration in Shakespeare's *Julius Caesar* serves as an excellent example for these social judgment principles. First Antony surprises the audience by coming to "bury Caesar not to praise him." He puts himself near their anchor for the situation and thus within their latitude of acceptance. But during his discourse, step by step, he increases the breadth of his comments into areas that initially would have been beyond the latitude of acceptance. He uses smooth transitions and innuendo to forestall the contrast effects that otherwise would have been likely. He first pins innuendo to the strong anchors of the audience's central values, such as bravery and honor, and then constrasts Brutus and the other conspirators to those values, thus putting them beyond the latitude of acceptance (see Kelly, Rokeach, and Festinger).

The second impact of persuasion through cognition involves memory and is related to the individual's capacity for remembering and acting on information, something quite separate from social judgment theory. Findings from the original Yale communications research of Hovland, Janis, and Kelley (1953) illustrate the manner in which this factor comes into attitude change. Here questions of when an individual is most influential and how long arguments can be retained have contributed to a number of generalizations about influencer-influencee communications (Zimbardo & Ebbesen, 1969, p. 21):

1   Present one side of the argument when the audience is generally friendly, or when your position is the only one that will be presented, or when you want immediate, though temporary, opinion change.

2   Present both sides of the argument when the audience starts out disagreeing with you or when it is probable that the audience will hear the other side from someone else.

3   When opposite views are presented one after another, the one presented last will probably be more effective. Primacy effect is more predominant when the second side immediately follows the first, while recency effect is more predominant when the opinion measure comes immediately after the second side.

4   There will probably be more opinion change in the direction you want if you explicitly state your conclusions than if you let the audience draw their own, except when they are rather intelligent. Then implicit conclusion drawing is better.

One sees that memory and judgment are implied to be somewhat limited and that a linkage of positive feeling with the proposed outcome is an important mediating factor. Further, this view of the thought processes of individuals emphasizes the role of presentation order and style on effectiveness and thus provides a bridge to the discussion of presentations, source of information, and phenomena.

Flow of Presentation of Events

Since the research of Hovland, Janis, and other communications theorists, a large variety of alternative sequences of presentation have been studied. Few simple conclusions have resulted from these studies, because most conclusions must be qualified by other moderating effects. Nonetheless, a few of the central findings of early research are noteworthy because they shed light on the effects of presentation order even if they cannot serve as universal prescriptions.

The first comments made by a speaker set the listener's mind and tend to be better retained than material presented in the middle because of the primacy of that information in the mind of the listeners. Similarly, the last material presented is held better than middle material because of its recency in the listener's mind. The last lawyer to speak in court must, for example, use this opportunity to destroy his opposition's statements and make his or her own argument stand out clearly (Nizer, 1961). The primacy effect dominates when a second side immediately follows the first, but the recency effect is most important when, as in court, the listener's opinion is evoked immediately after the second side has been presented.

In general, the more explicit and repetitive the message, the more it is accepted and retained. One qualification here is that more intelligent individuals tend to be unaffected in circumstances in which they draw their own conclusions. Here, implicit conclusions are the best presentation device; slogans such as "you can take Salem out of the country but . . ." actively involve listeners in the message, inviting them to complete it for the closure experience. This increases retention of especially brief messages and is known as the *Zeigarnik effect* (Zimbardo & Ebbesen, 1969, p. 110). As already noted, it is generally best to present both sides of an argument if the audience is initially hostile, because this increases attention. When the audience is friendly, alternatives should be reduced or even eliminated if no opposition is expected (Zimbardo & Ebbesen, 1969, p. 21). Another advantage of one-sided presentations is that they are simple and the listener can easily incorporate them. When a few points are condensed into catchy slogans, ease of repetition is added to simplicity. Feelings favorable to the adoption of an idea should be evoked before the idea itself is offered, rather than vice versa or simultaneously.

Innoculation against a persuasive message is possible according to McGuire (1964, 1967). Here, forewarning of the manipulative intent of a communication draws the listener's attention to that aspect and increases resistance to it. In contrast, a distraction during a presentation effort may lower the listener's resistance to manipulation. Counterargument in the listener's head is reduced and a general affective response is generated. It is noteworthy that affectively pleasing distractions increase response to the presentation while disagreeable or upsetting distractions have the opposite effect (McGuire & Papageorgis, 1961). Here again overall emotional impact is fundamentally important.

Source

> The creature man is best persuaded
> When heart, not mind, is inundated;
> Affect is what drives the will;
> Rationality keeps it still.

(Karlins & Abelson, 1970, p. 35)

The source of a persuasive communication is integral to the impact of a persuasive attempt. The personal characteristic most commonly cited regarding the source of a persuasion attempt is communication credibility (Hovland, Janis, & Kelley, 1953). Credibility is a function of many things, but trustworthiness and expertise relevant to the issue are central. A trustworthy source is apparently unbiased and honorably motivated. Walter Cronkite, during the fall of Nixon, was a highly credible scrutinizer of presidential power and thus a strong influence on the public.

The question then becomes, what contributes to credibility? Some researchers include station in life, dress, dignified bearing, apparent earnestness, and an authoritative manner (Anderson, 1967; Anderson & Clevenger, 1963). Moreover, cues change the fashion and the credibility of institutions or stereotypes. For example, in the early 1970s *Newsweek* reported an increased tendency for jurors to believe in lawyers with mustaches and long hair, in contrast to the slick Madison Avenue types.

Interpersonal attractiveness (Berscheid & Walster, 1970) is also an important source of persuasive appeal, but here it is difficult to distinguish between persuasion and identification. Walter Cronkite's wise, fatherly manner is no doubt attractive to many, especially in times of confusion. President Carter's friendly campaign smile made credible his claim of being a populist dedicated to openness in government, an important criterion for voters in the era after Nixon and the Vietnam war. Appearance in the media contributes to a person's credibility. The printed word and television especially (Walter, 1978) have the power to shape opinion; in many instances, this persuasive effect is independent of the particular person delivering the message. For example, the issues vividly portrayed on the evening news become *ipso facto* the issues that the viewing public "should" be concerned about. Satisfaction is derived from being "in the know" about world events and from the visual stimulation (consistency, cognitive/perceptual, and activation models of human functioning). In short, the most persuasive source of information personifies satisfactions relevant to the issues of interest to the audience.

Satisfaction is attained differently in the identification process, wherein the changee sees the model as being able to attain desirable satisfactions, and thus the changee wishes to become like the model. In persuasion the changee does not aspire to be like the model but rather, at least in a symbolic sense, to be liked by the source and to gain the comfort of conforming to the source's opinion on a particular topic. Anderson and Clevenger (1963) point out some additional source characteristics in their summary of studies on communicator "ethos" or image. Here attractiveness in its many facets comes into play. Dynamism, sociability, and apparent reliability are also attributes of importance (Griffin, 1967). Anderson (1971) emphasizes that as early as Aristotle, traits such as character, sagacity, and goodwill were important, and that it is the combined overall image held in the audience's mind that is the essence of ethos. In the case of Walter Cronkite, the media image transcends the man. Much depends on the audience, of course; this is one of the phenomena moderating persuasion.

Moderating Phenomena

Numerous social factors and environmental contexts affect or alter attempts to persuade. In psychological warfare, for example, the goals of opposition propaganda often include conversion of individuals. More pragmatically, there are also attempts to introduce divisiveness among opponents, to counteract alternative persuasive efforts and to consolidate influence over others within the formal domain of power. Here the chief mechanism is often merely to bring fears and discomforts to the central awareness or attention of a population so that they might have a predictable effect. The activation of these fears is seldom through threats but through "friendly" advice. The persuasion attempt in this case is more modest than that implied earlier but is potentially quite effective because of the highly volatile emotional issues often alluded to.

A second persuasion phenomenon is the police interrogation in which one policeman behaves threateningly and the other supportively toward the suspect. The alternation of threat and support builds emotional dependencies, trust, and a tendency to believe the "nice guy." The situation creates an ethos of credibility that then can be used to influence. Moreover, being confronted simultaneously with opposites affects a suspect's judgment.

Initiation rites, an often studied phenomenon, seem to create commitment to the group. According to Gerard and Mathewson (1966), the greater the pain experienced by a participant, the deeper the satisfaction derived from being in the group. Zimbardo and Ebbesen (1969) take these and other findings to support a consistency model of human functioning in which incongruities must be balanced by altered attitudes. If it is difficult to gain membership in a group it must be a good group.

Another phenomenon in influence is the character or conduct of the audience itself. Persons of low self-esteem, who are not threatened by the attempt, are more easily influenced than persons of high self-esteem. Active involvement results in more change than totally passive exposure to the message. Eye contact between audience and communicator creates a personal relationship and affects the potency of the source as an image in the mind of the audience (Nizer, 1961, p. 42). Intelligence and many other factors also must be acknowledged here, for, as noted above, it is through the wishes and needs of the audience that the persuasion attempt must naturally move.

Summary

An understanding of persuasion is central to appreciating the management of information for changing attitudes and behavior when there is no personal relationship between the source of the information and those to be influenced. Persuasion has two primary emotional components: to gain and hold the attention of the listener, perhaps through dynamic, forceful, or sexually stimulating presentation; and to offer satisfaction of needs conditional on acceptance of the message. Persuasive attempts must be comprehensible to the audience and initially not too divergent from the audience's present position.

The sequence of material in a persuasive attempt is important; the effectiveness of presentation devices depends on the occasion and on the audience's friendliness or hostility, intelligence, and involvement. The presenter of a persuasive message must have credibility, derived from personal traits and attending circumstances such as contemporaneous fashions and events and the role played by the media.

Zimbardo and Ebbesen summarize these aspects of persuasion in a four-stage model which considers "(a) the individual's initial position, (b) his attention to the communicator and the message, (c) comprehension of its arguments, examples, appeals and conclusions, (d) general and specific motivation for accepting its positions" (1969, p. 18).

Support

The role of the support process in change is quite distinct from those discussed so far. Other processes facilitate, encourage, and create pressure and direction for change; support "enables" change. Support refers to a physical, emotional, or symbolic contribution to individuals increasing their net stockpile of emotional capacity to cope with change. A discussion of the support process from each perspective, notably the individual therapeutic context, is preceded by a brief examination of the need for support.

Coch and French (1948), Hoffer (1964), and other social observers have documented emotional and behavioral evidence for individual resistance to change. Fear of loss, incompetence, and disorganization all fuel resistance to change. Reflection on the consistency and cognitive/perceptual models of human functioning yields a view of individuals as wanting to have a sense of continuity, predictability, and control in life. Absence of congruence-confirming feedback generates behavior directed at reestablishing some degree of control. In sociobiological terms, there is an underlying instinct for control that generates behavior in these situations. Emotion is the indicator of this underlying process and the fundamental emotion activated in change is fear—fear of loss, fear of overwhelming demands, fear of inadequacies being made manifest, and, ultimately, fear of death. The ethologist Bowlby's 1973 studies of fear in children described situations which evoked fear as having survival roots. Thus fear of strangers, loud noises, the dark, and rapid movements all have adaptive significance. Fear of change may also have fitness significance since our ancestors one million years ago saw very little change throughout their lifetimes.

The antidote to fear in the child is attachment and closeness to the mother, the life protector. Similarly for adults, interpersonal support and overt protection assuage fear and enable change. Consequently, support is a crucial ingredient in almost any effort to change behavior and contains a tight logical link to the life sciences model of human functioning.

Individual Perspective

Counseling and therapy have concentrated on just how the helper can best provide support to clients. Carl Rogers (1942, 1951, 1957) was the first to explore deeply the role of a supportive therapeutic relationship in individual change. For him, the crucial components were:

[1] The therapist experiences unconditional positive regard for the client.

[2] The therapist experiences an empathic understanding of the client's internal frame of reference and endeavors to communicate this experience to the client.

[3] The communication to the client of the therapists empathic understanding and unconditional positive regard is to a minimal degree achieved. (Rogers, 1957, p. 96)

The result of many years of investigation of these fundamental insights has been carefully articulated by Carkhuff and Berenson (1967), Egan (1975), Rogers and Truax (1967), and many others. Egan summarized the client-centered therapy conception of support as a broad helper role. Support is defined as the exercising of specific skills and capacities through a relationship in order to ease client fear and facilitate change. Therefore, since support is directed at reducing fear, it is the antithesis of coercion. This central fact is critical to the "unconditional acceptance" that Rogers so ably argues to be the essence of the therapeutic supportive relationship. Support requires "total listening" so that individuals know that they are being warmly and unconditionally understood and accepted. Support requires open and honest treatment.

Egan describes the skills of the supportive "helper" as: attentiveness, empathy, respect, genuineness, concreteness, and self-disclosure (1975, pp. 34–37). Attentiveness refers to "being with" or listening to the individual. Empathy shows the individual that what is felt or said is understood and appreciated. Respect involves valuing an individual's uniqueness and not disregarding his or her individuality or right to self-determination. Genuineness is similar to Rogers' and Truax's congruence (1967); helpers must be themselves and be comfortable with that behavior, rather than maintaining a superficial facade or playing a role. Spontaneous, nondefensive, consistent, self-sharing behaviors are hallmarks of genuineness. All of these traits are shown through physical expressions of caring and warmth although not all warmth need spring from this base. Concreteness aids individuals in specifying and objectifying their thoughts and perceptions. Self-disclosure implies a willingness to reveal one's self in the therapeutic relationship.

These helper skills if applied competently can result in "trust." "If I entrust myself to you, you will respond with care and skill to help me" (Egan, 1975, p. 110). The safety of a trust relationship, of course, is synonymous with fear assuagement and thus the discussion is brought full circle to the central notion of support. Skillful interpersonal support prepares the individual for change and makes the risks of change less ominous.

The impact of the facilitative conditions on client change has been thoroughly investigated (Mitchell, Bozarth, & Krauft, 1977; Parloff, Waskow, & Wolfe, 1978; Truax & Mitchell, 1971). "In brief all schools of psychotherapy appear to be in accord that a positive relationship between patient and therapist is a necessary precondition for any form of psychotherapy" (Parloff, Waskow, & Wolfe, 1978, p. 243). The Truax and Mitchell review found the facilitative conditions central to therapeutic success.

> These studies taken together suggest that therapists or counselors who are accurately empathic, nonpossessively warm in attitude, and genuine, are indeed effective. Also, these findings seem to hold with a wide variety of therapists and counselors, regardless of their training or theoretic orientation, and with a wide variety of clients or patients, including college underachievers, juvenile delinquents, hospitalized schizophrenics, college counselees, mild to severe outpatient neurotics and the mixed variety of hospitalized patients. Further, the evidence suggests that these findings hold in a variety of therapeutic contexts and in both individual and group psychotherapy and counseling. (Truax & Mitchell, 1971, p. 310)

However, after almost a decade of further study, the relationships are not as clear as one is initially led to believe. "The recent evidence, although equivocal, does seem to suggest that empathy, warmth, and genuineness are related in some way to client change but their potency and generalizability are not as great as once thought" (Mitchell, Bozarth, & Krauft, 1977, p. 481).

Being skilled in offering high levels of these conditions is every bit as important for leaders in experiential learning activities as it is for helpers in therapeutic settings.

Interactional Perspective

Interactional sources of support come from personal and group relationships. An examination of these relationships will enable us to appreciate more fully the elaborate social interplay of fear and anxiety with support and the role of trust. Janis (1968, pp. 80–90) showed that external threat results in anxiety to group members. Subsequent regression is expressed in greater needs for reassurance, and increased group identification by members follows. Similarly, Sherif and Sherif (1953) documented that relatively minor threats of intergroup competition lead to increased group solidarity. Cartwright (1968, pp. 91–109) argued that cohesion in groups ultimately rests on the mutual satisfaction of needs, and that a sense of security and commonality grows out of closeness, belonging, and involvement. The relevance of these latter needs in daily fear-evoking situations suggests the importance of affiliation tendencies in self-protection; affiliation is a key precursor to the development of supportive relations.

Additionally, individuals display a tendency to seek out one another when their opinions are shaken or when uninterpretable events lead to ambiguity about social reality (Festinger, 1957, p. 64). The group also may offer considerable support under conditions of external threat.

> In morale surveys during world War II, we found that many soldiers said they would not want to be shifted to any other unit because they felt safer with their own group. For example, a wounded veteran of combat in North Africa said: "The fellows don't want to leave when they're sick. They're afraid to leave their own men—the men they know. Your own outfit— they're the men you have confidence in. It gives you more guts to be with them."
>
> Now when a soldier says that "it gives you more guts" to be with the men in your own outfit, it is not merely because of the increase in actual protection he consciously anticipates. External threats foster increased reliance on the group by arousing a variety of basic psychological needs for reassurance, some of which are, of course, preconscious, or unconscious. (Janis, 1968, p. 83)

Individuals want support from people they are attracted to, and a relatively higher status enhances attractiveness.

The phenomenon of isolation can also be linked to notions of affiliation, and, ultimately, support. Under conditions of anxiety, isolation is experienced as loneliness, which is the acknowledgment or awareness of an unsatisfied need for affiliation. The anxiety can be triggered by ambiguity, threat, or hunger, and is reduced through support gained from being a part of a group of peers facing the same threats or difficulties. In this situation the support grows out of the individual's attraction to the others in the group, a condition resulting from the generated mutual trust. Therefore, as illustrated by the soldier, members' personal feelings of isolation in a group bind the group together and generate support.

The centrality of the support process has also been stressed by proponents of human relations training. Rogers' conception of encounter is brought to fruition in Gibb's (1972) T.O.R.I. growth sequence. Gibb encouraged the creation of supportive communities through training emphasizing trust, openness, and realization of interdependency. Giving and seeking support enables the participants to look at aspects of themselves that otherwise might provoke anxiety. Support as a necessary prerequisite to growth is provided through a climate of trust emphasizing acceptance. The notion of the role of trust and support in T-groups and sensitivity groups is consistent with Gibb's position. For example, Friedlander (1971) shows that the initial level of trust in sensitivity training groups greatly affects the degree to which the group accomplishes its growth goals. Support, resulting in trust, is seen as the mastic which holds these types of learning experiences together.

Social Perspective

Analysis of support from the social perspective leads to slightly different insights. Scott (1965), for example, states that a common sense of social reality and a common approach to problems is central to affiliative tendencies and that friendships are highly ecologically determined. That is, physical proximity and convenience dominate. It follows that similarities are the natural result of conformity demands of interdependent individuals. The process of support, though possibly resulting from a common base of experience and sense of social reality, is not overtly considered. A contrast here is provided by Brown (1965), who argues that a sense of solidarity in affiliative relations depends on similarity and, most important, status similarities. The key seems to be that all types of commonalities, from goals to threats to benefits, are valuable factors contributing ultimately to some form of support.

For applications to task-centered organizations, we look to Bowers and Seashore's (1966) explorations of Likert's (1961, 1967) notions of supportive relations in the workplace. Here, support is defined as an action that enhances another individual's feeling of personal worth or importance, not only in performance but also in coping with fears of failure in the face of external pressure. In terms of social reality and conformity, one can see that support must be provided simultaneously as an incentive to accept goal standards and as a compensation for other pressures inevitable in social groups. Finally, it must be stressed that, for Likert, the significance of supportive relations is in direct response to the inherent alienation of specialization in organizations. The lonely crowd is a by-product of modern organization.

There are many sources of support throughout society. Family, friends, romantic relationships, kinship groups, and communities are obvious. National identity, shared language, and culture also create support of no mean significance. One need only reflect on the fears of societal breakdown and resistance to changes such as "metrication." Formal religion is an often undervalued source of support. The first few lines of the Twenty-Third Psalm capture the tone of this support:

> The Lord is my shepherd, I shall not want;
> He makes me lie down in green pastures.
> He leads me beside still waters;
> He restores my soul.
> He leads me in paths of righteousness
> for his name's sake.
> Even though I walk through the
> valley of the shadow of death,
> I fear no evil; for Thou art with me;
> Thy rod and Thy staff, they comfort me.

A loving God who looks out for the individual makes the vicissitudes of life and its termination more understandable and bearable.

Summary

Identification, persuasion, and support are the change processes most directly related to the leader's presence and behavior. Since the leader is actively engaged in preparing participants for the learning experience, these processes are useful in identifying the desirable leader qualities that enhance learning. Modeling desired behavior, presenting information in a convincing manner, and providing comfort and support promote change.

CHAPTER FOUR

Restructuring and Channeling

*By accepting the universal
neurosis he is spared the
task of forming a personal
neurosis.*

Sigmund Freud

Two general categories are used to discuss the manner in which a social context can induce change in the individual. These are called the restructuring process and the channeling process. Restructuring refers to actual changes in the physical, legal, or social structure having direct effects. For example, lowered highway speed limits have resulted in reduced accident rates, and some would argue that increased speed limits could now have the same effect. A typology of restructuring is developed in this chapter, first to aid the reader in thinking systematically about the kinds of restructuring useful for specific change goals, and second as a gauge on the qualitative magnitude of specific restructuring attempts. The discussion of channeling is a very brief treatment of how some of the major social mechanisms (such as interpersonal reinforcement for conformity purposes) operate through norms and roles to guide and control individual behavior in a given social structure. The points here are that social forces can be brought to bear on the individual more subtly in channeling than in restructuring and that any structure or restructure requires channeling for its full change potential to be realized.

Restructuring

Altering an individual's environment is one means of changing behavior. Restructuring is a deliberate or planned reorganization of some aspect of the physical environment or social structure affecting an individual. Restructuring can be most comprehensively described from a social perspective. Following this, a brief treatment of restructuring from a personal and interactional perspective is provided.

Social Perspective

In change, the social structure can serve in a way that is fundamentally different from the channeling processes, that is, through changes in the structure itself. Reorganization, for example, implies alterations of roles, hierarchical relationships, and status. Much of the impact of reorganization on individuals is through the subsequent channeling effects of the final structure, yet the reorganization in itself is the fundamental change. Restructuring changes are in themselves complex and subtle. This section describes a number of alternative ways in which restructuring occurs and discusses salient aspects of these and their relationships to other change processes. To simplify and systematize the discussion from the social perspective, three basic modes of restructuring are considered: constitutional, organizational, and cultural island. The three restructuring modes are seen to have an increasingly broad impact.

For the discussion of each of these modes, a distinction is drawn between change activities pursued by the authority (in power) on the one hand and nonlegitimized authority (out of power) on the other. Figure 4.1 illustrates the six possibilities and provides common examples of change strategies associated with each.

The following discussion is directed at examining this sixfold conception of restructuring and begins with a treatment of the constitutional-procedural mode.

	Mode		
	Constitutional-Procedural	Organizational	Cultural Island
In power change advocates	A_1 Legislation Policy Directives Incentives	B_1 Reorganization Product to function Decentralization	C_1 T-groups Brainwashing
Out of power change advocates	A_2 Disobedience Protest Competing ideology	B_2 Sabotage Disruption Strikes	C_2 Counterculture In-group insulation

Figure 4.1   Modes of social restructuring.

Constitutional-Procedural Restructuring. The constitutional-procedural mode of restructuring is the least dramatic and most pervasive in organized society. According to the reasoning of the structuralists' school of thought in sociology, the individual in any social grouping inherently makes a contract with that grouping. The contract means exchanging a willingness to abide by accepted rules and procedures for the benefits of group membership. This includes accepting a status system and its related rules that in turn legitimize the articulation, alteration, and enforcement of broader group norms. These processes go on at both formal and informal levels, and high status individuals need to display and exercise the capacity that justifies their social position in order to legitimize their authority. To quote Simon (1945), "Legitimate authority is that which is followed without questioning." It does not matter whether this authority is related to constitutional legislation, corporate policy making, interaction norms, articulated behavior expectations, or information exchange procedures. The process is basically the same and is a powerful determinant of individual change.

The criticism that "you cannot legislate morality," often applied to civil rights legislation, both ignores the powerful impact that legislation actually has had and points to the limits of legitimate authority. It also reveals some confusion about constitutional-procedural restructuring. For, in fact, Kohlberg (1969) argues that the basis for moral judgments and related behavior varies with the style of development of a culture. Less advanced societies rely on legal procedures for establishing morality; more advanced societies use principle orientation. In short, the force of morals supersedes that of rules. His classification scheme is presented in Figure 4.2.

The application of these restructuring insights is straightforward. Much of experiential learning is based on rules for action in learning. Furthermore, common cultural principles, such as "taking responsibility" and reciprocity, are central to the legitimization of these rules and directly linked to the conduct of experiential learning.

Constitutional-procedural restructuring for the case in which the change agent is out of power is quite different. Here the central procedures include overt disobedience or protest, both of which assault the currently accepted rules. The Satyagraha movement of Gandhi (Bondurant, 1972, pp. 303–313) and its western successor, the civil rights movement in the United States, are based on this restructuring technique. It is noteworthy, however, that a common thread among change efforts is a personal code of conduct based on the highest moral principles of the culture, which serves as moral and quasi-legal proof of the legitimacy of change. For example, Bondurant (1972) analysed the Satyagraha (or truth force) technique of social action that emphasizes both noncooperation and nonresistance. At first the two responses seem incompatible but they both pivot on the principle that

Level	Basis of Moral Judgment	Stage of Development
I.	Moral value is defined by punishment and reward.	1. Obedience to rules and authority to avoid punishment.
		2. Conformity to obtain rewards and to exchange favors.
II.	Moral value resides in filling the correct roles, in maintaining order and meeting the expectations of others.	3. Good-boy orientation: conformity to avoid dislike and rejection by others.
		4. Duty orientation: conformity to avoid censure by authority, disruption of order, and resulting guilt.
III.	Moral value resides in conformity to shared standards, rights, and duties.	5. Legalistic orientation: recognition of the value of contracts, some arbitrariness in rule formation to maintain the common good.
		6. Conscience or principle orientation: primary allegiance to principles of choice, which can overrule law in cases where the law is judged to do more harm than good.

Figure 4.2 The classification of moral judgment into levels and stages of development. (Wilson, 1975, p. 563; based on Kohlberg, 1969)

the highest truth, not the greatest power, is the ultimate criterion. Thus, Gandhi typically attempted to develop and maintain an inner strength, self-reliance, and a code of discipline so as never to retreat from central principles or settle for something that contravened them. Objectives, strategies, and tactics were asserted but were secondary to the moral principles of their position (Bondurant, 1972, pp. 304–305). In short, these change efforts articulate and personify an ideology tightly linked to certain moral principles clearly beyond the reach of standard authority. The early civil rights movement proceeded similarly. It is pivotal in this approach that the moral principle be commonly held throughout the culture; it was natural, then, that civil rights leaders often were and are from the Christian clergy. It is also noteworthy that the change agent deviates from a "designated role" in life, in itself a major act of restructuring and central to the theme of disobedience.

In the field of experiential learning, one critical application of the "out of power" source of restructuring is significant. Quite simply, rules often cannot guide activities as well as fundamentally shared principles, and structuring by a rule may in fact automatically contravene these principles. It must be acknowledged that experiential learning is based on principles and involves a philosophy, point of view, or ideology quite at odds with some traditional methods of instruction. Clear linkages between the ideology and commonly shared principles must be made so that participants know what the learning experience will require of them.

Kelman's analysis of compliance, identification, and especially internalization in attitude change is also relevant here. Compliance refers primarily to reinforcement but could include coercion and was found to have an effect primarily under conditions of scrutiny. When scrutiny was absent, so too was individual change. Similarly, identification yielded change only when the object of identification was salient, or of special significance, to the changee. For internalization, however, change was a function of the relevance of the change to the individual's core values and beliefs, and was much more enduring than the other two types. The discussion of the Satyagraha movement shows that it is in fact an internalization change strategy. Thus out of power restructuring requires a tight linkage with widely held principles for the group sponsoring change. These principles, then, are central to a group's attempts to describe change goals and gain acceptance of both goals and procedures.

Organizational restructuring. Organizational restructuring can also be divided into in power and out of power components. The objects of organizational efforts are to control or direct human activity, instances of which are well documented by organizational sociologists, social psychologists, and environmental psychologists. For example, authority and control can be centralized or decentralized. When they are centralized, the chances of undesirable consequences can be reduced (negative control) and resources can be focused at will; when they are decentralized, the energy, flexibility, and innovativeness of the organizational subunits are increased. Job enlargement and job rotation are modest organizational changes involving principles of giving responsibility and authority. A rapid and obvious outcome of these restructuring efforts in routine jobs is that the individual experiences less boredom and more task-centered activation.

Reorganization from a product line, such as Chevrolet, Pontiac, and Buick, to a function organization, such as research, design, engineering, assembly, and marketing, theoretically has the effect of simplifying communications as well as creating economies of scale and more efficient distribution. Moving from closed offices to open office planning (Steele, 1973) alters communication patterns and conceptions about being integrated into the whole organization. Physical arrangements fall into this category and social scientists document the ways in which mere proximity influences social relations. For example, opportunities to interact during daily contact make friendships highly likely.

One example of physical restructuring referred to in Chapter 2 is offered by Jones (1972), in which rather than individuals solving a problem the problem was "solved":

> In northern Nigeria, the home of the Hausa tribe: . . . sleeping sickness reached epidemic proportions. Field surveys showed that in some areas up to 40 percent of the inhabitants had the disease. Tests revealed that the disease could be controlled by cutting the brush along the streams in which the tsetse fly, the carrier of the disease, bred. The Hausa people disbelieved that sleeping sickness was carried by the fly. Moreover, they regarded certain patches of brush along the streams as sacred and inhabited by spirits who would be angry if their abodes were disturbed. The clearing of the brush was successfully carried out only when pressure was applied by the British colonial officials through the traditional framework of native authority. (Jones, 1972, p. 258)

This example illustrates the link between coercion and restructuring; pressure here means enforcement through military action. Coercion alone would not have produced the desired results.

An experiental learning example is the impact of flexible seating. When participants can move easily in the learning environment, opportunities for interaction increase and the leader has greater choice of activities. Leaders are generally seen as legitimately in control of the organizational restructuring as long as it is within appropriate bounds or social norms. These boundaries are often much wider than assumed in most typical learning contexts. On the other hand, transgressions beyond the boundaries activate internalized moral principles and create anxiety and aggression. Thus an experiential leader can rightly call for group discussion, role play, and specific feedback procedures, and most changes will be absorbed quickly and efficiently by the group.

For persons out of power, a number of unpopular and sinister applications graphically describe the subprocesses involved. Examples are disruption and divide and conquer as separate entities. The purpose of disruption is to make difficult the actual functioning of the existing organization. The most obvious approaches here include strikes and sabotage. Sabotage can vary from monkey wrenches in assembly lines to bombs in the Nazi-controlled heavy water facility in Norway during the race to build the atomic bomb in World War II. Political "dirty tricks," such as phony letters attributing undesirable characteristics to campaign rivals, is a subtle variant on this approach and implies an inner sense of "all is fair in war." Terrorism such as hijacking planes has a three-pronged effect. The first is the temporary disruption of one or more facilities. The second is the generation of inconvenience and expensive security measures in airports which disrupt activity on an ongoing basis. And the third is to pit one group, the pilots, against another, the airlines, to create internal organizational stress.

The latter disruptive consequence resembles divide and conquer, an approach used by both in power and out of power groups which often involves coercion. The difference between disorganizing and simple coercion is that in coercion the object of influence still has some choice about changing; in disorganization this option is virtually nonexistent. Intervention is the goal and weakness is the result. In contrast, disobedience incurs distractions, but no direct attempt to weaken the other individual or group is implied.

The most common divide and conquer approach is simply to emphasize differences between identifiable groups, raise dissatisfactions, and stimulate action. For example, working class is pitted against ruling class, men against women, blacks against whites, French Canadians against English Canadians, and one department in a business against another. Lack of communications and personal contact is important for the success of this strategy, as evidenced by the police strategy of dividing prisoners for interrogation and offering contingencies that undermine trust and produce a "prisoners dilemma." Powerful contingencies are easy to illustrate:

1 You confess and your partner does not: you get six months.
2 You confess and your partner also does: you get two years.
3 You do not confess and your partner does: you get fifteen years.

Risk avoidance leads to disorganization.

Coercive reinforcements are important, but the disorganization of the mutual protection arrangement is more important. Chinese brainwashing during the Korean War showed ample use of this technique (Schein, 1956). For example, taking one prisoner away, feeding him well and putting him back in the group resulted in the group fearing he had become a traitor (which often was the case). Systematically eliminating leaders from groups to generate a general state of social confusion and alienation was also used.

The Fabian strategy is more limited in scope but is pervasive among mankind. Huntington (1972), for example, discusses the manner in which Mustata Kemal pursued political reform in the Turkish Republic in the 1920s. Briefly, he separated unpopular from popular issues to get initial changes that could then serve as a springboard for subsequent ones. He isolated separate sources of resistance on each issue and worked quickly to prevent coordination of resistance. Thus political opponents were divided and conquered on changes in laws, codes, the calendar, script (from Arabic to Roman), education, and industrialization.

The Germans used two forms of government in peacefully occupied countries such as Czechoslovakia and Denmark. The first was a large "official" cooperatively administered unit, and the second was the "unofficial, uncontrollable" extortionary Gestapo. Loyal resistance fighters and loyal moderates became mutual enemies in occupied countries and hence added to the general confusion. Mysticism heightened the fear-inducing qualities of the Gestapo. This divide and conquer strategy was based on the same principle as the lightening war "Blitzkreig strategy" which used speed and surprise as a source of disorganization and a limitation of resistance. Further, both used fear to reduce organizational response capabilities. For the Nazi divide and conquer strategy, confusion was a prelude to fear. For the Blitzkreig, fear was the fuse for confusion, which inhibited responsive organization.

The significance of these disorganizing restructuring efforts at first may not be apparent, and surely such interventions are not advocated within a learning experience. However, some points are worth making. First, many overzealous experiential leaders transcend "normal bounds" and in so doing unwittingly create confusion and fear. The power of a structure can carry out "learning," but the principle of volunteerism, which is argued to be essential to constructive, ethical, experiential learning, is violated. An example here would be a workshop on body awareness in which the leader "asks" participants to strip to their undergarments fifteen minutes into the session when exit is difficult. The unstructured leadership of a T-group can come close to this effect, depending on how enthusiastically the trainer believes in the need to unfreeze people. Coercion can come in many subtle forms in experiential learning and is a constant risk in disorganizing restructuring efforts. Support–feedback mechanisms and other safeguards must attend to any such possibilities. The ethical boundaries are far from clear, but ignorance, insensitivity, and a simplistic ideological conception of experiential learning processes are certainly major contributors.

Cultural Island Restructuring. Cultural island restructuring implies that the individual can be moved to a new culture within which the old ways fail to work and new ways are felt to be necessary for adequacy. T-groups and brainwashing are two methods of change that rely heavily on this mode, and they have often been mistakenly associated with each other. In reality, cultural island restructuring is the key element of indoctrination, whether the indoctrination is directed toward creating priests, Ph.D.s, or marines. Its elements are straightforward. Individuals are taken away from the props, social relations, and other structural comforts of their everyday lives. In a new situation, moreover, the urge to cope is activated. Old ways fail. In T-groups, for example, the individuals must talk about feelings and perceptions of each other, an activity not generally pursued with acquaintances. Intimacy is generated with subsequent activation of "fight or flight" defensive behavior (Bennis & Shepard, 1956; Bion, 1961). To facilitate this, the leader does not "lead" by telling the rules, setting the agenda, or leading the discussion. A social vacuum is created. If nothing is said, another norm is violated. The most "open members" get subtle reinforcement and feedback from the leader that shows others one acceptable alternative to the anxiety. Unfreezing has been accomplished via disorganizing followed by reorganizing. Then the new social norms are intricately constructed throughout the early phases of the group through feedback, conditioning, modeling, and other change processes.

Brainwashing shares the cultural island restructuring emphasis of sensitivity training and other growth-centered approaches, but is in fact quite differently applied (Bradford, Gibb, & Benne, 1964; Golembiewski & Blumberg, 1970). The first stage in Chinese brainwashing is an assault on all supporting beliefs, attitudes, and values of the individual. By contrast, a T-group focuses only mild criticism on a few of these. Second, it is obvious that a two-week sojourn to a growth center constitutes a different island than a prisoner of war camp where internment is essentially permanent. Third, starvation, forced marches, filth, and various harassments degrade, exhaust, and undermine much of the personal stability of the individual. Even twenty-four hour marathons are neither intended to, nor do create these stresses. Fourth, in Chinese brainwashing fear was often created by one means or another to undermine further the individual's position, whereas fear is not actively used in T-groups. Mutual indoctrination sessions in which someone asserts communist ideologies and attacks western positions and constant hammering on key ideological points in lectures are also elements missing in T-groups.

Additional disorganizing efforts of brainwashing include segregation by rank and race and the sabotage of subgroup efforts to punish collaborators. Individuals are interrogated to discover inconsistencies and thrown into prisoner's dilemma situations to further undermine solidarity. Rewards, punishments, and "new-speak" reconceptualizations are used extensively. These efforts are in dramatic contrast to a supportive, facilitative T-group leader and to the building of a pivotally important group support (Gibb, 1961). In short, while both T-groups and brainwashing use the cultural island, the manners in which they do so are fundamentally different. Gibb (1972) argued for imbedded groups, or communities within communities, and has pioneered T.O.R.I.: Trust, Openness, Realization of Interdependence. T.O.R.I. communities serve as cultural islands where an individual can go for rejuvenation. In most instances the cultural island is owned and operated by the system that wishes to use its forces in reeducation. Gibb's T.O.R.I. communities are more permanent islands where voluntary entry and exit are simple matters.

For people out of power, the cultural island can also help to maintain change. For example, the hippies of the 1960s rejected traditional values and built communes as islands (Roszak, 1969). Spontaneous cultural islands such as clubs are pervasive in free society. These organizations are characterized by inductions, indoctrinations, limits on memberships, and enforcement of pivotal values. They both reflect and create diversity.

As a concluding point, it is important to note that all restructuring is central to a number of experiential learning techniques. Kepner and Tregoe (1965), Delbecq, Van de Ven, and Gustafson (1975), and others offer guidelines for problem solving. John Wallen gives rules for good communications. Schwitzgebel and Kolb (1974) described a program for self-directed change, much of which is based on rules or sequences for change that may be pursued by the individual. In essence a model here suggests that the individual can create his own cultural island within which the rules are different from yet consistent with the demands of the greater culture. Change may then occur within the constraints of what is seen to be appropriate by the culture at large.

Individual Perspective

From the individual perspective, restructuring can be seen as internal or external. Examples of internal restructuring are the use of drugs and more direct medical interventions such as surgery. Examples of external restructuring include some approaches to family counseling wherein the physical structure of the home environment is altered to change the quality of the relationships in the family (Minuchin, 1965; Minuchin & Montalvo, 1967). One case, presented by Aponte and Hoffman (1973), described how focusing on and changing the structure of the interactions of the family was effective in curing an anorectic child, as well as in improving the general quality of the family's interactions. This approach is compatible with the work of communications theorists such as Jackson.

Interactional Perspective

From the interactional perspective, various aspects of the environment have been examined by environmental psychology (Ittelson, Proshansky, Rivlin, & Winkel, 1974; Proshansky, Ittelson, & Rivlin, 1970) and architecture (Bayes, 1967). The point here is the impact of environment on behavior. Color, room size, space, and many other specific environmental qualities influence the way individuals might respond in a given situation. For example, Richardson (1970) describes how different types and configurations of furniture can affect the atmosphere in a classroom. Desks in rows create certain expectations associated with the use of the classical methods, while soft chairs arranged in a circle create very different expectations. The quality of the physical learning environment is central to the success of the endeavor.

Summary

Restructuring, from an individual, interactional, or social perspective is a powerful means of changing behavior. Very few experiential learning activities do not, at some point, use this type of change process. Consequently, leaders should always be aware of opportunities for restructuring the environment to achieve a desired change.

Channeling

Channeling results from the impact of social and technological structural sources. The dimensions of social structure are norms, rules, roles, and status. Technological factors refer to task, physical structure, and organizational arrangements. Because of the unique relationship of each source to specific channeling dynamics, a sequential discussion organized around channeling sources rather than the three perspectives is most practical. Contextual models of human functioning dominate in this discussion but other models are relevant and noted where appropriate.

Norms

Social norms serve as standards for guiding individuals' behavior. George Homans' *The Human Group* (1950, p. 123) offered the following definition of a norm:

> A norm then, is an idea in the minds of the members of a group, an idea that can be put in the form of a statement specifying what the members or other men should do, ought to do, are expected to do, under given circumstances.

In a sense, a norm is an unwritten or informal rule. Sociologists (Scott, 1970) generally assert that norms channel individuals by providing a standard and rationale for exercising positive reinforcements and punishment. Actual reinforcements used and how they are arranged are also important.

Many studies (Schachter, 1968) document the manner in which conformity to group norms is induced. Typically, a deviant is increasingly interpersonally punished through argumentative or condemning transactions. Then, in the absence of change, the individual is isolated or rejected from the group. Liking and rejection are among the most potent forces in groups. The power of the group to punish plus the desire to do so are positively related to the cohesiveness of the group and the relevance of the issue. Cohesiveness in turn is a function of mutual similarities, attractivenesses, commonalities, and many other factors. Deviants who revert to conformity, or "sliders," experience dramatically increased positive reinforcement compared to longtime conformers.

Conditioning, however, does not by itself account for the tendency of individuals to adhere to social norms. For example, there appears to be an inner wish or instinct for some degree of synchronization within a group (contextual and sociobiological models), and this internal dynamic accounts for both the tendency to be part of a group and the emotional significance to the individual of group acceptance and rejection. Similarly, the channeling force of a commonly held normative idea can be further appreciated from a contextual view through examining the need for belonging (Homans, 1950) and affiliation motives (Mehrabian & Ksionsky, 1970, 1974). The need for a sense of social reality is another source of channeling pressure (Cartwright & Zander, 1968, p. 143). Both the cognitive/perceptual and contextual models of human functioning depict mental representations and symbolization as fundamental to a sense of control and effectiveness in life. Since social situations are enormously complex, norms serve as pegpoints around which a staggering amount of stimulation can be organized.

From the individual perspective, ideals can be seen as comparable to norms, providing guidance for individuals in much the same way that norms provide direction for groups. The importance of beliefs and values is reflected in the cognitive and contextual models of human functioning. The notion that "virtue is its own reward" speaks to the organizing function of ideals.

Discussion of the channeling aspects of norms for the social perspective can be divided into three views, the behaviorist, the factist, and the definitionist. The behaviorist position, exemplified by Homans, emphasizes the pinning of interpersonal reinforcements and cues to norms. The factists take a more conventional sociological view, asserting that socialization processes result in a sense of the appropriate being stored in the minds of individuals. The tendency to do what is appropriate is also stored. In short, conformity is a habit. What one conforms to depends not on reinforcements but on the clarity of the situation and previous socializations. In this view, authoritarians are merely individuals with a clearly prescribed and highly socialized sense of the appropriate. Social definitionists emphasize the rather sketchy and incomplete nature of norms and the role of the individuals' deep mental structure in reading and interpreting cues (Garfinkel, 1967). Here behavioristic and contextual models of human functioning are supplemented by cognitive/perceptual models; individuals are seen to draw constantly their own conceptions of ever-changing norms.

Rules

Rules for the most part are formalized and articulated standards for behavior enforced by overt institutionalized power. Because of their static nature they are not sensitive to subtle or even dramatic changes in the conditions out of which they were created. Consequently, though many rules are current, others are out of date or even insipid. Compared to rules, norms have a smaller gap between their demands for conformity and the perceived relevance of those demands. Consequently, even though rules are easier to interpret they can be more difficult to rank. In addition, rules lead to more obvious channeling than norms, because their existence implies a greater degree of legitimization and durability. Coercion is linked to them more easily. However, to the degree that conformity depends on compliance measures, overt positive reinforcements are more important for the channeling effectiveness of most rules than for most social norms.

Goals

In models of human functioning the goals of individuals are central. In general, individuals are seen as having an operational goal of making the world sensible so they can cope with it. Coping involves using abilities, developing abilities, making judgments, satisfying ongoing needs, and facing risk and anxiety. The overriding goal is to maximize internal consistency, minimize anxiety, and generate a stream of gratifications that meet a variety of biological and psychological criteria. In short, each individual has the potential for a highly complex goal structure identified by such watch words as competence, anxiety, enjoyment, and satisfaction. Which of these factors dominates at a given moment is determined in complex ways, but clearly the goals asserted in a situation tend to have major activating properties. Thus social organizational and societal stimuli continually activate various goals in individuals. In fact, it is probably a unique individual who can maintain a clear operational structure rather than allowing the environment to activate specific goals on a moment to moment basis.

Within organizations, where individuals experience widely differing social and task stimuli, and also in groups, overtly articulated goals serve as major perceptual and cognitive organizing factors. The stimulus of physical closeness has quite different channeling effects when the goal is enjoyment rather than survival. Group level of aspiration provides a goal against which individuals and group members assess behavior, much as in the case of norms. The resultant social dynamics are also similar, and in a sense goals can be seen as a specific form of group norm. Goals give individuals in group or organizational contexts clear expectations around which subsequent behavior can be organized.

Other relevant facets of goals include goal clarity, goal conflict, the effect of frustration of goal attainment, and individual versus organizational or social goals. Clearly articulated and universally understood goals serve as cognitive anchor points for individuals. Research in the field of social judgment theory documents the effects of such anchors on cognition (Kiesler, Collins, & Miller, 1969). Cognitive clarity also affects perception and response and further channels behavior. Finally, clear goals, like norms, serve as rallying points around which other social channeling forces can be focused in social groupings. Joseph McCarthy's "get the Communists" and Hitler's "get the Jews" approach serve as grim examples of how aggression and fear can be channeled with the aid of goals. In most cases, scapegoating allows the release of pent-up fear and hostility while furthering group goals.

Goal conflict often results in confusion and diminished channeling ability. Unrealistic or incompatible goals can lead to frustration and a variety of divergent outcomes, which are the antithesis of channeling. Effective large social units allow individuals to see their goals as consistent with and furthered by the attainment of the group goal. Sherif and Sherif (1953) call the individualized goals subordinate and the overarching, integrative goals superordinate. Individual/organizational conflict is limited by the degree to which goal congruence can be attained and by the degree to which the organization is seen to reciprocate the individual's willingness to submerge personal goals temporarily for the sake of organizational goals. Such credibility goes beyond the conditioning process, since it simultaneously relates to the widely held social norm of reciprocity (Blau, 1967). The teleological properties of goals explain their power and are the key to their separation from norms, a more behavioristic pegpoint for channeling.

Roles

Roles serve as a source of channeling in a variety of ways. While the first is reminiscent of the manner in which norms and goals have effect, the others are more subtle and complex. Two definitions of roles are useful. A role is defined either as a set of expectations with regard to fulfilling a formal social position or as a set of actual behaviors displayed by an individual in a given circumstance. The sociological view of roles is that a given role has a basic character that gives a holism to the set of expectations and behaviors (a parent role). The psychological view emphasizes specific individual behaviors that fulfill functions such as harmonizers and idea generators as group maintenance and task roles respectively.

A role can have both formal and informal specification. Like norms and goals, a role serves as an individual's cognitive reference point for a legitimization of the application of sanctions, for a focus of socialization and learning, and as a source of social reality. Because of the specific nature of roles, they serve as sources of identificatory learning and aid the individual in the choice of a model, vicarious reinforcement, observation, and the performance of acquired behavior and attitudes. In other words, roles help organize other change processes.

In addition to this central issue a number of more subtle and complex points can be made. G.H. Mead (1943) emphasizes a crucial function of roles in establishing a "generalized other" and thus the ontogenesis of self. This development of the self occurs through a three-stage process. In stage one the individual actually takes the role of others by pretending or role playing. In the second stage, the individual develops a mental representation of the generalized other, against which a self-evaluation can be made regarding appropriateness and effectiveness of role enactment. This latter point is highly relevant to the re-cognition process. In the third stage, effort is made to act within the bounds of appropriateness developed in stage two. No actual socialization or extrinsic reinforcement is involved in this role assimilation process, nor are modeling and identification fundamental. It is of further importance that stage two does not yield an immutable set of expectations but is a starting point from which actual role acquisition can be negotiated. Acquisition is a dynamic phenomenon, and the individual is both a role maker and a role taker.

As with goal conflict, role conflict affects channeling. Conflict, or lack of congruity, in role demands lead to anxiety, cognitive conflict, and a variety of other outcomes predicted by various models of human functioning (father versus corporation president). While mild conflict can be energizing, very high conflict tends to create confusion. Stouffer and Toby (1951) demonstrated that when an individual faces irresolvable competing demands and expectations for a given role, the effect is to choose one demand over others. Tendencies to force choices reduce the predictability of the channeling outcomes for a given role. The implication is that clear ranking of role expectations is important to ensure the desirable channeling effects.

The importance of roles as organizing aids for broad behavioral patterns results in the need for formal rituals for role transitions. Induction ceremonies, for example, graphically assert that the individual has moved from one role (citizen) to another (soldier), and that dramatic expectational changes will parallel the initially required changes in dress, grooming, and demeanor.

The final manner in which roles affect channeling closely parallels the use of goals and modeling. A given role is a tangible source of cues that describe, elaborate on, and make operative goals and social norms. The player of a role becomes the personification of the goals and norms represented by that role and thus models the given attitudes and behaviors. The channeling of roles in conjunction with identification processes has considerable impact on individuals' behavior. Demands for conformity to pivotal standards increase as one goes higher in a social structure. Any given social system or organization has standards that it desires to be preserved and followed by its members. The individuals at the top of these social units are very visible, and this visibility, along with the status and power conferred on them, encourages identification. Since individuals at lower levels of the social units are inevitably influenced by those in prominence, both the content of the role and its performance are of crucial importance.

Status

Status refers to one's formal and informal position in a social hierarchy and is implicated in the channeling process through both subtle and obvious means. Informal status is a function of prestige (esteem), preferability, and popularity. Formal status is primarily a function of the attributes of a role the individual occupies, and is both the creator and result of the power of the role. For example, an individual in a position of power can influence a group to engage in activities that use and value the position, thus increasing both the power and status of the position. Status serves both as a reward for individuals who make valued contributions to a social grouping and as a source of social reality. Just as individuals can use status and power to increase their own status, group members may prevent the person of lowest status from outperforming the highest status person in a domain valued by the group (Whyte, 1969). Here the payoff is clearly in the area of maintaining consistency and a sense of social reality. Since the status "system" provides meaning for a variety of stimulus sources, inappropriate role behavior by one person creates social confusion beyond that of the role alone (Homans, 1950).

A number of specific subprocesses by which status affects channeling can now be noted. First, the phenomenon of status liability refers to the inherent requirement of greater conformity from individuals of higher status. This especially applies to fundamental norms and values; individuals of high status are also allowed extra "idiosyncracy credits" denied to lower status persons in areas of less pivotal importance to the group. Kahn et al. (1964) and others have noted that status structures tend to equalize; for example, good income tends to correlate with a good education. Lenski (1966) takes this social consistency argument further, but subsequent research (Farden, 1973) indicates that the complexity of the social processes involved defy simplistic "if-then" reasoning. Communications are also affected by status; lower status individuals typically direct more communications toward higher status persons than vice versa. This channeling process tends to keep on top those who are on top. Status is also often used as a justification for behavior, expectations, and demands. For example, a company president might demand a certain quality of hotel room and services, or ghetto dwellers may feel that their lowly status justifies a looting spree.

Finally, Garfinkel (1967) emphasizes that status is a real possession in society and is an item around which big changes must be negotiated carefully. Criminal trials are to a great degree status degradation ceremonies because the citizen-to-criminal status transition is so dramatic. Rituals of promotion, retirement, election, and so forth further serve the purpose of formalizing status transitions. As organizers and as indicators of social reality they are inherently reinforcing and therefore an intrinsic source of channeling influence on individuals.

Technology

Technical structures providing sources for channeling include the tasks to be performed, the tools, equipment, or mechanization that form part of the task, and the organizational arrangements devised to achieve a given objective. These three sources usually operate simultaneously and serve to provide many cues which have impact, ranging from activation to role definition and clarity.

Models of human functioning focusing on activation and need achievement provide the first way of explaining the channeling effects of technical structure. At the simplest level, one can think of a technology as an array of tasks, each of which has a particular stimulus pattern and gives individuals specific behavioral cues. The tasks may trigger control or mastery responses. The individual attempts to be competent in the face of stimuli for which clear responsibility is perceived (White, 1959).

The channeling force generated by an individual's desire for mastery is reinforced by the role definition provided by the technology. A piece of equipment provides strong cues for defining an individual's role in that setting. Consequently, technologically articulated roles have a clarity that goes beyond what mere social structure can offer.

Since clarity and legitimization (Simon, 1957) of specific role demands can result from the technology, the need for a clear sense of reality, posited in the contextual and cognitive/perceptual models of human functioning, can be satisfied. Individual acceptance of technology is at least partially a result of this intrinsic reinforcement. Physical reality as manifested in the technology is more tangible than social reality.

Perrow's (1965) and Woodward's (1965) models provide examples of how technology affects differentiation and the distribution of roles in industrial organizations. For instance, in moving from unit to mass production, the span of control of first line supervisors increases, but at the same time clear meshing of technical and social roles becomes more difficult. In process industries, the technical role of management is built into the plant and thus a given manager is free to concentrate more on social roles.

Moving from batch to process organizations, levels of hierarchy increase. If control is viewed as one of the central purposes of organization, then the type of technology determines the necessary form of that control. For example, more supervisors are required for the same number of employees in unit production than for mass production.

In summary, technical structure, whether in the form of a toy for a child, a machine for a worker, a videotape playback unit for a student, or a questionnaire for an observer, tends to create a stream of stimuli that activate various processes within the individual. Channeling from technological sources is characterized by a sense of legitimacy and clarity assisting individuals in forming images of themselves and the world. Many of the other change processes can be readily linked to technology, producing potent mechanisms for individual change.

Summary

Restructuring is important in experiential learning because it is a tangible means of generating other change processes and promoting learning. An awareness of channeling highlights the importance of factors outside the learning context as well as the guidelines generated within it. The roles and expectations participants bring to the experience are often as important in determining outcomes as the activities in the learning experience itself. To be effective the leader must consciously use these two processes to advantage.

CHAPTER FIVE

Re-Cognition

*My greatest wish is to
remain lucid in ecstacy.*

Albert Camus

This chapter pursues processes that are all in one way or another concerned with changing cognition, or re-cognition. While only one major process is pursued, the reader will see at once that this chapter is as complex or more than any other in Part 1. The reason for the length and complexity of this treatment is simply that the subject requires it. In the years since Freud, a wide variety of sophisticated and profound techniques have been developed to alter mental processes, chiefly in the individually focused domain of psychotherapy. The existence of contradictory descriptors such as rational-emotive therapy, cognitive behaviorism, and paradoxical intention are indicative of the difficult territory through which the following discussion must proceed.

Re-cognition refers to a broad range of change phenomena having in common an element of altering the manner in which individuals actually process information. Since most of the wisdom in this area comes from clinical and individual psychology, the discussion is pursued primarily from the individual perspective. For the purpose of this treatment, re-cognition has been divided into six major functional subprocesses: rational, behavioral, suggestion, interference, memory, and complex. The reader will discover some similarities between re-cognition and other change processes such as conditioning.

Rational Restructuring

Rational restructuring builds heavily on cognitive psychology. It is stimulated by observations on the extent to which many problems in human functioning come from sources such as irrational beliefs about the self or others (McGuire, 1968; Rokeach, 1960), shortcircuited thinking (Beck, 1970), misattributions of causality (Schachter & Singer, 1962; Weiner, 1972), and absence of thinking or coping skills (Goldfried, 1971; Meichenbaum & Cameron, 1973b). An emphasis on the importance of the linkage between emotions and thoughts is implicit in rational restructuring approaches to change. Epictetus, a stoic philosopher from about A.D. 60, noted: "Men are not disturbed by things but by the views they take of them." Modern rational stoic/hedonists such as Albert Ellis echo this assertion.

Albert Ellis (1970; Ellis & Harper, 1961) pioneered one rational restructuring approach to re-cognition called rational emotive therapy (R.E.T.). In this approach, a leader confronts such irrational beliefs as people thinking that they must be loved by everyone for everything that they do or feeling horrible when things are not the way they would like them. Through a persuasive and philosophical argument, the individual is encouraged to explore beliefs and assumptions that are linked to negative outcomes consistently and scientifically, that is, rationally. Particular thinking dysfunctions now altered through this approach include arbitrary inference, overgeneralization, magnification or "catastrophizing" (Beck, 1970), dichotomous reasoning, oversocialization (Lazarus, 1971), selective inattention, inaccurate anticipation of consequences, and logical errors (Mahoney, 1974).

Further thinking aids that build on the confrontation and persuasion of Ellis' approach have been offered. For example, Mahoney (1974, p. 175) uses a mnemonic aid (ADAPT) to organize a sequence of response for individuals.

A   Acknowledge the sensation of distress (anxiety, depression, anger).
D   Discriminate the private events (both thoughts and images) which have just occurred (i.e., do a "covert instant replay").
A   Assess the logical bases and adaptive functions of your images and self-statements.
P   Present alternatives (i.e., generate private monologues or imagery of more appropriate, coping content) and then
T   Think praise (!) (i.e., reward yourself for having executed the entire sequence).

Thus in re-cognition individuals are not only persuaded and encouraged to change, but they are also persuaded to adopt an approach to problems that results in far greater, long-term change. In addition, the technique also depends on individuals sharing the belief system of the leader, a condition requiring significant rapid change through confrontative feedback, identification, and persuasion. In terms of changing beliefs, Mahoney (1974, pp. 238–239) noted the following important elements:

1 Isolation of the belief in a formal symbol system.
2 Relating the belief to existing structures.
3 Shared conceptual system between client and therapist.
4 Rehearsal.
5 Confirmation experiences (as positive reinforcement).

The key element of rational restructuring is the systematic treatment of the individual's assumptions and expectations with the result of altering cognitive set, frame of reference, and thinking patterns (Goldfried & Goldfried, 1975).

Self-Management

Kanfer (1975) described three self-management methods of a highly "rational" nature offering an additional expansion to the R.E.T. approach. These methods are self-regulation, self-control, and self-monitoring.

Self-Regulation.   Self-regulation focuses on "problem areas" where normal habits and reactions "do not work." The individual is guided toward making commitments to change and provided with a structure for the pursuit of change. The structure is simply a three-stage procedure: self-monitoring, self-evaluation, and self-reinforcement or shaping. Over time, the individual not only debunks faulty assumptions but also shapes thinking and coping patterns. More important, the use of a "rational" self-monitoring sequence becomes habituated and a new part of the individual's thinking processes.

Self-Control.   The second self-management method, self-control, is directed at destructive behavior and goes beyond self-regulation in a few important ways. First, the actively destructive individual generally gets some immediate pleasure from the action, and thus changed behavior is experienced as a loss. Therefore, positive consequences of change must be found or provided. Second, the destructive response to a critical stimulus can virtually preclude "thinking" at that moment. Consequently, individuals are encouraged to cultivate and practice a "controlled response" before potential exposure to randomly occurring, unwanted "triggers."

Self-Monitoring.   The third self-management method is simply self-monitoring, and it is actually inherent in all the rational processes discussed above. Nonetheless, it is more than a fragment of a method and can stand alone. Some rules for effective self-monitoring include:

1 Accurate record keeping.
2 Frequency counts.
3 Unobtrusive, convenient recording methods (low cost).
4 Graphing data for higher visual impact.
5 Rehearsal of the sequence of one to four and/or role playing.

Clearly the intent of all these procedures is to make control an ally rather than an enemy, helping individuals to satisfy desires rather to deny them.

Other self-management methods are noted in subsequent sections of the re-cognition discussion. However, at this point, Kanfer's (1975, pp. 351–352) summary is provided to show the strongly rational aspects of the approach.

Step 1 A behavioral analysis, including a description of specific problem behavior, positive and negative reinforcers appropriate for the client's strengths and skills, and the resources in the client's environment that can be enlisted to aid the behavior change process.

Step 2 Observation and self-monitoring of the target behavior.

Step 3 Development of a plan for behavior change. Negotiation of a contract that includes clear specification of the goals to be achieved, the time allowed for the program, and the consequences for achieving it, as well as the methods for producing the behavior change.

Step 4 A brief discussion with the client on the underlying assumptions and rationale of the techniques to be used.

Step 5 Frequent external verification of progress and of factors that have retarded progress, as well as reevaluation of the contract.

Step 6 Recording and inspecting of qualitative and quantitative data documenting the change.

Step 7 A self-reinforcement program that relies increasingly on the person's self-reactions, is sufficiently varied to avoid saturation, and is effective in changing the target behavior.

Step 8 Execution of new behaviors by the client in his natural environment with discussion and correction of his behavior as needed.

Step 9 Frequent verbalization of the procedural effects, the means by which they are achieved and situations to which they can be applied in the future.

Step 10 Continuing strong support by the helper for any activity in which the client assumes increasing responsibility for following the program accurately or extending it to other problematic behaviors.

Problem Solving and Coping Skills

Another rational re-cognition approach deals directly with the acquisition of *problem solving* behavior and *coping skills*. Miller, Galanter, and Pribram (1960, p. 171) assert:

In ordinary affairs we usually muddle ahead, doing what is habitual and customary, being slightly puzzled when it sometimes fails to give the intended outcome, but not stopping to worry much about the failures because there are too many other things still to do. Then circumstances conspire against us and we find ourselves caught failing where we must succeed— where we cannot withdraw from the field, or lower our self-imposed standards, or ask for help, or throw a tantrum. Then we may begin to suspect that we face a problem.

The most important message in problem solving is inherent in the term; problems are there to be solved, not avoided. Once problems are recognized, solving starts and, for this, a number of sequences are widely advocated.

Goldfried and Goldfried (1975, pp. 105–106) offer the following sequence as important for a problem solving "orientation to life":

1 Problem definition and formulation.
2 Generation of alternatives.
3 Decision making.
4 Verification.

Osborn (1963) and Parnes (1967) emphasize generation of alternatives through brainstorming; Hoffman (1965) emphasizes high evaluation and argument as mechanisms for generating deeper problem insights; and MacCrimmon and Taylor (1976) comprehensively review the vast organizationally centered wisdom regarding productive problem solving. All types of problem solving at the very least aid the individual to concretize options and outcomes; in this sense they are highly re-cognitive. While self-management focuses on the known, problem solving aids the individual in structuring the unknown.

Since today's education emphasizes mastery of the known, it does very little to prepare an individual to cope effectively with the unknown. Yet many of today's school children will be spending more than half their lifetime in the unknown world of the twenty-first century. To cope effectively with the unknown, an individual must have a well-developed ability to think. Thus, an education that will prepare today's student for a useful, fulfilling life in the twenty-first century must provide him with extensive, systematic instruction in the skills required for original, independent thinking and problem solving. (Olton & Crutchfield, 1969, p. 69)

Training in coping skills is quite different from problem solving in that the skill is focused directly on the anxiety arising from a given situation. Alternative titles for approaches falling within this category include anxiety management training (Richardson & Suinn, 1973; Suinn & Richardson, 1971), and stress innoculation (Meichenbaum & Cameron, 1973b). These approaches link directly to more behavioral approaches such as systematic desensitization, but the central elements of coping skills training are rational as defined here. Goldfried's (1971, 1973) approach, for example, includes:

1 A description of a rationale for the approach.
2 Relaxation training.
3 Construction and use of a multiple theme hierarchy or stress-related issue.
4 Training or practice in "relaxing away" anxiety induced by thinking about a theme-related scene.

Stress inoculation is even more rational (Meichenbaum & Cameron, 1973b). Here individuals are presented with the following steps:

1 A discussion of stress reactions.
2 Relaxation training.
3 Making coping self-statements such as cognitive monitoring preparation for stress and self-reinforcement.
4 Coaching or supervision in real stress situations.

Although all the rational approaches focus on behavioral events in varying ways, their major thrust is the direct intervention into the way individuals think about what they do.

Behavioral Subprocesses

The behavioral subprocesses in re-cognition emphasize the conditioning aspects of change. While conditioning has already been discussed, certain aspects of it especially apply here for two reasons: first, because in recent years behaviorists have expanded their paradigm to include cognition; and second, because many behaviorally based therapeutic interventions have a heavy internal or cognitive emphasis. Cognitive behavior modification serves as the starting point for the discussion of these subprocesses. Some particularly effective applications of cognitive behavior modification are systematic desensitization, relaxation, and counterconditioning. Mahoney (1974) organized many of these subprocesses under the general heading of covert conditioning.

Cognitive Behavior Modification

Kanfer and Goldstein (1975), Krumboltz and Thoresen (1976), Mahoney (1974), and Meichenbaum (1975) provide the orientation for this discussion. All these authors state that external (behavioristic) events are "mediated" by (covert) processes; an overt stimulus results in a correlative inner covert stimulus, leading to a covert response that is ultimately displayed in an observable correlative outcome. For example, punishment can dramatically affect the way in which external stimuli are responded to internally as well as externally (Mahoney, Thoresen, & Danaher, 1972). Similarly, internal images and even concepts (Proctor & Malloy, 1971) can affect external outcomes. Further, thought can have a reinforcement or punishment quality as Ascher and Cautela (1972) have documented. They encouraged subjects to imagine a noxious scene, then to imagine hearing a bell, the consequence of which was the elimination of the noxious scene. In short, this is cognitive negative reinforcement (C.N.R.). In subjects' subsequent attempts to "estimate the size of a circle," utterance of the word "bell" by the experimenter dramatically affected individuals' estimates. Thoughts change people behaviorally and can be considered covert operants or "coverants."

Covert Conditioning

Since 1960 many powerful change strategies have been refined to take advantage of the conditioning significance of thought. Of these, systematic desensitization is perhaps the most graphic and easily understood. The major target of this approach has been the "fear reaction" to particular stimuli (Morris, 1975; Wolpe, 1973). The actual procedure is preceded by the creation of an "anxiety hierarchy" which details degrees of fear evocation for different events within a theme and by relaxation training (discussed more fully later). The individual is then exposed to the lowest or least fear-evoking item in the hierarchy, then gradually exposed to higher and higher items while simultaneously being encouraged to "relax away" the anxiety. For example, an individual afraid of snakes might be placed in a room with the word "snake" projected on the wall. Once anxiety had been relaxed away, the word could be replaced with a picture and eventually with a real snake at less and less physical distance. Rather than depending on physical stimuli, imagined events can be used within the same systematic desensitization modality.

Relaxation training in itself is worthy of elaboration. Morris (1975, pp. 240–241) suggests the following sequence as illustrative of the instructions and actions involved.

1 Take a deep breath and hold it (for about ten seconds). Okay, let it out.
2 Raise both of your hands about half way above the couch or arms of the chair and breathe normally. Now, drop your hands to the couch (or, down).
3 Now, hold your arms out and make a tight fist. Really tight. Feel the tension in your hands, I am going to count to three and when I say "three," I want you to drop your hands. One . . . Two . . . Three.

4   Raise your arms again, and bend your fingers back the other way (toward your body). Now drop your hands and relax.

5   Raise your arms. Now drop them and relax.

6   Now, raise your arms again, but this time "flap" your hands around. Okay, relax again.

7   Raise your arms again. Now, relax.

8   Raise your arms above the couch (chair) again and tense your biceps until they shake. Breathe normally, and keep your hands loose. Relax your hands. (Notice how you have a warm feeling of relaxation).

9   Now hold your arms out to your side and tense your biceps. Make sure that you breathe normally. Relax your arms.

10 Now arch your shoulders back. Hold it. Make sure that your arms are relaxed. Now relax.

11 Hunch your shoulders forward. Hold it, and make sure that you breathe normally and keep your arms relaxed. Okay, relax. (Notice the feeling of relief from tensing and relaxing your muscles).

12 Now, turn your head to the right and tense your neck. Hold it. Okay, relax and allow your head to come back to its natural position.

13 Turn your head to the left and tense your neck. Relax and bring your head back again to its natural position.

14 Now, bend your head back slightly toward the chair. Hold it. Okay, now bring your head back slowly to its natural position.*

15 This time bring your head down almost to your chest. Hold it. Now relax and let your head come back to its natural resting position.*

16 Now, open your mouth as much as possible. A little wider. Okay, relax. (Mouth must be partly open at end).

17 Now tense your lips by closing your mouth. O.K., relax. (Notice the feeling of relaxation).

18 Put your tongue at the roof of your mouth. Press hard. (Pause.) Relax and allow your tongue to come to a comfortable position in your mouth.

19 Now put your tongue at the bottom of your mouth. Press down hard. Relax and let your tongue come to a comfortable position in your mouth.

20 Now just lie (sit) there and relax. Try not to think of anything.

21 To control self-verbalizations, I want you to go through the motions of singing a high note—Not aloud. Okay, start singing to yourself. Hold that note, and now relax.

22 Now sing a medium note and make your vocal cords tense again. Relax.

23 Now sing a low note and make your vocal cords tense again. Relax. (Your vocal apparatus should be relaxed now. Relax your mouth).

*The client should not be encouraged to bend his neck either all the way back or forward.

24 Now, close your eyes. Squeeze them tight and breathe naturally. Notice the tension. Now relax. (Notice how the pain goes away when you relax).

25 Now, let your eyes just lie there and keep your mouth open slightly.

26 Open your eyes as much as possible. Hold it. Now, relax your eyes.

27 Now wrinkle your forehead as much as possible. Hold it. Okay, relax.

28 Now, take a deep breath and hold it. Relax. (Notice the wondrous feeling of breathing again).

29 Now, exhale. Breathe all the air out . . . all of it. Relax. (Notice the wondrous feeling of breathing again).

30 Imagine that there are weights pulling on all your muscles, making them flaccid and relaxed . . . pulling your arms and body into the couch.

31 Pull your stomach muscles together. Tighter. Okay, relax.

32 Now extend your muscles as if you were a prize fighter, make your stomach hard, relax. (You are becoming more and more relaxed).

33 Now, tense your buttocks. Tighter. Hold it. Now, relax.

34 Now, search the upper part of your body and relax any part that is tense. First the facial muscles.
(Pause 3–5 seconds) Then the vocal muscles.
(Pause 3–5 seconds) The neck region.
(Pause 3–5 seconds) Your shoulder . . . relax any part which is tense.
(Pause.) Now the arms and fingers. Relax these. Becoming very relaxed.

35 Maintaining this relaxation, raise both of your legs (to about a 45 degree angle). Now relax. (Notice that this further relaxes you.)

36 Now bend your feet back so that your toes point toward your face. Relax your mouth. Bend them hard. Relax.

37 Bend your feet the other way . . . away from your body. Not far. Notice the tension. Okay, relax.

38 Relax. (Pause.) Now curl your toes together—as hard as you can. Tighter. Okay, relax. (Quiet . . . silence for about 30 seconds.)

39 This completes the formal relaxation procedure. Now explore your body from your feet up. Make sure that every muscle is relaxed. (Say slowly) —first your toes, . . . your feet, . . . your legs, . . . buttocks, . . . stomach, . . . shoulders, . . . neck, . . . eyes, . . . and finally your forehead—all should be relaxed now. (Quiet—silence for about 10 seconds.) Just lie there and feel very relaxed, noticing the warmness of the relaxation. (Pause.) I would like you to stay this way for about one more minute, and then I am going to count to five. When I reach five I want you to open your eyes feeling very calm and refreshed. (Quiet—silence for about one minute.) Okay, when I count to five, I want you to open your eyes feeling very calm and refreshed. Four . . . ; and, five.

Covert Control

Many thoughts having conditioning consequences occur "naturally" or habitually. Homme (1965) conceptualizes these as "coverants or operants of the mind."

According to this viewpoint, thoughts are early elements in a response chain. Subvocalizations such as "I'm dying for a cigarette" may precede and functionally activate an undesired target behavior (i.e., smoking). Utilizing Premack's (1965) differential probability definition of reinforcement, Homme suggested a programmed sequence for the modification of maladaptive coverants. According to this "coverant control" paradigm, stimuli which have previously elicited inappropriate coverants can become cues for coverants which are incompatible with the undesired target behavior (TB). For example, the individual can be trained to generate anti-TB coverants in the presence of TB stimuli. This is represented in the first two phases below.

1	2	3	4
TB stimuli	anti-TB coverant	pro-non-TB coverant	reward
Smoking stimuli	"smoking causes halitosis"	" I'll save money by not smoking"	coffee

To avoid terminating the response chain on an aversive element (phase 2), Homme recommends that a reinforceable behavior be inserted and then some reward (high probability behavior) experienced. Thus, an individual might encounter a cigarette machine. To counteract his usual "urge" for a cigarette, he engages in an anti-smoking coverant (e.g., "smoking causes cancer"). This is followed by a thought which is compatible with not smoking (e.g., "my food will taste better if I don't smoke."). This positive coverant is reinforced by engaging in a high probability (rewarding) activity, such as drinking a cup of coffee. (Mahoney, 1974, pp. 85–86)

Similarly, Meichenbaum (1975) describes the role of "voices in the head," or the individual's inner dialogue. Clearly his position is that modified self-statements result in further individual change. At some point, the modification of self-statements can be very similar to some of the systematic rational restructuring techniques already discussed, such as R.E.T. However, the point to be emphasized here is the existence of self-statements and their conditioning consequence. Change the statements and you change the conditioning contingencies.

Covert sensitization, covert reinforcement, covert extinction, and covert modeling roughly parallel the systematic desensitization-relaxation paradigm. For covert sensitization, the individual may be encouraged to imagine a problem such as overeating and then an aversive event (Cautela, 1967). For covert reinforcement, negative reinforcement might include imagining an aversive stimulus and then mentally shifting to a desired behavior while mentally getting away from the aversive image (Mahoney, 1974). For covert extinction, a stutterer might imagine that there was no negative reaction from others to stuttering behavior and might conjure up different situations in a systematic desensitization manner. Covert modeling involves symbolic rehearsal of appropriate behavior (Cautela, 1971). Kazdin (1973) found in this regard that "coping" rather than "mastery" imagined models were more effective in promoting change. A coping model, while less than perfect in performance, aids individuals in their struggle with inner issues such as developing a relaxing response during stress.

Environmental Control

Environmental control refers to controlling one's physical surroundings in order to generate or avoid specific stimuli. It is basically stimulus control and is noted here in addition to the conditioning because the central principle is "self-directed" stimulation. That is, rather than controlling one's thoughts to control covert stimuli, the individual controls the environment. This behavioral version of self-management provides the individual with suggestions and aids to promote control. For obesity problems, the suggestion is to keep little food in the house. The important thing is that the individual tries to control the situation in which he or she must cope rather than trying to cope with any and all situations. It is situation management with conditioning consequences emphasized.

Suggestion

In the sociobiological models of human functioning, it was noted that one of the most striking qualities of humans is their enormous susceptibility to influence. Wilson (1975) goes so far as to state that the human hunger for direction and structure makes people "absurdly easy" to manipulate. Nowhere in the change literature is this tendency better illustrated than for suggestion and related techniques. Torrey (1972) describes important leader characteristics that are valuable in inducing change in this regard. These echo points raised in the persuasion discussion.

> A patient's "faith" and motivation for improvement are determined by several factors: (1) the degree to which the therapist's ability to name the disease and its cause agrees with the views of the patient, (2) the degree to which the therapeutic techniques employed are considered by the patient to be of value in helping him, and (3) the degree to which the therapist's personal qualities match the patient's expectations of what a therapist should be like. (Coe & Buckner, 1975, p. 393)

Further, it is noteworthy that many other change techniques such as relaxation training depend upon suggestion and this type of leader presence because of the suggestion consequences.

At the most fundamental level, it is the expectations of the participants that create change (Coe & Buckner, 1975). Thus when a patient sees a doctor and is prescribed pills as part of the treatment, the patient may well change because of "faith" in the situation. In fact, the term "placebo" is derived from the Latin "I will please." Torrey (1972) argues that direct suggestions, symbolism, and magical formulas can enhance this expectational tendency. Thus the doctor's prediction that the pills will, for example, reduce tension can enhance expectations. The ritualistic procedures of a doctor's office plus the medical dress and other accouterments further contribute to this enhancement, just as dance, talismans, and fire aid the primitive tribal shaman. Similarly, the magic of primitive incantations is paralleled in today's society by the "miracle of modern chemistry." The "expert" and "trusted" often make suggestions that fit and are incorporated into the sets of expectations of others, thereby resulting in change.

The most formalized mechanism for this process is hypnotism, known in the eighteenth century as mesmerism or animal magnetism. Coe and Buckner (1975) offer some important orienting comments about this technique. First they acknowledge that "Unfortunately, the image of hypnosis as mysterious and bordering on the occult has caused some practioners to avoid using it, and persons who might benefit from it to shy away" (p. 398), but at the same time they assert its essential commonality with procedures already discussed:

> The usual procedure is to begin by administering an "induction," instructions that lead the subject from his normal "waking" state into the "trance" state. The client is often requested to gaze at an object while the hypnotist repeats a variety of suggestions, including those leading to relaxation, heightened awareness of sensations, and tiring of the eyes. (Coe & Buckner, 1975, p. 398)

In the typical induction sequence, the individual is encouraged to "drop" and "let go" of greater and greater degrees of self-control in specific areas, ranging from the focusing of vision and the relaxing and closing of eyes to allowing the body to sway and falling backward into the leader's arms. Physical involvement tends to make the words more tactile and effective. Mesmer used the laying on of hands and later large tanks of "mesmerized fluid" to aid in the induction process. "The more the subject becomes involved, the more likely it is that he will experience a subjective loss of control and allow responses to occur that would normally be suppressed" (Coe & Buckner, 1975, p. 403). However, it is important to note that the stereotype of the true surrender of will under hypnosis is unjustified.

Values in areas of criminality and sexuality are not likely to be transcended by the procedure. Rather, the success of hypnosis seems to lie in suggesting the right things, things desired or potentially desired by individuals wishing or willing to open themselves to that desire. Desire also relates to commitment and is discussed further in the next chapter.

On the other hand, suggestion can lead to suggestibility. Behavioral consequences can be dramatic, even theatrical. Levitt and Hershman (1963) surveyed physicians who use hypnosis, and Coe and Buckner summarize some of their results.

> The single best represented medical specialty was obstetrics-gynecology (11 percent). They reported using hypnosis with 12 percent of their patients to ease childbirth. On the average they claimed a three hour reduction in labor and a 60 percent reduction of chemical anesthesia. Surgeons made up four percent of the medical respondents and used hypnosis primarily as an analgesic agent. They estimated a 50 percent average reduction in the use of chemical anesthetics, and significantly reduced bleeding. (Coe & Buckner, 1975, p. 399)

Self-attributions and autohypnosis are important extensions and refinements of these insights. Individuals suffering from insomnia (Davison, Tsujimoto, & Glaros, 1973) and pain (Davison & Valins, 1969) were given ameliorating drugs during relaxation training. When subsequent attributions for change were assigned solely to the self because the drugs used were inert, subjects' changes were more enduring. Kulka (1972) found that for people with high internal locus of control (Rotter, 1966) achievement orientation affected this tendency; internal achievers were more likely to be affected by self-attributions than were externals and nonachievers. In autohypnosis the individual can be encouraged to use a simple pendulum in conjunction with relaxation training so that a deeper concentration is achieved. Post-hypnotic suggestion also can be given to aid individuals in relaxing themselves using the procedure, or a triggering word such as "relax" may be used (Suinn & Richardson, 1971). Deep breathing can also serve as a cue for self-relaxation.

Yoga (Eliade, 1969), psychocybernetics (Maltz, 1960), and many other self-help and dynamic and tactile meditation techniques emphasize these principles of expectationally centered change. Coe and Buckner (1975) point out that virtually all these approaches have a philosophy, a set of principles, or words that individuals repeatedly utter to themselves during self-absorbing physical activity or physical self-restraint. The yoga candle focuses attention, the reverse posture to rejuvenate organs adds magic, and the daily repetition, garb, and incantations are ritualistic.

Interference

The interference subprocesses in re-cognitive change can be considered in relation to information processing and other cognitive models of human functioning. Three particular techniques are discussed in this section: thought stopping, confusion, and imaginal flooding or implosion. The last technique is heavily associated with behavioral extinction processes but it is also relevant here.

Thought Stopping

Thought stopping is generally directed at the challenge of breaking mental patterns "mid-stride" so to speak (Bain, 1928; Wolpe, 1958, 1969). Thus R.E.T., in providing clients with rational thoughts, might need to be supplemented by preparatory stopping of irrational ruminations. Meichenbaum (1975, pp. 380–381) summarizes the procedure as follows:

1 The frequency and impact of the client's irrational self-verbalizations- (and images) are determined. The self-defeating nature of such thinking processes is discussed.

2 Thought stopping procedure begins with the client's closing his eyes and imagining himself in a real-life situation beginning to verbalize his obsessive thoughts aloud. The therapist shouts "stop" at the beginning of the obsessive thought. After several successful trials, the responsibility is turned over to the client.

3 Now the client begins his obsessive thoughts, saying them to himself subvocally and then the client shouts "stop" aloud in order to interrupt the obsessive thought sequence. This is repeated for several trials, initially aloud and then covertly.

4 In order to strengthen the client's ability to interrupt and sense that he can control his thinking processes, he is encouraged to produce an assertive statement to himself that is incompatible with the content of the obsession. Initially the expression of "stop" and the assertion is made aloud. Over a number of trials they are gradually made in lower and lower tones and eventually faded out to a covert level.

Rimm and Masters (1974) encourage individuals stuck on thoughts of a nervous breakdown not to use one single command but to covertly assert themselves: "Screw it! I'm perfectly normal!" This interference in the habituated thinking pattern clearly unfreezes individuals' behavior in areas where they have already chosen to change. Limits to the effectiveness of this procedure are hinted at by Mahoney (1971), who found that counting backward from seven to one actually increased clients' unwanted ruminations! In 1974, Mahoney emphasized the importance of linking this technique with other counterconditioning as well as focusing on imaginal rather than purely verbal interference mechanisms.

Confusion

The confusion technique (Erikson, 1964; Haley, 1967) differs from thought stopping in that the unfreezing effects are designed to overcome the individual's will rather than reinforce it. Here, a generally incomprehensible flow of words is provided to overcome resistance to the leader's influence.

> Thus the subject is led almost to begin a response, is frustrated in this by then being presented with the next idea, and the whole process is repeated with a continued development of state of inhibition, leading to confusion and the growing need to receive a clear-cut comprehensible communication to which he can make a ready and full response. (Haley, 1967, p. 183)

Confusion creates acceptance of leader suggestions of increased susceptibility to hypnosis (Coe & Buckner, 1975).

Implosion

Finally, implosion or imaginal flooding can be considered in this subsection although Krumboltz and Thoresen (1976), Mahoney (1974), and Morris (1975) all emphasize the behavioral qualities of the technique. Currently, implosion is primarily directed at the reduction of fear. An individual, fearful of snakes, imaginally embellishes scenes and rehearses fantasies of snakes for thirty minutes to an hour. When fear outcomes are not fulfilled, there results an effect on the fear similar to extinction. Of greater theoretical importance, however, is how intense imaginal flooding on a selected issue can alter inner thought sequences. Instead of trying to avoid unwanted thoughts, the individual overindulges them and thereby interferes with the normal thinking pattern; the hold of such thoughts consequently is reduced. As with thought stopping, the individual is again interfering with thoughts through an act of will in an effort to alter them.

Support for interpreting implosion as interference in nature is provided by Phillips (1956), who emphasizes that the outcome of interference is a new perspective on a sequence of events. For him, the important characteristic is that an expectation or assertion about the self becomes disconfirmed in a tension producing sequence which is itself counterconditioning.

Memory

If learning is defined as information acquisition, then memory-related change processes are perhaps the most significant unit in the analysis of individual change. Psychologists have studied memory extensively, and the body of knowledge is great, complex, and difficult to apply pragmatically. These complexities include such esoterica as neural analysis (Kesner, 1973) and many subjects that cannot even be touched upon in this section. Other points can only be briefly discussed, and it appears best to defer to Postman (1975) who offers some tight generalizations about the area.

As is well known, the major lines of evidence which have been invoked to support a functional dichotomy of memory processes include (a) the specificity of memory deficits in brain-damaged patients; (b) apparent differences in encoding related the length of the interval between input and retention test; (c) the effects of presentation modality on performance; and (d) the interaction of the serial position at input with a variety of experimental manipulations, with recall of the terminal items presumably reflecting output from STS (Short term Storage) and that of early and middle items from LTS (Long term Storage).

While models vary with respect to the characteristics assigned to the two stories, there is substantial agreement on the major functional differences between the hypothesized long-term and short-term systems. A useful composite summary of these differences was recently presented by Craik & Lockhart . . . : STS is a system of limited capacity in which information is maintained by continued attention and rehearsal. The format of the information is predominantly phonemic, probably also visual, and "possibly semantic." The trace is of short duration (up to 30 sec) and loss from the store occurs through displacement or "possibly decay." Retrieval is likely to be automatic or dependent on temporal and phonemic cues. Information that has been maintained by rehearsal in STS is transferred to LTS; a common assumption is that the probability of transfer is a direct function of the duration of an item's stay in STS . . . Once information has entered LTS, which has no determinate limits, it is maintained by repetition or organization. The format of the information is largely semantic but includes some visual and auditory representations as well. The long-term trace is of indefinite duration. Successful retrieval depends on the availability of appropriate cues and may be the outcome of a search process. Forgetting occurs when the stored information becomes inaccessible because of the loss of retrieval cues or discriminability is degraded through interference. (Postman, 1975, pp. 295–296)

Peterson (1977) emphasizes the role of "levels of processing" in another review of memory. His insights into change build on the original Craik and Lockhart (1972) extensions beyond LTS–STS. For example, Craik and Tulving (1975) demonstrated that semantic coding was a more helpful memory aid than visual coding. Similarly, words presented by the same voice are more easily encoded and retained. Further refinements in this view distinguish between episodic memory, memory associated with certain events, and semantic memory. Different encoding mechanisms control these processes, and, in the latter case, single, concrete ideas ordered in a simple, familiar pattern are best retained.

Ginsberg and Koslowski (1976) also discuss the importance of pattern recognition for storage or encoding. Klahr and Wallace (1976) note that information processing is facilitated by serial presentation of ideas. Wertheimer (1959) and gestaltist followers emphasize the role of "seeing" a total pattern, grouping, or structure. Order aids memory even when it is provided by the individual.

The role of the individual can also be considered from the perspective of sense-making efforts. Mastery tendencies alter retention, according to Ginsberg and Koslowski (1976). Implicit here is the attention resulting from individuals' attempts to learn, and the retention consequences of finding a "fit" between certain items and their mental structures. Similarly, Klahr and Wallace (1976) discuss the need for the "chunking" of information bits so that they fit more easily into the individual's semantic slots for long-term storage.

Application

Finally, we note Gagne's 1962 and 1968 studies of the need for learning hierarchies in which the individual processes conceptualizations from the simple to the complex. Gagne sees a need to balance repetition, similarity, and contiguity of items with the challenge of more complex and stimulating items and issues. His work states that it is not the intensity of a learning experience that affects memory, but the simultaneous challenge and comprehension, and the way the experience can be tied to other stores and inputs of information.

A moment's reflection on all of the memory material points out that this re-cognitive subprocess is the antithesis of the interference subprocess discussed above. Clearly, information accumulation is important in learning, but more often than not the task of experiential leaders is to facilitate *relearning* (Bennis, Benne, Chin, & Corey, 1976). The message from the memory literature is that relearning is highly incompatible with many fundamental cognitive processes central to retention. Leaders must know whether they are building on or going against participants' existing mental structures. The two circumstances have dramatically different pedagogical implications.

Complex Approaches

The complex re-cognitive change approaches do not fit into any of the preceding categories. Insights are provided by Frankl's logo therapy and Kelly's constructive alternativism. These approaches are rational in some respects but the way change is induced transcends simple rationality. Similarly, the areas of belief, countercontrol, and choice offer additional information.

Logo Therapy

Frankl's (1960, 1966, 1967, 1969) approach pivots on the interrelationship between will and cognition. By redirecting thoughts away from the self (dereflection) and by artificially attempting to assert exaggerated degrees of will (paradoxical intention), the individual develops cognitive detachment and, ultimately, self-control. The issue here is overcoming fears that arise when the self is the object of attention or inattention, but re-cognition is of a more general nature. Dereflection dismisses the self from perceived demands from the outside. Paradoxical intention, in a manner reminiscent of implosion, confronts an issue hyperbolically. Individuals try to direct all their will to doing what they do not want to do and paradoxically find that doing the unwanted thing is impossible. Humor plays a self-detachment role similar to those of paradoxical intention and dereflection.

Construct Alternativism

Kelly's 1955 theory of cognitive change is to some extent both the basis for and an elaboration of the systematic rational approaches already discussed. Cognitive change can occur in four ways that can be arranged in a hierarchy reflecting the significance of the change. These are:

1 Contrast reconstruction: here the individual slightly refines and redefines details in the old mental organizing systems. Information feedback might aid in comparing various outcomes with expectations that could lead to revisions.
2 Controlled elaboration: here the individual reorganizes an old system, collapses redundant categories, and increases precision.
3 Formation of new constructs: here the individual acknowledges that certain events are not well explained in the current system, and so creates or adapts new constructs in order to increase predictability and control of events. Disconfirming feedback may be valuable here. In the extreme, Goldfried, DeCenteceo, and Weinberg (1974) talk about the development of an entirely new cognitive set.
4 Reduction of constructs to impermeability: here the individual relaxes internal rigidities regarding the construct system used.

Kelly's approach to re-cognition emphasizes working with emotions as well as ideas. Through role playing and experiential emersion, events are used to test cognitive systems and to generate emotions. Aggression is an "active pursuit of constructive experience" and inherent in change. Hostility, however, is a "continued attempt to extort validational evidence in support of a personal construct which has already discredited itself" (Sahakian, 1969, p. 363). What is implied, then, is a complex strategy in which the indivdiual's system is challenged, leading ultimately to aggression but not to hostility. Sharp contrasts clarify choices. Leader tolerance and strong, clear reality guideposts are valuable contextual factors. Only a few constructs are concentrated on in any given time period and, in contrast to rational, behavioral, or suggestion methods, the total emphasis is on the individual's self-discovery. It is through the "enactment" of one's life with a given construct system in mind that an individual is able to test constructs and changes as the information dictates. Validation of a particular temporarily explored construct is often satisfying and effective in leading to the permanent adoption of the construct.

Other orientations regarding beliefs or rules for action have similarities with Kelly's position and point out some limitations of his approach. Mahoney, for example, agrees with Kelly's view at a general level.

In terms of cognitive-symbolic structure, Bem distinguishes between primitive beliefs (the "givens" of a system) and higher-order beliefs (which are vertically and horizontally interdependent elements). Primitive beliefs are implicit "leaps of faith" which do not demand experiential confirmation or formal defense. Examples are the belief in the validity of our own sense data and such assumptions as causality. Higher-order beliefs, on the other hand, may require confirmation and/or defense. They are not "unconscious" or "intuitive" and often form complex superstructures with both parallel and hierarchical organization.

It is worth noting here that, aside from some structural embellishments, social psychology has added little terminological refinement to some longstanding conventions in epistemology. The philosopher Charles Peirce (1878), for example, defined "belief" as "a rule for action" having three components: cognitive, emotional, and behavioral. He contended that a belief entailed (a) sensations to be expected, and (b) behavior to be prepared. In his famous treatise on "the Will to Believe," William James (1896) defended the role of emotional satisfaction in justifying belief. A pervasive focus in virtually every epistemological definition of belief, however, has been behavioral—i.e., a "willingness to act" upon some predicative assumption. This "performance accountability" is illustrated in the fable about an irreligious vacationer who accidentally fell over the edge of the Grand Canyon and found himself dangling precariously from a small shrub. As he hung agonizingly close to imminent death, he mustered an awesome prayer of faith and conversion. Suddenly, his cries for supernatural intervention were answered by a thunderous question from the heavens, "Do you believe?" Startled and inspired, the dangling convert cried, "Yes . . . oh, yes, I do believe!" The voice thundered back, "Do you really believe?" "Yes, dear God . . . I really, really believe!" There was a brief silence before the heavenly voice wryly responded, "Then let go of the shrub." (Mahoney, 1974, p. 229)

However, the issue of human drive for cognitive control and especially consistency is less pervasive for the more behaviorally focused change scholars. For example, Bem (1970) states:

> Inconsistency, they seem to be trying to tell us, motivates belief and attitude change.
>
> But I don't believe it. At least not very much. In my view, a vision of inconsistency as a temporary turbulence in an otherwise fastidious pool of cognitive clarity is all too misleading. My own suspicion is that inconsistency is probably our most enduring cognitive commonplace. That is, I suspect that for most of the people most of the time and for all of the people some of the time inconsistency just sits there. . . . I believe, in short, that there is more inconsistency on earth (and probably in heaven) than is dreamt of in our psychological theories. (Bem, 1970, p. 34)

And Mahoney (1974, p. 230) concludes that "consistency among beliefs or between beliefs is an acculturated value not an inborn circuit." Thus, for cognitive change, important issues are the degree to which a given belief can be isolated from an entire system and the degree to which leaders and participants already share a conceptual system. Mahoney's (1974) emphasis on the value of choice and perceived freedom is consistent with Kelly's position. Choice seems to be internally reinforcing and motivating to the degree that individuals will often strive to avoid or mitigate the reduction of personal freedom or restore lost options (Brehm, 1966). Kelly's emphasis on the individual's re-cognitive efforts coming out of self-directed coping is supported by Mahoney's behavioral observation that, in behavior therapy, individuals often demonstrate a high propensity toward "counter control." The point here is that highly conspicuous, manipulative, or coercive aspects of control stimulate oppositional or rebellious patterns.

In general, these insights on re-cognitive change focus on the limits of "forcing" new cognitions and beliefs on individuals and the importance of letting such changes crystalize within the thought structure of the individual. Rational, behavioral, and suggestion techniques all implicitly acknowledge this principle, but, in the subtle balance of enough but not too much, attention and inattention is best appreciated by Frankl. Through Kelly, one realizes that all the other processes do not really lead to cognitive change; rather, they prepare the backdrop, pave the road, provide support, and reduce blocks for the individual. Interference techniques also provide this second chance for the individual to change.

Summary

Re-cognitive change processes are present in some form in any attempt to change behavior. The dichotomy drawn between cognitive and experiential approaches, with the former concerned with thinking about issues and the latter with feelings and behavior, is simply not valid. Re-cognition has a central role in all learning experiences, regardless of their form.

CHAPTER SIX

Existential Change Processes

*I was in the process
before I started thinking
about the process.*

John Dean III (1973)

*The end of all thought
must be action.*

Aldous Huxley

Existential change processes rely most heavily and directly on actually altering some aspect of the individual. Activation is more simple than commitment or action; it is synonymous with the energizing of the organism or some aspect of it. Much of our being and adaptation is in response to the world as it is experienced, and activation is the pivotal point between perception and consequence. This discussion of activation explores the human capacity and need for activation, and a number of practical sources of activation for learning.

Commitment is a more difficult concept, referring to the coalescence and direction of the self and involving that almost metaphysical notion, will. A conflict of wills between the leader and the participant is most often counterproductive, but many coercive arrangements or unaware leaders unintentionally create this dynamic. A variety of other issues are also explored and conclusions drawn for limits, potentialities, and techniques for altering commitment and thereby change.

A discussion of the action change process closes the chapter. Central to the existential nature of action in change is engaging the individual in a struggle with an educational reality. The action change process acknowledges that learning is accomplished through living, and even implies that one of the most fundamental aspects of living is learning.

Activation

The activation process is highly dependent on the stimulation impinging on an individual and the manner and degree of the impact of that stimulation (Fiske & Maddi, 1961). Activation is intimately enmeshed with the change processes already discussed, in the sense that most of them can be thought of as engendering specific types of activation or stimulation. An exception is positive reinforcement, generally regarded as the complement to activation, because it leads to a reduction rather than an arousal of drive states. Positive reinforcement implies need satisfaction and in extreme cases results in satiation. On the other hand, coercion involves not only punishment but also the activation of fear and avoidance responses. Support assuages feelings of fear (Bowlby, 1973), and thus demonstrates deactivation potential but of a different nature than that of positive reinforcement. To further complicate matters, warmth in support also activates feelings that can fill the emotional void after assuagement of fear.

Activation is a crucial aspect of the impact of change on the central nervous system. The consistency models of human functioning, for example, indicate that the nervous system can handle large quantities of stimulation and that this stimulation is needed continuously. Individuals are said to become conditioned to a level and pattern of activation early in life and to seek out this consistent pattern later in life (Fiske & Maddi, 1961).

Individual Perspective

Many of the models of human functioning have the same general sense of individual nature. The life science models, cognitive/perceptual models, consistency models, and some of the fulfillment models (White, 1959) depict individuals as having evolved and developed to cope with a complex and subtle world and to gain control over it. The enormous perceptual capacities of humans allow for the incorporation of 10^9 fresh stimulus inputs every millisecond, 10^8 of which are visual. The eye oscillates through one half minute of arc about 100 times per second, and if these motions are compensated for by using electronic optical feedback devices, vision ceases in a fraction of a second (Ditchburn, 1955; Riggs, Armington, & Ratliff, 1954). The human brain makes decisions at a rate of twenty per second while absorbing, assembling, and comparing patterns of present and past data (Platt, 1961). The intensity, variety, and meaningfulness of stimulation affect the impact it has on the individual. Impact results in arousal (Mehrabian & Ksionsky, 1970, 1974; Mehrabian & Russell, 1973) and coping behavior.

In early stimulus deprivation studies, individuals were seen to experience mental confusion and hallucinations. More recently, Seudfeld (1975) and others have shown that internal mechanisms can be generated resulting in less disturbing internal responses. In short, the human brain has evolved to cope with enormous quantities of data and therefore constantly needs stimulus input. Riesen (1961) showed that mental development is highly dependent on stimulation and that in the absence of visual stimulation, for example, visual discrimination and reaction times are reduced. Stimulation leads to activation because the mind exists to engage when presented with stimuli. Understanding this engagement process is critical for understanding change.

Platt (1961) discussed beauty from an activation perspective. "It now appears that the requirements for aesthetic enjoyment are simply the requirements for perception itself, raised to a higher degree; and the essential thing in each case is to have a pattern that contains the unexpected" (p. 403). In short, the pattern gives a sense that all is well; the variety of the unexpected creates a pleasing level of activation. "The mind demands a pattern" (p. 410), but "has evolved to deal with continuous novelty of pattern" (p. 412). Music serves as a good illustration because it is a pattern of sounds with variations and alterations. In the song, "Three Blind Mice," a simple pattern is established, altered, and returned again, giving a sense of fulfillment, closure, and a more complex pattern.

Mehrabian and Ksionsky (1970, 1974) address the issue in a different way. Quite simply, they argue that activation or arousal is experienced by the individual as positive reinforcement. Thus, the first way in which activation affects change is through reinforcement. Platt also notes that the type of change particularly appealing to individuals contains pattern alterations that are not too extreme. Similarly, an activation interpretation of "need for achievement" explains the effects of moderate challenge as optimally activating, while low or high challenge leads to underactivation or overactivation.

Is there, then, an optimal level of activation and if so, what are its sources and characteristics? Scott (1966) summarizes the research as follows:

The relationship between activation level and performance is generally described by an inverted U. At low activation levels, performance is handicapped by lack of alertness, a decrease in sensory sensitivity, and lack of muscular coordination (all of which are due to insufficient cortical stimulation from the BSRF). At the intermediate levels of activation, performance is optimal, and at high levels performance is again handicapped by hypertensiveness, loss of muscular control, "impulsion to action," and in the extreme, total disorganization of responses. The direct evidence in support of this relationship is meager in that few if any investigations have obtained measures of activity in the brain stem and observed concomitant variations in performance. (Scott, 1966, p. 12–13)

In 1961, Young clearly demonstrated that pleasantness or unpleasantness of affective arousal resulting from stimulation is a function of both the intensity of stimulation and the individual's specific hungers. Pleasant arousal is a reinforcing activation and relates to homeostasis needs of the organism. In general, it can also be said that understimulation results in the unpleasant state of boredom and overstimulation, the aversive state of stress (Fiske & Maddi, 1961).

Adequate levels of stimulation result in a general activation of the limbic system of the brain. While this was once believed to lead to direct stimulation of specific portions of the lateral system through the reticular formation (Scott, 1966), it now seems that the stimulation leads to a general energizing of the entire brain (McGeer, 1977). The notion of the natural child in transactional analysis (T.A.) corresponds to the limbic system. Change through T.A. emphasizes strokes (stimulation) for the natural child (limbic system) supplying the energy necessary for change. In short the T.A. approach to change seems to fit with the neurophysiological characteristics of the activation process.

Interactional Perspective

From this perspective, several phenomena can be constructively related to activation. Among these, perhaps social facilitation is the most important. Discussions of social facilitation typically are divided between audience effects and coaction effects (Zimbardo & Ebbesen, 1969). It was found, for example, that chickens eat more grain when in the presence of other chickens than when alone, and that bicyclists ride faster in the presence of others than when alone. Relatively simple or well-learned responses tend to be performed better with coactors or audiences than are more complex or unlearned responses. In the latter case, the task itself has a large activation component and the additional activation of the presence of others yields stressful overactivation which diminishes performance. On the other hand, the visual and mental stimulation generated by the presence of others results in extra energizing. The feeding chicken constantly experiences activation of its eating drive when in the presence of other feeding chickens. "Facilitators," in growth environments such as encounter groups, create a warm atmosphere of trust and support that activates different aspects of the individual than does a competitive group atmosphere. Similarly, one individual's profound personal experiences has impact on others in the group and aids them in ways that go beyond identification processes alone.

Activation is also integral in the areas of sex appeal and charisma. In both cases something is activated in others. Sexual arousal and inspiration are similar to each other in this sense. Winston Churchill activated the aggressive determination residing in many individuals through his tone of voice, gestures, appearance, and verbal imagery; Elizabeth Taylor activates amorous instincts with a warm smile that, at some level, signals approval of the person at whom she is smiling. Important in this and the social facilitation application is the simple fact that people are an enormous source of stimulation for each other and therefore an important source of activation.

Social Perspective

Two areas easily noted from the social perspective are television and work. A moment's reflection on Platt's definition of beauty, pattern, and change gives a penetrating insight into the appeal of television. Game shows, police stories, variety shows, situation comedies, and nature excursions predominate in prime time programming. The patterns are relatively simple and predictable. Specific events are altered to give adequate variety. Visual stimulation is enhanced by color, action, and a paced alternation of the camera angle from one character to another every ten to thirty seconds. Since 10^8 of 10^9 stimulus inputs per millisecond are visual, television, and especially color television, is very stimulating visually. It gets people's minds off their troubles, allows "escape," and, in other words, entertains. It is significant that television programming is not so stimulating that it activates behavior that would take the viewer away from the set!

The issue of the work world is addressed by Scott (1966) who documented the performance consequence of routine jobs. Over time, repetition leads to boredom, or underactivation. This in turn results in decreased energy, less effort expended on the job, and thus lower performance; errors and mistakes are increased as are accidents in some cases. But simply increasing the complexity of a task does not increase performance, because any activation due to increased task difficulty is directed toward learning and mastery, not performance. The task is by definition more difficult, and performance is not increased and can be decreased. The individual, however, might be more engaged and satisfied in dealing with the more complex task.

Scott and Erskine (1977) also find support for the significance of activation of task activities. Their findings show that the arousal can be positively reinforcing, sufficiently so that extra reinforcement has little additional impact when tasks are adequately activating.

Commitment

The importance of commitment in changing behavior cannot be overstated, but its role in change has been casually and vaguely articulated. Paradoxically, this is the result of its centrality in change; it is often taken for granted that commitment exists and that it is mobilized by simple, well articulated, mechanistic means. It is seldom deeply reflected on. After a few general points, the following discussion looks at commitment from the individual, interactional, and social perspectives.

For the current analysis, commitment is defined as "the pledging or binding of the individual to behavioral acts or beliefs, attitudes and perceptions" (Kiesler & Sakumura, 1966, p. 349). The most simple and ubiquitous commitment tactic is the contract. Contracts are widely used in the behaviorist change approaches and also in a variety of psychotherapeutic approaches. Contracts can be overt (written or oral, with self or others), contingent (changeable, depending on outside occurrences), or implied. Implied contracts refer to informal agreements or directions determined by relationships (Dinoff & Rickard, 1969, p. 127). The use and signifiance of contracts in change is treated more fully in the analysis of commitment from the individual perspective.

The second point about commitment concerns its relation to the action change process. The action orientation of the experiential approach often blurs the distinction between these two processes. The experiential rule of thumb—to get involvement through active participation—seldom differentiates between commitment building, commitment utilizing, and other facets more specifically identified as action. For example, milling procedures that bring participants into immediate contact with each other involve action, but more importantly generate a feeling of involvement in and commitment to the learning experience. Subsequent participation in other activities such as role play or simulations, is made possible by the commitment already generated. Active behavior can be used to increase commitment to the learning process, a particular change goal, or the learning group itself. Then the commitment can aid in generating action. The two processes are highly interdependent and tightly linked.

The issue of participant involvement leads to the third general point. Typically, participant involvement is pursued aggressively in the experiential approach. One social science milestone often cited in this regard is Kurt Lewin's (1952) report on efforts to get housewives voluntarily to select meats of a less desirable character so that other cuts could be sent to the men fighting in World War II. An overt decision and public voicing of that decision was coaxed from the women. Dramatic change resulted. Kiesler (1971), however, raises the point that more recent change programs have often tried this approach only to have participants make the wrong decision! Mindful of the risks of oversimplification, Kiesler (1971, p. 33) offers five ways to increase commitment:

1 The more explicit, public, and otherwise unambiguous an act of commitment, the greater subsequent maintainance of the commitment (Hovland, Campbell, & Brock, 1957).

2 The more important the act to the subject, the greater the commitment (Sherif, Sherif, & Nebergall, 1965).

3 The greater the irrevocability of an act, the greater the subsequent commitment.

4 The greater the number of acts or their repetition, the greater the commitment (Kiesler, 1971).

5 The greater the volition perceived by the individual in performance of an act, the greater the commitment (Freedman & Steinbruner, 1964; Kiesler & Sakumura, 1966).

Within the above action dynamics one sees the importance of the consistency models of human functioning; an individual tries to hold attitudes and demonstrate behaviors consistent with previous public displays of attitude and behavior. One major view of commitment does in fact emphasize the consistency models of human functioning. However, important insights into the process are also provided by other kinds of models of human functioning.

Individual Perspective

The various models of human functioning discussed in Chapter 1 serve as an organizing device for this analysis of commitment. From the psychoanalytic-therapeutic tradition, insights from the conflict and fulfillment models of human functioning are most useful. From the social-psychological tradition, the cognitive/perceptual and consistency models of human functioning dominate. From the behaviorist tradition, issues such as contracting are considered. Finally, techniques and their relation to the traditions are outlined.

Psychotherapy. In the psychoanalytic-therapeutic tradition, commitment is pivotal. The therapist allows the individual to self-disclose and thereby build a sense of commitment to the therapist. The implied or overt contract of the therapist's protection and acceptance of the patient can result in transference. That is, the patient strongly identifies with the therapist. Modeling of analytical ego functioning and incorporation of new superego messages are major change outcomes.

Rank (1947) argues against the emphasis on identification in change, asserting that individuals need to commit to themselves rather than to a model. He sees as a major problem in therapy a conflict of wills (resistance) between therapist and patient. One solution to this problem is the reduction of the degree of surrender (commitment) necessary to the therapeutic arrangement. For this purpose, he proposes two approaches to establishing contracts that reduce the scope of surrender; first, limit the time of the therapeutic arrangement and thus the commitment implied, and second, make the desired outcome of the change effort explicit. Resistance is reduced because less conflict of will is generated. Further, when conflict of will does arise, it is more circumscribed and easier to cope with because of the limited scope established in the change contract.

It is important to note that Rank's ideas of will parallel those of Rollo May and other existentialists (May, 1969; May, Angel, & Ellenberger, 1958; Sahakian, 1969). In most models of human functioning, individuals are depicted as striving inwardly for something (e.g., competence, superiority, understanding, or survival of genes). Even conflict theorists such as Freud allow for a life instinct. According to May and other existentialists, these facets are manifested in what is generally called "will."

Will is both the cause and effect of commitment events such as decision making and planning. Trigg (1973) argues that will involves direction toward an object and that it includes impending action. Trigg's theory that commitment comes out of a belief system recalls the cognitive/perceptual models of human functioning as well as existentialism and fulfillment. The reader is reminded that at the beginning of this section commitment was seen to be intimately related to action. Here it is emphasized that commitment is, in essence, the mobilizing, solidifying, and focusing of will.

Rogers' client-centered therapy stresses the goal of patient self-determination through therapist acceptance. In a sense, Rogers has formalized Rank's notion that the key to successful therapy is the avoidance of the conflict of wills. In psychoanalysis, however, this is achieved by therapists restraining their own wills and not imposing them on clients, thus allowing the clients to assert their own wills. The therapist serves as a mirror, not a model. For Rogers, May, and the existentialists in general, commitment is the prerequisite to living actively and avoiding doubts. Commitment precedes true comprehension, not vice versa. To quote Frieda Fromm Reichmann, "the patient needs an experience not an explanation" (Sahakian, 1969, p. 266). Similarly, Kierkegaard asserted that "decision precedes knowledge" (Sahakian, 1969, p. 271), capturing the existential role of decision making in commitment as well as the notion that commitment precedes understanding and change.

Clearly, will and commitment are tightly linked. Various *dominating* wills have been advocated by different theorists. Freud, for example, argues that the will to pleasure dominates. For Adler, it is the will to power, and for Frankl, the will to meaning. At a certain level it does not matter toward what one is committed so long as one is committed. Commitment mobilizes will and creates the potential for action.

Social Psychology. A second perspective on the commitment change process comes from the social psychological tradition and uses the consistency and cognitive/perceptual models of human functioning. Kiesler (1971) reports three alternative explanations for the impact of commitment on individuals. The first centers on the phenomenon of cognitive dissonance avoidance, the second on attributions made by individuals about self and others, and the third on the impact of beliefs.

Dissonance reduction is favored by Kiesler's analysis. Basically the argument holds that any commitment by an individual results in a search for consistency that might result in change to fit the earlier commitment. In an experiment on minimal justification, Kiesler and Sakamura (1966) found that subjects who were paid less money to assert an arbitrarily assigned belief held more tenaciously to that belief in the face of subsequent criticism than did subjects who were paid more. The logic here is that decisions or assertions resulting from less outside pressure generate more dissonance. For the same reason, when individuals invest more effort on an attitude, they experience greater dissonance from later divergencies. Experienced dissonance of divergence is a function of expended effort (Aronson, Carlsmith, & Darley, 1963; Zimbardo, 1965). In short, if individuals can be encouraged to assert an opinion and to work actively for an idea, they will subsequently perform more significant acts to avoid dissonance. Hitler noted in this regard that "fellowship demands only passive appreciation of an idea, while membership demands an active presentation and defense" (Hitler, 1941, p. 849).

The second social psychological mechanism involves H.H. Kelley's (1967) attribution theory and reflects the cognitive/perceptual models of human functioning. Kelley asserts that confidence is based on previous consistency of response and that one infers attitude from one's own and others' response patterns. An act committed is evidence of inner attributes. Thus high energy expenditure can be seen as a chance for the individual to impute self-held attitudes (Kiesler, 1971, pp. 142–143, 173). Similarly, Heider (1958) argues that one's perception of one's self-responsibility is central to commitment. Choices are expressions of self-responsibility and are made to maintain consistency. The more extreme a choice, the stronger the attitude attribution required.

Finally, the third explanation for the holding power of commitment relates to associated beliefs. The stronger the underlying belief, the greater the resistance to attack (Kiesler, Mathog, Pool, & Howenstine, 1971). In an experiment exploring commitment levels, it was seen that forewarning of an upcoming attack on one's beliefs strengthened the more committed person's hold on those beliefs but weakened the hold of uncommitted persons. Here it is implied that the warning leads to a decision to defend or not to defend, which is in fact a specific commitment to the self. In general, the social psychologial perspective has a cognitive, consistency-seeking view of the role of commitment in change and resistance to change that is different from, but not incompatible with, the viewpoints already discussed.

Behaviorism. The third approach to commitment comes from the behaviorists. Very little analysis or discussion of commitment is offered, but the centrality of contractual commitments in behavioristic change efforts is clear (Gambrill, 1977; Krumboltz & Thoresen, 1969, 1976). A few generalizations can be made. First, contracts assume an exchange relation: x cost of change deserves y compensation. Compensation takes the form of the attainment of objectives as well as rewards. Second, the contract establishes the style of interaction and limits the client–helper relationship. Time limits on the contract and careful definition of evaluative methods are established, thus reducing resistance by limiting the scope of the change relationship. Typically, helpers construct guidelines to emphasize overt short-term goals, and give small, immediate reinforcement for accomplishment of goals (Homme, Csanyi, Gonzales, & Rechs, 1969; Patterson, 1971; Thomas, Carter, & Gambrill, 1971; Weathers & Liberman, 1975a, 1975b). The signature of parties is regularly called for on the actual contractual form, which increases the degree of commitment (Gambrill, 1977, p. 143).

In addition, however, even the behaviorists offer supplementary advice that hints at some of the issues already discussed. Gambrill argues for the need of reward contingencies to "secure the clients' involvement" (Gambrill, 1977, p. 77). Thomas (1976) and Thomas, O'Flaherty, and Borkin (1976) argue that contracting helps in the development of planning and decision-making skills, as implied by the existential argument. Dinhoff and Rickard (1969) note that contracts help clients learn that privileges entail responsibilities. Gambrill (1977, p. 398) argues that contracts must be seen as fair by all parties and be entered into in good faith. This is an excellent practical guideline for guaranteeing the personal respect that Rank saw as important in avoiding resistance. The behaviorists use contracts for planning, commitment building, legitimization of a conditioning process, demystification of the helper-client relationship, and development of a sense of responsibility. Again this is not incompatible with all that has been discussed thus far.

As a conclusion to this part of the commitment discussion, it is valuable to note the various approaches to gaining commitment used in a variety of change efforts. Below are five helper interventions listed in an increasing degree of incursiveness on the individual's will. Following the five points, each is explained.

1 Elicit assertion regarding goal, plan, outcome, or impending act.
2 Elicit decision regarding goal, plan, outcome, or impending act.
3 Encourage and evoke redecision regarding goal, plan, outcome, or impending act.
4 Encourage and facilitate temporary regression to child ego state or a symbiotic relationship.
5 Encourage and facilitate a major long-term regression for deep transference identification.

Explanations:

1 Assertion of a goal, plan, outcome, or impending act is the mildest and most limited form of commitment for change. As with the Kiesler experiments, the primary effect of assertion is to strengthen

resolve and mobilize will around the issue, and to reduce vacillation and susceptibility to alternative competing change influences. To be effective the individual must be serious in the assertion.

2 Decision involves goals, plans, and outcomes. Choice makes manifest and strengthens the underlying belief structures, priorities, and self-assessment of desires. According to the existentialists, the key aspect of decision making is confronting ontological fear and acting in the face of it. This confrontation requires an expenditure of energy (Holloway & Holloway, 1973).

   A helper's role in decision making and assertion is primarily to elicit the decision and to aid the individual in seeing the appropriateness or need for a decision (Gambrill, 1967; Krumboltz & Thoresen, 1969, 1976). In transactional analysis this approach is pivotal.

3 Redecision implies more than decision. Here a previous commitment that may have been made long before is reversed (Goulding, 1972). Early life experiences and attributions can be thought of as influences leading to the original decisions individuals make about themselves and how they deal with the world. New behaviors and attitudes may be incompatible with these earlier commitments. A redecision is a new decision that nullifies the old decision and allows change. The helper's job here is to aid the individual in seeing clearly the old decision, through graphic techniques such as psychodrama and sociodrama, and in exploring future ramifications of decision and redecision, through techniques such as fantasy. A climate of support and acceptance that encourages the needed explorations and aids cognitive flexibility are also needed (Goulding, 1972). Ideally, individuals see themselves at the "cutting edge" of time and are able to make clear decisions, taking responsibility for and control of their own lives. Transference would be an impediment to this fundamental goal and is therefore not encouraged. The expanding field of self-management techniques makes considerable use of these first three levels of the commitment change process (Kanfer, 1977, 1978; Schwitzgebel & Kolb, 1974).

4 Cyclical regression refers to temporary regression to earlier times or to more primitive modes of ego functioning where decisions were made and their consequences were felt. Primal therapy, gestalt therapy, and transactional analysis temporarily allow the individual to reexperience the totality of earlier events and patterns of living. When the individual comes back to the present and more mature levels of functioning, additional information and questioning can encourage and allow assertion, decision, and redecision. Here again the helper is a guide for and protector of the regression,

providing advice, issue clarification, and other ego support. Later, individuals make decisions and commitments for themselves that are more productive.

5 Major regression is more substantial than the momentary process just discussed. Major regression occurs slowly and subtly in a psychoanalytic relationship. The object is not to increase the client's immediate responsibility and self-control as in the previous four levels of commitment making; instead, confidence and trust in the therapist cause a gradual surrender of will through emotionally focused discussion. In T.A. terms, the child ego state of the client predominates, but the parent and adult ego states of the helper predominate. Ideally the helper is accepting, noncondemning, analytical, and unemotional. In the long run, the parent and adult ego states of the helper are incorporated by the client through transference (identification). This procedure requires a decision to give up control of one's own life rather than to assert more.

Interactional Perspective

The interactional discussion of commitment focuses on the interpersonal relationships that foster commitment. Such relationships are used to promote change in therapeutic groups, T-groups and many other group settings. Shostrom's 1976 "actualization therapy" provides a useful background conceptualization. He distinguishes between *I–it* relationships (traditional), *it–it* relationships (hedonistic), and *I–thou* relationships (actualizing and existential). Classic psychoanalysis grew out of the medical model and tends toward the I–it arrangement, where the doctor provides what is needed to fix the patient. By contrast, Otto Rank uses overt contracts or commitments to limit the incursion of the doctor's will over the patient's will, and thus is an early advocate of the mutual respect of an I–thou relationship. Carl Rogers and the existentialists extend this notion to emphasize the significance of interpersonal commitment. Faith in self and others is generated by a supportive and accepting relationship. According to this view, individuals attempting to gain control over their own lives should not be coopted. Here established limits on scope and duration of the relationship give the client freedom to choose. In contrast, behaviorists aim to depersonalize the relationship as much as possible, that is, to make the relationship mostly of an it–it (hedonistic) character. Contracts from these three therapeutic orientations might appear very similar, but, because different relationships are cultivated, the meaning of commitment can differ considerably.

T-groups, sensitivity training, and encounter make use of interpersonal relationships in change (Bradford, Gibb, & Benne, 1964; Egan, 1970; Golembiewski & Blumberg, 1970; Schein & Bennis, 1965). The overt contract is for open, honest, confronting relationships that produce intimacy; mutual commitment comes from participants' mutual vulnerability and emotional give and take. Classic psychoanalytic relationships sponsor dependence; existential, T.A., and behaviorist relationships encourage independence, but rely on interdependence. Therefore they pursue more complete, two-sided I–thou relationships than would be expected in therapeutic contexts. Encounter leaders try to create a climate within which intimacy, openness, and mutual commitment spiral and build on one another.

The relationship of commitment to intimacy is an interesting one. Milgram (1963) studied the willingness to coerce and found it inversely related to factors that might relate to intimacy (lack of personal commitment). Subjects were increasingly willing to inflict shocks of up to lethal strength to experimental confederates as the distance between themselves and their victim was increased. If greater distance and less intimacy increase the likelihood of coercion and perception of the relationship as an I–it variety, the opposite, no doubt, is true also. There is inherent commitment in relationships of mutual intimacy. Similarly, Kiesler (1971, p. 129) demonstrates that expectations of future interaction increase interpersonal commitment and commitment to issues attached to the relationship. For example, relationships among individuals of the same religious persuasion might cause those people to remind one another of their commitments and ties to the church.

Finally, commitment can be viewed in interactional terms using the social psychological construct of conformity. Here the channeling forces operate around the group norms and member expectations discussed in Chapter 4. The cohesion of the group, or, alternatively, the attractiveness of the group to the individual, affects conformity directly (Golembiewski, 1962; Kiesler & Kiesler, 1969). At one level this is indicative of members wanting to continue in the group and wanting to receive various benefits from the group. At another level, however, cohesiveness can be viewed as a sense of mutual commitment stemming from attraction and assured future interaction. In brief, channeling is at least partly a function of commitment. This interpretation is reinforced by Festinger, Schachter, and Back (1968), who found that conformity and conformity pressure increase when an issue is perceived as relevant to members. An important challenge to group belief awakens membership commitment, which in turn mobilizes pressure for conformity.

In summary, from the interactional perspective it is seen that depth and meaning of relationships carry the inherent commitment of vulnerability. Therapeutic relationships tend to be one-sided, with the surrender of will and vulnerability highest in the psychoanalytic arrangement and lowest in the behavioristic arrangement. For the behaviorists, contracts legitimize subsequent conditioning, limit the relationship, and avoid resistance. Existential and other modern approaches involve the establishment of a variety of relationships, but in general they tend toward equality while still allowing for one-sided vulnerability. In a sense, the massive support provided by the more intensive change approaches such as psychoanalysis or sensitivity training is the first intervention to elicit trust and openness and to foster the emotional dependence of the participants. Behaviorists tend to abhor this apparently unnecessary and perhaps counterproductive intrusion into self-direction.

Social Perspective

The social perspective offers additional insights into commitment varying from simple to profound. First, the operation of organized life entails an exchange relationship wherein the individual gives cooperation, conformity, and responsiveness in exchange for group benefits, organization, and societal membership. Membership always involves both privileges and responsibilities (Bendix, 1956; Mills, 1967; Ofshe, 1973; Wilensky & Lebeaux, 1965). In addition to being channeled, individuals choose both to take and make certain roles for themselves. In the world of work, modern organizations emphasize division of labor and separation of the individual from the final or complete product. There is a one-sided dependence: individuals depend on the organization far more than the organization depends on a given individual. It is noteworthy that some modern organizational theorists (Pfeffer & Salancik, 1978) virtually equate dependency with forced commitment, implying that the organization gets more commitment than it gives. Professional training, with its inherent costs, can also lead to further work-centered commitment (Wilensky, 1964). But Gouldner (1957) and Pelz and Andrews (1966) point out the dilemma of dual allegiance, wherein commitments to profession and employer are not always compatible.

Whyte (1956) in his classic book, *The Organization Man,* explores other ways in which organizations increase dependency and thus commitment in favor of the organization. Constant moving, for example, is identified as one way competing ties with friends and community could be broken. Training that is directed only to technical skills and pressures to conform to organizational value systems reduce the probability that well rounded, independent thinkers might make awkward choices. According to Whyte the social ethic is replacing the protestant ethic for commitment. Today, organizations like IBM even provide country clubs for managers so that family recreation takes place with other IBM employees, thanks to the graciousness of the "mother" organization. Similarly, large corporations in Japan have a paternalistic tendency with employees who are tightly bound to the organization. This is not a new phenomenon there and commitments are more two-sided than in North America.

Furthermore, increases in leisure time and outside interests, and the concomitant rise of hedonism, actualization, and individualism have broadened the competition for individuals' commitment. Thus organizations are prompted to search for more effective commitment-building tactics. Staw and Ross (1978), Steers (1977), and others have explored attitudinal and behavioral aspects of commitment in organizations. Age, education, ambition, and group attitudes all affect both behavioral and attitudinal commitment. As a prelude to these studies, Porter (1969) and Porter and Smith (1970) pointed out the problem of high performers showing low commitment in some organizations. The key seems to be in the goals of the organization; when they are highly congruent with the individuals' beliefs and priorities and when organizational procedures for rewards are clearly consistent with avowed central goals, commitment will be highest. The mechanism implied is the individual's broad and free choice of an employer from a wide variety of clearly defined and congruently organized alternatives.

This latter point leads to a brief comment on the nature of commitment in society. Bertrand Russell in *Freedom versus Organization* (1962) provides a succinct comparison of totalitarian and democratic societies. The strength of totalitarian societies is their capacity to direct action through conditioning, persuasion, or even coercion if necessary. The strength of democratic societies lies in the people themselves. When people choose leaders there is commitment to follow them, and when they choose to go to war they voluntarily will do things that totalitarian means can never direct. For historians, the capacity to defend national boundaries and unifying ideologies is the bottom line of the survival of political units. For Russell, democratic choice is the best way to build the commitment necessary at this level.

For the most part, commitment has been seen here as a positive force for change. Coser (1974), however, takes a competing view and one which is a worthy qualifier in conclusion. Looking at political loyalty, or commitment, Coser analyzes a variety of institutions, from the church to fifth century Persian, sixteenth century Turkish, and seventeenth and eighteenth century German regimes. In Persia from the time of Xerxes on, eunuchs filled all chief offices of state from advisers to generals. The reason, according to Coser, was relatively simple. Eunuchs were used widely as family servants and guardians so that the ruling family grew up in their trusted presence. No question of dual loyalty (family) need ever arise because of the very nature of a eunuch. Similarly, Lorenzo the Magnificent maintained the Ottoman empire chiefly through the use of Christian Renegades, who were separated from the rest of the population and kept financially dependent on the crown (Coser, 1974). The simple solution to commitment building was to pay the renegade army in cash rather than encourage the development of alternative holdings or income production.

Following the Thirty Years War and the decline of urban centers, the German princes formed coalitions with the outcasts of that society, Jews, to create a governmental apparatus of unconflicted loyalty. Within this structure, a confidential sense of mutual involvement and trust paralleled that of the ruling Persians and eunuchs. Coser's point from all this closely resembles W.H. Whyte's insights in *The Organization Man*. Greedy organizations command extra commitment by entrusting with power only those who lack significant competing loyalties. Further, these loyalties are actively sought through the use of dependency, tactics limiting competitive loyalties, and selection measures. In closed organizations, commitment may well be not the prerequisite but the product of demanding high performance when there is no time for outside activities.

As a final point, it is acknowledged that many commitment tactics are manifestly manipulative. This type of manipulation is assumed to be justified when it is "for their own good." A valuable ethical criterion from the existential therapies suggests cultivating capacities for self-direction and control.

Action

For a number of reasons, the action change process is the ideal topic for concluding Part 1. First, experiential learning is above all an action approach to change. Second, action naturally follows and is tightly linked to commitment. Third, action can be used as a vehicle for making summary comments about other change processes and the models of human functioning.

One general notion central to experiential learning is that an individual learns about an attempted action through effort and the way in which change processes such as feedback and conditioning can be linked to the person's behavior and very being. For example, a student of group psychology may sit, listen, read, write, and take examinations to learn about group processes. Through these procedures, the student could acquire cognitive information about groups but would be likely to learn very little about productive, satisfying, intimate group membership. This requires action in the form of participation in a group. It also demands the provision of linked and organized change influences. According to Wittgenstein, just as commitment precedes understanding, so action precedes personal change.

Four separate forms of action are noteworthy: *exploration, experimentation, practice,* and *performance.* Each form can be either symbolic or manifest. Symbolic action refers to mental processes such as fantasy and focused imagery, and manifest action to all other possibilities. It is immediately acknowledged that there is a fuzzy boundary between manifest activities such as problem solving and symbolic activities such as anticipation. But the distinction is not central to the way in which action affects change and so no further definitional clarity seems necessary at this point.

The four forms of action have implications for all other change processes since the elaboration of each change process is always through action or in juxtaposition to a given action.

Exploration refers to an individual's action in an unknown, ignored, or avoided domain. A highly supportive environment allows behavioral free-dom and encourages reactivity, uncensored responding, and a willingness to "go with the flow" of events. Exploration implies expanded freedom of action and security because of the absence of negative consequences. Old boundaries are transcended; inner processes and desires are allowed to surface and be experienced and externalized; habits are relaxed.

Experimentation is an extension of exploration with the addition of thoughtful analysis and planning. Choices are made between various ac-tion possibilities discovered through exploration activities or stored from previous experience. The choices are in harmony with the individual's total being, and have attendant hypotheses regarding outcomes. Data gathering and analysis must be linked to experimentation, making it more selective, systematic, focused, commitment-requiring, and commitment-building. Commitment marks a crucial difference between experimenta-tion and exploration.

Practice involves the active choice of behaviors possibly identified through exploration and experimentation. In addition to choice, there is the commitment dynamic of persisting in the behavior beyond simple "normal" bounds. Commitment is even more central to practice than to the previous two action modes. Thus practice increases behavioral pro-pensity directly through habituation and skill acquisition, and indirectly through commitment building.

Finally, *performance* involves an even greater commitment to open an action to one's own and other's judgments. It allows comparisons with standards, and invites conditioning even beyond that expected in practice. Self-image is confronted and tested; will is directed not at acquisition and refinement but toward a standard. The effects of other change processes such as feedback are different in performance than in other action modes because of the altered purpose and meaning of the action.

Some individuals consider every action performance in nature and con-sequently are inhibited and afraid of exploration. Others like to experi-ment but avoid making the commitment inherent in performance. Clearly, all learning arrangements need to provide the opportunity for several forms of appropriate action, but further effort must be directed at identifying individual participants' propensities for the different forms of action. For example, high support helps the performer to explore, and various commitment tactics assist the passive and indecisive in directing their energies toward consistent outcomes.

The Argyris theory (1976) and Argyris and Schon's (1974) description of their theory of action in learning is relevant here. They state that educa-tion is a "quest for discovery of the problems and concepts to help students understand and predict them" (Argyris, 1976, p. 653) and they describe the learning cycle in four stages (discover, invent, produce, and general-ize). Their concern is that many change efforts ignore this cycle and their research emphasizes the difficulty of producing invented actions based on discovery. To put this judgment in terms of the concepts in this chapter, many learning situations do not allow for or encourage sufficient exploration and experimentation. There is such an emphasis on performance and performance measurement in learning situations and within the normal population of participants that critical adaptive skills are absent. In fact their model I learning appears to be consistent with our practice and performance notions and they argue that about ninety-five percent of the students they have dealt with are so "locked into" that pattern that the flexibility and openness necessary for the total cycle is simply beyond them. Thus Argyris' call for expanded learning is consistent with this system, which emphasizes the critical importance of exploration and experimentation actions in sponsoring individual change.

The manner in which the four forms of action can be used for each of the other eleven change processes could be discussed more deeply at this point, but it is unlikely that discussion could tie all the change process material together. That task is pursued in an applied way in the analysis of methods in Part 2. As a conclusion to this chapter and to Part 1, comments concerning the relationship between commitment and action are offered, and some bridging notes are made on the models of human functioning in light of the role of action in change.

Commitment and Action

The commitment discussion contains many descriptions of the function of action and references to the pivotal role played by commitment. Commitment focuses the individual's will so that it can be directed toward an action. Figure 6.1 schematically deals with the role of will in the interrelationship of being and action. In the figure the individual is depicted diagramatically in a manner reminiscent of Lewin's use of concentric rings to distinguish among levels of privateness. Perceptions, attitudes, beliefs, and self-image are the layers of the sensory *input side* of the individual. Commitment is the final element of the individual's *output side* where core and other dynamics are translated into overt action. It is implied that reality exists for the individual both at a being and action level. Just as perception is commonly thought of as the "filter" of information affecting the individual's being, so commitment provides the parallel output side function of "transformer" between being and action.

In Figure 6.1, arrow 1 represents the notion that commitment and decision making imply action. Arrow 2 represents the notion that commitment is the prerequisite for living an active, goal-striving life and avoiding doubts (Trigg, 1973).

The tight relationship between action and commitment is further emphasized by "input side" arrows 3 and 4. These acknowledge the discussion of attribution theory in commitment. In brief, a given action accords the individual certain attitudes and beliefs. Arrow 5 allows for cognitive

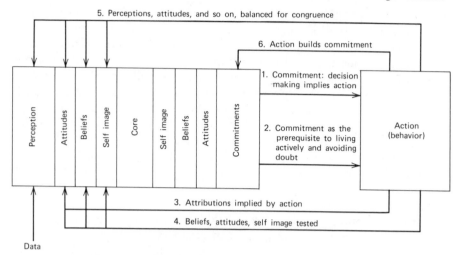

Figure 6.1   The role of commitment in being and action.

congruence-seeking through altered perceptions, beliefs, and self-image; its presence in this model stresses the limitations of cognitive dissonance theory's emphasis on perceptual distortion to deal with congruency seeking. Finally, arrow 6 serves as a reminder that action is fundamental to commitment building. It is the individual's investment of energy as evidenced by the number of acts, their explicitness, irrevocability, and importance, which is shown to generate commitment and to direct will.

It is also useful to note that the core of the person in Figure 6.1 has no arrows directly linked to action. By this it is implied that energy between the core and the external reality is rather "osmotically" or diffusionally related, and that the core is not directly changeable. The behaviorists' stress on observable behavior fits this model's valuing of action as the "window on the individual's world." In contrast, psychoanalytic efforts to penetrate the core do not take advantage of the vital role of action in commitment and thus are less congruent with the emphasis of this chapter.

Models of Human Functioning Revisited

Perhaps the most striking aspect of Figure 6.1 is its usefulness in reviewing the models of human functioning. In the *conflict* models, core, self-image, beliefs, and attitudes all exist in unsteady tension with the perceptual and commitment processes on the boundary of external reality. For *fulfillment*, commitment is the prerequisite to action which in turn is the prerequisite to the continued energizing and actualizing of the being. Core tendencies are "complicated" by beliefs. Congruency-seeking, testing, and attributional dynamics are best understood in the context of the consistency model. Perceptual screening and attendant attitude, belief, and self-image screening of information relate to the cognitive/perceptual models. The attributional arrow in Figure 6.1 is also primarily a cognitive/perceptual element. Qualitatively speaking, half of the individual's reality resides in action, and action must always occur within a context; hence the applicability of the contextual model. For *learning,* one need only reflect that all learning described by the models centers on overt acts and their consequences. Finally, the *life sciences* models, with their concentration on underlying instincts, energizing tendencies, and deep complexities heavily emphasize the core. It serves to aid in appreciating the core as something far beyond a "black box," complexly mediated by the external reality of the world of action.

However, of all models of human functioning, fulfillment highlights the importance of the thought behind Figure 6.1. Gordon Allport (1955), for example, was first to emphasize the importance of action in becoming a person. It was he who labeled action as the essence of existence and passivity as the essence of sickness. Similarly, existential psychologists like Rollo May (May et al., 1958) and countless others emphasize action in actualization, building on Kierkegaard's philosophical thesis that, ultimately, reality is totally a function of one's own acts. More specifially he stated, "Truth exists only as the individual himself produces it in action." A similar remark, central to Carl Rogers' philosophy, is used to begin Chapter 8. All in all, this discussion underscores the total and overwhelming importance of action to the experiential approach to learning.

The next step is to convert this information about change into a practical understanding of actual experiential learning activities. This goal is addressed in Part 2.

PART TWO

Applications

*Many persons might have
achieved wisdom had they
not supposed that they already possessed it.*

Seneca

Part 2 focuses on the actual use of experiential techniques in learning. Chapter 7 provides a practical description of the phases or sequence of events that constitute an entire experience. These are addressed under the headings planning, introduction, activity, debriefing, summary, and evaluation. Chapters 8, 9, and 10 contain descriptions and analyses of sixteen major teaching methods widely used in the field; these are grouped as central methods, classical methods, and supporting methods (Bligh, Ebrahim, Jacques, & Piper, 1975; Boocock & Schild, 1968; Brown, Lewis, & Harcleroad, 1973; Gage, 1976; Gage & Berliner, 1975; Hyman, 1974; Kemp, 1975; McKeachie, 1969; McLeish, 1968; Wittich & Schuller, 1973). In these chapters, each method is described in detail before material from Part 1 is brought to bear in the analysis.

Chapter 11 provides twelve dimensions that are guidelines for designing and conducting experiential learning activities and a simple decision-making model to aid in design. Some common issues encountered in using a wide variety of methods are discussed, and resolutions of dilemmas are suggested. Finally, Chapter 12 discusses the ethics of experiential learning, offers a "protected goods" approach to the issue, and provides an exploration of four key future directions.

CHAPTER SEVEN

Phases of the Learning Experience

*An acre in Middlesex is
better than a principality
in Utopia. The smallest
actual good is better than
the most magnificent
promises of
impossibilities.*

Francis Bacon

The six phases that are used to describe experiential learning are *planning, introduction, activity, debriefing, summary,* and *evaluation.* Aspects of this general sequence have been proposed for use in a variety of instructional situations (Davis & McCallon, 1974; Gagne, 1970, p. 304; Houle, 1972; Knowles, 1970, p. 297). Of particular interest are the key events in each phase, the roles and responsibilities of leaders and participants, and effects of specific leader and participant actions.

Planning

Planning has two components: the decision making regarding the design of the learning experience and the preparation for the specific components of that experience. Planning involves identifying learning needs, assessing leader capabilities and supporting resources, budgeting, establishing appropriate objectives, and designing and selecting suitable activities (Davis & McCallon, 1974; Knowles, 1970). The dimensions in Chapter 11 provide a detailed guide for planning.

The significance of preparation can be overlooked because of its simplicity. Often, experiential leaders can become overconcerned with process and interpersonal issues and assume that all necessary preparation is implicit in their own personal capacities. Similarly, classical leaders, over time, rely on their mastery of a content area and less and less preparation is deemed necessary. In reality, experiential learning requires a great deal of preparation well in advance of the event, including duplicating handouts, arranging for desired visual aids, checking room arrangements, and having all required materials on hand. Murphy's Law ("If anything can possibly go wrong, it will, and at the worst time") is particularly applicable to experiential learning. The remedies are double checking and having backup activities, two obvious actions that increase leader confidence and reduce distracting tension. The risk of technological catastrophy appears to increase geometrically with technological complexity. For example, a videotape recording and playback arrangement is many times more likely to break down than just a playback arrangement, and when a number of videotape units are used simultaneously, malfunction is almost inevitable. Many leaders unnecessarily let these risks inhibit their use of experiential technology.

Whenever feasible, it is also desirable to provide participants with an understanding of the learning experience prior to their involvement. The more likely that a learning situation will contain surprises, the more is this forewarning needed. For example, if partial or complete disrobing is part of a learning activity, participants should know this in advance rather than being confronted with the choice during the introduction of the learning experience or, worse, after they have become involved.

Some leaders attempt to compensate for lack of planning and preparation by relying on past successes, their personal charisma, and on the passivity and cooperativeness of participants. Subsequent emotional dynamics can erode the learning climate for participants and make thinking and taking corrective action nearly impossible for leaders.

Preparation without planning is generally the consequence of merely repeating past successes or attempting to "cook book" a workshop. Again, leader charisma can make such a prepackaged effort a superficially successful "dog and pony show." These leaders generally receive a great deal of praise for their excellent teaching and they naturally assume that participants have experienced correlative learning. Other leaders with less ability and charisma tend not to fair as well as they plug in their module and grind out the day. Either way, learning is seldom maximized by the prepackaged approach. Similarly, the absence of systematic preparation generally results in disorder and confusion and ultimately the expenditure of large amounts of energy that could have been directed toward learning.

Absence of backup activities when Murphy's Law intervenes can be even more important than the above. A two-hour hole in a two day workshop is painful and can overwhelm all other factors.

Introduction Phase

The introduction phase refers to two separate procedures: the general comments made at the beginning of any learning experience and the specific instructions that are given prior to an activity within that experience. The introduction to the total experience addresses themes, identifies and establishes participant expectations, and initiates desired social norms for learning. Introductions to specific activities are quite different. These include describing the activity, clarifying participant responsibilities, and making role assignments.

The *introduction to the total experience* is the first face-to-face opportunity leaders have to begin creating the desired learning climate and to make manifest the results of their planning and preparation. Their actions at this point set the tone for the entire experience (Knowles, 1970, p. 271). Important themes include involvement versus passivity, openness to experience and risk taking, process orientation, and leader and member responsibilities.

Learning through involvement has a "self fulfilling prophecy" quality in that leaders might say to participants:

> If you take a wait and see attitude and sit back, not becoming engaged in the activities, at the end of the experience you will say to yourself anything from "that was not too bad but I did not learn much" to "that was a complete waste of time!" On the other hand, if you become involved the odds are that your efforts will be rewarded and your reactions will be more in the order of "that was really enjoyable, I learned something!"

The leader can communicate this theme experientially as well as through verbal descriptions. Having participants introduce each other is one example of how involvement can be initiated and foreshadowed.

A second theme, *openness to experience,* implies not hiding behind defensive critical judgments of the proposed activities prior to their occurrence. This can be described to the participants as the "principle of suspended judgment" which states that learning is inhibited if energy is invested in a critical evaluation of the experience rather than in becoming involved. The participants are asked to trust the leaders' choices and decisions and suspend judgment until after the particular activity has been completed. A second component of openness and risk taking is for participants to be willing to give and receive feedback and to be as authentic as possible in the exchange.

In most lectures and seminars, *process* is never overtly considered but in experiential learning it is an integral part of the experience. Attending to process is important because the process, and not the content, often provides the most significant contributions to learning. In addition, a process focus further legitimizes the principle of suspended judgment by placing importance on going with the flow of the experience and considering for analysis the total experience rather than its individual components.

In a learning experience based on orthodox assumptions, an exercise is seen only as an illustration of a concept and the process generated by the activity is rarely considered in the discussion. Here, activities have content but no process functions. In experiential learning, however, the process generated by activities has much broader purposes and is often the lesson itself. Here content often serves the function of helping participants to organize and comprehend the significance of the processes they have experienced.

Responsibility for learning falls on the shoulders of participants as well as those of the leaders. It is useful to address this issue directly during the introduction. A mechanism is a psychological contract in which participants assert responsibility for voicing their needs and asking questions when something is not clear in exchange for the leader's agreement to be responsive to those requests and to meet them whenever possible. A colorful contract offered by one leader is: "I will not play Sir Lancelot if you will not play possum!" This refers to situations in which leaders see themselves as knights on white horses dispensing truth to the unwashed while many participants hope either to be cleansed magically or at least to escape the experience unscathed. Leader behavior displayed and participant actions evoked through the contracting process create norms that tend to last throughout the entire experience. Actions speak louder than words.

Another important part of introducing the experience is generating and *sharing* participants' *expectations.* Many facets of the participants' expectations have already been dealt with in the discussion of themes, but it is also desirable to have participants make their expectations overt in some systematic way. This provides the leader with valuable information for activity selection, pacing, and debriefing. Further, the sharing itself contributes to the desired group climate. It emphasizes participant involvement and clarifies for everyone what the starting point of learning is for the group. Finally, it provides a benchmark against which learning can be assessed at the end of the experience. The method of sharing expectations can vary depending on the size of the group. All participants first can be asked to list their expectations and then these can be shared individually if the group is small, or, if the group is larger, participants can form small groups to generate lists to be shared with the entire group.

When themes are not presented or are presented vaguely or ambiguously, participants face uncertainty, and this produces anxiety. Anxiety is accompanied by confusion and both of these emotional consequences increase "risk-avoidance" behavior and reduce involvement. In contrast, when too much time is spent lecturing on themes with little or no time for participant involvement, norms of passivity can become dominant.

Allocating insufficient time to the introduction can also inhibit participant involvement. If a one-hour lecture is followed by only five minutes of expectation sharing instead of fifteen to thirty minutes, participants learn that their involvement in the learning experience is not really important. A second problem area is the inappropriate choice of introductory activities in terms of length, complexity, and the degree to which they are confrontive or require personal disclosure. Too much too soon inevitably generates a great deal of fear and antagonism and is the most destructive error that can be committed in this phase. Consequently, the choice regarding the optimal amount of personal sharing is difficult, because without some immediate sharing, an essential group norm may never be generated effectively.

In addition to the general introduction, each learning activity requires specific orienting comments. The *introduction to a specific activity* is a relatively brief but essential task having a number of important elements. The first is describing the activity in sufficient detail to link it to the objectives and to give an overview that aids participants in organizing the experience in their minds. When too much detail is provided at the beginning of an activity, participants are often confused and may experience anxiety at wondering what to do or what will be expected of them. At a certain point participants' attempts to comprehend the detail compete with their ability to become involved, and, rather than respond naturally to the experience, they try to second guess what might occur or attempt to integrate the concepts with the experience prematurely. Too few instructions leave participants wondering what to do or where to go.

The second element is clarifying participant responsibilities. Clear, specific instructions are important here as is being directive and getting the activity under way smartly. Attempts to be overly participative by encouraging contributions and influence during this phase can result in failure to generate the momentum and organization necessary to initiate the activity. Participants can experience anxiety, frustration, irritation, and annoyance, because it appears that the leader is disorganized or possibly incompetent. They may lose faith that something good will happen. In contrast, the overly directive leader misses opportunities to attend to the emotional needs of participants and to clarify areas of confusion. As a result, participants can feel unimportant or coerced.

Other specific introduction items include making specific role assignments, eliciting requests for clarification, stimulating participant attention to subsequent instructions, and encouraging them to deal constructively with their feelings. Further, participants can be encouraged to articulate needs when appropriate. It is also important to provide simple reminders about themes such as the principle of suspended judgment. Finally, this is the point at which participants are moved clearly and directly into the needed configuration for the activity.

Activity Phase

The end of the introduction overlaps with the beginning of the activity phase. *Mechanical aspects* of conducting the activity include matters related to materials, physical space, and arrangement of participants. The availability of all necessary materials and their orderly distribution before and during the activity contribute to a sense of organization and provide the participants with cues to the appropriate behaviors for the commencing subphase of the activity. Equally tangible is the physical configuration of the participants. Many activities require specific accommodating physical spaces and strategies for moving participants in them.

Instructions have sequencing and timing components. First, sequencing requires that the leader understand and recall the instructions in the correct order for a given activity. Second, it is often desirable to give the participants a sense of the sequence of the subphases within the activity to reduce their uncertainty. Third, specific instructions should be provided at key moments between subphases to move participants smoothly into a new subactivity.

For timing or pacing, three points deserve emphasis. First, giving participants expectations about the amount of time allocated to the activity can contribute to their sense of organization and help them pace themselves. Second, adjusting the time in terms of the rate at which groups work on a task is important. This includes asking if more time is needed and providing it if necessary. The third is making participants aware when the end of the available time is approaching so that undealt with material can be surfaced or closure can be achieved. What is emphasized in these points is leader efforts to aid participants in managing their learning.

Important leader and participant behaviors during the activity phase include leader involvement and attending as well as the responsibilities of both leaders and participants throughout the activity. Involvement here refers to the extent to which leaders become actively engaged with participants in the task and not to their apparent interest in or concern for the participants themselves. Attending refers to observing, sensing, and listening to participants' needs and reactions resulting from their involvement in the activity. Overly involved and overly attending leaders are experienced as "meddling" by participants, and with low attending, the leader becomes a "distractor" and, in extreme cases, a "bungler." Leaders who are low in involvement and attending lose touch with participant dynamics and lack the necessary information to make process adjustments. They behave irresponsibly. The desired condition is for leaders to attend to but not to interfere with task activities. Leaders should be available to answer questions and make adjustments, but to be truly "responsible" they must do more.

Responsibilities

Leaders need to maintain an *awareness* of their own and others' needs and feelings and understand change dynamics. A lack of awareness results in inadequate information for responsible action, and too great an awareness has the potential of cluttering the leaders' minds and confounding their ability to act effectively.

Action consists of operationalizing the mechanical aspects needed and generating and maintaining participant concentration on the relevant facets of the activity. This concentration is facilitated by leaders adopting roles compatible with the theme of the activity. This role might be symbolic of a key emotional aspect of the activity. For example, in an interpersonal conflict exercise the leaders may role model a combative or aggressive stance that participants are encouraged to adopt. Other concentration-facilitating leader behaviors are captured in descriptive terms such as coaching, encouraging and supporting, energizing, and even cheerleading in addition to basic responsiveness and attending.

Participant responsibilities in the areas of awareness, action, concentration, and responsiveness are also important. The development of awareness by participants takes significant effort and a willingness to challenge their psychological defenses. Openness contributes to awareness, both directly and through feedback. Action includes following the instructions, becoming involved in the activity, and assuming necessary roles. To do so may require combating feelings of passivity and withdrawal, suspending judgment, and taking risks. The second component of participants' action is coping with stimuli generated by the activity and remaining responsible for themselves during this coping.

Concentration refers to efforts to avoid being distracted from the central theme of the activity and to avoid distracting others. Responsiveness implies participants' receptivity to the activity, the other participants, and the leader for the purpose of enhancing their own learning. However, participant responsiveness does not imply the same degree of interpersonal responsiveness and competence as that required of the leader.

Possible Inadequacies

Inadequacies during the activity phase are less problematic than those discussed for the earlier two phases. In short, conducting the activity is easier than planning or introducing it; however, some inadequacies do exist. Missing or incomplete material or instructions reduce the organization, and the activity may never get off the ground. Similarly, when material and instructions are present but are fragmented and disorganized, participants often become confused and frustrated. Fast pacing limits involvement because participants feel rushed and the activity is not given sufficient time to have an impact. Pacing that is too slow reduces involvement and concentration. The process wanders. Participants feel harried and inadequate in the former and bored in the latter. It has been our observation over the years that most inexperienced leaders underestimate the needs of participants and tend to pace the activities too fast, sometimes by 200 to 500 percent rather than simply 10 or 20 percent. An example is alloting 10 minutes to a group task when 30 minutes is needed.

The behavioral consequences of leader task overinvolvement or lack of attending have been identified. The "meddler" frustrates participants and undermines their sense of responsibility for their own learning. The "bungler" not only frustrates but also irritates or angers participants who either withdraw or become aggressive and lose confidence in the leader's ability to manage the situation. The "irresponsible" leader leaves some participants feeling unimportant or vulnerable or both. Further, a very real danger exists here that destructive situations will develop and go unnoticed. The primary effect is for participants to hold back from the experience, consequently curtailing their future learning.

If individual participants lack the energy or willingness to get involved, the learning experience can stagnate or possibly stop completely. Second, if participants are not responsive to instructions or to the activity, things can get sidetracked. Criticism can confuse and frustrate and, in the extreme, can immobilize other participants and evoke defensiveness in the leader. Risk avoidance reduces openness. It is an error to believe that the activity is learning. If learning is likened to the process of making flour, then participants' feelings and behaviors are the grain and the activity is the millstone. Conducting an activity without participant risk taking is like trying to make flour without grain.

The activity phase is pivotal to the learning experience. Here successful planning and introduction come to fruition and the personalized information is generated for consideration in the debriefing and summary phases. Without these latter two phases, activities merely stimulate participants, generate random data, and serve as little more than entertainment.

Debriefing

Debriefing is primarily a discussion of the completed activity and provides detail, order, and meaning to the participants' experiences. It is easy to underestimate this highly critical phase and thus move prematurely toward closure and the summary phase. This discussion of the debriefing phase considers content, process, and generalization aspects of the learning; issues of participant-centered versus leader-centered approaches to the procedure; and, finally, inadequacies.

The content–process distinction is highlighted and takes on new significance in the debriefing phase. The content of the activity consists of the subject and the techniques used to illustrate it. Generally, the techniques are vivid for participants at this point, and often they need an opportunity to talk about them; the amount of attention paid to the content depends on the type of the learning experience.

The debriefing of process can be divided into three modes: feedback, sharing, and reactions to feedback and sharing. Leader interventions here include allocating time, suggesting guidelines as to how participants might proceed with the debriefing, setting a responsive and open tone, modeling the giving of feedback, and cueing the observers through specific questions or focusing comments.

Feedback comes from those performing an observer role for an activity, from other participants, and, to a limited extent, from the leader. Constructive feedback is specific, based on behavioral observations, nonevaluative, and provided in such a way that its recipients can incorporate the information into their own experiences (see Chapter 2). Sharing combines self-disclosure with listening, reveals subjective impressions, personalizes the experience, and generates support. Exchanging reactions to the feedback and sharing underscores the importance of openness and keeps the debriefing on track. Finally, in debriefing, generalizations from the activity to other situations or issues can be made.

Responsibilities

Leaders need to provide adequate organization for the debriefing such as a topic outline of points to be discussed. Further, if reactions to the experience are important and sharing among a large number of people is desired, the leader's personal involvement can elicit this information much more quickly and effectively than can structured techniques. Leader attention aids in creating a congruent summary for participants and helps the planning of future activities. It is the responsibility of the leader to build a bridge between the debriefing and summary by presenting ideas and concepts that foreshadow the summary and by extracting key participant responses. Leader support is always useful.

During the debriefing, participants are responsible for giving feedback if they were observers and for sharing reactions to the experience and the feedback if they were in the activity. By seeing the debriefing as an important part of their learning they are expected to invest energy in the discussion and ask questions of the leader when they need clarification.

Possible Inadequacies

Inadequacies of procedure, time, and process are noteworthy items here. Possible procedural inadequacies include too little or too much sharing and feedback, a preponderance of trivial or destructive information, and disorganization. Without feedback and sharing, group *esprit de corps* and support fail to materialize and the information and energy generated in the activity are dissipated. Too much feedback or feedback on too many issues can create confusion, reduce involvement, and inhibit support. In the destructive case, participants can be hurt or frightened by other participants, causing them to withdraw. A final procedural inadequacy is disorganization. A break for lunch or coffee between the activity and the debriefing phase can fragment the learning experience. Not only is the emotional momentum for debriefing reduced but also the specific feelings and reactions related to the activity are more difficult to recall. Thus giving feedback, deriving meaning from the feedback, and sharing and exchanging reactions are all impeded.

When insufficient time is allocated to the debriefing, participants are stopped "just when they get going." Much of the best part of the learning experience is thrown away and can result in resentment toward the leader and wariness toward becoming involved in the remainder of the learning experience. This is probably the most common way in which lecturers and more directive experiential leaders violate participation. When in doubt, allow more time. In the extreme, when little or no time is allowed for debriefing, there is a qualitatively different result. Learning objectives are not linked to the activity and the entire experience is seen as either irrelevant but enjoyable or silly and a waste of time.

The final possible inadequacy involves failing to develop the appropriate content or process emphasis during debriefing. Participants can spend time discussing the mechanics, intricacies, or even irrelevancies of the activity and never address any of the salient issues. Leader involvement and direction on this issue is critical. In general, debriefing provides information and mental clarification and facilitates acquisition and retention. It also increases the probability that future learning endeavors will be productive.

Summary Phase

The summary phase, like the introduction, involves both the specific activity and the entire experience. For both types of summary the primary task is to assist participants in increasing their storage and recall of the learning achieved in the preceding phases and in developing cognitive structures for organizing and giving meaning to the experience.

The summary of a *specific activity* has several important components. The first is highlighting and giving perspective to the content and process issues most central to the learning objectives. The second is integrating theoretical and empirical research with the participants' experiences in the learning situation. The third is building generalizations about the learning and exploring possible applications in an effort to give additional meaning and value to the completed activity. Leader and participant roles during this phase appear very similar to those in a lecture; however experiential leaders also share their feelings and reactions with participants, and any lecture material should be linked closely to participant experiences. Further, brevity is desirable since the experience has already provided the explanation. Flexibility and responsiveness to participants' requests for elaborations are invaluable, even when they deviate from "the prepared text" or are difficult to relate closely to a solid discipline source.

No other phase requires more active leader behavior than the summary phase. Since adequate planning provides the basis for substantive comments and the leader's attending behavior during the activity and debriefing identifies specific linkage points, the summary confronts the final challenge of putting it all together. Participants need to share reactions, ask necessary questions, and attempt to integrate the ideas with the experience.

The *summary of an entire learning experience* is concerned with the integration of the learning experience and the transfer of salient learning to other settings and situations. As a caution, leaders can highlight the differences between the culture created in the learning environment and the culture of the back home setting. For example, focusing on and dealing with feelings is central to many experiential learning activities, but in normal work environments such direct expressions are rarely considered legitimate. They can make the individual appear self-centered; they can threaten and intimidate others; they can expose vulnerabilities to others motivated to hurt the individual; and they can generally diminish and detract from the tasks of a work organization. Further, the typical learning situation provides much greater support for emotional expression and behavioral experimentation than does a work organization. In a learning environment, there is a similarity of expectations among participants that is not to be found in outside groups. Other transfer aids are establishing goals, planning, and contracting. A buddy system for sustained support is timely. Additional advice on where, when, and how behavioral experimentation is appropriate, feasible, and safe is also useful. A warning to the wise is that when the meaning and significance of terms are not known by others, the participants' new learnings appear to others as mere labeling and jargon and are alienating.

Possible Inadequacies

As for each of the preceding phases, there are consequences for learning if errors or omissions are committed in the summary phase. If the summary is omitted or performed in a perfunctory manner, participants are deprived of an opportunity to reflect on and integrate the experience, and this absence is often accompanied by inadequate debriefing time. The emotional consequences for participants can vary from mild confusion or frustration to disdain and disillusionment. All these feelings tend to reduce involvement over time, either mildly or dramatically, with corresponding effects on learning. A lack of perceived relevance provides a focal point for other dissatisfactions and can be used to justify avoiding future involvement. Insufficient conceptual linking can have similar consequences.

The second issue is the leader's openness. Because leaders must address questions and challenges and deal openly not only with participants' feelings but also with their own, interpersonal competence is critical in the summary. Refusal to deal with these issues can leave participants feeling violated. If leaders address these questions in a closed and incongruent manner, participants are left suspicious and wary. These feelings can lead to withdrawal or to aggressive attacks on the leader and the experience. The credibility of the leader and the experience and even experiential learning in general is eroded and the energy shifts away from the planned learning objectives.

The third issue, the transfer and application of learned material to back home problems and situations, is always difficult and deserves significant effort. Inadequacies in dealing with the transfer of learning can be considered within three broad categories of effects: suboptimizing, naive, and evangelical responses.

The most common response to the absence of addressing transfer issues is a suboptimized participant reentry into the back home environment. Upon returning from the class or workshop, participants may experience frustration and disappointment because their new skills or ideas do not work outside the learning situation. Consequently they shed their newly acquired behavior.

However, leader errors or omissions concerning transfer can be potentially more damaging. Naive participants assume that there are no problems associated with directly applying the new learning and are unaware that neither they nor the environment are ready for the impending confrontation. Good intentions cannot replace a clear set of guidelines for applying new skills. When rejection, humiliation, and exploitation occur, the entire learning approach is discredited. Paradoxically, these circumstances seldom come to the leader's attention. In some circumstances leaders may feel an unqualified sense of success when participants ultimately experience profound failure.

In the absence of guidelines, some participants may respond evangelically, trying to convince everyone that they are right. They force their ideas on their situation, use labels or jargon, and fail to respond to the impact they are having on their environment. They become intolerant, critical, and demanding of others, which can have a number of detrimental effects on the way others view them and the learning experience. Because of this reaction, the evangelists never complete the final stage in the learning and remain insensitive to feedback from their environment. Even in the more simple case of merely undeveloped, nonspecific, or unrealistic goals, participants may feel overwhelmed by the difficulty of implementing their learning upon reentry and may feel isolated in the absence of the support of the group. They can withdraw from the challenge of establishing a set of realistic goals and consequently apply their learning in a haphazard manner at best.

Evaluation

Evaluation can be defined as the efforts taken by the leader to determine the effectiveness of the learning experience. The evaluation can be of a single activity or of the entire experience. The placement of this phase at the end of the sequence does not imply that evaluation only occurs at the end of one or a group of learning activities. Evaluation is an ongoing concern that must be considered first during the planning phase. There are many excellent discussions of the theory behind and implementation of evaluation procedures (Bloom, Hastings, & Madaus, 1971; Kirkpatrick, 1975; Steele, 1973; Tuckman, 1979). Greenfield (1978) has compiled an annotated bibliography of twenty-three major references in evaluation, and the reader is referred to these sources for a thorough treatment of the subject. The purpose of this discussion is to highlight the importance of evaluation as a part of experiential learning by looking at some general issues related to evaluation and identifying some guidelines for leaders to use in their evaluation efforts.

The first issue concerns whether the evaluation is formative or summative (Bloom, Hastings, & Madaus, 1971; Scriven, 1967). Formative evaluation refers to efforts during a learning experience to make ongoing changes in that experience to improve its effectiveness. Summative evaluation refers to efforts at the end of a learning experience to determine the extent to which learning objectives have been achieved.

The second issue concerns whether information is gathered formally or informally (West & Foster, 1976). The formal gathering of information involves the use of questionnaires, surveys, or other standardized measures. The use of formal procedures requires that they be developed or selected during the planning phase of the learning experience. The informal gathering of information occurs through casual or spontaneous conversation, solicited or unsolicited participant comments, and leader observations of the learning experience. An informal approach to evaluation typically is unplanned.

The two issues can be used to form a 2 × 2 table to identify four broad types of evaluation (Figure 7.1). Formal formative evaluation (Cell I) is comprised of planned procedures to gather information used to make adjustments to the learning experience or to provide feedback to participants while the activities are in progress. An example is assigning trained observers to monitor a group's interaction using a behavior checklist or some other standardized instrument or procedure. The information then can be used to alter the design of future activities for the group and to

	Formative	Summative
Formal	Cell I	Cell II
Informal	Cell III	Cell IV

Figure 7.1   Types of evaluation.

provide participants with feedback as to how to improve their learning.

Formal summative evaluation (Cell II) is comprised of planned procedures to determine whether the learning objectives of the experience have been achieved or to assess other consequences of the learning experience at or after its conclusion. For education, if the acquisition of information was the objective, then procedures requiring participants to demonstrate their knowledge would be used. If the purpose of the learning experience was to provide participants with skills, then simulated or real activities could be used to check if participants can perform the desired behaviors. If the purpose of the learning experience was to change the participants' attitudes or feelings, then these areas could be examined systematically to see if changes had occurred.

Informal formative evaluation (Cell III) is comprised of information that leaders receive simply because they are present in the learning experience. They might observe that a large number of participants cannot perform a given task, or they might be told in response to a question that an activity is too difficult, confusing, or really terrific! Most of the ongoing adjustments that leaders make during an activity are based on this type of evaluation.

Informal summative evaluation (Cell IV) is comprised of information leaders receive at the conclusion of the learning experience that they can use to determine whether the experience has been successful. These data include reports from participants concerning their reactions to the activities and situations in which they have applied the concepts and skills addressed.

A third evaluation issue is the degree of objectivity of the information used. Information at the objective end of the continuum is observable, verifiable, and relatively free from bias. Examples are questions dealing with the acquisition of knowledge, physical measures such as weight, or measurable performance on a given task. Information at the subjective end of the continuum is based on opinion, perception, and feeling. By definition it is biased and its true meaning cannot be readily verified. Examples are self-reports regarding reactions to material learned in a situation or participant observations of other participants' behaviors. Both objective and subjective information belong in an evaluation, and information gathered through formal means such as questionnaires tends to be more useful (Kirkpatrick, 1976).

Perhaps the issue of greatest importance is what specifically is to be evaluated. Participants' reactions, learning, behavior, and results are four distinguishable items (Kirkpatrick, 1976). Reactions refer to participants' emotional responses or attitudes toward the learning experience and, as noted earlier, are often the only thing "evaluated," especially in experiential circles. Learning refers to knowledge and skills that participants acquire. Behavior refers to the transfer of the material learned to settings away from the learning experience. Results refer to outcomes such as more rapid career progression, reduced absenteeism, or increased profits attributed to the learning program.

In addition, Smith, Neisworth, and Greer (1978) and Tuckman (1979) urge that the contributions of all aspects of the instructional milieu be considered in an evaluation. These components include the instructional program or methods (structure), the leader, the participants, the subject or content, and the environment (setting and climate). In general, it seems apparent that this level of evaluating a learning experience contributes to the variety of perspectives available in the evaluation and thus increases its potency and potential usefulness.

The procedures for evaluation vary, but a number of simple guidelines are noteworthy. Four steps in any evaluation are: (1) identify the objectives of the experience and state them in a measurable form; (2) design a program that will function so as to meet the objectives; (3) identify the kinds of information to be gathered and develop instruments or procedures to obtain it; and (4) assess participant change and the program's strengths and weaknesses in achieving its intended objectives. Further details and statistical procedures related to conducting evaluations are widely available (Fink & Kosecoff, 1978; Morris & Fitz-Gibbon, 1978; Tuckman, 1979).

Much of the evaluation that usually occurs in experiential learning is informal. The challenge is to use more formal means of formative and summative evaluation and to systematize informal evaluation efforts. One step in this direction in terms of formal evaluation is to invest much more energy in stating the objectives for the experience. To be effective, the nature and details of the evaluation must be considered during the planning phase. Evaluation is easier when objectives are overt, comprehensive, and detailed. This topic is treated thoroughly in Chapter 11 under the heading "Types, Purposes, and Objectives." Readers do not have to be experts in statistics and research design to evaluate their efforts (Thomas & Friedman, 1978) and can benefit from using a variety of approaches.

Chapter 11 elaborates a pragmatic conceptual system of informal evaluation that is useful for analyzing and organizing the complex processes that occur in experiential learning in such a manner that ongoing adjustment is possible.

Conclusion

Emotions and behaviors are the greatest source of informal evaluative judgments, and some salient points from this chapter can now be systematized. The level of energy, the feelings participants hold about themselves as they enter the experience, and the feelings generated in response to the learning experience are three important factors. The interaction of these three factors dramatically affect participant behaviors. An array of possible correlative behaviors resulting from these interactions are identified in Figure 7.2. The figure distinguishes among low, moderate, and high levels of energy. Low levels relate to passive behavior and high levels relate to active behavior. Each energy category is paired with a positive and a negative emotional state. A positive state means the participants' involvement in the learning experience is not contaminated by other issues in their lives and they react favorably. Their anxiety is relatively low, and they can concentrate on the activities. A negative state means participants are preoccupied or upset and these feelings compete with involvement. Unfavorable expectations toward the experience may exist and anxiety is relatively high. These conditions exist independent of the learning experience and are brought to it by the participants.

Once in the experience, participants have a broad range of emotional reactions to the specific events that occur. Some of the more common feelings are happiness, confusion and frustration, disappointment, fear, and anger. Just as participants' feelings toward specific activities change, their energy levels and emotional states vary. Consequently, any participant is capable of a wide range of reactions within a given experience.

Several of the behavioral descriptions in the cells in Figure 7.2 require some explanation. One of the most common undesirable participant reactions is withdrawal from the learning experience. This withdrawal takes many forms. In Figure 7.2 the term "detaching" refers to participants

Energy Level/Emotional State

Feelings generated by experience	Positive emotional state		Negative emotional state	
	High to Moderate Energy	Moderate to Low Energy	Low to Moderate Energy	Moderate to High Energy
Anger	Aggresive challenging, demanding clarification or changes, describing feelings	Behaving in a distracting manner and/or disengaging	Behaving in a distracting manner and/or withdrawing	Hostile, aggressive attacking and/or total withdrawing
Fear	Requesting clarification and reassurance, describing feelings, seeking peer and leader support	Seeking support and/or disengaging	Withdrawing	Aggressive attacking, withdrawing
Dissappointment	Questioning the experience, attempting to solve or work through problems	Behaving in a distracting manner and/or disengaging	Withdrawing	Aggressive challenging, discounting, and/or withdrawing
Confusion and /or Frustration	Asking for clarification, attempting to solve or work through problems	Behaving in a distracting manner and/or disengaging	Behaving in a distracting manner, disengaging	Aggressive challenging, discounting, and/or withdrawing
Happiness and/or Contentment	Participating enthusiastically, actively engaging in activities, open, lively	Participating pensively, contemplatively	Participating partially, detaching somewhat	Participating but distractedly

Key:

☐ = Zone I   ▦(vertical lines) = Zone III

☰(horizontal lines) = Zone II   ▦(grid) = Zone IV

Figure 7.2 Typical participant behaviors resulting from various feeling, energy level, emotional state combinations.

175

becoming uninvolved in a specific activity for a finite amount of time. This is the mildest form of withdrawal and is focused away from the current activity. For example, a participant that does not like solving puzzles might become detached from that particular task but become immediately reinvolved in the next task. The term "disengaging" refers to more substantial withdrawal from the learning experience. Here participants not only question their involvement in a specific activity but also begin to insulate themselves from the entire experience. For example, if a group discussion becomes too personal, some participants might begin to question the validity of their involvement in the entire learning experience. As a result they disengage. The term "withdrawing" is used to signify those situations in which participants psychologically or physically remove themselves completely from the learning experience. This includes even getting up and leaving! In Figure 7.2 the use of the term "withdrawing" implies that all three responses are possible; "disengaging" means that only the first two kinds of withdrawal are likely; "detaching" indicates that the more extreme forms of withdrawal will probably not occur for that cell. Thus leaders can attend to both emotional and behavioral issues to maximize their effectiveness in making informal formative evaluations and in acting on these evaluations.

The cells toward the top right of the figure represent increasingly disruptive reactions to the learning experience. Additional order is provided to the matrix by grouping the cells together in terms of the disruptive potential of the behaviors within them. These groupings or zones are represented by different codes: a blank space represents no disruption, or the entirely positive condition (Zone I); horizontal lines represent mild disruption, a somewhat positive condition due to activation (Zone II); vertical lines represent moderate disruption, or the somewhat negative condition (Zone III); and vertical and horizontal lines represent extreme disruption, or the negative condition (Zone IV). No learning experience exists exclusively in any one zone. Even the most desirable condition for learning does not fall entirely in Zone I. The zones themselves represent groupings of behaviors and their concomitant feelings but do not translate directly into measures of effectiveness.

One way of looking at effectiveness in terms of zones is to estimate the percent of time spent by participants in each of the four zones. Figure 7.3 presents a representative percentage breakdown for four levels of effectiveness: optimum, adequate, suboptimum, and inhibitory.

No Zone IV experience exists for participants in the optimum case and almost none in the adequate case. In contrast, for the suboptimum and inhibitory cases, an increasing percentage of participant experiences fall into Zones III and IV with a corresponding decrease in Zone I experiences.

Different percentages can be used to describe the four levels of effectiveness, but it is unlikely that optimum or adequate effectiveness is ob-

Level of Learning Effectiveness	Percentage of Participant Experience in Each Zone			
	I	II	III	IV
Optimum	50 or more	45 or more	Up to 5	0
Adequate	40 or more	50 or more	Up to 9	Up to 1
Suboptimum	30 or more	58 or more	Up to 9	Up to 3
Inhibitory	30 or less	58 or less	9 or more	3 or more

Figure 7.3   An example of the relationship between participant experience in the four zones and learning effectiveness.

tained without a significant portion of participant experience occurring in Zones I and II. The destructiveness of Zone IV experiences cannot be emphasized enough, and even the presence of a very small proportion of these experiences can have a dramatically negative effect on everyone's learning. Zone II behavior is a major source of activation within the learning environment. In the optimum and adequate cases this energy is directed positively toward the learning objectives while in the suboptimum and inhibitory cases the energy usually is invested in behavior counterproductive to learning. While a great deal of Zone II experience is inevitable within any learning situation, it is the presence or absence of the other three zones that actually determine the relative effectiveness of the experience.

Returning to Figure 7.2, the behavioral descriptors in each cell, when compared with those in other cells, can be used to provide a general appreciation of the nature of the entire zone and the differences among zones. It is emphasized that this information can serve as a means of formative evaluation and thereby provide a basis for the ongoing adjustment of the learning processes. While specific remedial steps may be different for different phases, Figure 7.2, together with Figure 7.3, apply diagnostically to all the phases of the learning experience.

CHAPTER EIGHT

Central Methods

The only kind of learning which
significantly influences behavior is
self-discovered or self-appropriated
learning—truth that has been assimilated in experience.

Carl Rogers

There are five methods that are central to experiential learning: simulations, exercises, group interaction, role playing, and body movement. Other methods such as the classical case method could be argued to belong here also but are more conveniently discussed subsequently.

Simulations

Simulations (and games) are models or representations of some facet of the human experience. Sets of rules, guidelines, and materials are used to provide a structure that in turn illustrates, reflects, approximates, or duplicates some other process, event, or condition. Perhaps more than any other method, simulations are uniquely flexible in their application to a large number of topics yet also rich in their potential for tapping many underlying change processes. Four broad classifications of activities are possible: games, simulations, nonsimulation games, and simulation/games.

Games are competitive activities with sets of rules and specified goals; outcomes are determined by skill or chance or a combination of the two. Although general principles may be abstracted from playing them, they are intended to stand for themselves and do not represent any other facet of reality. Poker, chess, and baseball are examples. *Simulations* are attempts to reproduce, in simplified form, some aspect of reality so that others, by being immersed in a prescribed format, can experience a facsimile of that reality. Either roles or resources might be defined, but goals or specific participant actions are not. Participants are free to behave in any way they think appropriate within the parameters of the simulation. Examples of this type of activity are the NASA Lost on the Moon Task and SIMSOC (Simulated Society). *Nonsimulation games* are games based on knowledge within a given subject area; winning is contingent on mastery of the content. These activities are desirable for several reasons.

> The gaming situation itself, and the social interaction with peers in an atmosphere that suggests fun rather than classwork, appear to be sufficiently appealing to induce students to devote willingly increased time and energy to learning the requisite skills . . . In this type of game, knowledge of results is usually immediate, and repeated plays reinforce learning. (Seidner, 1976, pp. 225–226)

Simulation/games combine aspects of games and simulations. There are specified participant goals within a set of rules, but, in this case, the format and rules are designed to reflect some aspect of reality.

Simulations are widely used for many purposes in a variety of disciplines (Gibbs, 1974; Twelker, 1969; Zuckerman & Horn, 1973) and many authors have documented their nature, design, use, and effectiveness (Avedon & Sutton-Smith, 1971; Boocock & Schild, 1968; Gordon, 1970; Lewis, Wentworth, Reinke, & Becker, 1974; Livingston & Stoll, 1973; Seidner, 1976; Twelker & Layden, 1972).

Any other method or methods can form an integral part of a simulation, especially group, 2, 3, and 4 person interactions, and role playing. For example, a simple group decision-making simulation might include the following:

1 Solving a problem abstracted from a case study.
2 Giving each participant different segments of specific content necessary for solving the problem.
3 Assigning participants different roles for conducting themselves in the discussion.

This activity involves role playing, group interaction, case study, and time to enable participants to prepare themselves for the discussion. In addition, some participants could be assigned the role of process observer, recording the actions of the other participants discussing the problem and then giving them feedback on their performance during the debriefing phase. Combining process observation with simulations or any other experience-based method adds an important component to the learning experience.

Simulations can produce a wide variety of effects. They can motivate by generating enthusiasm, stimulate inquiry, personalize and integrate aspects of the human condition, promote cognitive and behavioral skill development, change attitudes and enhance empathy, promote personal awareness, and transform the basic character of the instructional environment (Lewis et al., 1974, pp. 43–45). The compelling reason for their popularity is twofold. First, they actively and directly involve participants in the learning processes. Second, they permit simultaneous treatment of interpersonal interaction, process objectives, and information and skills related to a given content objective.

When using simulations, leaders have to be aware of many important considerations. They must know the characteristics, logistical requirements, and probable impact of the activity so that they are in a position to judge its suitability for the context and objectives of the learning experience. Ideally, leaders would first have been participants in the same or similar simulations. Leaders need to develop the ability to remain disengaged from the activity and the sensitivity to know when and how to intervene. All the guidelines discussed in Chapter 7 are of particular relevance, since a large component of successful experiential learning centers around the use of simulations. Although the term simulations is used to signify all of the specific experiential methods discussed in this section, the reader is reminded that simulations, games, nonsimulation games, and simulation/games all have distinguishing characteristics affecting their usefulness at a given time and in a given place.

Analysis

Simulations use and depend upon the change processes of support and restructuring. A *supportive* climate and supportive leader behavior is valuable in neutralizing participant resistance to involvement in the early phases. Specific supportive leader interventions include:

1   Giving expectations about the duration and intensity of the activity as well as likely outcomes.
2   Providing a physical arrangement and the necessary materials for the activity.
3   Providing adequate privacy for the participants.
4   Being responsive to participant requests, questions, and other needs.

Leader warmth, caring, and authenticity are supportive.

Restructuring also occurs during the introduction phase and is the central change process used in simulations. Of the six types of social restructuring discussed in Chapter 4, simulations primarily depend on the reorganization type (see Figure 4.1). By changing the roles, social norms, or interaction patterns, simulations provide new structures within which participants must respond. The activity is much more than the mere illustration of ideas. The immediate consequence for participants in simulations is a rather high degree of *activation*, which in turn provides the energy to sustain the activity, making leader interventions for this purpose virtually unnecessary. The associated *action* has participants exploring concepts and behavior in pursuit of a given learning objective and allows for individual experimentation. Costs of these actions are minimized by the "game" atmosphere in the activity. Rehearsal, practice, and performance are less important than exploration and experimentation.

Participant involvement in simulations opens the door for the immediate effects of *feedback* and *channeling*. Because of the interactive nature of most simulations, participants begin receiving dynamic feedback almost immediately. They are constantly confronted with the impact of their behavior in terms of task requirements and reactions from other participants. During the debriefing phase, they receive static feedback concerning their involvement. This tends to be informational, but leader style and the norms of the learning experience can affect the degree of confrontation dramatically in this phase.

The social nature of the interactions creates a new social reality. This new reality generates its own set of *channeling* forces. For example, in an intergroup competition simulation, a given participant reference group quickly establishes internal mechanisms that allow that group to cope with the new structure of the simulation. Some members in the group would be likely to experience fear during the activity, and thus group cohesion tends to increase as a means of self-defense.

Participant involvement also generates a type of *identification* leading directly to the ready acquisition of effective behavior when that behavior is clearly demonstrated. The acquisition process may be immediate, occurring during the simulation, or it may occur after the simulation has been completed. Identification among participants can increase the likelihood of the acquisition of effective behavior.

Activation, action, channeling, and identification combine to increase participants' *commitment* to the learning experience by stimulating and tapping their individual wills through the realism of the total situation. Ideally, the leader and the learning situation do not compete with individual wills, but provide the context within which they can operate. Resistance to change is thus minimized and commitment often is increased.

Re-cognition also occurs during simulations. Self-monitoring and self-management techniques, for example, can be used to increase participants' ability to gather and use dynamic feedback during the activity. Similarly, specific suggestions and expectations articulated before or during the activity affect how participants think about the simulation and consequently experience it. Direction contributes significantly to learning.

Persuasion can be used effectively to underscore the important issues raised in the simulation. When a message is paired with a stimulus source of high emotional impact the message is more likely to be assimilated. Furthermore, effective persuasion stresses the use of a very small number of implicit conclusions; strong feelings and few points lead to ease of retention.

The activation and action generated by the simulation also have a *positive reinforcing* quality related to the overall learning experience. Leader praise of participant feedback and particular participants' behavior during the simulation is valuable as well.

Exercises

Exercises are activities used to engage participants directly with the content of the experience or with each other. They consist of step-by-step procedures that are clearly defined and intended to provide opportunities to become familiar with and practice skills, to generate feelings and reactions, and to facilitate participants' movement through the learning experience. For example, exercises directed at teaching skills contain written material and require participants to read, write, and become involved in some form of behavioral practice, possibly in the presence of an observer for feedback purposes. Many programmed instruction sequences also fall within this category.

Exercises generally involve some form of action. An example is to give participants each an apple or orange and have them study it and then describe it to the other members of their group. The apples are then collected and the participants are asked to try to find their own apples. This specific activity can be used to illustrate stereotyping and prejudice. Another type of exercise does not have a direct relationship to the content of the learning experience but is used to facilitate some aspect of its process. For example, there are many structured sequences for introducing participants to each other, increasing their comfort level, and moving them from one activity to another. If a large group were watching a film and then were asked to discuss their reactions, they might be asked first to find one person they had not yet talked with and to spend several minutes exchanging views. Then each dyad might be asked to find two other dyads whom they felt might have different reactions than theirs to the film; hence groups of six would finally discuss the film. These three types of exercise can be found in published sources such as the *Handbooks of Structured Experiences for Human Relations Training* (Pfeiffer & Jones, 1969, 1970, 1971, 1973, 1975, 1977), or can be developed by the leader to meet the particular needs of a learning design.

The availability of exercises has made it much easier for leaders to become familiar with and to use experiential methods. However, there are possible problems associated with this availability. Published sources of these materials, such as Pfeiffer and Jones, include step-by-step directions for conduct, but ignore whether the leaders using them have any knowledge of their potential impact. Easily implemented procedures for heightening awareness and creating feelings give leaders the power to generate data that they might not be able to manage. In such cases, there is a tendency to underutilize all the phases of the learning experience, thus in a sense trivializing the activity itself. Selected exercises should be compatible with the type and objectives of the learning experience, the participants' expectations, and the leader's capacities.

Analysis

The change dynamics characteristic of exercises are *action, feedback,* and *conditioning.* In contrast to simulations, their general purpose is to generate action in a circumscribed area. They are more focused than simulations; there is less exploration and experimentation, and more rehearsal and practice.

Re-cognition and *persuasion* are important early in the learning process, especially as preparation for the actual exercise. When the learning has a cognitive component, such as for interpersonal competence, the first concern of the learning arrangement must be for re-cognition. Practically, this means that new constructs must be described, illustrated, and presented in such a way that the participants can inculcate them. Kelly's (1955) construct alternativism is an example of the models of human functioning assumed here. The major purpose of persuasion, generally, is one of *commitment* enhancement. It is often useful to make overt the costs and benefits of the material to be learned, and to use examples with which people can identify. Involvement is generally the object of these efforts. Evoking participant reactions to examples is of direct value.

The important goal in the introductory phase is readying participants to direct their will toward the task of acquiring skills linked to the new constructs. Herein lies a pivotal distinction between the use of ideas in exercises and the use of ideas in a lecture presented for their descriptive interest. Here, it is only necessary and desirable to use a few constructs providing a framework for understanding the exercise. In a simulation, however, the ideas tend to emerge from the experience and are elaborated on *post hoc,* so the conceptual structure can be more abstract. In the former case, giving individuals prior ways of thinking about the experience by setting expectations and making suggestions as to how they might cope with high probability outcomes during the exercise is central to the actual success of the exercise itself.

As with any activity, the *action* in an exercise should have an important *activating* quality; much of this comes from task challenge, participant coaction, and interaction. Exercises often may appear very simplistic, especially to adult participants who have not pursued learning in as tightly structured or directed a manner for a long time. Nevertheless, the presence of others attempting the same activity serves as a source of social *support* and eases embarrassment.

The character of the action can be different for different exercises. Skill-building exercises focus on practice and performance action. Awareness exercises, possibly involving body movement, are primarily exploratory and experimental in nature. The action generated by all exercises is dependent on the structure or set of steps and procedures given, but the *restructuring* is much less dramatic than in simulations. Restructuring involves articulating rules for interaction, and these rules are generally restricted to specific behaviors. The overall reorganization typical of simulations is not desired; indeed, one might say that the restructuring is legislative rather than organizational.

The activity provides a context and source of *feedback* and *conditioning.* Interpersonal feedback about consequences, when paired with clear criteria, serves a negative feedback function enabling participants to focus tightly on learning objectives. Thus negative feedback is positively reinforcing because knowledge of results leads to improved performance and an intrinsic sense of achievement. Additional positive reinforcement is of an operant nature, caused by the genuine enthusiasm and positive regard one participant extends towards another when effective behavior is demonstrated. Thus rules discouraging mutual criticism but encouraging informational feedback help participants avoid unnecessary emotional costs during learning, and produce an emphasis on positive reinforcement of performance.

Channeling aids in keeping participants at the task. *Identification* occurs during and after the activity. Participants who perform tasks correctly are models providing incentives and cues for others. In the debriefing and summary phases, success stories and learning insights are vividly shared, thus allowing further identificatory learning. The leader, through praise and supportive comments, positively reinforces this process. Consolidation and long-term retention are facilitated by extending the period of activation beyond the period of activity itself, and by using repetition and recall during the debriefing. *Persuasion* focuses on the few rules that need to be assimilated and on a few fundamental points of learning. The sharing process dominant in debriefing can encourage retention, aid in solidifying participant conclusions, and increase the commitment to apply learning in the outside world.

Group Interaction

Group interaction as an instructional method is surpassed in popularity only by the lecture. Group interaction may also incorporate role play, body movement, fantasy, instrumentation, and audiovisual techniques. Tasks, projects, and simulations also typically use group formats and group interactions here are an integral part of the learning. However, without the structure provided by the task or simulation the group would have no context. Various types of groups are also used as the primary vehicle for discussing ideas and reactions generated by other methods, but, again, these groups could not function without the prior experience to provide the substance for their interaction. The above distinguishing characteristics of groups can be classified into two situations, one in which the group is the experience and the other in which it is the context for other experiences. It is from this point that a more detailed description and analysis can be pursued.

Group Interaction as the Experience. The T-group is an excellent example of a group procedure that stands by itself (Benne, Bradford, Gibb, & Lippitt, 1975; Bradford, Gibb, & Benne, 1964; Golembiewski & Blumberg, 1970; Lakin, 1972; Schein & Bennis, 1965). T-groups have been described in terms of the following purposes (Schein & Bennis, 1965, p. 35):

1 To increase self-awareness, self-insight, and self-knowledge.
2 To increase awareness, insight, and knowledge of other individuals.
3 To become familiar with the characteristics of group process, specifically those factors that facilitate or inhibit the group's functioning.
4 To understand interpersonal behavior in groups.
5 To develop diagnostic skills for identifying and understanding individual, group, and organizational behavior.

These conditions are achieved in a group setting exclusively through group interaction. Participants are requested to talk about what is happening in the group and to devise their own structure and format for doing so with very little direct assistance from the trainer (leader). Simulations, role playing, body movement, and other specific techniques for providing structure and generating data are of peripheral value.

The group interaction has a number of distinguishing characteristics. Through an atmosphere of trust and group support, participants are encouraged to talk about their feelings and reactions towards other members of the group and the group process in the here and now. Any discussion of events outside the group is discouraged. "Attending to feelings as they are felt and understanding what evokes those feelings is a constant concern . . . One learns from participating in the group process, from observing that group process, and from reflecting on it" (Shaffer & Galinsky, 1974, p. 200). As a part of this procedure, participants are encouraged to disclose their feelings and give and receive feedback. As the group progresses, it develops norms that regulate how its members deal with each other. These norms establish limits for the disclosure and feedback processes; they can range from urging participants to be polite and take turns to having them confront certain issues or individuals.

The T-group interaction inevitably generates a wide range of strong feelings and reactions that make this group method a very potent learning activity. Even though participants might acquire knowledge and learn specific interpersonal skills within this format, the actual processes that occur stimulate personal growth. Thus the "T" in T-group, which stands for "training," can be and has been misleading.

Other groups are less purely interaction oriented (Back, 1972; Egan, 1970; Rogers, 1970; Schutz, 1973; Shaffer & Galinski, 1974). An encounter group is a representative example of the use of a group as the principal method in combination with other methods. An encounter group can be defined as

> a method of human relating based on openness and honesty, self-awareness, self-responsibility, awareness of the body, attention, feelings, and an emphasis on the here and now . . . Encounter is therapy insofar as it focuses on removing blocks to better functioning. Encounter is education and religion in that it attempts to create conditions leading to the most satisfying use of personal capacities. (Schutz, 1973, p. 3)

The encounter group stresses physical action and nonverbal exchange, incorporating many methods within the group format in order to achieve its goals. Body movement, role play, psychodrama, fantasy, dance, instrumentation, and an infinite variety of exercises combining aspects of these methods are used in addition to the group interaction to generate feelings and reactions in the group. The leader's task, besides monitoring the group process, is to select and implement various other methods to facilitate individual and group movement. These group experiences are very intense and even more personally focused than a T-group. They definitely fall within the personal growth type and possibly the therapy type of learning experiences.

Syndicates are another example of group interaction (Bligh et al., 1975). A syndicate is a small group without a leader that meets over an extended period of time to address either a real or a simulated task. In addition to the content of the task, participants learn from the relationships and issues that evolve as a consequence of working together in this format. Other methods, such as readings, written tasks, and process observation, can be used, but the nature of the group would be its distinguishing characteristic. Unlike the encounter group, syndicates tend toward educational, training, and professional development goals.

Groups as a Context for an Activity. A group format is used for many learning activities wherein other methods define the actual content of the experience (Pfeiffer & Jones, 1975; Zuckerman & Horn, 1973). For example, simulations often put participants into groups to carry out the activity, and groups are also used as vehicles for discussing information presented through other methods (Bligh et al., 1975; Davis, 1976; Gage & Berliner, 1975; Gall & Gall, 1976; Hyman, 1974; McKeachie, 1969). Discussion groups can be convened to explore reactions to a lecture, film, field trip, or to examine a wide range of topics. McKeachie (1969, p. 37) identified eight purposes for which a discussion format may be used:

1   To use the resources of members of the group.
2   To give students opportunities to formulate application of these principles.
3   To get prompt feedback on how well the leader's objectives are being attained.
4   To help students think in terms of the subject matter by giving them practice in thinking.
5   To help students learn to evaluate the logic of and evidence for their own and others' positions.
6   To help students become aware of and to formulate problems which necessitate information to be gained from reading or lectures.
7   To gain acceptance for information or theories counter to folklore or previous beliefs of students.
8   To develop motivation for learning.

A typical example of the use of a discussion group within an experiential learning design is the leaderless small group, in which exchanges of views and reactions to certain ideas or events generated during the activity phase are possible. Discussion groups can also be used during the introduction phase for expectation sharing and goal setting and as opportunities for involvement after lectures during the summary phase. McKeachie's eight points underscore the importance of this use of group interaction, but it is important to keep in mind that the use of a group for discussion purposes differs from its use during the activity phase. Even though discussion groups are an indispensable part of most experiential learning designs, they seldom are the only experiential component (Miner, 1978).

In using a particular group format, leaders should be aware of several important points. First, if a T-group or encounter group is to be included as a part of the learning experience, its potential impact must be compatible with the type and objectives of the experience and the expectations of the participants. In addition, leaders must have the specialized skills necessary for conducting the activity. Of the skills required for conducting any of the experience-based methods, these are probably the most difficult to acquire. Second, when a group discussion is used in a design, efforts should be made to give participants clear guidelines for the discussion and to incorporate formally the results of their deliberations into the learning experience through group reports or other means. If guidelines are unclear and accountability for performance is absent, the discussion may fail to achieve the impact intended.

Two, Three, and Four Person Interaction.   Dyads, trios, and quartets are specific types of interaction formats that are better suited to some purposes than larger group interactions (Bligh et al., 1975; Schutz, 1967). These configurations can be the principal method in the experience, either by themselves or in conjunction with other methods.

> The charge to each member of the dyad is to try to understand the other, learn how to give and take from the partner, and how to produce creatively with him. The objective is to provide an opportunity for each participant to learn to express himself and receive the expressions of another in such a way that a relationship can be built. (Schutz, 1967, pp. 71–72)

Groups of three or four can identify and discuss expectations or evaluate learning outcomes at the end of the experience. In a simulation, participants can gather in small groups to discuss objectives, plan strategies, and execute tasks. Small groups can quickly exchange reactions to feedback, a film, or a lecture.

During the introduction, smaller groupings make discussion easier, and time and facilities may make small groupings more practical. Leader–participant dyads or trios are probably the only suitable format for providing potentially sensitive feedback to individual participants and for counseling or coaching a participant who is agitated or having problems.

There are very few difficulties associated with the use of this method. Nevertheless, leaders should make sure that participants understand the activity and how to proceed through it to prevent them from wasting time or becoming sidetracked. Errors to avoid include such things as providing a programmed sequence for dyads establishing a higher level of intimate exchange than participants are expecting as an introductory exercise in an educational type of experience (Jones & Jones, 1974).

Analysis

The analysis of the group interaction method is divided into three parts: the group as the central experience, for example in T-groups, the group as a context for other experiences, and the group as a vehicle for reflection on a given learning experience.

Groups as the Central Experience.   Many analyses of T-groups, encounter groups, and sensitivity training groups have been offered over the years (Bion, 1961; Bradford, Gibb, & Benne, 1964; Cooper & Mangham, 1971;

Egan, 1970; Mann, 1967; Schein & Bennis, 1965). Many of these discussions are excellent and this current analysis cannot be as comprehensive. What is offered here are analytical insights (based on Part 1) capturing the essential elements that actually induce change.

The T-group is the classic example of the group as a central experience. The most obvious change process present in a T-group is *restructuring;* dramatic realignment and redefinition of social norms take place. Reorganization of interaction patterns also occurs, and leaderlessness is an example of this. Together these changes create a cultural island even if the T-group is not held in a retreat setting. Because of the high levels of ambiguity, this restructuring can easily confound participant expectations. For example, the persuasion attempts by a leader common to most groups are absent in T-groups. Criticisms of T-groups as tantamount to brainwashing (Harvey, 1971; Manley, 1971; Odiorne, 1970) are accurate in that restructuring is both dramatic and powerful. However, the active and violent coercion characteristic of brainwashing is nonexistent in T-groups. Nonetheless, it is important to acknowledge that some degree of inherent coercion exists in the absence of traditional or expected structures, though it is mild and relatively passive in nature.

This subtle, coercive element is critical to a T-group's power to change individuals; participants tend to experience high levels of anxiety and thus feel the urge to *action.* The resulting high levels of *activation* help to overcome inhibitions and create the possibility of tapping further change processes. This is a delicate process. In the somewhat confused early state typical of a T-group, the cultural island is created slowly by the leader. Hints for an acceptable minimal structure are provided, forming a system of rules for social interaction that center on giving and receiving *feedback* and expressing and responding to emotions. This structure usually is embraced eagerly by participants, who accept the evolving rules partly in order to dissipate their high levels of activation.

The information exchanged by participants in the resulting interaction perpetuates the activation–action cycle. Pacing and reinforcement efforts by the leader are directed primarily at regulating the momentum of the dynamic and avoiding too much too soon.

Highly confrontive feedback is often criticized by traditionalists as being coercive. This may or may not be true in any given case. It is possible to conduct T-groups with noncoercive levels of confrontation and here leader judgment and skill are key. It is one thing to create a high level of anxiety and pain and quite another to cultivate fear. The latter is seldom constructive in a T-group context; it is not necessarily part of the approach but rather derives from leader style, values, and capacities (Lieberman, Yalom, & Miles, 1973).

In terms of *conditioning,* the leader encourages intimacy and feedback by using eye contact, nods, and other gently reinforcing behaviors. Any other conditioning occurs as a part of the group interaction and is inherently a part of the *channeling* process.

In the T-group, restructuring, conditioning, and feedback change dynamics are primarily directed toward *re-cognition.* A number of conceptualizations are typically presented that aid participants to adjust their view of the world and themselves. For example, the Johari Window concept (Luft, 1963) is particularly useful, because, in describing a model for desired participant interaction, it supports the change encouraged through other means. It provides an alternative construct through which individuals can view themselves in relationship to others.

A third layer of change processes serves to buttress these dynamics. Participants provide *support* for one another via initial friendship and mutual attraction derived from subgroups. This seeking and providing of mutual support is at first directed at resisting the leader's pressures for openness and intimacy, but, because it alleviates anxieties, the support process is paradoxically the direct enactment of the leader's directions. The support process creates intense personal loyalties and a sense of closeness which, over time, result in increased group *identification.* The observation and vicarious reinforcement aspects of the identification change process are facilitated in the group by the openness of behavioral expressions and emotional intimacy. Intimacy is closely linked to both observation and reinforcement, and when they exist at a high level, the group also has a high degree of power to influence individuals via *channeling.*

In summary, high anxiety early in a T-group leads to the need for and provision of support and the open expression of feelings. Both of these dynamics increase identification. Support and channeling also pull the participants into personal *commitment* to one another and to the group. In essence, individuals are not allowed to deal with each other in traditional ways (I–it) or in merely hedonistic ways (it–it). They are virtually forced or channeled into existential relations (I–thou) (Shostrum, 1976). Because of the strong engagement of individual will in the latter type of relationship, it is argued by the existentialists to be a most powerful commitment. This third cluster of change forces tends to increase the potency of the previously discussed change processes and increases group cohesion, which in turn acts as a positive feedback loop for the entire third grouping of change processes. This increased cohesion is analogous to turning up the heat on a burner, perhaps why "good" T-groups find it almost impossible to deal with the breakup of the group at the end of the learning experience.

In contrast to T-groups, we can examine briefly the syndicate as another use of the group as central experience. Syndicates do not generate the intensity or directness of *feedback,* nor do they establish I–thou relationships and the intimacy associated with them. Consequently, *commitment* in a syndicate is less personal and more circumscribed; the task facing the syndicate not only provides the rationale for the activity but also serves as an outlet for the participants' energies. The task allows people to respond to a structure already available or familiar to them, so *restructuring* is also minimal.

Unlike the T-group, a syndicate seldom turns energies back into itself, and thus energy levels are seldom sufficient to overcome interpersonal inhibitions. Using the metaphor of a nuclear reactor, syndicates rarely reach critical mass, whereas competently led T-groups virtually always do. Therefore, social interaction and self-discovery are less intense in a syndicate than in a T-group. On the other hand, because syndicates tend to resemble normal work and task groups, the learning attained is more easily integrated into the participant's task-centered life. *Re-cognition* is seldom directly pursued in a syndicate context, whereas in T-groups major reorientation often occurs, and changes in such fundamental cognitive elements as social prejudices, beliefs, self-esteem, and ego strength are well documented (Cooper & Mangham, 1971).

Group processes, observations, and feedback within a syndicate produce quantitatively and qualitatively different learning than in a T-group. Education, training, and limited professional development often occur in syndicates, but in T-groups little pragmatic training is likely; the primary consequence is personal growth and therapy with the purpose of helping individuals share life intensely and directly with one other (Egan, 1971).

Groups as a Context. Even when the group is not the focus of the learning activity, the vast majority of experiential learning occurs in a group context. As the group itself becomes less central to the learning and as interpersonal issues among members cease to be the prime focus, there is a dramatically reduced need for *restructuring* and *commitment* building. A blend of *support, identification, feedback,* and *conditioning* is the hallmark of the type of restructuring appropriate in a "contextual" group. Thus, instead of cultural island restructuring, a minor legislative change directed toward personal safety is pursued. Particular norms, in addition to the giving of feedback, could include a charge to participants to take responsibility for their learning and to ask for clarification. The major emphasis, however, is on the generation of *support* within the group in order to facilitate exploration, experimentation, and other forms of *action* that otherwise might be inhibited through fear or because of underactivation.

Identification allows participants to learn through the observation of the actions of others. Interpersonal *feedback* occurs at various stages and is usually static rather than dynamic. Feedback in this case, because of the function of a contextual group, is generally controlled through development of norms and guidelines that define areas appropriate for feedback and encourage it to be informational rather than confrontational. The encouragement of supportive norms within the group is also typical in this use of group interaction. Similarly, the conditioning emphasis is on positive reinforcement contributing to the supportive nature of the group as a context.

Commitment building typically takes the form of a psychological contract between the leader and participants. This contract often emphasizes the participants' freedom to control their degree of involvement in ensuing activities and their level of commitment to the learning situation (Berte, 1975; Brown, 1978; Mack, 1979). *Coercion* is avoided; support and encouragement are offered as aids to participants' efforts in becoming engaged in the learning experience. *Persuasion* encourages experimenting and self-monitoring.

The role of *channeling* is also less aggressive in contextual groups than in T-groups or encounter groups because of the voluntary arrangements and lack of intimacy. Consequently, it must be more circumscribed and, for legitimacy, must be linked to the pursued activity. Support can help to channel the sharing of reactions, mutual encouragement, and positive reinforcement for involvement.

Activation, as noted above, centers on a moderate but sustained level of pleasant feelings and results from interpersonal interactions—joking, coffee breaks, stretch breaks, and periodic movement. *Re-cognition* can be encouraged through self-management procedures such as systematic self-observation in the form of journals or diaries.

Groups as Vehicles for Reflection. In the final phases of group activity, *support* becomes far less pivotal to the learning process. Instead, clear procedures for analysis, reflection, and planning help participants to synthesize and transfer learning. This legislative type of *restructuring* serves as a halfway house between exploration and application. The sense of closure thereby attained positively reinforces previous involvement. The aim of the new structure is to reduce *activation* for a number of purposes: first, to avoid distractions created by overactivation at this point; second, to avoid the sometimes painful experience of being left up in the air; and third, to create the relaxation associated with decreased activation serving as positive reinforcement for decisions that might come out of discussion.

Channeling, feedback, persuasion, commitment, and *identification* are all marshalled in this application of the group towards the purpose of *re-cognition.* The central rule for channeling is that participants take responsibility for implementation of the material covered. Feedback is limited and focused; more emphasis is placed on knowledge of results and information. Confrontation, if it occurs, is on a content or cognitive level.

Identification is important here for individuals who were less actively involved during the learning experience. Participants can see similarities between models and themselves. Commitments to further actions must be obtained from participants. Announcements of decisions made and mutual promises for contracts enhance commitment through their explicitness. The structure of the analysis, reflection, and planning should direct the participants clearly toward the goal of making and sharing these decisions.

Persuasion by the leader takes the form of presenting learning generalizations and summary conceptualizations tightly anchored to the participants' emotions and thoughts from the experience. Recency effects and communication research studies emphasize that only a few such points can be made and that their durability depends on brief articulation and even catchy or humorous slogans (Zimbardo & Ebbesen, 1969). Finally, group support can be evoked by the leader to reward participation and reinforce learning.

Role Playing

Role playing is a popular and engaging method of instruction in which participants assume a prescribed perspective or set of behaviors. It is used in many different settings for many purposes (Corsini, Shaw, & Blake, 1961; Elms, 1969; Hyman, 1974; McKeachie, 1969; Maier, Solem, & Maier, 1957; Moreno, 1946, 1964).

> Role playing may be defined as a method of human interaction that involves realistic behavior in imaginary situations. It is a "spontaneous" technique, since participants act freely rather than from a script. It is a "make believe" kind of situation, where people act as though what they were doing was "for real." (Corsini, Shaw, & Blake, 1961, p. 8)

Much of the rationale for the role playing method has been derived from Jacob Moreno's work on psychodrama (Moreno, 1946, 1953, 1964). He found that action and acting, spontaneity and creativity, and a focus on the here and now generated a catharsis for both the actors and the audience. This emotional release is central to the learning that occurs in these situations. All of Moreno's psychodramatic techniques can be adapted for use in nontherapeutic settings simply by changing the content of the role play.

Basically, role playing requires participants either to assume another individual's identity and act as they believe the other individual would in a given hypothetical situation, or to be themselves and react as they imagine they might in unfamiliar or troublesome hypothetical situations. The method may be used either alone or in conjunction with other methods.

Many simulations place participants in roles as an integral part of the activity; the case study method can be transformed into a more aggressively experiential mode by having participants actually play the roles described in the case; and very often role playing or psychodrama is used for identifying and highlighting issues or for giving participants the chance to focus their attention more intensely and directly.

The structure of the roles and the context within which they are to be acted out significantly affect the viability of objectives. As a method, role playing is as appropriate in an educational experience as it is in therapy. Beyond its engaging and energizing nature, role playing is useful for (McKeachie, 1969, p. 115; Maier, Solem, & Maier, 1957, p. 3):

1 Providing opportunities for participants to demonstrate and/or practice knowledge and skills they have learned, including managing their feelings.
2 Illustrating principles related to the subject under consideration.
3 Providing an appreciation of the importance of emotions in determining behavior.
4 Enhancing participants' awareness of and sensitivity to their own and others feelings, attitudes, and behavior.
5 Promoting attitude and behavior change by placing participants in novel, atypical, or conflictual roles.
6 Highlighting the importance of practice in developing effective interpersonal skills.

Leaders should be aware that participants might be threatened by having to perform in front of their peers. The activity should be carefully introduced and participants engaged diplomatically. It is also important that the activity addresses issues in a way compatible with the stated objectives of the experience; use of a role play should not change the type of the learning experience. For example, a role play in an educational experience, if improperly managed, could quickly become overly personal.

Analysis

As with simulations, the change analysis of role playing begins with *restructuring*. Specific rules for role play are offered, and hence the individual's social contextual world is reorganized. This reorganization is less physical than in simulations, but it is equally tangible. In fact, tangibility in the description of the role is of paramount importance to its usefulness. The tangible restructuring, in a *supportive, noncoercive* climate, allows the participants to identify with the characters in the roles and, most importantly, to project themselves into those roles. This *identification* is somewhat different from the observational identification emphasized in many other methods. The reader is reminded of Mead's symbolic interactionism, in which it is argued that the primary manner in which people construct and modify their social selves is through seeing other people's roles, playing them, and generating and generalizing insights acquired while playing a role. People are intrinsically motivated to "try on" the and outside the learning experience, other participants and friends exchange informational feedback on which comparisons, judgments, and decisions are made. Most participants are eager for feedback and sharing in the debriefing phase, and channeling can further encourage this process. In addition to the behavioral learning emphasized in role playing, a significant amount of *re-cognition* also occurs.

Mead's theory of symbolic interactionism states that the opportunity provided by role playing of putting one's self in the shoes of another enables individuals to adjust and expand their conception of how others might experience a given role relationship. This in turn adds subtlety and complexity to individuals' conceptions of their relationships with others in any particular social context. This might be labeled *social contextual competency* in contrast to the interpersonal competency (IPC) of Chris Argyris (1970) and others. Interpersonal competence stresses a stripping away of roles and a capacity to generate high degrees of personal intimacy. Social contextual competency (SCC) relates to constructive and effective performance across a variety of roles, including the relatively low intimacy interactions common in everyone's life. These relationships have received little attention during the past two decades of experiential learning research.

Persuasion, near the end of the learning sequence, is best directed toward implementation rather than conclusions. Participants are encouraged to make decisions about the effectiveness of the specific actions and about themselves and their conduct in relationship to others. They are encouraged to try out new behaviors in their own lives, and, for areas in which this is possible, *commitments* are elicited.

Body Movement

These activities can range from relaxation techniques to a wide variety of physical exercises and are generally used to develop and enhance personal awareness. The importance of body awareness, movement, and contact as a vehicle for promoting growth and change has many advocates (Barlow, 1973; Brown, 1973; Feldenkrais, 1972; Lowen, 1958, 1967; Reich, 1949; Schutz, 1967, 1971, 1973; Weir, 1975). These methods range from breathing and relaxation exercises to massage and other forms of physical contact such as arm wrestling or shoulder pushing. They are used for energizing, heightening awareness of different parts of the body, mobilizing feelings, and confronting and reducing tension. The methods in this category provide an alternative to verbal exchange for bringing issues to a participant's awareness. The advantages of the techniques are twofold: first, in many situations they succeed in providing access to certain issues where verbal exchange could not; and, second, they generate data more graphically than is possible merely through the use of words.

As awarenesses become more vivid and as willingness to share them increases, body movement becomes more appropriate for personal

roles of others. This is obviously true for children who dress up
or play with dolls and toys, but it is also true for adults. Th
contextual model of human functioning might be assumed when
ing role playing. In contrast, an experiential leader who assum
behavioristic orientation might actually reduce the potency of th
by overstressing reinforcement and punishment.

Channeling plays an important part in directing participant
First, the norms of the learning experience help participants to (
inhibitions and to attempt things that otherwise might be inti
Second, the structure inherent in the role serves as peg points f(
channeling into the social dynamics that the role and role playi

In combination, the foregoing factors create a full spectrum
within a role playing activity. Participants can explore the worl
experience of others much as children might explore grown-u
Participants can experiment either with self-generated behav
attitudinal alternatives within role playing or with ideas and ac
vided prior to the role play or noted in the introductory phase
suggestions for actions to be attempted could also be made durin
play. Performance applications emphasize using responses in the
that have been learned in another situation, with arrangements
participants to make relatively specific refinements. Role playing
erful technique because so many alternative functions of actic
pursued within a given role play. Thus, participants with wide
needs and levels of development can all be accommodated.

Conditioning and *activation* are tightly linked to action. Int
role playing is positively reinforcing because of human proclivit
on" that with which they identify. The release of this natural ten
an activation consequence because it acknowledges that the ac
intrinsic in addition to being a result of the stimulation that occu
role play. In colloquial terms, one could say that role playing is
entertainment characterized by pleasant and engaging stimul
tivated through projection and spontaneous fantasy. Audience |
into a drama sustains activation and drive release as the action
These same points apply to a certain degree to simulations, but
ing provides more structure for identification and generally bu
carious and action-centered conditioning. It takes less imaginat
come involved in role playing than in some other methods. The
of role playing is central to its power, and its power is highly d
on the fun participants have. Hedonistic fun is pleasant stimul;
pled with drive release and positive reinforcement in low-risk c

Feedback has a complex function in the role play. The dyna
back which occurs interpersonally during the actual role play r
situation real, facilitates involvement within the activity, provide
reinforcement, and contributes to the participants' *commitme*
identification with the role. During the debriefing and summa

growth and therapy and less so for education and training. Similarly, when body methods are used to allow feelings regarding personal or interpersonal issues to surface, or when they are used to help participants confront and work through aspects of their behavior, they are best confined to a personal growth or therapeutic experience. These techniques are common and effectively used alone or within an encounter, personal growth, or therapy group format. *Joy, Expanding Human Awareness* by William Schutz provides a clear description of the variety of methods available and their respective applications.

Leaders conducting experiences using body methods first should know the technique well in terms of its implementation and potential impact; previous personal experience of the technique as a participant is a near prerequisite. Second, they should choose a technique primarily because of its compatibility with the learning experience overall and the specific objectives within it, not because of its potency. And, finally, leaders must appreciate that, generally, participants may be threatened by these techniques. Consequently, participant readiness and pacing of events are more sensitive issues in using these techniques than they are for more familiar, less engaging methods such as a group interaction or a film presentation.

The body methods discussed above are used as the actual learning activity. However, some types of body methods can be used as a part of the introduction for ice breaking, or at specific points throughout any type of learning experience for warming up, relaxing, or energizing functions (Feldenkrais, 1972; Hendricks & Wills, 1975). Consider the following relaxation exercise:

> . . . close your eyes . . . tense every muscle in your body at the same time . . . legs . . . arms . . . jaws . . . fists . . . face . . . shoulders . . . stomach . . . hold them . . . tightly . . . now relax and feel the tension pour out of your body . . . This activity can be repeated several times and combined with deep breathing. (Hendricks & Wills, 1975, pp. 46–48)

The use of body methods in this way is very different but no less important than its more central uses. Feelings and reactions generated either in support of or as a diversion from the major focus of the activity rarely, if ever, need to be formally considered, even though they have a direct impact on the quality of the learning experience. Leaders should not select techniques that generate too much data and hence detract from the learning experience.

Analysis

As with many of the other experiential methods, effective use of body movement requires *support*. There are physical, expectational, and contractual components of support. The physical components can include a variety of factors that reduce inhibition and generate a feeling of safety. For example, if particularly large groups are engaged in movements tapping deeply personal feelings, a relatively large amount of space per person and perhaps subdued lighting might be valuable. Other physical contributions might be the presence of a number of leaders or aids throughout the room. Furthermore, fears may arise from the possibility of physical danger or unwanted contact with others. For these issues and others, question and answer sessions during the introductory phase and a tight, structured presentation with regard to possible outcomes, risk, and protections are important. Relationships between participants and the leader need to be contractually established via the leader's personal commitment regarding his or her own conduct, as well as the leader's assertions regarding the appropriate conduct of the session. In exchange, participants may be expected to abide by the safety requirements of the session; quite clearly, support is linked to *commitment.*

Action is the epitome of the body movement method and it is through action that *activation* and *re-cognition* occur. Beyond what has already been said about activation for other methods, three additional points are noteworthy here. First, in some body movement activities the ultimate goal is simulateously to create energy around specific issues and to engage in a change effort on those issues. For example, the "two chair" gestalt technique brings out psychological conflict in a given individual, and at the same time is used by the therapist to clarify the conflict for the individual. Further, the energizing can be used to create a confrontation of the conflict, and thus to form a new gestalt for the individual.

This leads directly to the second point, that of focusing the individual's energy through body movement. In a variety of learning situations, activation levels are already adequate, but participants are unable to bring the threads of their learning together. Physical acting out of a prescribed set of behaviors serves to amplify the issue considered. For example, an intimacy activity such as mirroring highlights many issues of personal control by focusing participants' attention on one another. Simple, momentary actions such as stretch breaks allow for the dissipation of body tension that otherwise could inhibit learning.

The relationship of activation to *re-cognition* is crucial. Body movement inevitably entails recentering of the individual's consciousness. While this shifting of the individual's center of attention is different than the thought stopping sequence described in Chapter 5, it has similar consequences, that is, the reduction of unproductive thinking patterns. In body movement, physical activity creates emotion that engrosses the individual's attention. In contrast, in a more passive circumstance one might focus one's center of attention on the same nonproductive thoughts. Thus body movement is not only inherently re-cognitive, but, as discussed for activation, it also provides a basis for further re-cognition. Other re-cognitive sources that link to body movement include a variety of "suggestive" possibilities. As part of the introduction and debriefing, one is told that such and such action will surface feelings and increase "centeredness." Action seems to increase certain suggestibilities.

The above change processes can occur with or without *restructuring.* In the absence of restructuring, the intensity of the activity is relatively low, but with restructuring the intensity can be exceedingly high. For mild experiences such as group "mills," used for social ice breaking, any structural transitions can be relatively smooth and minor. This is true also for movement from one configuration in the learning experience to another, as the group begins or concludes a given activity. An example is moving from a lecture format to triads or vice versa, movement which takes a significant proportion of workshop time. In terms of activation this is certainly not wasted time.

Restructuring of the body movement domain can have direct activation and re-cognition consequences. "Dynamic meditation," for example, might include darkening a very large room, providing music, and requiring blindfolds. The result is a dramatic shift of energy to the body so that the body drives the mind and not vice versa. For example, est (Erhard seminar training) uses rules in many ways to confound participants and create a "cultural island." Restriction of movement over extended periods of time can increase tension; this not only activates participants but also sets them up motivationally for bioenergetics or other movement activities. Increased intensity for a given set of movements is the result. Here, the support and commitment provided in a body movement activity should be geared realistically to the degree of intensity that the experience can or will generate.

In addition to the primary processes already discussed, *feedback, conditioning,* and *coercion* are significant. The central feedback for this method is dynamic and proprioceptive, that is, feedback from the participants' bodies. Interpersonal feedback is primarily in the form of sharing experiences, the major value of which is the dissipation of some of the excess energy generated during the activity and thus movement to closure. Classical conditioning occurs when accessed feelings are paired with clear thoughts, goals, and behavior. This pairing is pervasive both during and after the activity. One possible unintended consequence is associated with overactivation. Feelings generated can go beyond anxiety and discomfort to fear and pain, and, in such cases, the activity itself might be experienced by participants as punishing or coercive.

The one legitimate, although potentially dangerous, use of coercion in establishing and conducting body movement activities is in the creation of the physical confrontation between different elements of the individual's personality. Actual participation in expressing aggression may well coerce participants into something beyond what they anticipated, with or without leader involvement.

The central paradox in body movement is that both support and coercion can coexist in such a large measure. It is incorrect, however, to assume that the support exists in spite of coercion. Quite the contrary. Dramatic levels of support must be provided because of the coercion potential; in fact, the presence of the coercion is dependent on the high levels of support. The critical element seems to be a clear commitment within the learning situation that coercion will be limited and will be used to further the individual's will rather than to subjugate it. This encourages individuals in their struggle for growth. It is this double-barreled effect in some body movement activities that contributes so significantly to their impact. The complexities and subtleties of managing the coexistence of support and coercion probably explain why so many body techniques have come and gone, having failed to generate and maintain a broad base of acceptance.

Channeling, persuasion, and *identification* are not central. Channeling linked to group support provides social reality, thus legitimizing and reducing inhibition for involvement. For persuasion, leader credibility is important in the domain of support and commitment. For example, credibility aids in leader efforts to create the right tone; timing of interventions is critical for optimal emotional impact. Mild participant identification with the leader occurs as a function of the personal confidence inspired. Group identification also occurs, and, although it too is generally mild, it is an additional source of support, modeling, and vicarious experiencing. Opportunities for observational learning are abundant even though what is learned vicariously often differs markedly from what would be learned through active involvement.

An additional comment concerning commitment is necessary. The high involvement of the activity tends to create high levels of commitment to ideas and motivation. It is the leader's personal responsibility to aid participants in their efforts to draw insights and generalizations from the experience and to implement them. For many participants, this intensity clarifies feelings and issues which can aid the leader in this commitment-making process. Unfortunately, since insights are often clear it is often too easy for leaders to ignore the later phases of action planning and commitment building. But when this additional planning is actually done, the learning experience is greatly strengthened and the probability is increased that transfer back home will occur.

Summary

Participant action is the theme that is central to the methods in this chapter. The effectiveness of these methods rests in the fact that the actions they generate foster the development of many other change processes. Most experiential learning activities rely on the use of one or more of these methods.

CHAPTER NINE

Classical Methods

*When all else fails, read
the directions.*

Anon.

The classical methods have been in use for hundreds of years and are widely accepted by traditional educators. These include the case method, the lecture, reading, and written tasks. Group discussion is also a classical method, but it was mentioned in Chapter 8 as a facet of group interaction. The relationship between classical methods and experiential learning is the prime focus of the following discussion.

The Case Method

The case method is a complete approach to learning centered on the reading and discussion of case studies. It is a common yet very distinctive mode of instruction. The classical approach to case studies, developed at Harvard University (McNair & Hersum, 1954; Towl, 1969), is the instructional format in many schools of business and law; it is very different from simply using case studies as a part of a learning experience, though the details of actual situations described in the cases can be used in many learning settings. In most other contexts, case studies are used in an ad hoc or moderate way, with variable effectiveness (Dooley & Wickham, 1977; Reynolds, 1978).

The central objective of the classical case method is to

enable the individual to meet in action the problems arising out of new situations of an ever-changing environment. Education, accordingly, would consist of acquiring facility to act in the presence of new experience. It asks not how a man may be trained to know, but how a man may be trained to act. (McNair & Hersum, 1954, p. 2)

This objective can be directed toward education, training, or professional development (Dooley & Wickham, 1977). Cases are used to simulate the decision-making challenges of the real world. Participants are given written, detailed, factual descriptions of organizations and specific circumstances confronting them. Their first task is to become familiar with this information through

> careful reading, some experimental figure work to discover the relationships inherent in any financial (or other) data which might be presented, and some thought about the significance and solution of what seemed the most important problems. (Carson, 1954, pp. 82–83)

Preparation for the class case discussion at the heart of the procedure also provides incentive for this familiarization process. In the class, participants are asked what the relevant facts are, what action they would take, and what the reasons for those actions are. The entire experience consists of dialogue between leader and participants and among participants around responses to these and similar questions based on the content of the case under consideration.

While pursuing these questions, the leader plays several roles: discussion leader, resource person, helpful expert, evaluator or summarizer, and judge of performance. The responsibility of the leader is to foster the independent thinking of the participants by challenging their ideas and pushing them to the limits of their understanding, not providing them with information or answers.

> Confronted with cases as a medium of learning, the student experiences a gradual growth in the maturity of his point of view, but the path is not smooth. His mental reactions run successively from great interest and natural curiosity to confusion and some degree of frustration, and then to various degrees of skepticism. In the long run progress seems to be rapid. The student grows in analytical ability and in power to discriminate among relationships of different kinds. (Carson, 1954, pp. 85–86)

The class discussions are engaging because of the competitive spirit that exists among the participants and the quick changes in thought demanded of them. Even though the exclusive focus of the discussion is the content of the case, the dialogue, questions, and challenges generate "pit of the stomach reactions which can hardly be termed academic" (Schoen & Sprague, 1954, pp. 80–81).

In addition to individual study and class discussions, the case method can be used with groups of various sizes and may incorporate lectures, small group discussions, audiovisual methods, and process observation. However, the classical case method generates a different atmosphere than that fostered by the use of other methods. It cannot be combined with simulations or role playing in the same way that they can be combined with each other because of this climate, yet cases themselves can serve as useful additions to many experiential arrangements.

In using this method, leaders have to be aware of the unique characteristics of the approach: its impact, necessary support facilities, and the types of content to which it is best suited. The method is useful for teaching many business and law subjects but would be less appropriate for teaching skills in other disciplines such as counseling or psychotherapy or for transmitting a set body of knowledge or information. Leaders also have to be able to gather or write case material appropriate to their intended objectives and to learn the skills necessary for conducting class case discussions.

Analysis

Analysis of the case method is best discussed under two headings, the "classical approach" and the "moderate approach," in which many of the dynamics of the classical approach are absent.

Classical Case Method.   The classical approach begins with and is dependent on a dramatic *restructuring* of the usual classroom experience. In essence, the structure of a classical case class is essentially a microcosm of the courtroom or competitive business environment; by this symbolic representation of real conditions, the classical case approach maximizes application and minimizes problems of transfer in learning. One might even speculate that the adversary tradition in the legal system and western societies' common law, built up through cases, provides the justification for restructuring of cultural island magnitude. Thus it also can be said that the restructuring provides the basis for realistic socialization of participants within their career environments.

Three other change processes are linked tightly to restructuring. These are *channeling, feedback,* and *conditioning.* The competitive structure results in a high degree of interpersonal aggression and provides a constant reminder that the goal is success and status in the classroom. Weakness is more often scorned than pitied and never defended by fellow students (Cohen, 1973). The first objective of personal behavior in the classroom is to avoid losing; the second is to win. Thus *coercion* predominates and conditioning is a mere appendage. Feedback is evaluative, confrontative, and primarily content-centered. The conditioning associated with evaluative feedback is positive reinforcement for adequate performance and punishment for poor performance. Systematic written assignments buttress the punishment–avoidance dynamic. In sum, the channeling, feedback, and conditioning are all part of the coercive nature of the arrangement; fear seems to be the dominant emotion in many first-rate law and business schools.

Coincident with the above change processes, *identification* with the leader is often very powerful, being a complex mixture of love and fear. The demanding and sometimes personally punitive nature of the leader creates an effect that goes beyond conditioning. Moreover, the leader demonstrates successful argumentative behavior while putting down students, thus constantly and persuasively asserting his or her own credibility and thereby increases the likelihood of convincing participants to accept direction. Participants learn to use fear in a competitive context via identification. Fear is introjected (Redl, 1942).

Within the classical case method, the prime source of *support* is the structure and predictability of classroom activity. High levels of participant *activation* and much active involvement in case analyses result from the combination of coercion, conditioning, identification, and *persuasion*. Participants receive some practice early in the experience, but the *action* emphasis is on performance.

The high fear activation generates considerable *commitment*, if for only survival purposes. Commitment is to the activity and to one's self. This suggests I–it relationships, within which the "I's" all attempt to assert their wills on the "its," the other participants and the instructor. The battle of wills further energizes the competitive environment. Although the classical case method creates a powerful cultural island restructuring, as does the T-group method, it is antithetical in process to the T-group approach where an alignment of wills is ideal. Both methods have potent capacity to unfreeze participants through the stripping process; sensitivity training is more personal and the classical case approach is more coercive.

It appears that the classical case approach uses competition and a generally "defensive climate" to activate mastery needs in participants (see White on fulfillment in Chapter 1). The tendency for cases and discussion to lead participants up blind alleys and into traps, combined with leader control in the form of focusing discussion on particular topics, sparking controversy, avoiding digressions, and bringing about predetermined conclusions, can also create a contest of wills between the leader and participants and a feeling of "being had."

What happened was that some of the most vocal executives felt that they had been manipulated by the faculty member into competing with each other. The result was that, during the next class, one of the most vocal members announced that he wasn't going to get "caught" again, and he then retreated from future discussion. The observer noted that the rate of participation initiated by the other executives in the class session diminished significantly. In order to keep the discussion alive, the faculty member had to call on the executives more often. Also, for the first time, several executives were observed to say in response to the faculty member's summary of their views, "No, I did not say that. My position was . . . ." (Argyris, 1980, p. 294)

There is strong motivation among participants to *perform*, but the classroom dynamic also creates resistance and leads to rebellion. This dynamic appears to occur even if role plays or other techniques are also used with the classical case approach.

One serious problem then is that *exploration* and *experimentation* are limited in the classical case method, or, to use Argyris' terminology, no double-loop learning occurs. Single-loop learning is distinguished from double-loop learning as follows:

> Learning may be defined as the detection and correction of error. Learning that results in the detection and correction of error without changing the underlying policies, assumptions, and goals may be called single-loop. Double-loop learning occurs when the detection and correction of error requires changes in the underlying policies, assumptions, and goals. A thermostat is a single-loop learner because it detects when the room is too hot or too cold. A thermostat would be a double-loop learner if it questioned why it was set at 65 degrees or why it was measuring heat. (Argyris, 1980, p. 291)

Argyris asserts that the pressure, developed through the classical case method, forces participants into preprogrammed actions of a "model 1" nature that are primarily defensive in character (Argyris, 1976; Argyris & Schon, 1974, 1978). Behaviorally, the participants cling tenaciously to the past even though they may assimilate and become facile with new content of the case. It thus appears that the goals of training, professional development, and personal growth cannot be achieved with this method; only education can be pursued. The limits here are also significant because cases need to be "company specific" for lessons to be useful (Argyris, 1980). The limits on transferability of learning should be further researched, because the apparent major strength of the case approach is its tangible applicability.

Finally, besides acquiring knowledge and competitive skills, participants in this intense learning technique experience significant *re-cognition*. Here it is the implosion of the work load that probably has the most significant change impact. But the *persuasion* and the constructs with which the participants are urged to consider their world are also important. In conclusion, the most profound thing about the classical case approach is its conscious effort to evoke a conflict of wills in such a way that whatever the participants do they lose the battle and succumb to the model.

The Moderate Case Approach. In the moderate version or versions of the case approach, the case serves as the vehicle through which the participants can project themselves into a hypothetical situation (Dooley & Wickham, 1977). Thus, the change dynamics in this method in many ways can resemble those of simulations and role playing, rather than those of the classical case method. The first difference is that the case can provide an alternative structure, but participants are not necessarily placed in a restructured social context. In other words, their *restructuring* is hypothetical rather than real. A *supportive* group context serves the same function for the moderate case approach as it does in most other experiential learning contexts.

In contrast to the classical approach, the moderate approach does not set the case at center stage. Instead, the case is an appendage, illustration, or expansion of some other aspects of the class. *Channeling, feedback, activation,* and *conditioning* are attenuated in the use of the moderate case approach. For channeling, nothing beyond the typical small group discussion norms apply. Typically, one can assume that the topic is attended to and the task and coaction cause activation. Interesting and useful discussion is positively reinforcing. The absence of formal evaluations increases the likelihood of these positive exchanges and is an important part of the supportive, low-risk context. Feedback in the form of knowledge of results satisfies curiosity for information. Advocates of high student autonomy often underestimate the power to influence via timely presentations of information. The *coercion* of the classical method is strenuously avoided except during written case analyses, which are done individually and formally evaluated.

By contrast, *identification* is highly important. Participants can fantasize about the case, project themselves into it, and personalize the discussion rather than remain detached from it. They need the opportunity to observe the contributions of others closely, so that they do not either scramble to prepare their own contributions or, through lethargy, allow themselves to drift away from the discussion. This attentiveness requires both exciting cases and eager participants, conditions which are often not met.

Persuasion has a number of purposes here. First, the leader needs to convince participants of the learning implications of identification and involvement. During the discussion the leader needs to encourage the making of cognitive linkages between case material and other relevant content, as well as the application thereof. Interesting illustrations demonstrate the emotional impact of persuasion. The actual discussion is the *action* and is of moderate intensity, in contrast to the high intensity discussions of the classical method. Thus activation levels are relatively low and very much depend on the level of interest that can be kindled in participants.

The president of the Western Academy of Management recently decried the problem of inadequate quality and quantity of case material for general use; no doubt herein is the crux of the problem, because the case itself carries a much greater burden for generating activation in the moderate approach than in the classical approach. The individuals who learn most in this approach are intrisically motivated, highly disciplined self-starters, but generally low *commitment* is all that can be expected. Thus the moderate approach should be supplemented, first by increasing participation (Miner, 1978) and second by making use of other experiential methods (Gadon, 1977).

In summary, then, the hallmarks of the moderate case approach are: (1) avoidance of coercion, (2) dependence on identification with the case and, (3) discussion of cases in a low-risk context. Since the learning situation generates only low levels of activation and commitment, the moderate case method is not as truly "experiential" as the other methods already discussed.

The Lecture

The lecture or verbal presentation is the most popular and widely used method of classroom instruction (Bligh et al., 1975; Gage & Berliner, 1975; Husband, 1949; McKeachie, 1969; McLeish, 1976).

> As a teaching device it is undoubtedly the most economical method by which the individual can present in an individualized and continuous argument the general framework for understanding the fundamentals of a particular subject, emphasizing the key concepts and involving the audience in reflective thought that moves in time with the on-going performance. An air of studied improvisation gives the lecture its salient character, that is, an extended conversation that has developed into a monologue because of the intensity of student interest in the thoughtful contribution of the master. (McLeish, 1976, p. 253)

The effective lecture engages the participants in a creative listening and thinking process by stating problems and guidelines for their resolution and not simply by providing solutions (Odiorne, 1977). Still, it is important for the lecturer to be credible, observably knowledgable, and committed to the material. The effectiveness of a lecture is enhanced by organizational factors such as an outline, clear transitions, highlighting important points, and pauses for reflection. Questions are helpful for stimulation and for diversity (Gage & Berliner, 1975). Controversial illustrations and evidence also add stimulation. Most important is that participants are encouraged to grapple with the content as it is presented rather than just being passive receptacles.

In using the lecture, leaders need to keep a number of points in mind. Because of the convenience and flexibility of the lecture format, care must be taken not to slip into its overuse; it should be a supplement and provide perspective to the experiential component of the learning activity. In experiential learning the lecture is used in support of the experience-based methods. The entire quality of the learning experience is transformed if this relationship is reversed. However, errors in the opposite extreme should also be avoided. The assumption that the participants will make connections themselves without having them presented is unwarranted. And when these connections are not made, the effectiveness of the learning experience is reduced.

Analysis

There are three kinds of lectures: the pure or ideal lecture, the classical lecture as found in most public educational contexts, and the experiential learning lecture.

The Ideal Lecture.   The ideal lecture is voluntary and thus *commitment* to the subject or to the person is assumed. It then becomes the presenter's opportunity and responsibility to influence through *persuasion,* that is, to present the information in such a way that its emotional and cognitive elements have the desired impact.

In this regard, the distinction between persuasion and *identification* becomes somewhat artificial, because sources of credibility such as physical attractiveness and status are also sources of identification. The kind of identification that is critical is the intrinsically satisfying relationship with what Redl (1942) called the "patriarch" or "leader" types. We recall here that identificatory learning does not result only from external reinforcements accruing to the model but also from the reinforcement inherent in the relationship between participants and model.

Channeling can be useful in creating vicarious reinforcement when social norms such as interrupting the speaker with applause are encouraged. The applause granted a political speaker, for example, is at once an expression of agreement with what the speaker has said (commitment) and also an overt reinforcement of the speaker that some participants will experience as vicarious reinforcement.

Interest, challenge, and emotionally laden content increase *activation* as does proper delivery in terms of loudness, pitch, quality of tone, articulation, pronunciation, cadence, and emphasis or the variation in loudness, pitch, tone, and cadence (Walter, Austin, Beattie, & Heflin, 1978). Stylistic or logical alterations, such as the injection of humor, can be used to relieve tension, create a friendly atmosphere, and establish a positive climate. Simultaneously, these contributions provide *positive reinforcement* for participants who often perceive the latter contributions as *supportive* and indicative of leader acceptance. This acceptance can encourage further identification.

In addition to the conditioning, identification, and persuasion elements, *re-cognition* can occur through the rational, suggestive, and complex mechanisms. By building on shared beliefs and perceptions, a lecturer avoids resistance, and new information fits easily into a listener's rational system. Not only can participants accept some new ideas or make some commitments to action, they might also begin to think in a new way. Through suggestion, participant readiness can be increased and participants can be covertly sensitized to issues otherwise out of their sphere of awareness (Torbert, 1972). Attributions and suggestions about participants, their world, or the causal nature of a variety of variables can also be powerful. Kelly's (1955) construct alternativism and its four-level hierarchy of cognitive change is an illustration of a complex mechanism by which a lecture can lead to re-cognition. That is, the leader might attempt only to alter participants' views of themselves within their own mental system (contrast reconstruction) or might attempt to aid participants in the formation of new constructs to replace old ones.

Participant actions are limited in the lecture approach, yet *action* is of major importance in building commitment. In writing notes, participants actively decide what parts of the delivered message are worth organizing, summarizing, and recording (Odiorne, 1977). Thus the two key criteria for commitment—personal volition and explicit outcomes for decision making—are both present. More explicit, active expressions of opinion about the message, such as applause, are also important commitment builders. For the most part, the action called for from participants is of the performance variety, different in purpose from action in other experiential methods. Action affects commitment and aids participants in focusing their attention on the speaker's message. In other methods action indicates activation, while involvement is cultivated for commitment building. In its pure form, the lecture has cognitive commitment procedures that are direct and immediate.

The Classical Lecture Method. The classical lecture method presumes that the change processes discussed for the ideal lecture are present, but because of limitations on voluntarism in public education and the presence of evaluation and competition, the climate can become defensive. Because of potential *coercion,* participants become concerned to avoid incurring the overt displeasure of the lecturer and to achieve a good grade or avoid a bad one. Performance-centered *feedback* heightens the coercive climate.

Thinking may be more focused but is also likely to be less free. *Identification* may be through fear rather than love or admiration (Redl, 1942). *Overactivation* can occur if too much emphasis on evaluation exists and can have "interference" *re-cognitive* effects. Typically the element of evaluation provides the activation that may be absent from less than ideal lectures. *Commitment,* emanating from engaging the participants' will, is low for most people. Commitment tends to be in spite of most participants' will rather than because of it, and is a direct function of coercion. It is a compliance rather than internalization mode of conduct.

The Experiential Lecture. The experiential lecture is short, focused, and intended to provide structure or suggestions that facilitate *re-cognition* during the activity. It is generally limited to one or two specific, relevant ideas by which participants can perceive, think about, and discuss the actual activity. *Persuasion* and *support* directed at participant involvement are generally present. Coercion is avoided. *Feedback* is primarily supportive, not confrontative and not linked to evaluation. It is noteworthy that participants often request feedback comparing their interactions with other groups. This feedback appears to be positively reinforcing and generally these curiosities are satisfied easily. It is often fun. *Positive reinforcement,* however, is important not only because it contributes to the supportive climate and can be used to give closure to the experience, but also because it represents another opportunity for rewarding participants for their involvement.

Reading

Reading the printed word is the most available and flexible format for transmitting knowledge and is probably the most important learning tool an individual can possess (Bligh et al., 1975; Braken & Malmquist, 1970; Cook, 1977; Jennings, 1965; Johns, 1974; McKeachie, 1969; Rothkopf, 1976; Williams, 1976). Participants can read and discuss short items before or after an activity. Experiential learning is often seen as being biased against some of the more traditional methods of instruction such as assigned readings. It is possible to overlook the value, if not the necessity, of supplementing the experiential component with reading activities. Reading adds a stable instructional system to the experience-based facet of the learning activity, an unstable instructional system (Rothkopf, 1976, p. 93).

Analysis

The fundamental purpose of readings is to provide a straightforward set of constructs for *re-cognition.* Kelly's contrast reconstruction is the most simple level at which this can occur. In this case reading materials build on the participants' current system by adding detail or providing moderate change. A more ambitious goal can also be pursued, that of aiding participants in the formation of new constructs. When readings are presented before an activity, the new constructs provide the participants with a cognitive map shared by others in the group that can guide behavior and interpretive responses to the activity. When provided after an activity, the new constructs can be rapidly assimilated by participants, since at this point they are activated and tend to be attempting to make sense of their experience (see the ethnomethodology discussion under contextual models of human functioning in Chapter 1).

Readings also generate *activation* and *commitment*. Prereadings can ready participants for an activity by evoking desires and aiding in goal setting. *Persuasion, identification, feedback,* and *conditioning* can buttress the re-cognition effectiveness of a given reading. Clear, credible information paired with emotionally appealing examples or illustrations tightly anchored to emotionally significant aspects of the activity are persuasive. Similarly, the vividness and perceived relevance of events in readings affect the reader's identification with the material. Descriptive results of actions or policies presented are in a sense an aspect of feedback of special significance to the highly invested, involved reader. Readings that entertain or provide answers to questions already in the minds of participants contribute positive reinforcement. An overload of applications or too broad a scope prevents adequate linkage of the reading material to the experience. *Coercion, support, restructuring, channeling,* and *action,* as discussed for the other methods, are of little direct or immediate relevance to the use of readings in experiential learning.

Written Tasks

Written tasks are an important component of most learning situations and are the primary means used for documenting what has been learned (Bligh et al., 1975; McKeachie, 1969). Log books aid in generating attention, strengthening memory, and summarizing data by requiring participants to spend some time each day recording their ongoing reactions to and thoughts about the learning experience. Participants also could be encouraged to take notes during lectures or summary discussions or at any time a particular event strikes them as significant.

Important benefits of written tasks include the generation of a permanent record, a basis for self-evaluation over time, a vehicle for integrating experiences and other wisdom, and a source of evaluation of the experience itself.

Analysis

As for a number of other methods discussed already, it is important that written tasks in an experiential learning context be integrated with the actual activity and should be relatively easy in the sense that they draw on existing skills of participants rather than trying to build new skills. The *action* is performance rather than experimentation in character and the central outcomes of the action are of a *commitment*-building and *re-cognition*-inducing nature.

The explicitness of placing perceptions, opinions, and observations on paper as well as having to make choices in that act affect the degree to which participants direct their will toward the challenge associated with the written task. Attention and perception are focused. Systematic reflection and systematic recording of memories, thoughts, and observations can have significant re-cognitive impact on one's mental organization. In transactional analysis training, for example, participants are encouraged to reflect upon and write down memories regarding values, habitual emotional reactions, parental modeling, attributions and indoctrinations, and significant events that comprise the script. To do this they are guided with a set of categories that lends itself to a plan of action for change.

Another way in which written tasks affect re-cognition relates directly to self-monitoring re-cognition techniques. Here keeping records of behavioral events aids individuals in overcoming perceptual biases, assumptions, and beliefs, and can increase their ability to be more accurately aware of "objective reality." Further, such monitoring activities provide the basis for other self-management activities such as planning and self-conditioning.

Evaluation is avoided since writing often serves as a way for participants to assimilate a desired structure or approach to issues; the combinations of writing and *action* provide sufficient activation for learning even when no evaluation is included. In fact, the instructions, guidelines, or series of questions that direct the writing activity are often structured to serve many functions such as *support*. Punishing and *coercive* contingencies that inevitably accompany evaluation can confuse these already complex dynamics. *Activation* and *conditioning* are generally high because of the totality of the experience and the personal nature of much that is written.

Written tasks can be used in a variety of ways for *feedback*. Participant interpersonal feedback is more systematic and specific when a written preparation is required. The process of feedback can be facilitated through written procedures such as anonymous sharing. Finally, written tasks have long-term learning consequences. In addition to supplementing the individual's memory regarding insights, decisions, and action plans, the written material serves as a focus of *identification* with one's self as one experiences learning. And this can be self-reinforcing.

Summary

Effective experiential learning relies on the use of the classical methods. Case material can be used to link the learning experience with real situations. Lectures, readings, and written tasks provide structure and organization especially useful for re-cognitive change. Though these methods do not form the central part of the learning experience, they are indispensable to its ultimate success.

CHAPTER TEN

Supporting
Methods

*The perfected man does not
interfere in the life of
beings, he does not impose
himself on them, but he
helps all beings to their
freedom.*

Martin Buber

The supporting methods in experiential learning for the most part cannot stand by themselves, yet they can contribute much to the effectiveness of a learning design. These methods include: process observation, alone time, fantasy, audiovisual methods, instrumentation, and projects and field experiences. The section on audiovisual methods is much longer than the others because of the different uses of the various techniques and because video tape feedback can be used as a central experience as well as in support of other methods.

Process Observation

In this procedure some participants watch others in a simulation, role play, or similar task within the actual learning setting. Participants may subsequently be asked to give feedback to those they have observed or share their impressions and reactions to the events they witnessed. Some audiovisual methods are useful for facilitating this observation–feedback process. Observers focus upon nonverbal and verbal behavior such as (South, 1972, pp. 131–132):

1　Body configuration—position of head, arms, trunk and legs.

2　Body state—muscle tone, alertness, attention, involvement.

3　Movements—nods, gestures, eye contacts, positioning with respect to others.

4　Voice tone, inflection and pitch.

5　Speaking speed.

Observers then provide feedback to the participants on the relationship between these behaviors and feelings, involvement, influence and influence style, goal setting, leadership, decision making, group task and maintenance functions, group atmosphere, membership, roles, and norms (Pfeiffer & Jones, 1972, pp. 21–24). In order to focus their attention on *how* the discussion is progressing, observers need to be disengaged from *what* is being said. For this reason it is important for observers to maintain a detached objectivity at all times.

There are many different systems for organizing observations (Bales, 1970; Flanders, 1970), and the choice of categories, their comprehensiveness, and specificity is determined by the objectives of the experience, the nature of the activity, and the observation skills and sophistication of the participants. Observing, giving feedback, and receiving the feedback can be useful to both observers and participants and can occur during the learning activities or be used away from the formal learning setting. In the latter instance, the individual's normal routine is monitored.

Process observation can be used in conjunction with experience-based methods such as simulations, role playing, and dyad and group interactions, and can be greatly enhanced by being combined with instrumentation such as rating scales and audiovisual methods, especially video recording and playback. Process observation lends behavioral validation to the learning experience norm of participants' responsibility in learning. When observers give feedback to participants away from confounding leader–participant dynamics, the potency of their contributions and the importance of observers in learning are underlined.

Written observer forms or verbal guidelines are generally useful to focus observers' efforts and to link observations with other aspects of the learning experience. Guidance for giving feedback also is needed and generally encourages descriptive, tentative, and nonevaluative exchange (Hanson, 1975). Leaders should attempt not to confound the participant observation–feedback process with their own comments and reflections if they wish to foster the participants' feelings of responsibility for their learning.

Analysis

Process observation appears to most inexperienced experiential leaders as the most simple and obvious method available. Contrary to role playing, however, effective use of process observation requires precise and firm leader direction. Common social or learning interaction norms must be transcended. Thus, the pivotal change process is *restructuring* and the first concern of the leader is to provide adequate *support* and *persuasion* to guarantee that the restructuring is successful.

The reason that support and persuasion are important is that they assuage inhibitions and counteract unproductive norms. In this society, it generally is not considered polite to tell people what you really think of them or to watch them too closely. Observers can thus feel embarrassment or even fear and be reluctant to perform the activity. A persuasive message about the importance and legitimacy of accumulating accurate and detailed information provides justification for this initial deviation from normal social intercourse. Support and persuasion can also overcome inhibitions about talking directly about feelings with strangers or in relatively large groups. For example, process observers are required to adopt a "here and now" focus in their observations and subsequent feedback and discussion. These social norms are more consistent with T-groups than with normal learning or social circumstance. Also, some observers identify with the participants' discomfort of being observed during the activity and with their fear of being put on the spot by the observers' feedback. This raises fears of hurting others, saying something wrong, going too far, and the possibility of social rejection. Observers also experience performance anxiety about being able to observe anything of value and to provide meaningful feedback to the group. By symbolically taking on the role of the "leader," they increase this vulnerability. In the extreme, they can be perceived as vain, disloyal, wasteful of other people's time, and even blundering.

The establishment of the observer role also runs counter to some other general learning norms, for example, singling out a few participants to be treated differently than the rest. More important is the way in which this arrangement alters the norm of responsibility wherein the leader is no longer the source of learning. Thus the initiation of the observer role is a critical contribution to the overall restructuring for other methods. This reorganization type restructuring clearly shifts the responsibility to participants, as advocated by Argyris (1980), through the articulation of specific roles and the physical separation of observers from the rest of the group. A high sense of responsibility is evoked when there are expectations of being observed and giving and receiving feedback. This performance pressure is highly *activating* and leads to two primary *re-cognition* dynamics for the observers. As the process observers focus in on other participants, they rapidly absorb or inculcate constructs and even the entire construct system of the observer guide.

The process of being an observer encourages putting one's self in the place of others in a kind of vicarious role playing situation. Thus many of the re-cognitive dynamics discussed for role playing are experienced by the observers. *Identification* also can have powerful learning consequences for observers as they report and become excited about specific acts, behaviors, styles, or strategies of participants that were seen to be particularly effective. The quality of identification possible in this experiential method is fundamentally different from the other methods discussed because the individual is free of interaction obligations in the short term and thus free to focus complete attention on observation. Once the structure is accepted by participants, the explicitness, perceived importance, and overt *action* of process observation builds *commitment.* Following an activity, participants nearly always show great curiosity about what observers might have seen. If the observed participants are given copies of the observer guides prior to receipt of feedback, the coherence and meaning of the feedback is increased and also the constructs can be more readily absorbed, resulting in re-cognition.

It is essential that *coercion* be avoided and perhaps the two most important antidotes to coercion are lack of evaluation and active support from the leader and fellow participants. A tone of "keeping it constructive" is of further value since *conditioning* emphasizes knowledge of results and positive reinforcement. Punishment is as counterproductive as coercion because it reduces the long-term viability of using the method. Obvious protection from evaluation is useful.

Feedback is enhanced by group identification, a sense of congruence between one's self, the pivotal values of a learning experience, and fellow participants in the learning arrangement. Some discussion following the actual observer feedback can be valuable for clarification, airing of feelings, and equalizing of participant status. Leaders can also encourage the exchange of mutual and explicit pledges of commitment with regard to change at this point. Still it is important to avoid undercutting the delegated responsibility of the observers.

Alone Time

Alone time refers to giving participants the task of thinking about some aspect of the learning experience in a segment of time set aside especially for that purpose. It aids participants in summarizing and organizing their experience and can be a prelude to having participants discuss or act on the focus of their consideration. For example, in a personal growth workshop, a participant could be assigned to be alone and reflect on the events he has experienced. He is to focus on himself, his feeling, and his relations to others and to practice the techniques of fantasy . . . (and) . . . association . . . This activity provides an opportunity for the participant to explore himself and to provide a framework and support for introspection of a serious nature. (Schutz, 1967, p. 62)

For many people this is an electrifying experience. Several report that they had never used their time alone in this way before. For many, it affords an opportunity to consolidate experience.

Analysis

Alone time is totally focused on *re-cognition.* It initially involves *restructuring* in the form of decentralization as the entire responsibility for the learning process is charged to the participant. Leader *support* and *persuasiveness* are necessary initially to encourage participants into this mode. The action of re-cognition centers on participants' exploration of feelings, thoughts, insights, and other information. These explorations are linked with two important phenomena. The first is the individual sorting out what is desired from a variety of possible outcomes; these desires then become the bases for decisions such as goals for further change. In short, desire grows into active will and thus *commitment.* The second is an increased sense of mental organization around the issues addressed in the learning experience. This mental restructuring tends both to direct will and be directed by it. The combined effects of the re-cognitive and commitment dynamics are increased self-monitoring and increased self-management. Most important, alone time is provided at particular points in the learning arrangement when other methods have provided participants with a rich set of stimuli with which to cope.

Fantasy

Fantasy and guided imagery can be used in a variety of ways to expand awareness and help people explore their thoughts and feelings. Fantasy is sometimes assumed incorrectly to be mere relaxation or digression, but to the experiential leader this is not the case. Fantasy methods use the images and symbols that form the substance of much of an individual's mental activity in the service of achieving greater self-awareness, understanding, and growth (James, 1929, pp. 378–379). The use of methods such as free association and varieties of dream analysis is well established in therapeutic settings (Freud, 1962; Jung, 1961) and these procedures and variations of them have been adapted for use across a broad spectrum of learning experiences (Schutz, 1967, 1973; Perls, 1969a, 1969b, 1969c; Hammer, 1967; Hendricks & Wills, 1975).

The primary means of implementing this strategy in a learning experience is through the use of guided or directed fantasy, imagery, and day-dreaming. There are many different types of these procedures. Often they initially involve the use of mood setting statements, body movement, or breathing exercises to increase participant relaxation. Once relaxed, with eyes closed, participants might be told a stimulus story or asked to visualize some scene, event, or starting point for the fantasy (Stevens, 1971). The leader or guide then identifies or suggests symbols or images, proposes directions, or encourages confronting and overcoming obstacles. For example:

> An object is broken—the guide helps the person put it back together.
>
> A person dreams of flying—the guide helps the person to go to the end of the flight, to find out who or what is there, and to bring back something of value to share with the group.
>
> A person dreams of climbing stairs—the guide helps him or her reach the top.
>
> A dreamer is being attacked—the guide helps fight the attackers.
>
> A child falls—the guide encourages him or her to continue the fall until he or she falls *somewhere.* (Hendricks & Wills, 1975, p. 71)

Through questions and suggestions, participants construct a fantasy experience that they can relate to some other facet of themselves or the learning experience.

Another technique involves teaching participants to remember and work with their dreams. In this method, focusing on dreams is based on the premise that:

> Man discovers his deepest self and reveals his greatest creative power at times when his psychic processes are most free from immediate involvement with the environment and most under the control of his indwelling balancing or homeostatic power. The freest type of psychic play occurs in sleep and the social acceptance of the dream would, thererefore, constitute the deepest possible acceptance of the individual. (Stewart, 1969, p. 164)

Participants can be taught how to remember, continue, and complete their dreams either with or without the assistance of a leader for the purpose of making the information contained in dreams accessible for use in waking activities.

Fantasy methods generally aid individuals to become aware of aspects of themselves or their circumstances that might otherwise be avoided or lost. Fantasy activities can be combined with any of the other methods and productively used to:

1   Relax or energize participants.

2 Introduce novelty, variety, and diversity to the learning experience.

3 Allow maximal freedom and exploration of personal issues.

4 Generate creative ideas, information, or alternatives for a given situation.

5 Promote introspection and reflection.

6 Help participants integrate various aspects of the learning experience.

In using these methods, leaders should have considerable experience as participants in fantasy activities. It is important to create an atmosphere in the group conducive to fantasy work and not to select inappropriate symbols or to guide the fantasies in directions that might surface problems beyond the scope of the learning experience. When used as a part of an educational experience, failures in staging or guidance most often result in the fantasy having very little or no impact. However, when used in personal growth or therapy, poor guidance could have more serious consequences. Participants can become overwhelmed with feelings and images or be left in an unresolved and very agitated condition.

Analysis

Fantasy involves a thinking *action* rather than a behavioral one and emphasizes a particular kind of thought that goes beyond mere reflection. Thus, the thinking that occurs in alone time typically lacks important elements discussed here. For this discussion, it is useful to distinguish between the action of engaging in the fantasy and the action of sharing the fantasy. The learning arrangement is typically *restructured* in a decentralized way in preparation for the initiation of the actual fantasy. Desirable arrangements here include comfortable seating, sufficient distance among participants so that a sense of abandonment is possible, appropriate lighting, quietness, and privacy. The emphasis is on eliminating external demands other than those provided directly as a precursor to the activity.

Within this setting a number of leader behaviors are valuable in initiating fantasies for participants. The leader, through demeanor, tone, and topics addressed, provides *persuasive* communications that set the emotional tone for the learning activity. Implicit in this tone is the appropriate *activation* level as well as the desired carrying feelings for the fantasy. Simultaneously, and perhaps with the same communication, the leader needs to create in the minds of participants an understanding of the support within the learning situation and inherent in the leader as a person. Depending on the arrangement, communications can also be directed at providing a set of concepts that can be used by participants to structure their fantasy experiences. The final element of this overall

preparation involves making specific suggestions that enhance participants' emotions, expectations, and mental imagery and then provide the
final springboard for the actual fantasy. Stevens provides a long yet useful
example of the verbalizations from a leader that can launch and guide a
fantasy:

Wise Man

I want you to imagine that you are walking up a trail in the mountains at
night. There is a full moon which lets you see the trail easily, and you can
also see quite a lot of your surroundings . . . What is this trail like? . . . What
else can you see around you? . . . How do you feel as you walk up this
mountain trail? . . . Just ahead there is a small side trail that leads up higher
to a cave that is the home of a very wise man who can tell you the answer
to any question. Turn off onto this side trail and walk toward the wise man's
cave . . . Notice how your surroundings change as you move up this trail and
come closer to his cave . . .

When you arrive at the cave, you will see a small campfire in front of the
cave, and you will be able to faintly see the silent wise man by the light of
the dancing flames of the fire. . . . Go up to the fire, put some more wood
on it, and sit quietly . . . As the fire burns more brightly you will be able to
see the wise man more clearly. Take some time to really become aware of
him—his clothes, his body, his face, his eyes . . .

Now ask the wise man some question that is important to you. As you ask
this question, continue to watch the wise man, and see how he reacts to what
you say. He might answer you with words alone, or he might also answer you
with a gesture or facial expression, or he might show you something . . . What
kind of answer does he give you? . . .

Now become the wise man . . . What is your existence like as this wise man?
. . . How do you feel and what is your life like? . . . What is your attitude
toward this visitor who questions you? . . . How do you feel toward this
visitor? . . . What do you say to your visitor—whether in words, gestures, or
actions? . . .

Become yourself again and continue this dialogue with the wise man. Do you
understand what he is saying to you? . . . Do you have any other questions
to ask him? . . . How do you feel toward the wise man? . . .

Now become the wise man again, and continue this conversation . . . Is there
anything else you can say to your visitor? . . .

Become yourself again. You will soon have to say goodbye to the wise man
. . . Say anything else you want to before you leave . . . Just as you are about
to say goodbye to the wise man, he turns and reaches into an old leather bag
behind him, and searches in the bag for something very special to give to
you . . . He takes it out of the bag and gives it to you to take home with you
. . . Look at the gift he gives you . . . How do you feel toward the wise man
now? . . . Tell him how you feel . . . and slowly say goodbye to him . . .

Now turn away, and start walking back down the mountain trail, carrying your gift with you. . . . As you walk back down the trail, look at the trail carefully, so that you will remember how to find your way back to the wise man when you want to visit him again . . . Be aware of your surroundings, and how you feel. . . .

Now keep your eyes closed, and bring your gift with you as you return to this room . . . Take some time now to examine this gift in more detail . . . What did he give you? Really discover more about it . . . Touch it . . . smell it . . . turn it over in your hands and look at it carefully . . .

Now become this gift. Identify with it and describe yourself. What are you like as this gift? . . . How do you feel as this thing? . . . What are your qualities? . . . What do you do, or how can you be used or appreciated? . . .

Now become yourself again and look at the gift and see if you can discover even more about it . . . Do you notice any change in it, or anything that you didn't notice before? . . . Now put this gift away carefully and safely in your memory, . . . and say goodbye to it for now . . . (Stevens, 1971, pp. 183–185)

At this point during the actual activity, participants embark upon free association from the point of departure provided. Possibilities are limitless since no physical constraints exist. Consequently, the activity is of an exploration variety. Following a brief fantasy of one to five minutes, participants are "brought back to the room" and are typically encouraged to write down an account of their experience. The reflection, remembering, and recording of the fantasy serve the initial function of self-monitoring *re-cognitive* change. The combined effects of the exploration and the self-monitoring in stage one of the action is typically labeled awareness expansion (i.e., personal growth) and is primarily re-cognitive in nature. Individual *commitment* grows immediately out of this awareness since desires quite often surface and are made tangible. This initial level of commitment and associated enthusiasm paves the way for the second stage of the action.

The sharing stage of fantasy work is characterized by further leader *support*, interpretive structures, and motivational suggestions. These focus on the challenge of guiding individual participants to work with fantasy material and to think about its meaning and implications. Leaders are more specific in their comments yet less directive at this stage. The leader must avoid co-opting the participant's effort to explore the personal issues raised if the desired loosening up of assumptions is to be maximized. The participant begins by sharing the fantasy and then immediately works with it for additional learning. "Work" is defined as further exploration into facets of the fantasy, experimentation with reprogramming or adjusting the fantasy, practice of particular skills or responses to particular elements in the fantasy, and performance of desirable behavior based on the fantasy.

Re-cognition during the sharing phase can be even greater than in the actual fantasy. In this regard coping training and anxiety management principles are helpful as long as they are not used to avoid the work. Similarly, most of the principles of rational control can come into play during sharing. Working with fantasies is also typically directed at issues of generalization or making connections between the fantasy images and real life issues. Responsive leadership and a relatively low-risk climate are useful to the individual since fear often blocks progress. Finally, self-management procedures such as making specific plans for action provide closure for the participants and a basis for the continuation of change.

Commitment grows out of many aspects of sharing. For example, participants learn to approach and deal with problems in a new way. Decisions made that are based on the fantasy often aid in the resolution of conflicts, provide impetus for movement in desired directions, and increase commitment to identified areas for immediate development and change. Overt sharing and working with fantasy material in the group increases commitment to the whole fantasy process and increases the likelihood of its subsequent usefulness.

The discussions of sharing and working to this point have stressed the impact on the individual, but the effect on others is also important. The ideas of *activation, channeling,* and *identification* are useful here. These processes tend to initiate or sustain other people in pursuing their own fantasies throughout the balance of the learning experience. Consequently, if the fantasy procedure is used repeatedly, these change processes form a cycle which contributes to the power of the learning experience. Broad sharing of the fantasies and using a variety of orienting themes enrich the learning and minimize the chances that individual participants will be "left out" because they could not become engaged using one specific theme. *Feedback* and *conditioning* are limited to judicious encouragement of particularly vivid, clear fantasies, constructive sharing, and work. *Coercion* is to be avoided.

Audiovisual Methods

Audiovisual technology is an increasingly important and rapidly expanding instructional methodology (Armsey & Dahl, 1973; Briggs, Campeau, Gagne, & May, 1967; Brown, Lewis, & Harcleroad, 1973; Kemp, 1975; Leifer, 1976; Thompson, 1969; Unwin, 1969; Wittich & Schuller, 1973). Its popularity is the result of the diversity and impact it brings to instructional situations, and the reduced cost and increased availability of much of the hardware associated with its use. The techniques can be roughly grouped into five categories: graphic presentation methods such as blackboards, flip charts, wall diagrams, and photographs; models and life demonstrations; still and moving projected aids such as slides, film strips, overhead projectors, and films; audio systems such as record players and audiotape recorders; and video systems such as closed circuit television and video recording and playback (Duncan, 1969).

This methodology can be used to aid information transmission in an experiential learning design. Audiovisual techniques can also generate supporting information in a variety of ways. Audio and video recording and playback can be used to record a group's action during a task, and this material can become the focus of the debriefing process or simply be made available to participants to listen to or view at their leisure. In addition, participants may be shown photographs, slides, or films as a stimulus to provoke thoughts and feelings or to generate discussion around a certain theme.

Concepts and ideas can be clarified or emphasized through the presentation of various visual or auditory cues. Through these techniques, participants can be helped to understand, integrate, and place into perspective their thoughts, feelings, and behavior resulting from involvement generated by some other method. After participating in a group problem solving task that created interpersonal conflict among the participants, the group could be shown the film *Twelve Angry Men* to illustrate how conflict was managed in a different group situation.

The use of audiovisual methods is pervasive; they have been used traditionally to complement lectures, readings, and written forms of instruction and are integrated with many other methods, like process observation, in innumerable ways. More recently, entire learning activities have been based on the recording and playing back of participant behavior using videotape. In these situations the technology becomes an indispensable part of the process. The Interpersonal Process Recall (IPR) system developed by Norman Kagan and his associates (Kagan, Krathwohl, et al., 1967) is a case in point:

> [IPR] provides participants in a recently concluded diadic encounter with maximum cues for reliving the experience by means of video-tape playback. The participants view the playback in separate rooms and are encouraged by interrogators at significant points in the playback to recall feelings and interpret behavior. Parallel reactions are obtained from the participants through simultaneous interruption of the video-tape playback. (Kagan, Krathwohl, & Miller, 1963, p. 237)

There are also many audiotape programs designed to facilitate group interaction in the absence of a leader; these groups have no direction except the audiotaped instructions.

When using these methods, leaders first must have a working knowledge of the probable impact of the different audiovisual methods; second, have the necessary skill or expertise to locate or develop the desired materials; and third, be able to operate the necessary equipment. Because of the powerful impact of this technology, care must be exercised in the choice of audiovisual techniques that fit the objectives of the learning experience and the expectations and readiness of the participants. The following is an illustration of an unfortunate event from the "Harvard University Visiting Professors Case Method Program."

> Perhaps the complexity and difficulty of observing and interpreting what went on in a class would be suggested by referring to the videotaped closed-circuit television playback of case discussions in 1964. This seemed, at last, the answer to Robert Burns' wish: "To see ourselves as others see us!" Without detouring to discuss this experience, it is important at least to note that during the viewback of a case discussion when one participant said to another: "There! See what I mean when I say you are a Cheshire cat?", the group became more self-conscious than was anticipated or could be constructively managed in the program as it was designed.
>
> Less sharp tools of observation seemed to be more tolerable and allowed the life of the group to mature in a different way. (Towl, 1969, p. 160)

Analysis

A wide variety of audiovisual methods are currently available, if not yet widely used. These methods can be used in four different modalities: presentation, discussion, sharing, and feedback. In this analysis, the most common usage, presentation, will be reviewed first. Then each of the other three modes, with their increasingly complex dynamics, is explored.

Presentation Mode. Flip charts, graphs, models, demonstrations, slides, and films are widely used for presentations in both experiential and nonexperiential settings. Their prime value, in addition to increasing the amount of information that can be transmitted, centers on the change processes of *persuasion, activation,* and *identification.* The persuasive power of the media is well documented (Liebert, Neale, & Davidson, 1973; McLuhan, 1951). Vivid, emotionally orchestrated films featuring credible spokespersons can often make points that no instructor or other method alone could hope to achieve. Similarly, physical models or graphic presentations carry with them a kind of credibility and legitimacy which have a strong persuasive significance. The activation aspect is perhaps obvious and most leaders typically use such aids to add energy to the learning experience.

Films and television have the additional change potential of providing vivid sources of identificatory learning. Walter (1975a, 1975b, 1975c, 1978; Walter & Miles, 1974) emphasized the power of this change process, and Donald Roberts has consistently asserted that for children, the identification power alone of television is sufficient to qualify it as virtually a third parent. Critical factors in the effectiveness for specific learning include clear learning objectives, observable and manageable behaviors, and proper vicarious reinforcement.

The aspects of the above change processes are mutually consistent. They make the learning material more vivid, concrete, and personally real for the individual; they aid in developing a new way of seeing. This richness is very important in capturing high levels of participant attention. *Re-cognition* is thus facilitated as the interfering thoughts of the participants are minimized or avoided. Here, suggestion is similar to persuasion. That is, a consistent pattern of assumptions, expectations, and motivational states can all be addressed or developed simultaneously. Various constructs can be made more concrete for the individual and hence more readily internalized. Finally, audiovisual techniques can be linked easily to other methods, such as a lecture or group discussion.

Discussion Mode. In the discussion mode, the audiovisual methods are an integral part of the discussion rather than an antecedent to it. For example, a film can be stopped at many points, during which issues and questions are discussed by participants; a thirty minute film becomes the basis for a two to three hour learning experience. This use of audiovisual methods implies a significantly *restructured* learning situation. A unique aspect of this restructuring is that participant attention shifts back and forth between the film and the discussion of it. This can be time consuming and potentially confusing to some participants, but for most it reduces the demands on maintaining attention, structures the discussion, and increases *activation.* The activation energizes interaction and a spirit of inquiry, and since the structure requires alternating periods of passivity and activity, clear messages to get involved are repeatedly received by the participants. Thus *channeling* as well as restructuring is facilitated. These discussion dynamics, in addition to the presentational dynamics already discussed, have a number of predictable effects, including:

1 Highly focused and predictable involvement.
2 Relatively high levels of *commitment* due to the periodic nature of the required involvement.
3 Generally high quality of discussions.
4 Rapid and credible *feedback* to participants about reactions, understanding, and decisions made in response to the film.

The enriched potential for feedback in this mode further activates performance-oriented *action.* It is unfortunate that physical facilities are often suboptimal for this use of audiovisual methods. Switching from bright lights to darkness has aversive conditioning consequences, and long waiting periods between stopping the film and moving to discussion can allow the energy to dissipate. Thus leader *support* in this mode needs to be primarily directed at practical, logistical matters such as these.

Sharing Mode.   The sharing mode of audiovisual methods might at first seem very similar to the discussion mode but significant differences are noteworthy. For example, sharing often is facilitated in small groups by such aids as magic markers and newsprint or materials for creating collages. The *restructuring* required for this mode is decentralization. In contrast to treatment of issues in task-centered activities, participants here are encouraged to face themselves and explore more freely. In addition to delegation elements, restructuring emphasizes the goals of exploration and information sharing and establishes rules and expectations concerning timing and the subsequent character of the sharing process. These social structure elements become critical guideposts for the natural *channeling* tendencies among participants. Further, since sharing may involve self-disclosure or evoke fears of negative evaluation, a supportive physical and social climate is useful. This is especially true when information to be shared is extremely revealing and personal, as it is in collage building.

Restructuring allows for two different *action* stages, preparation and actual sharing. During the preparation stage, action takes the form of exploration or performance, and can be similar to that associated with fantasy and tasks respectively. In addition to the rich information created, the action generally leads to relatively high involvement and a sense of creative ownership. It generates both *commitment* and *activation.*

In the sharing stage, the action is usually of a practice or performance nature. Primary change processes operating include *feedback, identification,* and *support.* Feedback comes from the reactions of other participants and the leader. The existence of other information juxtaposed with one's own has significant informational value and aids the participant in developing a better perspective on both the self and the issues at hand.

For identification, two points are noteworthy. First, during stage one of this sharing mode, involvement leads to increased identification with issues and with others (House, 1979). Second, the actual sharing process has identification dynamics because of vicarious reinforcement consequences of group liking and admiration. The degree to which the sharing is personal affects the degree to which learning about highly personal issues occurs. Since certain participants are well liked or particularly attractive, the information and feedback given by these individuals is often more powerful than anything the leader may say.

The support of a nonevaluative climate is as important in the second action stage of sharing as it is in the first. Often the quality and quantity of sharing is such that a large proportion of participants may feel overwhelmed, inadequate, or unable to build on what was discovered. Supportive efforts by the leader should encourage individual reflection and growth and help in the exploration of possible implications.

As with other audiovisual modes, the entire learning arrangement has pervasive *re-cognition* implications. Included here are an altered sense of how to approach problems and issues, how to deal with others, and how to monitor one's self. The tangible reminders provided by the media also assist participants in remembering material covered. Persuasive comments by the leader are for the most part irrelevant and could inhibit learning. *Coercion* needs to be avoided.

Feedback Mode. Audiovisual feedback generally is pursued within small groups engaged in some activity. There are three direct consequences of recording these activities. First, the awareness of being recorded is highly *activating*— perhaps overactivating for videotape. Second, the arrangement requires some relatively predictable and overt *action* sequence. Third, the technology and the physical arrangement have a *channeling* effect in terms of a demand for performance, which not only results in activation but also in a focusing of participant behavior. Clear guidelines give participants a sense of direction and avoid unnecessary frustrations.

Feedback, readers will recall, is inherently confrontational and dynamic rather than static. Videotape feedback, by definition, is confrontational because it invariably contains fundamental information about one's self-image. Since self-image, according to Mead, is to a great degree a function of the physical realities of early life experiences, the participant inevitably experiences incongruities between assumptions about the self and what appears on the video monitor. This confrontational element was revealed in the research of Resnik, Davidson, Schuyler, & Christopher (1973), wherein tapes of hospitalization intake procedures for individuals who had attempted suicide were kept and shown to the patients in therapy. This extreme action was reserved for individuals who denied ever being self-destructive or who attempted to remove themselves from treatment prematurely. Such confrontations are seldom actively pursued, especially in an educational experience, but the power of videotape recording and playback to provide such fundamental self-image confrontation should not be ignored. An unintentional confrontation is an ever present possibility.

Another major videotape feedback risk is overactivating participants or engaging them in learning tasks beyond the scope intended. A tangible and overt activity is useful in guaranteeing that the self-image issue is dealt with simply and effectively. In the absence of adequate conditions, confrontations could generate fear, with the result that the entire learning arrangement is experienced as highly *coercive.* On the positive side, this potential for overtly confrontative feedback is indicative of the enormous richness of this method.

A variety of opinions exist concerning the timing of feedback to maximize its usefulness. Kagan, Krathwohl, and Miller (1963) advocated instantaneous feedback as an ongoing subprocess within the group. At first this appears very similar to the "start-stop" sequence described for films, but because feedback rather than new information is being provided, the process is infinitely more powerful. Thirty seconds of replay can generate an hour of discussion. In other approaches, Geertsman and Reivich (1965) showed feedback of the previous week's group meeting at the beginning of each therapy session; Goldstein (1966) did not show videotapes in family therapy until the fifth session, lest the feedback be too confrontative too early in the therapy process. The latter approach retains the activation and information aspects of the feedback but sidesteps the risks of confrontation. The length of feedback is also worthy of attention. Geertsman and Reivich (1965) showed full forty-five minute playbacks, but Danet (1968) warned against overloading individuals with information. Stoller (1968) suggested that each segment should terminate once a comprehensible bundle of information had been presented to the participant.

It is often valuable to provide specific cues concerning what to watch for in the feedback, and to provide interpretive structures for viewing it. These *re-cognition* contributions serve to minimize unintentional confrontations and focus the individual's perceptions in a way that allows maximum incorporation, organization, and retention of the information provided. A second re-cognition aspect relates to the richness of the V.T.R. feedback process. Even at nonconfrontational levels, there is an effect tantamount to imaginal flooding. Further, the idea of self-monitoring is epitomized by the observation of videotape feedback and thus the tendency to self-monitor is increased through the experience of receiving videotape feedback.

Three other important change processes are *conditioning, commitment,* and *identification.* Since observing video tape feedback releases participants from the demands of social interaction, they often can perceive more clearly their overt behaviors and the consequences of these behaviors. Clear perception of outcomes may have intense reinforcing and punitive consequences. This point should not be confused with observed versus intended behaviors, which are the substance of confrontation. The vicarious conditioning of video feedback is potentially very powerful. Additionally, direct identificatory learning is also available as a participant observes the successes and failures of others with the clarity and detachment that the video feedback offers. The vivid and undeniable qualities of V.T.R. feedback can have significant commitment consequences. During feedback most participants have at least one or two insights that are felt intensely. Debriefing can encourage sharing and decision making about future behavior and thus encourage commitment toward long-term change. Multiple sessions are more useful than a single session since adjustment to novelty is needed.

The activation, confrontation, conditioning, and coercion possibilities of videotape feedback make the *support* from both the group and the leader of fundamental importance and thus a very low participant/leader ratio is desirable. This support is essential in reducing the punishing aspects related to the intensity and vividness of the feedback and the fear-evoking potential related to self-image. In an earlier age, critics of progress asserted that people were not intended to fly. Some people might now assert that people were not intended to see themselves on videotape! Still, the total experience provides rich double-loop learning, in contrast to other uncomfortable methods such as the classical case approach (Argyris, 1980).

Instrumentation

Instrumentation, which here is considered to consist of standardized paper and pencil procedures for assessing various aspects of personal, interpersonal, or group functioning, traditionally has been used primarily for research purposes (Kiesler, 1973). However, this method is useful in experiential learning (Pfeiffer & Heslin, 1973; Pfeiffer & Jones, 1975) to heighten participant awareness of issues and to provide them with feedback on personal characteristics, group process, and a variety of other relevant conceptual and theoretical matters.

Instrumentation is a flexible technique. A questionnaire can be used in much the same way as role playing, fantasy activities, or body movement exercises are used to generate cognitive and affective reactions. The process of responding to the instrument is engrossing, personal, and, at the same time, a concrete experience of a perhaps vague topic. A questionnaire can also be used as an alternative to a film presentation or as a supplement to lectures or readings to help participants organize their thoughts and reactions to an activity. Instrumentation can be incorporated into most designs to meet a variety of needs such as:

1 Providing an opportunity for immediate, low-risk involvement where direct interpersonal exchange might be too threatening.
2 Providing objective, concrete feedback and immersing participants directly in the data generating and feedback processes.
3 Familiarizing participants quickly with terminology, constructs, and theory.
4 Generating information against which participants can assess their movement and leaders can assess the effectiveness of the overall experience in achieving its objectives.

The type of instrumentation and its location in the design depends on the specific objectives of the experience, the expectations and other characteristics of the participants, and the nature of the other instructional methods involved.

Leaders must have a working knowledge of the ethics involved in using instrumentation. These methods should not be used for purposes for which they were not intended (e.g., using interest inventories as indicators or predictors of success in a particular area). Care should be taken not to use instruments that might address topics beyond the scope of the objectives of the experience, such as measuring and discussing central personality issues in an educational experience. Participants should not be seduced into revealing information about themselves that might be damaging to them. Participants must have absolute control over their scores and make their own decisions about data sharing. Leaders should be familiar with the administration and scoring procedures as well as the structural and interpretative depth of the instrument. Finally, it is useful to foster a "non-clinical, open, and experimental" climate in which instrumentation is used (Pfeiffer & Heslin, 1973, p. 24).

Analysis

Re-cognition and *feedback* are the central change processes in the use of instrumentation. The two major sources of re-cognition correspond to the *action* of filling out the instrument and that of analysing, reviewing, and sharing its results. The first action can involve either exploration or performance. Curiosity about one's self tends to be activated as is a desire to answer questions raised and to understand. Desire, of course, is the basis of *commitment* building.

Participants' "sense-making" efforts for a given instrument have immediate re-cognition consequences. First, the construct system used in the instrument can be partially internalized. Second, the actual engagement of the participant in questions related to self, others, or the context often constitutes a significant shift in thinking. Third, in addition to raising questions, many instruments subtly suggest answers or directions for answers and thus immediately provide influence that participants often adopt. Cognitive theorists and contextual theorists such as ethnomethodologists emphasize the universality and centrality of the human propensity to attempt to make sense of their experience (Garfinkel, 1967).

The second major source of re-cognition is a direct result of the feedback. During feedback, the conceptual system underlying the instrument can be explained to and adopted by the participants. The explanation is then illustrated by the revealed information. The individual gains perspective on the self relative to others and in this way the constructs in the instrument are made tangible, concrete, and a part of the participant's reality. There can be a simultaneous alteration of the statements about the self in light of the data, and there is an increased tendency and capacity for self-monitoring along the dimensions of the instrument. All these contribute to self-perspective and an altered definition of social reality.

The more one monitors the self, the more one tends to self-monitor all behavior. The degree to which feedback and self-monitoring can be linked to learning payoffs affects their *conditioning* consequences for the learning experience. Repetition of feedback over time increases the effects of the material.

Instrumentation provides very persuasive and specific feedback. Feedback can be closely related to highly credible relevant research. Finally, because of the tightness of the structure of a given instrument, there are typically a small number of specific conclusions or courses of action that can be articulated and linked to the participants' immediate comprehension and emotional disposition.

Again, is feedback informational or confrontational? Many instruments produce information that is at least mildly surprising to participants. This is highly *activating*, but if the degree of confrontation is too great, participants find it easier to resist the learning by discounting or criticizing it, and supporting one another's negative reactions. When dealing with uncomfortable, unavoidable results, participants can feel *coerced*. The degree to which confrontational feedback can be used in the group is a function of the accumulation of conditions that make a given confrontation viable. These include a well developed social structure in the learning experience legitimizing confrontation and relatively high levels of *support*. Instrumentation alone seldom yields constructive confrontations. In fact, the use of highly confrontive instruments in an inadequate environment can be termed incompetent or unethical. The degree to which feedback is informational or confrontational is also moderated by the style and *persuasiveness* of the leader. The more the leader asserts that participants should accept and believe the results, the greater the potential for confrontation. Singling out a given individual increases confrontational dynamics.

Identification is implicit since many instruments are conceptualized from an ideal. For example, a given instrument on leadership inevitably articulates a model of the highly successful or ideal leader. Ideal scores naturally relate to successful "real world" individuals who are the recipients of numerous rewards. Ideal scores can become virtual objects of identification. Thus, identification motivates and reinforces the desirable changes suggested by the instrument. Conditioning, support, and channeling have minor roles to play, primarily as adjuncts to re-cognition as described above. Restructuring and coercion are not particularly relevant to the instrumentation method.

Projects and Field Experiences

Real tasks or projects refer to activities in which participants are required to be involved as an integral part of their responsibilities either within or outside the learning context. These activities are generally complete in and of themselves, for example, a group convened for the purpose of planning and organizing a party or dance or a committee set up to resolve problems in a student residence. Observing or becoming a part of ongoing events in settings away from the learning experience is a field experience. This includes site visits, either foreign or domestic travel, providing service, work-study, and internships or in-service training (Duley, 1974; Quinn & Sellars, 1974). Experiences ranging in length from several hours to several years could be appropriate depending upon the type, objectives, and context of the learning experience.

Projects and field experiences can be readily combined with many other methods, especially simulations, role playing, process observation, and self-directed methods such as reading and writing. The former two methods, when used prior to the task or field experience, can orient participants to the setting and its possible dynamics and help them clarify their learning objectives. In addition, these and other methods can be used as focal points at specific times during the experience to provide feedback (Angus, 1974). Structure is provided by observation and recording of events and reactions, and reading for additional perspective makes the learning experience more comprehensive and permits evaluation of its effectiveness. Some specific techniques include reading from a list of recommended titles, writing up critical incidents (Flanagan, 1954), keeping a log book or journal, and writing a final report or summary.

There are a number of issues leaders need to keep in mind when using real tasks and field experiences. The selected activity must be compatible with the objectives of the experience and must be a suitable means for addressing those objectives. Is it worth the time and effort? Real tasks are best when combined with other methods. For field experiences, developing and maintaining liaison relationships with individuals in the field are essential. Often greater skill at observation and analysis is needed in field experiences than for other experiences. Thorough documentation is also useful since in many cases considerable time can pass between the experience and discussion with others. Overall, these methods produce rich and varied experiences relevant to education, training, professional development, personal growth, and therapy but face significant logistical constraints on their successful implementation in an experiential learning design.

Analysis

Projects. Projects and other tasks are used in experiential learning in a manner similar to the moderate case study method. The first change process to be noted is *persuasion.* The leader attempts to establish conceptual anchor points, realistic expectations, and a desirable emotional tone in an effort to make the participant's experience constructive. Second, the *restructuring* is in essence a relaxing of the rules and structures of other learning situations in order to allow greater degrees of participant self-direction; in other words, a more decentralized learning structure. The absence of structure allows for greater participant freedom to engage in the *action* that directly relates to the project itself, and thus the project serves as the major structuring element. The *activation* resulting from the action is generally higher than for the moderate case approach, but, as with cases, intensity of involvement and activation is a function of a variety of factors. For projects, *commitment* is primarily a function of the perceived relevance of the project. Thus challenge, apparent usefulness, richness of the task, apparent applicability to real life, and intrinsic gratification all contribute to commitment.

Because of the relatively moderate intensity of the approach, *re-cognition* is also generally moderate and involves participants seeing themselves differently in relation to others and the world. They may identify more with aspects of the world that were unknown or hazy prior to the project. *Channeling* has the limited function of maintaining a group atmosphere within which high personal autonomy can be preserved. Similarly, interpersonal *feedback* is minimal and the dynamic and static feedback is linked to tasks.

Coercion and *conditioning* both might be related to evaluation procedures. Evaluation can be emphasized or de-emphasized, with a primary purpose of focusing participants' attention on the task and guaranteeing action and activation. When coercion and conditioning are intense, the liberal character of the learning arrangement is fundamentally altered. Commitment through relevance and re-cognition through identification are probably squeezed out by the high activation–fear dynamic; learning becomes more cognitive and conceptual, as in the classical case approach. Finally, *support* for exploration and experimentation is of less significance here than for some of the methods discussed above. Relevant support is task-centered in nature; the leader provides task expertise and a task structure. The certainty provided by the structure of the task is also supportive. In general, projects and tasks are richer in potential than moderate cases, but in the absence of emphasis upon evaluation, perceived relevance is the pivotal criterion for success. It is a more decentralized approach than the other experience-based methods.

Field Experiences.   As with projects, field trips can also benefit from the proper *persuasion* to set tone and expectations. However, in contrast to projects, the *restructuring* is more dramatic since the physical environment is changed; reorganization is not merely decentralization, but a totally new experience. The *action* is more physical and tangible; involvement and *activation* are relatively higher if a degree of perceived relevance and evaluation are held constant. Involvement, *commitment,* and perceived relevance can probably be affected by the length of field experience, and greater temporal immersion is more probable in field experiences than in projects. Tangible sources of *identification* are abundant, and leader comments are often useful in maximizing participant success in making links between their inner world and the object of the field trip. This is the central *re-cognitive* component for field experiences.

Coercive evaluation is infrequent in field trips where evaluation is often more open-ended and participant directed. *Conditioning* is restricted to positive reinforcement of participant efforts to relate the experience to course content and generally to their own lives. *Support* is very important and, in addition to providing a proper atmosphere, it is most fundamentally experienced in the form of proper logistical and physical arrangements. *Feedback* is less central except in work-study program situations where the participants are actually required to become involved in the setting.

Conclusion

The central dilemma raised by an analysis of these sixteen methods is the difficulty of retaining and systematically using the information. A summary of the sixteen methods and their most important subtypes is juxtaposed with the change processes in Figure 10.1. The presence and importance of each change process for a given method is indicated by the presence or absence of horizontal and vertical lines. The purpose of this scheme is to offer a general, visually vivid, but nonquantitative indication of these contributions. A blank space in a cell indicates important or pivotal contributions by the change process for the method. Horizontal lines in a cell indicate mild to moderate contribution. Both horizontal and vertical lines in a cell indicate relatively little contribution of a given change process to a given method.

Perhaps the most obvious and predictable generalization arising from Figure 10.1 is the importance of *support* for many methods that might be stereotypically associated with the modern "growth scene." As is expected, classical methods, lectures, reading, writing, and the classical case method do not rely on support. It is noteworthy, however, that neither do instrumentation nor presentational audiovisual methods.

The second point is the *absence* of *coercion* for the effective use of most of the methods, except the classical case method, some body movement techniques, and some forms of group interaction. For lecture, reading, and writing it can be seen that coercion is generally linked to evaluation; it may be used to overcome limitations resulting from low commitment in participants or inadequacies in lecture presentations.

The third point relates to the issue of *re-cognition*. A striking aspect of Figure 10.1 is the pervasiveness across methods of re-cognition change processes. The centrality of re-cognition has thus far gone unrecognized in experiential learning because of the concern for the emotional and behavioral aspects of change through the approach. Still it seems logical that if feelings change, cognitive elements probably also must change to aid in a new steady state.

Finally, the central methods have much more emphasis on *activation, commitment,* and *action* than methods in the other two groups. This helps to explain their potency and self-sufficiency in a learning experience.

Reflection on Chapter 1 in light of Figure 10.1 yields a new appreciation for the degree to which the conflict, fulfillment, learning, and especially

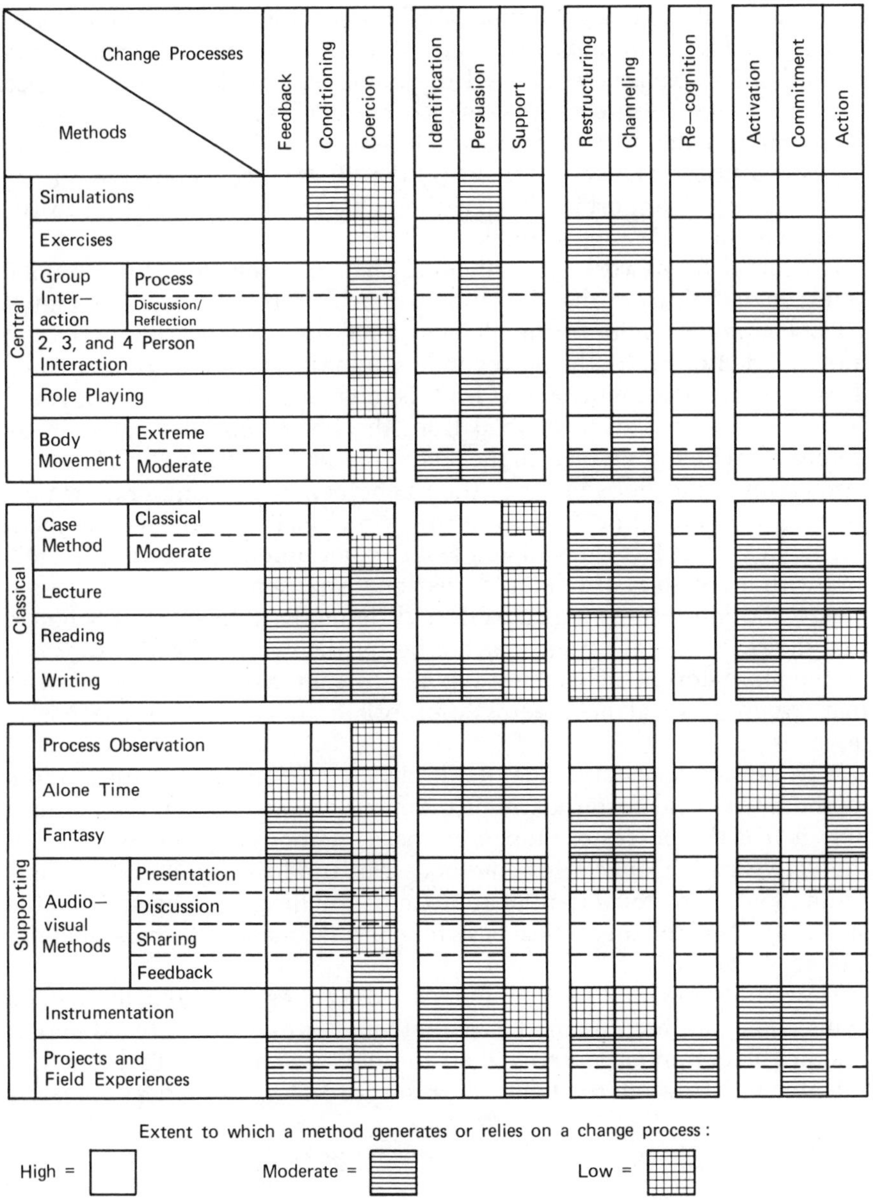

Figure 10.1 Presence of change processes for a given method.

235

the contextual and cognitive *models of human functioning can and must be balanced when promoting change.* Modern experiential learning, until recently, has heavily emphasized the fulfillment model, and it is hoped that the perceived necessary balance explored in this volume will be helpful in broadening the theoretical base upon which experiential learning is explained. The consistency and the life sciences models of human functioning are important in that they clearly add appreciation to the actual meaning of many variables.

A general framework for individual change is the most fundamental issue emanating from the above discussions and the summary of Figure 10.1. The applicability of the change processes across a wide variety of methods demonstrates the power and usefulness of the conceptual system. This general applicability allows leaders to pursue a new *systematic eclecticism,* one that is distinguished from the borrowing and patching together of techniques typical in the field. This new eclecticism can be based instead on the leader's views of the phenomenon of change rather than on a single model of personality or intervention. This analysis of methods perhaps can stand as a model and first step for others who can ultimately and with increased latitude tailor learning experiences to the capacities, needs, and interests of participants and themselves. In short, it is hoped that the reactionary "my approach is better than your's" will be replaced by the more flexible eclecticism typified by statements like "for me with that group this balance seems appropriate to generate these consequences."

Advocacy of eclecticism does not imply an opinion that the use of more methods will yield better learning and more change. In fact, the message here is that the processes tapped by many methods are so powerful that the active use of only a few methods can produce significant change. Limitations on the experiential approach, until now, have come from the lack of a systematic theoretical basis for considering possible combinations and aggregations.

The reader may well say that understanding does not lead to immediate application and that this analysis of methods has done more to aid understanding experiential learning than to guide its conduct. True enough. Chapter 11 is now offered in an effort to address these practical concerns.

CHAPTER ELEVEN

Conduct and Design of Activities

*Chance favors the
prepared mind.*

Louis Pasteur

For this discussion, twelve dimensions, useful in thinking about conducting learning activities, are placed into four groups or clusters. These clusters—Target, Contextual, Influence, and Organizational—provide the overall framework for the discussion of these dimensions and of the elements in the design–decision-making formulation developed in this chapter. A brief overview of each cluster and its dimensions precedes the more complete discussion.

THE TARGET CLUSTER

The target dimensions are concerned with what the learning experience is attempting to achieve. It was Seneca who said "When a man does not know what harbor he is headed for, no wind is the right one." This cluster includes the types, purposes, and objectives of a learning experience and the subject. It defines what the learning experience hopes to achieve. *Types* of learning experiences, as noted in the introduction, are education, training, professional development, personal growth, and therapy. Within any type or combination of types of learning experiences, different *purposes,* involvement, awareness, insight, and change can be pursued. Finally, all learning experiences have specific *objectives* that fall into three domains: cognitive, affective, and psychomotor or behavioral.

In any learning experience, it is possible to pursue a large number of topics or *subjects.* For example, training can be oriented toward the development of mechanical skills such as typing or complex interpersonal skills such as empathy. Since the type of learning experience is described partially in terms of objectives and purposes, these latter categories are treated first in the discussion of the Target.

Types, Purposes, and Objectives

The expected outcomes of any learning experience can be stated in terms of *objectives,* and these aid the leader with organization and design. They also aid in linking different aspects of the learning experience, and they provide a basis for evaluation.

In this discussion, objectives are considered to fall into three general domains: cognitive, affective, and psychomotor (Bloom, 1956; CSC/Pacific, Inc., 1972a, 1972b, 1972c; Krathwohl, Bloom, & Masia, 1964; Ringness, 1975). The cognitive domain consists first of activities related to remembering and recalling information or knowledge, and, second, of skills and abilities such as problem solving related to working with that knowledge. A taxonomy of objectives for the cognitive domain proposed by Bloom (1956) includes the following general categories: knowledge, comprehension, application, analysis, synthesis, and evaluation. The affective domain contains objectives that are concerned with feelings and emotions. A taxonomy of objectives for the affective domain developed by Krathwohl, Bloom, and Masia (1964) has the following categories: receiving, responding, valuing, organization, and characterization by a value or value complex. Objectives in the psychomotor domain focus on movement and include motor skills such as typing, physical tasks such as push-ups, and perceptual motor behaviors such as language skills. A schema for classifying objectives in the psychomotor domain emphasizes perception, set, guided response, mechanism, and overt response (Simpson, 1972, p. 50–55).

In addition to objectives, a learning experience can be viewed in terms of its *purposes:* involvement, awareness, insight, and change. The purposes are a more general way of describing a learning experience than are the objectives. They refer to how participants are expected to approach and deal with the learning tasks rather than to the nature of the tasks themselves.

Involvement refers to the degree to which participants become engaged in the assigned activity. If it is a body movement exercise, do they perform it? If it is a role play, do they take a role and act it out? If it is a group discussion, do they enter into the conversation? Figures 7.2 and 7.3 and the discussion of phases in Chapter 7 point to the importance of involvement in learning effectiveness. The relationship between positive involvement and the change processes underscores why this is so. If participants do not become involved in the activities, they greatly reduce their opportunity to receive feedback and positive reinforcement. With low involvement, activation is correspondingly low and the amount of interpersonal exchange necessary to generate support and channeling processes such as group norms and expectations do not occur. With low involvement there is little or no action and consequently commitment to the learning experience is minimal. Participant lack of involvement reduces opportunities to develop awareness, insight, and change. This is also why the manner in which the leader sets the themes discussed in the first part of Chapter 7 is so important.

Awareness refers to participants' internalized perceptions of various facets of a topic and the linking of those perceptions with knowledge they already have. This is qualitatively different than just listening to a topic presentation. Awareness differs from information accumulation in that here the participants bring their current knowledge to bear in response to the learning situation. New information discovered or generated during the involvement is highly contiguous to old knowledge and therefore its integration with old learning is facilitated. For example, after learning about the different group roles, participants could use that information to interpret the behavior in a discussion group by identifying the roles as they actually occurred.

Insight occurs when a sufficient level of awareness is achieved resulting in the emergence of an integrating or unifying concept or idea. At this time fragments of information are brought together in a unified total picture or gestalt. In terms of the group roles example, insight is descriptive of the process when participants gain a realization of the roles they themselves play. The significance of attaining these insights is undeniably apparent to participants. It helps them organize and retain their learning and reinforces their participation in the learning experience. Chapter 5 provided a detailed description of the kinds of change that might be expected to occur through awareness and insight, thus emphasizing the importance of the pursuit of these two purposes in a learning experience. In addition, awareness and insight are viewed as important contributors to change and thus laudible purposes when one reflects on the conflict and fulfillment models of human functioning discussed in Chapter 1.

Change can be specific or broad, and it can deal with attitudes or behavior. Specific change may refer to acquiring attitudes or skills that can be addressed in a circumscribed manner. Demonstrating the ability to type or to use communication skills such as paraphrasing are examples. Broad change refers to issues that cannot be separated easily from an individual's total personality or behavior. Examples include changing the way an individual approaches and deals with other people or acquiring a complex set of skills such as empathy. If change was a goal in the learning experience dealing with group roles, participants would be expected to act on their awareness and insight and demonstrate constructive change in the way they behaved in the group discussion.

Each *type* of learning experience contains certain patterns of objectives and purposes. The types, education, training, professional development, personal growth, and therapy, represent five different themes, and more than one type is usually needed to describe a given learning experience. It is important to note that the five types are not meant to represent the kinds of learning experiences that occur in specific settings. For example, the schools are responsible for education, but that does not mean that education is the only type of learning experience that occurs in that setting. Similarly, the use of the word "training" in sensitivity training bears little or no resemblance to the heavy personal growth emphasis typical of that learning experience. It is important not to confuse the types with currently popular labels such as sensitivity training, management development, transactional analysis, est, or whatever.

Education is characterized by an emphasis on objectives in the cognitive domain. Objectives in the affective domain may be addressed but are pursued with much less intensity than the cognitive objectives. Psychomotor objectives, beyond academic skill development, are not emphasized. All of the learning purposes, involvement, awareness, insight, and change can be pursued in the cognitive domain, but insight and change in the affective domain is less appropriate. Educational experiential learning can have an emphasis on the content regarding personal and interpersonal issues, but if the issues themselves are considered, they are addressed without confrontation and at very low levels of intensity.

For example, participants interested in social issues could get involved in a simulation to heighten their awareness of competition among different groups in society. The simulation could include content directly related to the interaction among various interest groups in a community. Debriefing here focuses on the relationship of the simulation dynamics to what participants have read or experienced in other situations regarding the topic. Feelings and reactions to the experience are shared, but they are not a central concern of the group. There are expectations for participant change in the form of increased cognitive understanding of how society might work, but participants are not expected to gain awareness or insight into or change their own behavior as a result of their involvement in the experience.

Training is characterized by an emphasis on objectives in the psychomotor domain and generally results in participants being able to perform some specific skill or set of skills in an improved manner. Consequently, involvement and change purposes are skill-centered, and awareness and insight are subsidiary. For example, in learning how to type, the potential use of the skill is proposed as a rationale for acquisition, but knowledge of the history or background of the development of the typewriter is irrelevant. If the acquisition of this latter information were the goal of the learning experience, it is education, not training. For communication skills such as paraphrasing, the same emphasis applies.

Beyond providing a framework within which the skill is presented, participants do not need to know anything about the larger issues of effective interpersonal relationships to learn how to paraphrase. Here they concentrate on the specific components of paraphrasing and ways to apply the skill. As a result of mastering the skill they might gain awareness and insight about themselves, but these two purposes are not pursued directly in the learning experience.

Professional development is concerned with something more complex, and, consequently, cognitive, affective, and psychomotor objectives are all involved. Skills are buttressed by cognitive material for understanding and by affective material for self-direction and coping with others. Greater personal involvement than for education and training is required because of the complexity of the constellation of skills and the need to place them into perspective and integrate them into a coherent style. Even though the involvement can be intense and personal, the skills, not the participants' personalities, are the focus of this type of experience.

In professional development there is a relatively high need to create broad awareness and insights for the participants about the personal significance of the skills. The context within which the skills are used, the interrelationships among different skill areas, and the relationship of the skills to the context are also of great importance to attitude and behavior change. While awareness and insight are only directed toward information or content in education and are merely incidental in training, they are critical in professional development. Most supervisory skills workshops have some professional development emphasis. Participants are encouraged to practice specific skills in job related role play or simulations in such a way that they learn about various aspects of their own behavior.

Personal growth is oriented toward increasing participants' understanding of some aspect of their lives as well as their ability for self-management. It is a preventive and developmental process rather than a remedial one (Amundson, 1978). It is directed toward helping adequately functioning individuals to become more effective rather than toward helping inadequately functioning individuals to cope. Participants are encouraged to become more open to their life experiences, to increase their adaptiveness through identifying and experimenting with alternatives, and to explore the direction and meaning of their lives. Consequently, all three domains of objectives are involved with emphasis on the affective domain. Cognitive objectives are pursued as they relate to the individual's personalized understanding of problems. For example, for the topic "group interaction," cognitive objectives around group processes such as learning group roles are pursued as they directly relate to participants' behavior, but they are not ends in themselves. In education, cognitive objectives can stand alone; in personal growth they are used in conjunction with objectives from the affective and psychomotor domains.

Personal growth, because of its personal focus, is a very engaging experience for participants, affecting involvement, awareness, insight, and change. Changes in attitudes and behavior can include increases in participants' self-management ability, ego strength, self-esteem, and self-acceptance. In personal growth the person, not the skills, takes center stage.

Sensitivity groups, encounter groups, and est are familiar examples of personal growth. Specific communications skills such as paraphrasing might be presented primarily as an aid to participants in their search for self understanding. The immediate impact of the application of the skill predominates over skill acquisition and refinement. Not only is the personal focus much stronger, but the intensity is also much higher.

Therapy involves participants whose dysfunction is sufficiently great to motivate the use of even more intense and comprehensive change arrangements. The participant needs to learn how to cope in an improved way. Significant discomfort, rather than vague dissatisfactions or high aspirations, is the central motivation for moving into therapy. Therapy is primarily remedial rather than preventive or developmental. Objectives from all three domains are involved and require integration through a tight philosophical framework.

As for personal growth, the four purposes are all important in therapy. Paradoxically, participant discomfort often results in extremely high involvement, which can be a barrier to the development of awareness and insight. Consequently, reducing participants' high anxiety resulting from "over-involvement" is often pursued. For the other types of learning it is just the opposite. Some examples of therapy are thematic groups for alcoholics, the chronically unemployed, and families with problems. The topics addressed in these groups can be examined by any of the other types of learning experiences, but in those situations the needs and expectations of the participants are very different, as are the methods used to deal with the subject.

Summary

Figure 11.1 is offered as a summary of the types, purposes, and objectives discussion. The relationship between the purposes and objectives are presented for each type. In addition to the three domains of objectives, an integration category has been added to reflect the extent to which attempts are made to integrate the three kinds of objectives within a particular type of learning experience. There are five levels of emphasis of a particular purpose for a particular objective. The emphases range from high to low.

Generally, all the change processes are involved for all types, but as one moves from education toward therapy support and commitment become more central. It is also emphasized that, in practice, learning experiences are combinations of the five types. A consideration of group roles might be forty percent education, thirty percent training, fifteen percent profes-

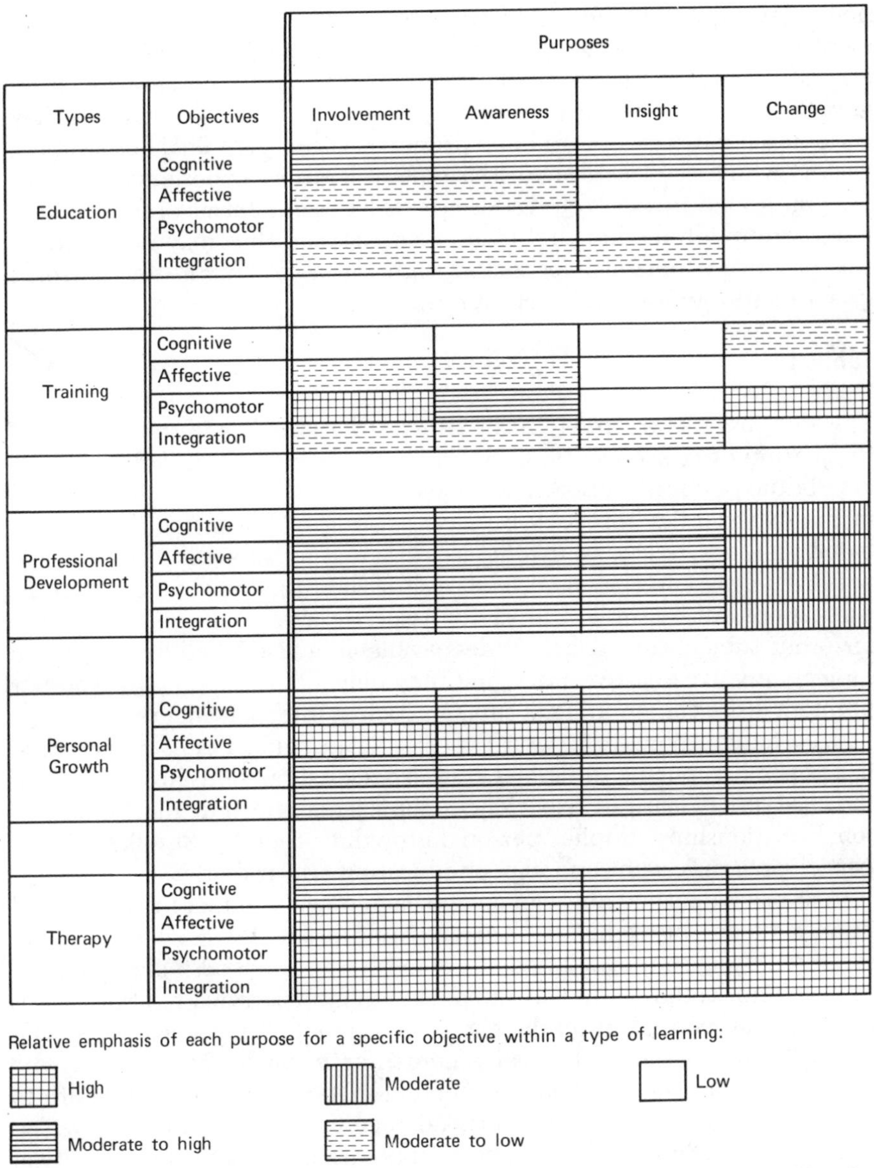

Purposes

Types	Objectives	Involvement	Awareness	Insight	Change
Education	Cognitive	Moderate to high	Moderate to high	Moderate to high	Moderate to high
	Affective	Moderate to low	Moderate to low	Low	Low
	Psychomotor	Low	Low	Low	Low
	Integration	Moderate to low	Moderate to low	Moderate to low	Low
Training	Cognitive				Moderate to low
	Affective	Moderate to low	Moderate to low		
	Psychomotor	Moderate	Moderate to high		Moderate
	Integration	Moderate to low	Moderate to low	Moderate to low	
Professional Development	Cognitive	Moderate to high	Moderate to high	Moderate to high	Moderate
	Affective	Moderate to high	Moderate to high	Moderate to high	Moderate
	Psychomotor	Moderate to high	Moderate to high	Moderate to high	Moderate
	Integration	Moderate to high	Moderate to high	Moderate to high	Moderate
Personal Growth	Cognitive	Moderate to high	Moderate to high	Moderate to high	Moderate to high
	Affective	High	Moderate to high	Moderate to high	Moderate to high
	Psychomotor	Moderate to high	Moderate to high	Moderate to high	Moderate to high
	Integration	Moderate to high	Moderate to high	Moderate to high	Moderate to high
Therapy	Cognitive	Moderate to high	Moderate to high	Moderate to high	Moderate to high
	Affective	High	Moderate to high	High	High
	Psychomotor	Moderate to high	Moderate to high	Moderate to high	Moderate to high
	Integration	High	High	High	High

Relative emphasis of each purpose for a specific objective within a type of learning:

- High
- Moderate
- Low
- Moderate to high
- Moderate to low

Figure 11.1   The relative emphasis of objectives and purposes for the five types of learning experiences.

sional development, and fifteen percent personal growth. A body movement workshop for helping professionals might be fifteen percent training, fifty percent professional development, thirty percent personal growth, and five percent therapy. Leaders need to know what it is they are doing if participants are to be properly placed. As a final observation, leaders who are unclear about the type of learning experience they are designing tend to use preferred methods like some forms of body movement, group interaction, and video feedback and thus may unintentionally produce a personal focus and high intensity suitable for personal growth and therapy but inappropriate for education.

Subject

This dimension is relatively straightforward and refers to the content of the learning experience, be it group problem solving, marketing strategies, or the political process. The choice of subjects is somewhat restricted in the experiential approach because existing materials for experience-based methods, to a large extent, are designed for subjects related to self understanding, interpersonal relationships, and the human aspects of organizations, for example, University Associates Press materials. Materials for other subjects are generally less available and thus addressing these subjects involves costly and sometimes difficult development. Another problem is the confounding of subjects such as interpersonal relationships with certain purposes or types of experiential learning. For example, while it is possible to pursue the subject "interpersonal relationships" for any of the five types of learning experiences, some leaders assume that "interpersonal relationships" implies personal growth or therapy. Simultaneously, participants may want and expect education and training.

Conversely, participants can coerce each other into more personal and intense modes of exchange than are appropriate for a given learning situation, because they assume a previously experienced technique such as encounter is the "right way" to deal with interpersonal relations. Thus an important constraint on the choice of a subject is participant expectations. Mismatches reduce involvement. For instance, participants who come to a learning experience expecting material on personal health to include diet and exercise but instead receive information on how the body's systems fight disease will be disappointed. The activating quality of the topic itself is also a consideration. Still, one of the real strengths of the experiential approach is its potential for accommodating any subject for which the leader has comprehension and relevant pedagogical skills.

THE CONTEXTUAL CLUSTER

The contextual dimensions describe the human, physical, and temporal aspects of the environment of the learning experience. This cluster includes participants, group size, physical resources, and scheduling. Are the *participants* students, professionals or lay people, male, female, young or old? Is their involvement in the learning experience voluntary or compulsory? The *size* of the group can vary from three or four people in a therapy session to groups of fifteen or more involved in simulations, lectures, or other activities. The *physical resources* dimension is concerned with the actual setting for the learning experience and the budget available to finance it. Location, size, flexibility, type of seating, potential for privacy, and the general quality of the environment including factors such as lighting, heating, ventilation, and decor are included. *Scheduling* has four major components: the number of sessions, their length, the amount of time between them, and when they are held in terms of day of the week and time of day. Does the group meet on four consecutive Saturday mornings for two hours, for an hour on the second and fourth Tuesday evening of each month for four months, or all day on a Sunday?

Participants

Participant characteristics or qualities and their possible implications are discussed in terms of general and specialized abilities, personality, background, including past experiences and expectations concerning the learning experience, age and sex, the voluntary or compulsory nature of participant involvement, and the composition of the group. As one author concluded: "The magnitude of the effect of any given characteristic is small, but taken together the consequences for group process are of major significance" (Shaw, 1971, p. 86).

Common sense and substantial evidence indicate that *general ability or intelligence* is positively related to the amount of information learned, the rate of learning, or both (Cronbach & Snow, 1977, p. 496). Research supporting this statement has focused for the most part on narrow and specifically defined learning tasks and not on the broader processes usually addressed in many experiential learning activities. Nevertheless, some extrapolation to the experiential approach described here for this and the following issues is reasonable. For a high ability group, experience-based methods that allow for more self-directed involvement such as leaderless groups for tasks, projects, or discussion may be preferred. A faster pace and a greater emphasis on participant directed process observation and feedback is useful.

For a group of lower ability participants, more time might be spent describing the themes in the introductory phase and classical methods could be used to provide additional structure to assist the participants in understanding the experience. Examples are printed guides or outlines of the material to be covered and more frequent periodic lecturettes to refocus the attention of the group. Generally less reliance on totally self-directed activities like leaderless discussion groups is desirable.

Few clear, simple generalizations with respect to the impact of the broad range of participant *personality* variables on the learning processes can be stated (Cronbach & Snow, 1977; McGrath & Altman, 1966). However, participants who are highly anxious, introverted, or defensively motivated have been shown to profit from instructional designs demanding less self-direction (Cronbach & Snow, 1977, p. 469). Thus it is useful here to define participant responsibilities clearly during the introductory phase, and to persuade them of the value of their adopting and acting on the themes. If the group appeared to be highly motivated (Zone I in Figures 7.2 and 7.3), then self-directed experience-based approaches are a viable choice, whereas if the majority of the participants appeared to be defensively motivated, classical methods or experience-based methods that provide a more definite structure for their learning are more appropriate.

A participant's *background,* experience, education, and associated expectations affect learning. For example, certain individuals are not able to identify with a given role in a role play or to understand sufficiently the context that a simulation intended to create. Some degree of compatibility between the methods, materials, and participant background is desirable. Prior experience in a learning situation or with a learning procedure is positively related to participants' future performance on similar tasks (Cronbach & Snow, 1977, p. 506; McGrath & Altman, 1966, p. 58). Their past experiences, consistent with the introductory phase themes, contribute to a readiness for and responsiveness to the experiential approach. Less time is needed to brief them about the characteristics and requirements of experiential learning and a greater emphasis can be placed on self-directed experience-based methods for the previously initiated. The use of complex simulations or role plays requiring a great deal of background reading in a very short time is probably less appropriate for a group of participants who might have finished high school than for a highly educated group.

A safe assumption is that most participants have had little or no direct involvement in experiential learning and have expectations consistent with use of the classical methods. Thus emphasis on the introductory themes at the beginning of the learning experience is important. In terms of anticipated outcomes, it is useful to check that participant expectations for learning are consistent with the types, purposes, and objectives selected for the experience. This is achieved through the overt sharing of expectations as one of the first activities. The results of this sharing enable both leaders and participants to make adjustments.

Social participation increases and social interaction becomes more differentiated and complex with increasing *age* (Shaw, 1971, p. 181). Two implications follow from these points. First, when an experiential approach is used with school aged participants, the experiences need to be designed and paced so as to generate and sustain the interaction necessary for learning to occur. For example, a group discussion using the Magic Circle technique at the elementary school level requires much more direct leader intervention than a similar discussion with high school students. The point made earlier about the use of self-directed, experience-based methods versus more structured experience-based and classical methods also applies here. The content and complexity of the tasks addressed is also a function of age, with younger groups being less interested in certain topics and less able to cope with the use of certain methods. For example, adolescents, when compared with older individuals, find talking about interpersonal skills less relevant and have difficulty with process observation and giving feedback.

In terms of the *sex* of participants, women in groups on the average tend to be less assertive, less competitive, and more conforming with the majority when compared to men (Shaw, 1971, p. 182). This leads to complexly different learning climates with regard to cooperation, activation, and so forth. The male/female combination in a group also calls for attention. The relative number of men and women in a group can be placed in five broad categories: all men, all women, evenly balanced, a few men, and a few women. Groups containing men and women tend to be more engaging because the presence of both sexes adds an activation component to the exchange that is absent in a completely male or female group (Schutz, 1971). The male/female composition of a group affects the content of the discussion and the manner in which it proceeds. In a group with a few women, those women may feel alienated and intimidated while the men may feel inhibited in making casual remarks. Men in this type of configuration often become cautious and competitive.

There are several points related to *group composition* that are relevant here. Learning experiences are often easier to conduct when the group is homogeneous (Terborg, Castore, & DeNinno, 1976). Similarity of background factors such as level of education, social class, and work experience can contribute to mutual attraction among members within the group but can reduce the potential for a variety of reactions to the experience.

Heterogeneity of abilities is an issue when the differences within the group are great. Activities designed and paced for the high ability group leave the low ability group confused and frustrated while activities designed for the low ability group fail to challenge and activate the high ability group, whose members become distracted, bored, and possibly angry. Involvement is lost in either case. Generally, when dealing with adult groups, the age composition of the group is an issue only if it affects the participants' interest or ability to be involved in the learning experience.

Compulsory, in contrast to *voluntary,* attendance creates one of the crucial dilemmas facing the experiential approach (Corey & Corey, 1977, p. 122–124) because experiential learning depends on voluntary involvement. Giving participants a choice as to whether they become involved in a particular activity at a certain point is absurd if their physical presence at the activity is compulsory. No simple solution exists, yet voluntary aspects of the learning clearly must be seen as significant and real by the participants. Care must be taken to avoid giving participants the feeling that they are being dragooned into activities. People can be coaxed into involvement by creating an atmosphere of trust and by choosing activities with an interesting and engaging quality.

Group Size

Group size simply refers to the number of participants in the learning experience. As the size of a group changes the dynamics change (Hare, 1962). Consequently, the feasibility of certain techniques changes with size. It is possible to identify some broad, size related characteristic processes. Four somewhat arbitrary delineations of group size are used in the following discussion (see Figure 11.2). Dyads, trios, quartets, or nongroups are particularly useful configurations in providing support, exchanging information, tutoring, and personal counseling, as well as skill-centered supervision. However, they are less suitable when a wide variety of group roles and processes are desired.

The small group is one of the primary configurations used in experiential learning.

> The optimum size for a small discussion group may be five members since members are generally less satisfied with smaller or larger groups. In smaller groups members may be forced to be too prominent and in larger groups they may not have the opportunity to speak. In the group of five, strict deadlocks can be avoided and members can shift roles quickly. (Hare, 1962, p. 245)

Small groups allow for a variety of group dynamics and facilitate learning by providing security, social need satisfaction, stimulation, and motivation. Large groups typically offer fewer opportunities for leader–participant interactions and limit the intensity with which personal issues can be pursued.

Groups larger than fifty, such as those typically encountered in confer-

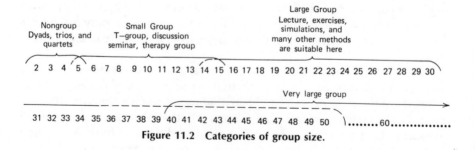

Figure 11.2   Categories of group size.

ences, require uniquely charismatic leaders, special facilities, supporting technology, a cooperative group of participants, and often considerable administrative support. The chances for confusion increase with the size of the group as do the difficulties in dealing with the confusion. In large or very large groups, the gregarious, outgoing participants tend to dominate.

Group size has important relationships to several of the change processes. Identificatory learning (Bandura, 1969; Bandura & Walters, 1963) is enhanced when there is a variety of models to observe. If the group is very small, not only is the number of potential models reduced, but also, because of demands to be involved, participants have far less opportunity simply to sit back and learn through observation and reflection. In terms of feedback, support, activation, and channeling, an inverted U shaped relationship (Fiske & Maddi, 1961; Scott, 1966) exists. Opportunities for feedback increase up to a certain size (fourteen to eighteen) and then decrease as the group gets larger. A similar relationship exists with respect to support and activation though both of these processes can be created at fairly high levels in dyads, trios, and quartets. For channeling, a small group (e.g., eight to twelve) is necessary to generate norms and group expectations and these can be very powerful, as in a T-group. However, as the size of the group increases, the potency of its specific channeling impact is reduced. For example, participants in a very large group are as or more likely to be influenced by channeling forces that are generally present in the culture than by forces generated in that particular group.

One of the most important leader decisions in designing experiential learning activities is in the choice of methods. The relationship of group size to the use of a particular method is presented in Figure 11.3. The methods in Chapters 8, 9, and 10 are arrayed against the four sizes of groups described in Figure 11.2. A blank space indicates that size places no restrictions on the use of a method; horizontal lines indicate that size places selective restrictions; vertical and horizontal lines indicate that size restricts the use of a method. Details of the size–methods relationships are examined below.

The use of experience-based methods in many instances is restricted by size. Fewer than five participants are insufficient to generate the dynamics necessary for many simulations, process groups, and the classical case method. A large group restricts the use of process and discussion groups. Role playing, moderate case discussion, audiovisual discussion, sharing, feedback, and tasks and projects are also more difficult here. For extremely large groups, many experience-based methods are very difficult to use.

The classical methods can be used without difficulty with any group size with the exception of the moderate case approach, because it relies on small group interaction. This is generally true as well for the supporting

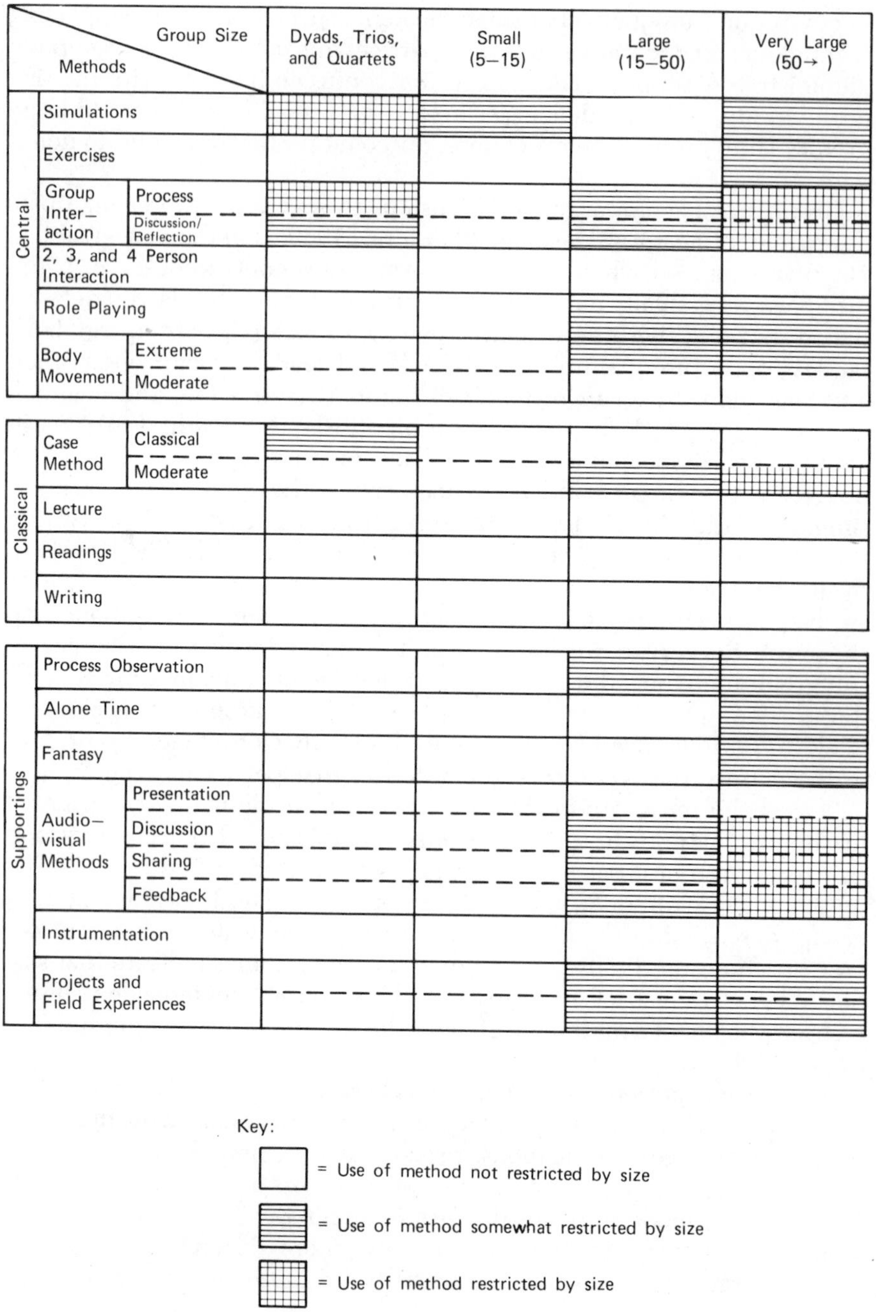

	Group Size → Methods	Dyads, Trios, and Quartets	Small (5–15)	Large (15–50)	Very Large (50→)
Central	Simulations				
	Exercises				
	Group Interaction — Process				
	Group Interaction — Discussion/ Reflection				
	2, 3, and 4 Person Interaction				
	Role Playing				
	Body Movement — Extreme				
	Body Movement — Moderate				
Classical	Case Method — Classical				
	Case Method — Moderate				
	Lecture				
	Readings				
	Writing				
Supportings	Process Observation				
	Alone Time				
	Fantasy				
	Audio-visual Methods — Presentation				
	Audio-visual Methods — Discussion				
	Audio-visual Methods — Sharing				
	Audio-visual Methods — Feedback				
	Instrumentation				
	Projects and Field Experiences				

Key:

☐ = Use of method not restricted by size

▤ = Use of method somewhat restricted by size

▦ = Use of method restricted by size

Figure 11.3 Relationship of group size to use of different methods.

methods except process observation, the discussion-sharing of audiovisual material, and video feedback procedures.

The relationship of group size to types, purposes, and objectives is worth noting. Figure 11.4 represents the restrictions placed on the pursuit of a type of experience by the size of the group. Again a blank space indicates no restriction; horizontal lines, some restriction; and horizontal and vertical lines, considerable restriction.

Education is not restricted by size, but pursuit of each of the other four types is restricted for the upper ranges of the large group and for the very

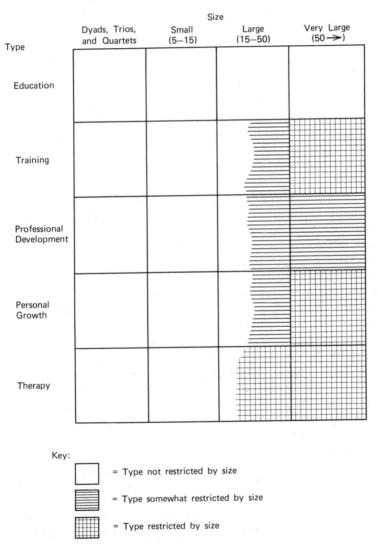

Figure 11.4   Relationship of size to type of learning experience.

large group. Training is difficult in very large groups because of the emphasis of skill development. Personal growth is at best risky and at worst inappropriate in large or very large groups. Therapy is inappropriate here. Many other observations on these interrelationships inherent in Figures 11.3 and 11.4 are left to the reader.

Physical Resources

Physical resources consist of the budget for the learning experience and the facility where it is held. *Budget* is a major consideration for workshops that must support themselves financially and thus affects group size, physical setting, the number of leaders, and choice of methods such as renting films and videotape equipment. You cannot do what you cannot support.

The characteristics of the *facility* include its location, size, furnishings, flexibility, and decor (Steele, 1973). When the setting fails to meet participant expectations or the requirements of the activities, the percentage of undesirable feelings and behaviors increases (Figure 7.2). The authors recently attended a conference of a highly experientially oriented professional organization that had too little space for popular sessions, was too warm and stuffy on hot days, and had a constant background hum that was distracting to many. The combination of these factors not only failed to facilitate learning, but actually inhibited it.

The setting has support, channeling, and activation implications. A carpeted, comfortably and warmly furnished room can be supportive. Adequate lighting, heating, ventilation, proximity to washrooms, and possibly refreshments further contribute to participants' feelings of being supported. They are able to relax in this atmosphere and this leads to a willingness to become involved. In contrast, hard, cold walls, bare floors, wooden chairs, and drab colors are inherently unsupportive. An amphitheatre with fixed seating elicits norms and expectations in participants. Conversely, rooms in which participants sit in small groups with movable chairs generate different and more interactive dynamics. In terms of activation, subdued lighting and very soft furniture in a carpeted room with pleasant decor is underactivating and might be more conducive to sleeping than to learning! An "out of doors" setting is an example of an overactivating environment. The objectives of the learning experience rarely can compete with the activation generated by sitting outside in the shade of a tree on a bright, fragrant, warm, breezy day with birds singing, leaves rustling, and people walking by.

The choice of method is closely related to the nature of the physical setting. Simulations usually require flexible furniture in an area sufficiently large to accommodate subgroups. When separate work areas are desirable for task or discussion groups, satellite rooms or room dividers are necessary. Body movement methods usually require a private carpeted area. The classical case method works best in very large groups where all can see their competition and where all can be seen. An accessible video system in a self contained area is often more effective than an arrangement that has to be assembled and dismantled at each meeting.

In general, a warm, supportive facility is more important for personal growth and therapy than for education, training, or professional development, but larger, more flexible spaces are usually useful for the latter types of experiences. Retreat environments are consistent with personal growth and therapy because comfort and especially privacy are crucial when high levels of intensity and a personal or interpersonal focus are pursued.

Scheduling

The number of sessions, their frequency, length, and the day and time of sessions are of interest in this discussion.

Different scheduling configurations produce different effects (King, Payne, & McIntire, 1973). A number of hourly sessions held at regular intervals is preferable for the dissemination of information, but, for many experiential activities, longer sessions are more desirable. Extended sessions can stand alone or be used very powerfully in conjunction with a series of shorter sessions. Extended sessions generate intense involvement, and reactions from the involvement can be systematically discussed and analyzed at the group's subsequent meetings. Manipulating the schedule provides the leader with opportunities to influence the processes and outcomes of a learning experience beyond the choice of methods.

One-hour sessions typically do not offer sufficient time for many of the experiential techniques to tap underlying change processes. Since time for interaction and involvement is limited, so are feedback, channeling, and support. Though the participants may be activated, opportunities for action are restricted with a corresponding impact on the participants' commitment to the learning experience. Two and three one-hour sessions on a weekly basis inhibit the generation of ongoing support and channeling since the processes created in one session tend not to carry over from week to week. Long "marathon" sessions provide the best opportunity for the development of these change processes but reduce the time for the reflection and integration necessary for some forms of re-cognitive change.

The impact of scheduling on the generation of the change processes is a result of the methods that can be used within a given time configuration. Generally, it is more desirable to have more than one-hour sessions for experiential methods, especially if adequate time is to be spent in the introduction, debriefing, and summary phases. If simulations or role plays are used in a one-hour session, the solution is to design them so that they can be completed in fifteen to twenty minutes, leaving sufficient time for feedback, discussion, and integration. Experience-based methods can be readily used in sessions that are three hours or longer. The classical methods can be used in any scheduling configuration but are best suited to shorter sessions (one hour). Sessions consisting solely of lectures, readings, and written tasks lasting for more than three hours are deadly!

Choice of day and time of day is also a factor. For example, biweekly sensitivity sessions for university students held in the evenings have the advantage that participants can return home after the experience. If the sessions were held during the day, participants would immediately have to cope with other pressures and responsibilities and consequently have little or no time for reflection.

THE INFLUENCE CLUSTER

The influence dimensions are the factors which actually make things happen in the learning experience—the active ingredients. This cluster includes focus, intensity, interaction, and orientation. It describes how the topic is approached. The *focus* refers to whether attention is directed primarily at the content, the attitudes and emotions of participants, the interactions among participants, or some combination of the three. Thus focus is closely related to the target cluster. The terms personal, interpersonal, and content are used to identify each emphasis.

The *intensity*, depth, or level of a learning experience is concerned with the extent to which any particular topic or theme is pursued. The treatment can vary from general and broad to specific and penetrating. For example, the intensity is usually low when children in a classroom are asked how they feel about a certain experience, but in a therapy or encounter group the intensity of the exchange of feelings around a given issue is typically quite high.

The mode of *interaction* among the participants and between the participants and the leader is the interest here. In a lecture, participants are detached from each other and the communication from the leader is one-way, whereas in an encounter group both participants and leaders are involved in intense interpersonal exchange.

The *orientation* dimension has three facets: place, time, and theoretical approach. Place has two locations, the learning setting and away from the learning setting, or "here" and "there." Time is broken down into past, present, and future. Theoretical orientation refers to the model or models of human functioning and change that the leader uses in understanding and affecting participant behavior. For example, in an encounter group the place/time orientation is here and present; that is, participants are concerned about events presently occurring in the group meeting. The theoretical orientation can be any one of a variety of combinations of models of human functioning, but fulfillment is probably dominant. In a task group, planning an interviewing schedule to gather information for a project, the place/time orientation is there and future. Participants are discussing their future actions, which will take place away from the meeting room.

Focus

Ruth Cohn (1969, 1972) used the terms "I," "We," and "It," corresponding to the personal, interpersonal, and content foci respectively. She defined these components as follows:

> The "I" encompasses the psychological experience of each person at any one point in time, whether or not this experience is expressed . . . The "We" refers to the interrelationships within the group at any one point in time and to the awareness on the part of at least some participants that they are in a distinct, unique group with its own particular dynamics, interconnections and concerns . . . The "It" refers to the theme or task that the group meets to consider . . . All groups gather with some sort of focus, however implicit, and . . . the more this focus is explicitly stated and intentionally kept in the forefront of the consciousness of both the leader and participant, the more successful will be the group-process and outcome. (Shaffer & Galinsky, 1974, p. 249)

An understanding of the focus dimension can be expanded by examining its relationship to the types, purposes, objectives, and subject dimensions. The choice of a type of learning experience really determines the focus of that experience. Education typically has a content focus while personal growth and therapy have a personal and possibly an interpersonal focus. Professional development usually has more of a balance among the three foci. Note also that the choice of focus is not determined by the choice of subject.

Negative dynamics can result when participant expectations and actual focus diverge. If participants come expecting to talk about content and are required to talk about themselves, they might react with defensiveness, withdrawal, or anger (Zones II, III, and IV, Figure 7.2). In contrast, participants expecting to talk about themselves and each other may become bored, withdrawn, or angry if they do not have an opportunity to do so. A theoretical orientation centering on conflict or fulfillment models of human functioning (Chapter 1) often implies a personal focus for increased participant personal understanding. On the other hand, a contextual theoretical orientation emphasizes group processes and thus an interpersonal focus is likely. Still, some learning and cognitive theorists see the content as the most important and much less concern is given to personal and interpersonal issues.

An interpersonal focus may generate high activation for change while a content focus might provide a better re-cognitive change arrangement. Experience-based methods such as simulations and role play allow simultaneous pursuit of the three foci while classical methods emphasize content. In a simulation that addresses group conflict, participants learn about their personal reactions in a conflict situation and see how others in the group are affected by the conflict in addition to learning some general principles related to conflict.

Intensity

For a content focus, intensity refers to the amount of detail, the comprehensiveness, and the thoroughness with which the subject is pursued. Chapter 1 treats the conflict models of human functioning less intensely than does a personality text and less yet than a book on Freudian psychology. Consistency between intensity and participant skills, abilities, and expectations is of obvious importance. Material that is too detailed or advanced creates participant frustration, and material that is too simple or general produces boredom.

For a personal or interpersonal focus, intensity refers to the extent to which participants are expected to become personally and emotionally involved and introspective in regard to themselves and their relationships. Dealing intensely with interpersonal issues may frighten participants. In general, a personal and interpersonal focus increases the intensity when confrontational feedback is used. High levels of intensity are very activating and stimulate action. Some forms of group interaction, like encounter groups and body movement methods requiring physical contact such as cradling and rocking, create very high levels of intensity for a personal or interpersonal focus. The use of process observation, especially with videotape feedback, has a similar impact. For a content focus, the classical case method uses competition to generate high intensity. For a personal and interpersonal focus, an increase in intensity is accompanied by a shift in type from education to personal growth and therapy. At a more subtle level, intensity can also be used to differentiate therapy from personal growth. Much legitimate criticism of personal growth activities is the direct result of those activities being pursued at a therapeutic level of intensity without adequate leadership or preparation.

Some Interrelationships

Figure 11.5 shows how the type of learning experience changes with variations in focus and intensity for a given subject. The content, interpersonal, and personal foci are arrayed vertically and three levels of intensity, low, medium, and high, are arrayed horizontally. The subject in this example is interpersonal relationships but other subjects could be innovative business practices, negotiation skills, organizational behavior, life planning, career exploration, and adjusting to single parenthood.

For a content focus and low intensity (cell 3), we have education. Here

Focus

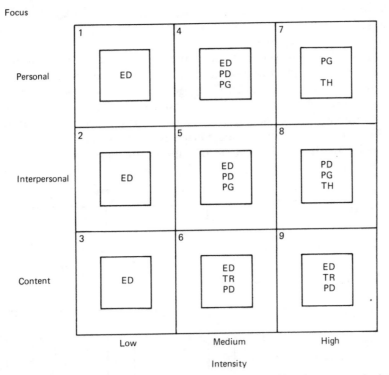

Figure 11.5   Type as a function of focus and intensity for the subject interpersonal relation-ships.

participants might watch a film on the subject and discuss their reactions to it in small groups. For medium and high intensity (cells 6 and 9), training and professional development also occur. Representative activities here are practicing communication skills in dyads and planning strategies for implementing the skills in a relationship at work or at home. For an interpersonal focus of low intensity, again the learning type is education (cell 2). Activities here might be working on a task in a group and then receiving feedback from observers on the roles assumed by the group members in the discussion. At medium levels of intensity, professional development and personal growth are likely, and at high levels of intensity therapy occurs. Examples of cell 5 activities are observing video feedback of a group interaction, identifying the dysfunctional roles, and performing a subsequent task.

For a personal focus, the same pattern as the one just described exists for low and medium levels of intensity (cells 1 and 4), but professional development is not present when the intensity is high (cell 7). Typical activities falling in cell 1 are having participants symbolically explore their strengths and weaknesses. At a higher level of intensity, participants need more investment and commitment and leaders need increased knowledge and skills. The focus determines the nature of participant commitment and leader expertise.

An example of a subject not concerned with interpersonal relationships further illustrates how the type of learning experience changes with shifts in focus and intensity. The subject "innovative practices in business" is representative of the kinds of topics that are presented experientially in many seminars and workshops. These relationships are presented in Figure 11.6. The major difference between Figures 11.5 and 11.6 is that personal growth and therapy do not appear in Figure 11.6.

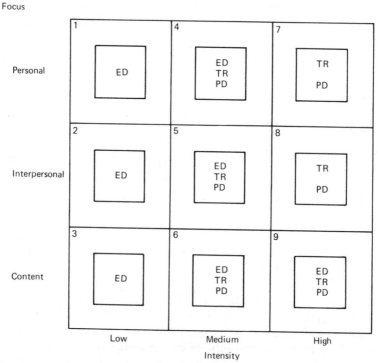

Figure 11.6   Type as a function of focus and intensity for the subject innovative practices in business.

Interaction

The next concern is with the kind of exchange that takes place between leaders and participants and among participants during the learning experience. Does the leader interact with the participants or is the exchange primarily one way? Do participants talk to each other or do they converse only with the leader? The range of possibilities for leader–participant

(L–P) and participant–participant (P–P) interactions is presented in Figure 11.7.

The vertical axis in the figure represents P–P interaction and varies from low at the bottom to high at the top. Low P–P interaction occurs in situations where participants talk with or engage each other at a minimal level. On the other hand, high P–P interaction consists of ongoing exchange that is central to the learning activity. The horizontal axis in the figure represents L–P interaction and varies from low on the left to high on the right. Low L–P interaction is found in any mode that does not involve two-way exchange such as in lectures or leaderless discussion groups. The sixteen instructional methods are placed in Figure 11.7 according to the interaction patterns they use. While a wide variety of possible interactions do exist, it is also seen that there is a definite interactional character consistent with a given method.

Some observations about the relationship between interaction and some of the change processes are relevant at this point. Without moderate to high levels of interaction, interpersonal feedback is restricted. Much of the conditioning that occurs in the learning context is transmitted through interaction. Support is established and maintained through the exchange participants have with each other and with the leader. In addition, interaction is one of the primary means for generating activation. Finally, since some form of verbal exchange is a major part of almost all learning experiences, interaction comprises a large part of the action that takes place. As interaction increases the number of change processes present and their impact also increases. It is not surprising, then, that high intensity change associated with personal growth and therapy almost always occurs with moderate to high L–P or P–P interactions.

Orientation

The orientation dimension has three components: place, time, and theoretical perspective. *Place and time* components are summarized in Figure 11.8.

In a group meeting to work on a task or project, all six time/place orientations are possible. When the participants summarize what they covered at their last week's meeting, the orientation is here and past (cell 1). When they present the task related activities they had been involved in during the week, the orientation is there and past (cell 4). When the group exchanges information regarding how they are working on the task at the moment, the orientation is here and present (cell 2). This differs from Schein and Bennis' notion of "here and now" since their label assumes a personal or interpersonal focus. For them, "here and now"

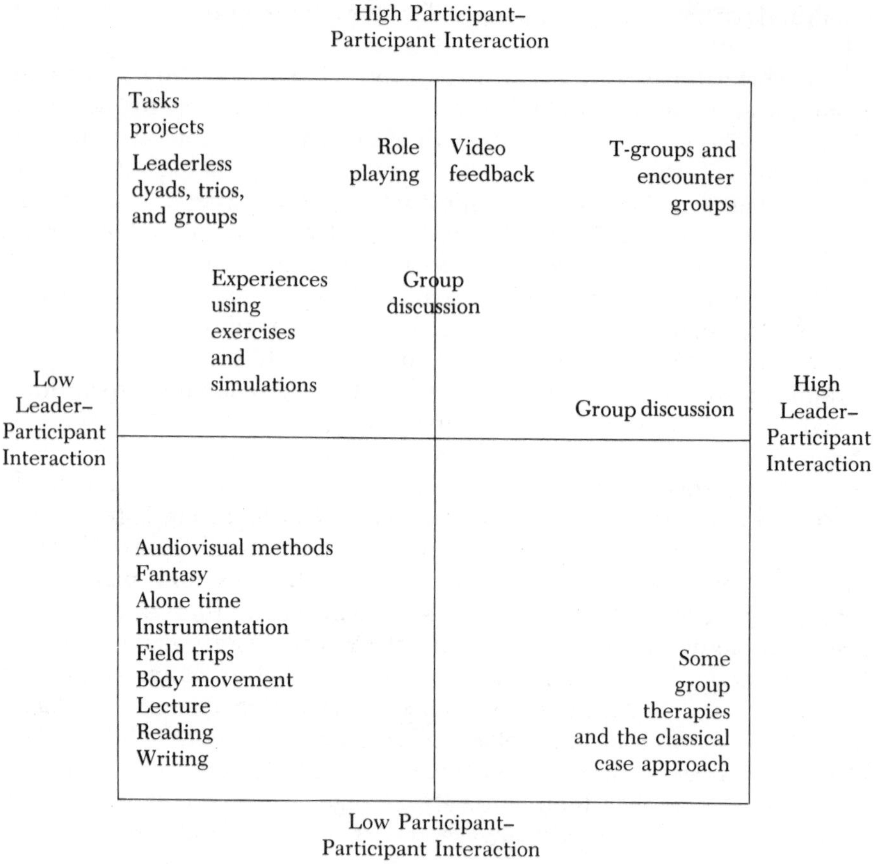

High Participant–
Participant Interaction

Tasks projects Leaderless dyads, trios, and groups	Role playing	Video feedback	T-groups and encounter groups
	Experiences using exercises and simulations	Group discussion	
			Group discussion
	Audiovisual methods Fantasy Alone time Instrumentation Field trips Body movement Lecture Reading Writing		Some group therapies and the classical case approach

Low
Leader–
Participant
Interaction

High
Leader–
Participant
Interaction

Low Participant–
Participant Interaction

Figure 11.7   Leader and participant interactions.

means that the focus of examination . . . is the *experienced behavior* of the delegates, nothing more or less . . . In other words, here and now learning is based on experiences which are shared, public, immediate, direct, first hand, unconceptualized, and self-acknowledged. (Schein & Bennis, 1965, pp. 38–39)

When the participants discuss the status of other groups' projects at that point in time, their concerns are in the present, but they are talking about events that are occurring outside of their particular group (there and present, cell 5). When the group plans what it will do at its next meeting, the orientation is here and future (cell 3). Finally, when participants plan what they will do individually with respect to the project during the next week, their place/time orientation is there and future (cell 6). Dealing in the "here and present" is potentially more activating and intensity inducing than other orientations. Most experience-based methods are "here" oriented while the classical methods tend to be more "there" oriented, and the supporting methods can be either. Process groups and similar methods require a present orientation but time orientation is less constrained.

A variety of orientations are suitable for the five types of learning, but the theoretical orientation of the leader affects place/time possibilities. For example, Freudians are concerned with events that occurred "there" in the past while behaviorists are concerned with events that are occurring "here" in the present. When the focus is personal or interpersonal, a "here and present" orientation generally increases intensity.

Theoretical orientation has two major components, views of models of human functioning and preferences for change processes inherent in the use of various methods. Psychoanalytic, Rogerian, or behavioristic schools of thought are predicated on different models of human functioning, and these different conceptions inevitably lead to different learning designs and interventions. For example, in terms of motivation, some approaches to human relations training hold that frustration is central to the unfreezing process and thus important for change (Bradford, Gibb, & Benne, 1964). Rogerians, on the other hand, see the fulfillment of needs such as acceptance as central for change (Shaffer & Galinsky, 1974). Further, a behaviorist might have a preference for exercises that focus on discrete, identifiable behaviors, while an existentialist might use leaderless groups to address the same issue.

Leader preferences for various change processes also exist. Explaining what to do and how to do it to participants reflects a different theoretical perspective from demonstrating the desired behaviors or letting participants discover them for themselves either through feedback or observation. Similarly, delineation of conditions in which personal growth or therapy can be performed vary for different theoretical orientations.

		Time		
		Past	Present	Future
Place	Here	1	2	3
	There	4	5	6

Figure 11.8 Place and time orientation matrix.

THE ORGANIZATIONAL CLUSTER

Social and technical structure and leadership are the two factors that specify how the learning experience will proceed. Structure addresses the selection and use of the methods discussed in Chapters 8, 9, and 10 for generating and directing participant behavior. These methods provide social and technical structure. Social structure includes the organization resulting from the channeling processes such as norms, roles, goals, and expectations. Technical structure is the organization resulting from tangible aspects of the methods, such as printed materials and equipment. Different learning experiences rely on different amounts of social and technical structuring. For example, a T-group is highly socially structured, a field trip or film presentation is more dependent on technical structure, and a role play or simulation require both. The other organization dimension, leadership, is treated following the structure discussion.

Structure

Social structure provides the source for the channeling processes discussed in Chapter 4. Since the social structure required for experiential learning is different from that required for classical methods, the leader's theme setting efforts during the introductory phase are crucial. Typical social norms made explicit here are the sharing of feelings and perceptions, active involvement in the learning experience, responsiveness to the leader's request for specific behaviors, and participant-centered responsibility for learning. The latter theme is buttressed by participants' immediate involvement in expectation setting and sharing activities. The norm of involvement is linked to giving and receiving feedback. The norm of participant responsibility for learning contributes directly to commitment.

Two quite different examples of social structure are demonstrated in T-groups and the classical case method. T-groups use norms of openness, spontaneity, dealing with feelings, and focusing on ongoing behavior. The "unstructured" social structure of the T-group places high responsibility on participants and allows the leader subtly to reinforce desired behavior. The classical case method emphasizes ongoing evaluation, displayed competence, and winning in a highly competitive and even coercive environment. Fear is sublimated into aggressiveness, and the result is often an intense, highly charged exchange. The necessary social structures for the lecture method center on the acceptance of the leader as an authority. Many of the supporting methods also rely on the participants' acceptance of authority.

Interaction is an important correlate of social structure. When L–P and P–P interactions and intensity are high with a personal and interpersonal focus (i.e., encounter groups), the norms, roles, and expectations of the resulting social structure have a very strong channeling influence on participant behavior. On the other hand, when L–P and P–P interaction and intensity are low and the focus is on the content, the resulting social structure exerts a less compelling influence on the participants.

Technical structure is provided by those facets of the learning experience that are tangible and are overtly directive. The assignment of roles and the use of certain materials and equipment are examples.

The methods are the source technical structure. Simulations create elaborate series of events and interactions within which participants are required to respond. These structures are initially established by the rules and materials of the simulation, and even though they generate a social structure of their own, the social structure would never materialize without the technical structure that created it. The simulation "Star Power" is a representative example in which a three-class society is developed through a process of bartering. In other methods, participants are assigned roles, taken on field trips, or asked to respond in a set sequence within an exercise. In all these cases the tangible aspects of the methods provide structure. The same is true for the classical and supporting methods. Readings, written assignments, pictures, films, questionnaires, observation guides, and video equipment all provide cues which influence the way participants behave and thus constitute technical structure.

Technical structures cannot stand alone and need to be buttressed with social structure. "Cook book" approaches to experiential learning often fail because their predominant or exclusive focus is on issues related to technical structure and pacing. Adequate supporting social structure is assumed but often neophyte leaders do not build this.

In closing, it is reemphasized that some groups of participants require more structure than others. Individuals with highly programmed jobs and individuals who have experienced or are experiencing highly programmed education may have learned to require a high degree of structure, regardless of the kind. On the other hand, individuals who are accustomed to operating autonomously and who have more self-directed learning experiences, may learn best and be most comfortable in formats with less structure.

Leadership

The leadership dimension is comprised of knowledge, skill, personality, style, and number of leaders. Knowledge and skill refer to information and its application gained through formal schooling, professional workshops, and experience. Personality refers to leadership qualities such as friendliness, trust, excitement, and enthusiasm, which promote the conditions required for effective experiential learning. Style refers to the manner in which the leader conducts the learning experience, that is, the way knowledge, skills, and personality are blended into a consistent pattern.

For *knowledge,* most university programs at the masters and doctoral levels should adequately prepare leaders in particular content areas. In addition, programs with a clinical training component such as clinical psychology, counseling psychology, or social work provide for *skill* development related to their respective content areas. A dilemma arises because experts in particular disciplines tend to assume that this expertise in and of itself is sufficient to enable them to lead learning activities in both experiential and classical modes. They ignore that some skill development is necessary to conduct learning activities. This problem is exacerbated by the fact that no universally accepted approach exists for training experiential leaders.

The major skills required for conducting experiential learning activities, in addition to expertise in a content area, are interpersonal competence (Arygris, 1962), the ability to use intervention techniques such as confrontation or feedback, the ability to provide facilitating aspects of social and technical structure, an appreciation of interpersonal and group dynamics, the ability to pace the activities appropriately, and the ability to generate desirable dynamics and avoid undesirable ones (Corey & Corey, 1977). In conclusion, the leader should be able to approach the experiential learning processes in Gallelian as well as Aristotelian modes. That is, the leader should be as comfortable dealing with underlying dynamics (Part 1) as with overt, observable components of the experience (Part 2).

Pacing can be divided into two components, the rate at which material or activities are presented and the timing of specific comments or interventions. If material is paced too slowly and participants are given more time than they need, activation suffers, but if they are rushed, they fail to become engaged in the activity. Leaders' timing of specific interventions is a function of their awareness of what is happening in the learning experience at that point and of their particular theoretical orientation. Scheduling five minutes for dyads to work on an exercise is a pacing decision but deciding when to interrupt them during the task to provide additional information or suggestions is concerned with timing. Some leaders prefer to wait until participants are really lost and confused before they intervene; others intervene to prevent confusion from occurring; still others choose not to intervene at all.

There is no ideal *personality* profile for experiential leaders (Bergin & Garfield, 1971, p. 896). Nevertheless, some personality traits are desirable (Corey & Corey, 1977; Getzels & Jackson, 1963). The first group of traits clusters around the term *openness,* which includes social openness or extroversion, intellectual openness or cognitive flexibility, and tolerance for ambiguity. These traits allow participants to feel accepted and comfortable in the learning environment. The second group of traits are encompassed by the term *consistency.* There are two kinds of consistency: the first is congruence among the feelings, statements, and actions of the leader at a given point in time; the second is the consistency of all three of these over time. Leader predictability by the participants is based on these two types of consistency. A third personality trait that serves as a foundation for openness and consistency is *self-esteem* or *ego strength*. The relevance of self-esteem is documented by research such as Rubin's (1967) study of laboratory training, which showed that tolerance of ambiguity and ego strength were positively related. Finally, the leaders' *energetic* quality is a trait that mobilizes the entire learning experience and aids in overcoming participant inhibitions.

Style refers to the general attitude and degree of directiveness assumed by the leader in the learning experience (Gordon, 1955; Tubbs, 1978; White & Lippitt, 1968). A directive style is one in which the leader tells participants what to do and provides structure and information that directs their behavior. A nondirective style is one where the leader permits the participants to function autonomously or provides broad guidelines within which participants can respond. A successfully conducted learning experience requires both directive and nondirective leader behaviors at different points in the process. Directive leader behavior is recommended for decisions surrounding the outlining of objectives, building social structure and expectations, and choosing sources of technical structure. Directive behaviors are needed during the introduction to set themes and in the summary to provide conceptual structures to assist participants in understanding the experience. They are selectively required during the activity and debriefing in the form of providing rules and procedures to be followed and for moving participants from activity to activity.

Nondirective leader behavior is appropriate for decisions regarding the participants' level of involvement, their choice of behavior at different points in the learning processes, the extent and the degree of intensity with which they choose to share their reactions to the activities, and the integration of their personal goals with the overall objectives of the experience. The essence of experiential learning rests in participants having choice in these areas.

For the classical methods, especially the lecture, a directive style is usually required while the experience-based methods typically involve the use of both styles. In a lecture, leaders assume their role is to communicate information, and they maintain control of the participants through the dissemination of information and the resulting patterns of interaction. On the other hand, in a Rogerian oriented sensitivity group, the curriculum evolves out of the interaction of the participants and any effort on the part of the leader to impose an agenda or overtly direct or change the process is considered inappropriate. If leaders approached a sensitivity group with a directive style, the interaction necessary for the development of the change processes such as feedback, support, activation, and channeling would not occur. Similarly, if leaders attempted to deliver a lecture in a nondirective style, they violate participants' expectations and fail to create the required channeling, persuasion, and re-cognition influences. The question is not which style is best, but which style or combination of styles is appropriate for a given situation.

The two most common errors made by leaders in terms of their choice of style are first, choosing a nondirective stance on theoretical or philosophical grounds rather than on the requirements of the situation, and, second, being overly directive in participant-centered aspects of the learning experience. For example, in terms of the first point, nothing is more frustrating to participants than leaders who fail to provide a clear sense of the type, focus, and orientation for the learning experience or a framework within which they can choose. Leaders often behave in this manner out of a need to be democratic or participative when in fact they have failed to meet their responsibilities. On the other hand, some aspects of experiential learning such as generating expectations or giving feedback require that the participants manage their involvement in the activities. Leaders who try to direct and control participant behavior in these situations sabotage the entire experience and are seldom able to diagnose that it is their directive style that is the reason the learning experience is not effective.

Aspects of a leader's style determine how activities are introduced and conducted, how methods are used, and how participants are treated during the learning experience. Since so many acceptable alternatives exist, it is not possible to prescribe one correct approach.

There are several advantages to having *more than one leader* when conducting a learning experience (Pfeiffer & Jones, 1975, pp. 219–229). Team leadership offers a greater variety of leader contributions (Lundberg & Lundberg, 1974). These include an increased capacity to attend to the processes within the experience and a more comprehensive mixture of knowledge, observations, style, and personality. In addition, more than one leader provides participants with a greater variety of models, reduces the tendency for them to become dependent on the leader, and increases the likelihood that important issues are brought into clear focus. To exploit this potential, co-leading arrangements require compatibility between leaders plus a considerable personal commitment and investment of energy. Some of the potential problems are incompatible theoretical orientations or approaches to pacing and competition with each other or the participants for time to present material. If the leaders review and share their expectations and are able to adjust their behavior during the learning experience, these disadvantages can be avoided. Co-leadership is especially desirable when dealing with large and very large groups, if for no other reason than to simplify the logistics of managing the learning experience. Tasks like dispensing handouts, answering questions, and providing guidance for participants can be performed more quickly and effectively.

DIMENSION INTERRELATIONSHIPS

It is possible to study the interdependencies of the twelve dimensions systematically. In Figure 11.9 all the possibilities are considered. The matrix in Figure 11.9 illustrates three categories of dimensional interrelationships: high, variable, and low. Horizontal and vertical lines indicate a high relationship between the two dimensions, that is, a change in one directly affects the other. For example, the physical setting determines the maximum size of a group that can be accommodated. A blank space indicates relatively low interdependence between the two dimensions, that is, a change in one can be made without affecting the other. For example, the choice of subject does not depend on group size or room size. Horizontal lines indicate more complex relationships where a broad range of possibilities exists or where a third dimension can affect the pair. For example, interaction varies with group size, but is also affected by different physical settings. If one dimension constrains the other less directly or less tightly than in the case of a *H* designation, it receives a *V* designation. Also, when one dimension is related to another in highly subjective and complex ways, a *V* designation is given. An example here is focus (personal, interpersonal, and content) or orientation (place, time, and theoretical).

With the significance of *H, V,* and *L* in mind, a number of observations based on Figure 11.9 can be made.

1   The centrality of the types, purposes, and objectives dimension is shown by the four *H*s and seven *V*s and no *L*s.

2   The subject is highly independent of all but three dimensions: type, participants, and leadership.

3   The participants dimension places no heavy constraints on the learning design except for type and intensity, as evidenced by the low number of *H*s.

4   Group size is highly independent of subject, participants, scheduling, focus, and orientation. It is highly related only to physical resources but has complex relationships with the remaining dimensions.

5   Physical resources is another relatively independent variable, but is highly related to group size and has variable relationships with types, participants, scheduling, intensity, interaction, required structure, and feasible leadership.

6   Scheduling is independent of subject, size, focus, and orientation, and has variable relationships with the remaining dimensions.

7   The focus is highly dependent only on the type and leadership and relatively independent of subject, size, physical resources, schedul-

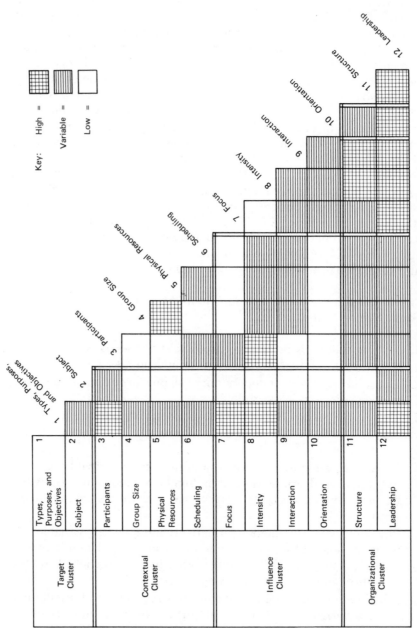

Figure 11.9 Matrix of hypothetical relationships among dimensions.

ing, and intensity. Its relationships with participants, interaction, orientation, and structure are much more complex.

8   Leadership and structure are the sources of intensity and therefore are highly related to it. The high relationships with type and participants speak for themselves. The complex relationships with group size, physical resources, scheduling, interaction, and orientation illustrate that these dimensions are major moderators of intensity. For example, groups of smaller sizes meeting in longer sessions and more frequently over a given time are more suitable for highly intense and personal exchange.

9   Leadership and structure determine interaction patterns and consequently are highly related to them. Constraints on interaction possibilities can be imposed by group size, physical setting, and scheduling. Guidelines are established for interaction by the desired intensity, the theoretical orientation, and by an interpersonal focus. Theoretical orientation includes assumptions about appropriate kinds of interaction and an interpersonal focus requires some form of participant–participant interaction in order to exist.

10   Leaders determine the orientation of the learning experience. Also, certain orientations require specific leader knowledge, skills, and styles. For example, a "here and present" orientation with a personal and interpersonal focus requires a high degree of leader interpersonal competence and process skill. Further, structure affects the feasibility of an orientation and orientation helps to determine the appropriate structure. Focus, intensity, interaction, and types are moderately linked with both place/time and theoretical orientation.

11   Structure has high mutual interdependence with intensity, interaction, and leadership. It is moderately constrained by group size in that choices of structure are limited for very small and very large groups, and has complex relationships with all the other dimensions except the subject.

12   Leadership, like types, purposes, and objectives, is highly or complexly related to all the dimensions.

These observations may appear overwhelming, but by moving to a cluster analysis, a meaningingful reduction of the complexity is possible.

CLUSTER INTERRELATIONSHIPS

This discussion provides a means for using the four dimension clusters as a system for designing experiential learning activities. The four clusters

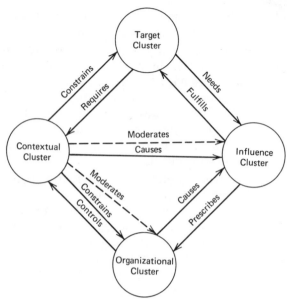

Figure 11.10   Dimension clusters and their relationships.

are bound together by a complex set of reciprocal relationships. These relationships are illustrated in Figure 11.10.

The target cluster is placed at the top of the model since the learning experience is oriented around the types, purposes, objectives, and subject. The target *requires* certain conditions in the context and *needs* certain patterns of the influence dimensions for the desired change. The contextual cluster *constrains* the target and organizational clusters but also *causes* certain influence processes to occur as well as having a moderating effect on the impact of some of the influence dimensions. The influence cluster *fulfills* the target and *prescribes* the needed structure and leadership for creating the desired influences. Finally, the organizational cluster *controls* the contextual dimensions and *causes* the influence processes to occur.

The discussion of the interrelationships among the clusters proceeds on a pair by pair basis: target–context, target–influence, organization–influence, organization–context, and context–influence.

Target–Context

Education, training, and professional development require participant homogeniety around skills, abilities, and level of preparation. It is also desirable that the subject be compatible with participants' expectations. Therapy is more feasible when participant involvement is voluntary, when the group size is below about eighteen, when a private, secure, and comfortable physical setting is used, and when sessions are scheduled so that follow-up is possible. The requirements for personal growth are similar.

Conversely, the participants' background, skill level, expectations, and, to some degree, age and sex, influence the choice of type of experience and the subject to be considered. For example, the expectations of a group of college students in a class on introductory management precludes intense personal growth. Similarly, as group size increases, the pursuit of professional development, and especially personal growth and therapy, becomes more difficult. Generally, the participants, group size, and scheduling place more constraints on the type of learning experience as one moves from education to therapy. A physical setting with fixed seating severely restricts the pursuit of therapy and personal growth. The most common errors in designing experiential learning activities falling within the target–context relationships concern the pursuit of personal growth or therapy: when participants expect education; when the group is too large; or when there is insufficient time.

Target–Influence

A well formulated theoretical orientation that unifies the influence contributions into a consistent pattern is always useful, but this is especially so for therapy. Therapeutic change also needs a personal focus, high intensity, and high levels of P–P and/or L–P interaction. Personal growth has similar needs. Professional development needs only moderate intensity when the focus is personal and a balance among all three foci. Training needs a content focus with a moderate to high intensity. Education needs a low intensity if the focus is personal or interpersonal.

Organizational–Influence

All the influence processes occur as a result of the leader's behavior or as a result of the social and technical structure created or selected by the leader. For example, using small groups to discuss reactions to an experience causes moderate to high levels of P–P interaction, and, depending upon the leader's directions, can also cause a personal and interpersonal focus at the desired levels of intensity. Conversely, when a personal focus and high intensity are desired, a supportive social structure has to be developed and methods like group interaction selected. In addition, the leader here has to have the appropriate clinical skills.

Organizational–Contextual

In some cases, the leader decides how many and what kind of participants will be involved in the learning experience and where and when it will be held. However, when aspects of the contextual dimensions are set, they constrain the choices available to a leader in terms of structure and interventions. For example, the use of a simulation is not feasible if the session is very short. The use of some audiovisual methods is constrained if the facility has windows without blackout curtains and no projection screen is available. In addition, the contextual cluster also has a moderating effect on the impact of the organizational cluster. A method such as group interaction has a different impact when used in a warm, comfortable physical environment as compared to a cold, uncomfortable one. Participants will engage in personal exchanges more readily in the former.

Contextual–Influence

Group composition factors such as age and sex affect interaction. Heterogeneity may inhibit P–P interactions. The moderating effect of the context is similar to its moderating effect on the organizational cluster. For example, as time increases, a personal focus becomes more likely, and if it already exists, its intensity will probably increase. A comfortable setting also increases intensity for a personal or interpersonal focus.

DESIGN DECISION MAKING SEQUENCES

There are three alternative temporal sequences for designing experiential learning activities: one for situations where there are considerable constraints, one for situations where there are moderate constraints, and one for situations where there are minimal or no constraints. These three alternatives apply in designing entire learning experiences, modules within them, or one specific activity. The first design step, regardless of the nature of the experience, is to determine the amount of constraint in the context. Once this information is identified a design sequence can be selected.

The Constrained Case

An example of the constrained case is a typical high school setting. The participants are grade eleven and twelve students in a guidance class that meets for three one-hour sessions a week for one term. There are thirty-five students in the class. The group meets in a classroom with movable desks. The topic of the module is career education. In this situation, the context and the target are determined. The sequence presented in Figure 11.11 represents the order in which design decisions are made.

1 In this situation, all aspects of the context are taken as given.
2 Within the context, the first approximation of the target is established (primarily education). However, there is often latitude for the choice of specific topics within the general subject. Some exam-

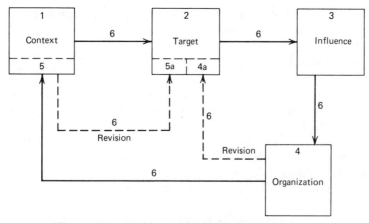

Figure 11.11 Decision model for the constrained case.

ples are identifying different groups of occupations, providing participants with opportunities to discover their own interests and attitudes with respect to careers, and examining the different tasks related to different careers.

3 The needed influence patterns are selected to meet the target. A content and personal focus are necessary but moderate or high intensity for either are inappropriate. P–P and L–P interaction is desirable and "here and present" and "there and future" place/time orientations are required so that participants can examine their present values and project what they will have to do to meet their future needs.

4 Appropriate organization probably builds on the use of lectures, reading, audiovisual methods, and, possibly, role playing. Guidelines for group discussion are desirable, self-administered interest inventories could be used, and field trips to local businesses or guest speakers are planned.

4a If the desired structure or leadership is not available, there is a revision of the target. For example, if none of the members of the community are able to come to the school when the class meets, rescheduling or substituting different methods may be required. Alternatively, aspiration levels for the target may be reduced.

5 The context is created or altered within the restraints. A noon-hour meeting is arranged for the representatives to come and speak to the students.

5a When necessary alterations cannot be made, the target is revised again. Revisions were possible so the target does not have to changed.

6   Steps 1 through 5 are reviewed and minor adjustments are made if necessary. This is essentially "fine tuning."

The Moderately Constrained Case

A group of fifteen graduate students in a personnel management course have requested a one day workshop to look more closely at the interview process. In this situation, the participants, group size, and length of the experience are determined, as is the subject, but other aspects of the context and target are not specified. This is typical of many of the situations in which leaders have to function. The sequence in Figure 11.12 represents the order of design decisions for this case.

1   The given contextual variables are noted. In this case, the participants, their number, and the length of the experience are known.
2   For the target, the general subject for the workshop has been chosen and the nature of the setting and participant group rules out therapy or an exclusive emphasis on personal growth as approaches to the treatment of the subject.
3   The remaining aspects of the target are defined. A 50 percent professional development–50 percent personal growth combination is chosen since the participants were more interested in understanding their own interviewing behavior than simply in being exposed to some techniques. Topics are selected such as questioning techniques, handling silence, and reading nonverbal cues.
4   The needed influence patterns are identified. An even balance among the three foci are desired with moderate to high intensity for content and moderate intensity for personal and interpersonal

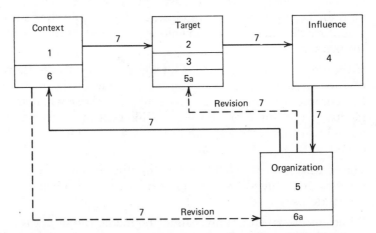

Figure 11.12 Decision model for the moderately constrained case.

issues. A "here and present" place/time orientation and opportunities for high levels of P–P and L–P interactions are also required.

5   Appropriate organization is selected or developed. Role play outlines are generated and video equipment for recording and playback is reserved. A film is ordered on nonverbal communication.

5a If desired structure or leadership is not available, the target is revised. The film and equipment are available whenever needed so no revision is necessary.

6   The context is created or altered within the restraints. A Saturday is selected and a comfortable room suitable for video playback and discussion is booked.

6a When necessary contextual conditions cannot be found, alterations to the structure and leadership are made. If alternative organization is not available, the target is revised again (5a).

7   Steps 1 through 6 are reviewed and minor adjustments are made if necessary.

The Unconstrained Case

An organization wishes to develop and conduct a series of learning experiences dealing with facets of interpersonal relationships for its membership. The specific content of the experiences is to be determined by the members' expressed needs. Financial resources, within reason, are available to support the designed program, including hiring leaders and renting necessary facilities and equipment. In this situation, most aspects of the context are not determined and the choice of target is left to the leader's discretion. The sequence presented in Figure 11.13 represents the order in which design decisions are made here.

1   The target is selected. The leader, after an appraisal of the organization's wishes and an assessment of participants' needs, decides that the first learning experience will be on managing feelings at work. A balanced combination among training, professional development, and personal growth is chosen. It is assumed here that leaders have the competencies to implement the choices they make.

2   The context is determined. Twenty-five volunteers express a preference for a two-day weekend retreat experience. A resort close to the community with adequate facilities is reserved.

3   Needed influence patterns are identified. A balance among the three foci and moderate intensity are desired. High P–P interaction and "here and present" and "there and future" place/time orientations are needed. Participants learn the skills in the present but also look to applying them in other situations.

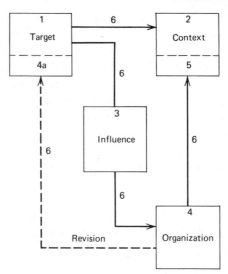

Figure 11.13   Decision model for the unconstrained case.

4 Appropriate organization is selected or developed. Exercises on interpersonal communication skills and observation guides are assembled. Work-related role plays are developed.

4a If the desired structure or leadership is not available, the target is revised. No revision is necessary here.

5 The context is created and controlled. Specific instructions are given to the resort regarding schedule, space, and furniture requirements for different activities.

6 Steps 1 through 5 are reviewed and, if necessary, minor adjustments are made.

CONCLUSION

These three decision sequences assist leaders in ordering their thinking when designing experiental learning activities. By clustering dimensions and using this relatively simple decision analysis format, systematization of the vast number of factors in conducting experiential learning can be sufficient to avoid a wide variety of oversights as well as confusion. Further, the four clusters of dimensions serve a pragmatic organizing function that allows subsequent reflection and analysis in light of the more analytical material provided in Part 1. Thus, Part 2, in total, provides the reader not only with a "menu" and a "recipe book" for preparing and conducting experiential activities, but also serves as a systematized base from which fundamental questions about various aspects of the field can be pursued.

CHAPTER TWELVE

Ethics and Future
Directions

*A teacher affects
eternity; he can never
tell where his influence
stops.*

Henry Brook Adams

Before considering the future of experiential learning, it is essential to confront the issue of ethics in this field. Ethical principles have been embedded in our analysis thus far, and of course are implicit in many of the techniques described. But the ethics of experiential learning have not been formally and fully explicated. This omission has caused confusion within the field and allowed criticism from without. Hence the following discussion is timely and necessary. The growth of experiential learning as a discipline depends on the integrity and strength of its foundations.

The study of ethics is as complex as it is important, and approaches vary from the subjective to the absolute (Frankena, 1963; Oldenquist, 1965). Tests for ethical sufficiency can be applied to either actions or outcomes. For example, the American Psychological Association in its "Ethical Standards for Psychologists" (1963) details principles and example actions around issues of misrepresentation, public statements, confidentiality, client relationships, and so forth. This is paralleled for group leaders by Olsen (1971) and Beck (1971). Alternatively, others discuss "problems" and issues around which problems arise in various activities such as sensitivity training (Benne, 1959; Jenkins, 1960; Lakin, 1969).

Perhaps the best ethical principle in experiential learning is the same as that of the medical profession: *Preneum Non Nocera*, first of all do no harm. But certain learning situations are by nature highly competitive;

within professional schools in a university, for example, students are encouraged to compete for the top grades that everyone cannot attain. Moreover, it is often not within the power of an individual to ignore or bypass the standards or traditions of the learning institution. "Harm" can therefore occur in an experience as the result of dynamics beyond the control or predictive ability of the leader. The dilemma is that if a leader must invest a great deal of energy in anticipating and preventing such outcomes, little would remain for facilitating learning. No leader can be perfect in this regard, of course, but an obvious conclusion is that it is ethically dubious to overstimulate or "hype" existing competition just to extract a "motivation" effect. There can be no "formula" for dealing with the necessary level of competition versus overstepping reasonable bounds, but leaders should be cognizant that the issue exists. Therefore, the guidelines offered here are not behaviorally prescriptive, but take the form of principles by which leaders can assess their own behavior, first, in terms of personal competence, and second, in terms of a set of "goods" and their protection.

Conducting experiential learning requires skill, experience, and an understanding of behavioral dynamics. One of the objectives in writing this book has been to establish a set of constructs by which leaders might recognize and measure the inadequacies of their own approach. Awareness of the field's complexity, the myriad techniques available, and the operative differences among them should stimulate a flexible, openminded understanding of the discipline. Dogmatically held beliefs, unrealistic goals, and a closed mind can not only limit a leader's effectiveness, but can also cause harm. Abuses of the past, such as the overuse of the "open classroom" or the emotional casualties of encounter groups, might have been avoided through more broadly based leadership skills. When leaders are sensitive to the number of leader-centered change processes and the dynamics of identification, persuasion, and support, they should then be able to adjust their performances accordingly. Knowledge of human functioning can be applied not only to participants in a learning experience, but to oneself; continuing to develop one's self, being open to various influences, and sharing a leadership function with others of complementary style and ability are important preliminaries to effective leadership and ethical sufficiency. Competence in this field is elusive and difficult to measure, but the consequences of incompetence are highly observable, harmful, and hence unethical.

Leaders can pursue ethical sufficiency by aiming to protect three specific possessions or "goods" of the participants. These are freedom, self-esteem, and privacy (Walter, 1975; Kelman & Warwick, 1978).

It has often been argued that effective change of individuals involves some degree of manipulation and hence a violation of individual freedom. Kelman (1965) prescribed a "constant, informed, free choice matrix" for participants in learning. He maintained that individuals need to be provided with continuous choice points throughout a learning experience at which they can voluntarily alter their involvement in light of what has already happened and their anticipation of what might happen next. This deliberate, careful solution to the protection of freedom can work well in small group or low pressure situations, in nonuniversity workshops, for example. But it is not applicable to the classical case method in a highly competitive system such as the Harvard Business School. In the former case, ethics and pragmatism are often mutually consistent; during a workshop with senior, experienced people in an organization, for instance, individuals may resent the sudden lack of free choice which they perceive as manipulation. They might subsequently refuse to participate, or at best dissipate the energy that would generate effective learning. Such a group would benefit from a free choice matrix. In the business school classroom, however, giving students the chance to opt out of the tightly structured progress toward the solution of a problem clearly is incongruent with the whole program, and once again the learning process would be disrupted. Here, commitment to the approach from the outset is essential to its effectiveness, and potential students need to be thoroughly informed prior to making a commitment to such a program.

Therefore, it seems unrealistic to insist, as Kelman does, that freedom must never be reduced, since, while no harm may be done, neither might any learning be acquired. As an alternative principle, freedom can be treated as an inviolable basic right of the participants. With this in mind, the solution is to provide certain realistic choices and to maximize voluntarism. This notion allows for highly directive leadership and strict limitation of participant choice at various points in a learning experience.

A second good, self-esteem, has been shown to increase as a result of sensitivity training (Rubin, 1967). Although little research has been done on the impact of other experiential techniques on self-esteem, its fundamental antecedents have been articulated. Self-esteem seems to depend on the following:

1 Seeing purpose in life (Frankl, 1967).
2 Not being used by others solely to promote their ends (Hagen, 1962).
3 Having some control over one's life (Rotter, 1966).
4 Maintaining some level of competence leading to control (White, 1959).

Experiential learning need not reduce self-esteem; the issue here is not avoiding manipulation *per se* but avoiding exploitive or preemptive acts or arrangements. The enthusiastic leader, however, can easily step over certain bounds, or the activities combined with group dynamics can sweep some people along against their will. Unfortunately, those who are so carried and those who are often not inclined to protest aloud or to resist workshop dynamics are those already lacking in self-esteem. Maintaining self-esteem, therefore, requires active effort by the leader in aiding and supporting these individuals. When choices are given, mechanisms for opting out need to be included. Those who choose to opt out need protection. Argyris (1980) argues that this protection is best when it comes from the structure and dynamics of the learning arrangement. Protection that comes merely from the leader sponsors dependencies and thus can have esteem reducing implications. Still, a leader's efforts to shift the focus away from someone overcome by anxiety is a supportive act; it may surprise other participants but it may also generate a more trusting, caring learning climate.

The third good is privacy. Until recently, the word "privacy" has been literally taboo in the experiential scene. Interdependence, intimacy, and authenticity were "in," while independence, isolation, and role play were "out;" openness was desirable and stoicism was suspect, confrontation encouraged and mutual avoidance denied. In this era, privacy became an anachronism, and the insights of a previous generation concerning its nature were lost. In 1948, Lewin conceptualized privacy as a series of concentric circles. In the central insulated zones, intimacy occurs with special people in unique relationships. Personal autonomy depends on one's ability to protect this inner self from censure or ridicule by others. Great personal danger occurs when one's mask is stripped away while others maintain theirs. Rogers (1956, 1961) implies that forced or indiscriminate incursions on privacy can be counterproductive to the development of intimacy, its very purpose.

Reubenhausen and Brim (1966), discussing the importance of privacy in the relationship between professional psychologists and their clients, were struck by the absence in the psychological realm of the guarantees present in the legal realm. The appropriate conduct of sensitivity training, for example, becomes much more obvious when one accepts the "right of freedom of the individual to exercise his own discrimination about what he reveals and communicates about himself and what he chooses to withhold from communication to others" (Collier, 1968, p. 9). Walton and Warwick (1973) correctly point out an inherent violation of this right in a human relations training context, where a participant might well be labeled inadequate or even sick if unwilling or unable to be "open and honest" with the group.

It becomes clear that privacy is both synonymous with freedom and a prerequisite to freedom when power imbalances exist. One straightforward conclusion, then, is that self-disclosure in experiential learning is safest and thus most ethical when limited to the "narrowest extent possible," and when used only for the stated purpose. This limitation is moderated by the initial set of mutual commitments for the learning experience; thus the argument has returned to the issue of freedom of choice in the classroom.

As a closing point, Kelman's notion of a matrix is useful. The above discussion aids in the description of the critical cells of such a matrix. What do participants want out of an experience and what are they likely to get (Pinder, 1977)? What are their concerns, needs, and desires? What mechanisms and protections are appropriate and necessary? How much must be publicly and broadly shared, and how much can be shared implicitly or with just a few people? Only in extremely competitive arrangements does this matrix need to be "filled in" at the onset of the learning experience, yet the issues should be clear in the leader's mind in order to maximize the invitation for participant influence as well as responsiveness to influence attempts. Ultimately, highly ethical behavior is highly pragmatic.

Future Directions

First, we must ask if the use of experiential techniques will increase. Critics have asserted that "despite its promises, experiential learning has a number of difficulties which rob it of its full meaning" (Green & Taber, 1978, p. 889). But, because of growing appreciation for the importance of participation and involvement in learning, the answer to the question is surely in the affirmative. The reason is at once simple and profound. Effectiveness is increased when learning is based on and directly related to the participants' experience, when there is some participation in design, and when there is some choice concerning personal behavior. This belief is well established in modern theories of learning; by 1953, Cantor (quoted in the introduction to Part 1 of this book) had a clear notion of the characteristics and qualities of experiential learning, and in many ways his work reflects that of Dewey (1938), who advocated progressive learning instead of traditional learning. Critics such as Green and Taber (1978) are really concerned with shortcomings of specific aspects of experiential learning, rather than the whole approach. Critics in the 1960s and 1970s attacked the conduct of certain activities and the subjects addressed by the fledgling discipline; these challenges have been considered by House (1979), Bradford (1980), and others.

Second, we must consider the demands of contemporary trends. Currently, there is evidence of a cyclical return to the "basics" of education in the school system and a preference for pragmatism by students looking for marketable skills and job training. Economic uncertainty has resulted in financial conservatism in institutions. But experiential learning can easily address itself to practical and immediate solutions, in fact, more so than can traditional teaching techniques. Further, in a rapidly evolving culture there is a compelling need to change the emphasis from standards established in the past to requirements articulated by current conditions. Experiential involvement of participants in learning is clearly present-oriented; traditional learning is founded on the assumption that what was to be learned was, for the most part, static and known. In *No Limits to Learning—Bridging the Human Gap*, 1979, Botkin, Elmandjra, and Malitza of the Club of Rome assert that our world's survival depends not only on our ability to devise technological solutions to global problems of hunger, pollution, and conflict, but also on our ability to develop methods of learning consistent with today's complex demands.

One paradoxical phenomenon occurring simultaneously with the education backlash and the insistence on pragmatism is the questioning of authority and growing resistance to manipulation. Argyris (1980) notes evidence of this in learning situations, but ubiquitous controversies over nuclear power, civil liberties, and so forth are also partially the result of concerns in these areas. At the same time, there is increased respect for the rights of the individual and a greater faith placed in the value of the individual as a source of information. Thus, just as participant goods such as privacy and freedom are reasserting themselves as ethical guidelines, so subjectivity is coming into focus as a resource in learning. Less tangible phenomena, such as feelings, are becoming legitimate discussion points; authority, represented either by a leader or by the content being addressed, cannot discount the relevance of this material to the learning process.

Four ways of setting objectives in a learning experience can show how emphasis is shifting away from established authority:

1 The leader presents the objectives.
2 The leader presents the objectives and invites comments and suggestions for revision.
3 The leader and the participants collaborate on the establishment of the objectives.
4 The participants establish the objectives and use the leader as a consultant and resource.

Traditionally, option 1 was considered the norm and option 2 was considered progressive. However, option 2 now can be seen as normal and 3 and 4 as more appropriate.

We must look beyond immediate, essentially concrete demands to those more deeply personal and transcendental. While formal learning institutions are challenged by the press to become more pragmatic, people generally have more leisure time, greater personal opportunities, and an expanded sense of the "quality of life." Flanagan (1978, pp. 139–149), in a comprehensive study, provided an outline of the areas comprising quality of life:

Physical and Material Well-Being
- Material well-being and financial security
- Health and personal safety

Relations with other people
- Relations with spouse (girlfriend or boyfriend)
- Having and raising children
- Relations with parents, siblings, or other relatives
- Relations with friends

Social Community and Civic Activities
- Activities related to helping or encouraging other people
- Activities related to local and national governments

Personal Development and Fulfillment
- Intellectual development
- Personal understanding and planning
- Occupational role
- Creativity and personal expression

Recreation
- Socializing
- Passive and observational recreational activities
- Active and participatory recreational activities

A large portion of our society has the leisure to seek self-improvement and growth, and the existentialism and humanism of this century give direction to the search for meaning. Specific issues come and go, but the search for "wholeness" remains. Sensitivity training, encounter groups, and TA have been replaced as popular movements by est and Life Spring. An alienated age "encounters" to increase intimacy; its passive, uncommitted successor responds with enthusiasm to est. New approaches to experiential growth will continue to be created to meet the needs of particular populations and times.

Since the current hunger seems to be for spiritual or transcendent values, it is reasonable to expect growth psychologists and psychiatrists to address subjects of a more metaphysical nature and for the clergy to become more experiential. According to the knowledgeable, synthesis of eastern and western religious notions will probably be the content of these new efforts (Campbell, 1962, 1964, 1968, 1979). In fact, est has been somewhat maligned for precisely this quality. On the other hand, the significance of est and the "Moonies" lies within the experience, not the philosophy. Fears of the Moonies underscore the need for overt ethical guidance of the experiential approach as it touches larger numbers of people in more personal and profound ways.

Finally, there is a need for increased depth and richness in the preparation of leaders. Historically, many experiential leaders have become emotionally committed to a technique or school of thought because of a highly satisfying personal experience (e.g., encounter) or a strong identification with a particular cognitive system and set of values (e.g., Transactional

Analysis). They were enthusiastic amateurs, but the field of experiential learning suffered from the unpredictability and undependability of such practitioners. Subsequent leaders decided to add some experiential activities to their otherwise traditional pedagogical repertoires, sought "cook book" solutions and benefited from such as those offered by University Associates. Similarly, text books in a variety of areas have been "experientialized." As House (1979) observed, because of the superficiality of these latter efforts, results have been marginal and vulnerable to criticism. Fortunately, using the experiential approach for "illustration" in education has yielded nothing worse than disappointment, disillusionment, and withdrawal of those who have failed. In contrast, the excessive zeal of the new convert in the 1960s did greater overt damage. Our current problems are not trivial, but there are indications of some maturity in the discipline that was lacking just five years ago. It is hoped that the descriptions of various models of human functioning, change processes, and experiential methods provide a comprehensive enumeration of areas worthy of greater exploration and study. Thus, leaders can decide for themselves in which area to invest for greater depth and competence. Development will be long-term and aggregative for most people in the era we have entered.

A recent series of studies (Nelson & Foster, 1980) substantiates the anticipated increase in the use of experiential techniques. The authors asked more than 900 Canadian university teachers to identify their teaching needs. Becoming more skilled at discussion techniques and group work were ranked one and two respectively, and it was recommended that workshops be developed to provide the necessary training. Leaders are calling for more "in-depth" training and development, and seem to have a more realistic sense of how much time and energy the development of the needed skills really requires. Currently there is a proliferation of aids and opportunities growing in response to this maturation. The literature takes the form of textbooks, journals such as *Exchange,* and many popular psychology paperbacks. Self-help sharing groups, such as the American Society for Training and Development, the Organizational Behavior Teaching Society, and the Organizational Development Network, expand leaders' understanding and competence. Most professional societies sponsor "Preconference Workshops," which make available uniquely skilled leaders to a wide variety of people. Institutes such as National Training Laboratories and the Western Behavioral Institute provide more in-depth (one week to one month) retreat experiences. University Associates offers traveling workshops for different professional skill areas. Many university counseling and organization development programs pursue skill-oriented learning. Other traveling workshops of two days to two weeks are likely to evolve as desired skills become more clearly perceived, articulated, and developed (Walter, 1975; House, 1979).

Argyris' concerns about leader actions in the classical case method show that virtuosity with a technique and subsequent praise from participants are not sufficient tests of leader development. The extra dimension that he advocates is that the leader's "theory in use" allow and facilitate "double loop" learning or development beyond one's assumptions, habits, and frame of reference (Argyris, 1976, 1980). Perhaps the most important guidance toward this goal is provided by the ethical principles discussed earlier in this chapter. The absense of manipulative and defense-evoking leader actions is necessary if participants are to look at themselves as they must to accomplish double loop learning. In short, leaders need to cultivate being potent without being poisonous.

In this expanding, evolving field, there is a need for more systematic and interdisciplinary research. It seems certain that no single school of thought should dominate or ignore the contributions of others. It is hoped that this book aids in the building of a broad interdisciplinary foundation on which further progress can be made. Guidelines for and guidance of the development of this field are needed (Foster, 1980; McKeachie, 1974). The consequences of various leader interventions and different learning designs need to be examined more closely and more comprehensively than they have in the past. Much exploration, experimentation, and progress has been accomplished in the years since Dewey's revolution. It appears that the future will be characterized by systematization, consolidation, and enrichment.

References

Abrams, P., & McCulloch, A. *Communes, sociology, and society.* Cambridge: Cambridge University Press, 1976.

Adler, A. *The practice and theory of individual psychology.* New York: Harcourt Brace and World, 1927.

Adler, A. Individual psychology. In C. Murchinson (Ed.), *Psychologies of 1930.* Worcester, Mass.: Clark University Press, 1930.

Adler, A. *What life should mean to you.* Boston: Little, Brown, 1931.

Adler, A. *Problems of neurosis.* New York: Harper Torchbooks, 1964.

Allport, G.W. *Becoming: Basic considerations for a psychology of personality.* New Haven, Conn.: Yale University Press, 1955.

Allport, G.W. *Pattern and growth in personality.* New York: Holt, Rinehart & Winston, 1961.

Amundson, N.E. The problem of therapeutic models for school counseling. *Counselor Education and Supervision,* 1978, **18**(2), 158–160.

Anderson, J. Giving and receiving feedback. In G.W. Dalton, P.R. Lawrence, & L.E. Greiner (Eds.), *Organizational change and development.* Homewood, Ill.: Irwin, 1970, 339–346.

Anderson, K.E. *Persuasion: Theory and practice.* Boston: Allyn & Bacon, 1971.

Anderson, K.E., & Clevenger, T., Jr. A summary of experimental research in ethos. *Speech Monographs,* 1963, **30,** 66–70.

Anderson, L. Belief defense produced by derogation of message source. *Journal of Experimental Social Psychology,* 1967, **3,** 349–360.

Angus, E.I. Evaluating experiential education. In J. Duley (Ed.), *Implementing field experience education: New directions for higher education.* San Francisco: Jossey-Bass, 1974, 77–84.

Angyal, A. A theoretical model of personality studies. *Journal of Personality,* 1951, **20,** 131–142.

Angyal, A. *Neurosis and treatment: A holistic theory.* New York: Wiley, 1965.

Annett, J. *Feedback and human behavior.* Middlesex: Penguin, 1969.

Aponte, H., & Hoffman, L. The open door: A structural approach to a family with an anorectic child. *Family Process,* 1973, **12**(1).

Ardrey, R. *The territorial imperative.* New York: Atheneum, 1966.

Ardrey, R. *The social contract.* New York: Atheneum, 1970.

Argyris, C. *Interpersonal competence and organizational effectiveness.* Homewood, Ill.: Dorsey, 1962.

Argyris, C. The integration of the individual and the organization. In G.B. Stather (Ed.), *Social science approaches to business behavior.* Homewood, Ill.: Dorsey & Irwin, 1962.

Argyris, C. Conditions for competence acquisition and therapy. *Journal of Applied Behavioral Science,* 1968, **4,** 147–177.

Argyris, C. *Intervention theory and method: A behavioral science view.* Reading, Mass.: Addison-Wesley, 1970.

Argyris, C. Dangers in applying results from experimental social psychology. *American Psychologist,* 1975, **30,** 469–485.

Argyris, C. Theories of action that inhibit individual learning. *American Psychologist,* 1976, 31(9), 638–654.

Argyris, C. Double-loop learning in organizations. *Harvard Business Review,* 1977, **55**(5), 115–125.

Argyris, C. Some limitations of the case method: Experiences in a management development program. *Academy of Management Review,* 1980, 5(2), 291–298.

Argyris, C., & Schon, D. *Theory in practice.* San Francisco: Jossey-Bass, 1974.

Argyris, C., & Schon, D. *Organizational learning.* Reading, Mass.: Addison-Wesley, 1978.

Armsey, J.W., & Dahl, N.C. *An inquiry into the use of instructional technology.* New York: The Ford Foundation, 1973.

Aronson, E., Carlsmith, J.M., & Darley, J.M. The effects of expectancy on volunteering for an unpleasant experience. *Journal of Abnormal and Social Psychology,* 1963, **66,** 220–224.

Ascher, L., & Cautela, J.R. Covert negative reinforcement: An experimental test. *Journal of Behavior Therapy and Experimental Psychiatry,* 1972, 3, 1–5.

Avedon, E.M., & Sutton-Smith, B. *The study of games.* New York: Wiley, 1971.

Back, K.W. *Beyond words: The story of sensitivity training and the encounter movement.* New York: Russell Sage Foundation, 1972.

Bailey, P. *A.M.A. Archives of General Psychiatry,* 1960, **120,** 361.

Bain, J.A. *Thought control in everyday life.* New York: Funk & Wagnalls, 1928.

Bakan, D. *The duality of human existence.* Chicago: Rand McNally, 1966.

Bakan, D. *Disease, pain, and sacrifice.* Chicago: University of Chicago Press, 1968.

Bakan, D. *Slaughter of the innocents.* San Francisco: Jossey-Bass, 1971.

Baker, F. *Organizational systems: General systems approach to complex organizations.* Homewood, Ill.: Irwin, 1973.

Bales, R.F. *Personality and interpersonal behavior.* New York: Holt, Rinehart & Winston, 1970.

Bandura, A. Social-learning theory of identificatory processes. In D.A. Goslin (Ed.), *Handbook of socialization theory and research.* Chicago: Rand McNally, 1968.

Bandura, A. *Principles of behavior modification.* New York: Holt, Rinehart & Winston, 1969.

Bandura, A. Psychotherapy based upon modeling principles. In A.E. Bergin & S.L. Garfield (Eds.), *Handbook of psychotherapy and behavior change.* New York: Wiley, 1971, 653–708.

Bandura, A. *Social learning theory.* Englewood Cliffs, N.J.: Prentice-Hall, 1977.

Bandura, A., Blanchard, E.B., & Ritter, B. Relative efficacy of desensitization and modeling approaches for inducing behavioral, affective and attitudinal changes. *Journal of Personality and Social Psychology,* 1969, **13,** 173–199.

Bandura, A., & Huston, A.C. Identification as a process of incidental learning. *Journal of Abnormal and Social Psychology,* 1961, **63**, 311–318.

Bandura, A., & Kupers, C.J. Transmission of patterns of self-reinforcement through modeling. *Journal of Abnormal and Social Psychology,* 1964, **69**, 1–9.

Bandura, A., Ross, D., & Ross, S.A. Imitation of film-mediated aggressive models. *Journal of Abnormal and Social Psychology,* 1963a, **66**, 3–11.

Bandura, A., Ross, D., & Ross, S.A. A comparative test of the status envy, social power, and secondary reinforcement theories of identificatory learning. *Journal of Abnormal and Social Psychology,* 1963b, **67**, 527–534.

Bandura, A., & Walters, R.H. *Social learning and personality development.* New York: Holt, Rinehart & Winston, 1963.

Barash, D.P. *Sociobiology and behavior.* New York: American Elsevier, 1977.

Barlow, W. *The Alexander technique.* New York: Knopf, 1973.

Bartel, N.R. *Locus of control in middle and lower class children.* Unpublished doctoral dissertation, Indiana University, 1968.

Bateson, G., Jackson, D.D., Haley, J., & Weakland, J. Toward a theory of schizophrenia. *Behavioral Science,* 1956, **1**, 251–264.

Bayes, K. *The therapeutic effect of environment on emotionally disturbed and mentally subnormal children.* London: Unwin Brothers, 1967.

Beck, A.T. Cognitive therapy: Nature and relation to behavior therapy. *Behavior Therapy,* 1970, **1**, 184–200.

Beck, C.E. Ethical practice: Foundations and emerging issues. *Personnel & Guidance Journal,* 1971, **50**(4), 320–325.

Beegle, C.W., & Brandt, R.M. (Eds.). *Observational methods in the classroom.* Washington, D.C.: Association for Supervision and Curriculum Development, 1973.

Bem, D.J. *Beliefs, attitudes and human affairs.* Monterey, Calif.: Brooks/Cole, 1970.

Bendix, R. *Work and authority in industry.* New York: Wiley, 1956.

Benne, K.D. Some ethical problems in group and organizational consulting. *Journal of Social Issues,* 1959, **15**(2), 60–67.

Benne, K.D., Bradford, L.P., Gibb, J.R., & Lippitt, R.O. *The laboratory method of changing and learning.* Palo Alto: Science & Behavior Books, 1975.

Bennis, W.G., Benne, K.D., Chin, R., & Corey, K.E. *The planning of change.* New York: Holt, Rinehart & Winston, 1976.

Bennis, W.G., & Shepard, H.A. A theory of group development. *Human Relations,* 1956, **9**(4), 425–437.

Bergin, A.E., & Garfield, S.L. (Eds.). *Handbook of psychotherapy and behavior change: An empirical analysis.* New York: Wiley, 1971.

Berkowitz, L. Words and symbols as stimuli to aggressive responses. In J.F. Knutson (Ed.), *The control of aggression: Implications from basic research.* Chicago: Aldine, 1973.

Bernard, H.W. *Personality/applying theory.* Boston: Holbrook Press, 1974.

Berne, E. *What do you say after you say hello?* Beverly Hills, Calif.: Grove, 1972.

Berscheid, E., & Walster, E. *Interpersonal attraction.* Reading, Mass.: Addison-Wesley, 1970.

Berte, N.R. Individualizing education by learning contracts. *New directions for higher education #10.* San Francisco: Jossey-Bass, 1975.

Berzon, B., & Solomon, L.N. The self directed therapeutic group: Three studies. *Journal of Counseling Psychology,* 1966, **13**, 491–497.

Bieri, J. Complexity-simplicity as a personality variable in cognitive and preferential behavior. In D. W. Fiske & S. R. Maddi, *Functions of varied experience.* Homewood, Ill.: Dorsey, 1961.

Bieri, J., Atkins, A.L., Briar, S., Leaman, R.L., Miller, H., & Tripodi, T. *Clinical and social judgement: The discrimination of behavioral information.* New York: Wiley, 1966.

Binswanger, L. *Being-in-the-world: Selected papers of Ludwig Binswanger.* New York: Basic Books, 1963.

Bion, W.R. *Experiences in groups.* London: Tavistock, 1961.

Blau, P.M. *Exchange and power in social life.* New York: Wiley, 1967.

Bligh, D., Ebrahim, G.J., Jaques, D., & Piper, D.W. *Teaching students.* Devon: Exeter University Teaching Services, 1975.

Bloom, B.S. *Stability and change in human characteristics.* New York: Wiley, 1964.

Bloom, B.S. (Ed.). *Taxonomy of educational objectives.* New York: McKay, 1956.

Bloom, B.S., Hastings, J.T., & Madaus, G.F. *Handbook on formative and summative evaluation of student learning.* New York: McGraw-Hill, 1971.

Blumer, H. *Symbolic interactionism: Perspective & method.* Englewood Cliffs, N.J.: Prentice-Hall, 1969.

Bondurant, J.V. Satyagraha as applied social-political action. In G. Zaltman, P. Kotler, & I. Kaufman (Eds.), *Creating social change.* New York: Holt, Rinehart & Winston, 1972, 303–313.

Boocock, S.S., & Schild, E.O. (Eds.). *Simulation games in learning.* Beverly Hills, Calif.: Sage Publications, 1968.

Boss, M. *Psychoanalysis and daseinanalysis.* New York: Basic Books, 1963.

Botkin, J.W., Elmandjra, M., & Malitza, M. *No limits to learning.* Oxford: Pergamon Press, 1979.

Bowers, D.G. *Systems of organization management of the human resource.* Ann Arbor: University of Michigan Press, 1976.

Bowers, D.G., & Seashore, S.E. Predicting organizational effectiveness with a four-factor theory of leadership. *Administrative Science Quarterly,* 1966, **11**(2), 238–263.

Bowlby, J. *Attachment and loss,* (Vol. II). *Separation anxiety and anger.* London: Hogarth Press, 1973.

Bradford, D. President's Address. *1980 Annual Organizational Behavior Teaching Conference.* University of Southern California.

Bradford, L.P., Gibb, J.R., & Benne, K.D. (Eds.). *T-group theory and laboratory method: Innovation in re-education.* New York: Wiley, 1964.

Braken, D.K., & Malmquist, E. (Eds.). *Improving reading around the world.* Newark, Del.: International Reading Association, 1971.

Brehm, J.W. *A theory of psychological reactance.* New York: Academic, 1966.

Briggs, L.J., Campeau, P.L., Gagne, R.M., & May, M.A. *Instructional media: A procedure for the design of multi-media instruction: A critical review of research, and suggestions for future research.* Pittsburgh: American Institute for Research, 1967.

Brown, D.R. Learning by objectives: A contracting approach to teaching organizational behavior. *Exchange: The Organizational Behavior Teaching Journal,* 1978, 3(1), 34–37.

Brown, J.W., Lewis, R.B., & Harcleroad, F.F. *A V instruction technology media and methods.* New York: McGraw-Hill, 1973.

Brown, M. The new body psychotherapies. *Psychotherapy: Theory, research and practices,* 1973, **10**,(2), 98–116.

Brown, R. *Social psychology.* New York: Free Press, 1965.

Bruner, J.S. On perceptual readiness. *Psychological Review,* 1957, **64**, 123–152.

Bucher, B., & King, L.W. Generalization of punishment effects in the deviant behavior of a psychotic child. *Behavior Therapy,* 1971, **12**, 68–77.

Buck, R. *Human motivation and emotion.* New York: Wiley, 1976.

Buckley, W. (Ed.). *Modern systems research for the behavioral scientist.* Chicago: Aldine, 1968.

Burton, A. (Ed.). *What makes behavior change possible?* New York: Brunner/Mazel, 1976.

Butler, R.P., & Jaffee, C.L. Effects of incentive, feedback, and manner of presenting the feedback on leader behavior. *Journal of Applied Psychology,* 1974, **59**, 332–336.

Campbell, D.T. On the conflicts between biological and social evolution and between psychology and moral tradition. *American Psychologist,* 1975, **30**, 1103–1126.

Campbell, J. *The masks of God: Oriental mythology.* New York: Penguin, 1962.

Campbell, J. *The masks of God: Occidental mythology.* New York: Penguin, 1964.

Campbell, J. *The masks of God: Creative mythology.* New York: Penguin, 1968.

Campbell, J. *Symbol and Psyche.* Speech for The Vancouver Institute, University of British Columbia, 1979.

Campbell, J.P., & Dunnette, M.D. Effectiveness of t-group experiences in managerial training and development. *Psychological Bulletin,* 1968, **70**(2), 73–104.

Campbell, S. Graduate programs in applied behavioral science: A directory. In J.W. Pfeiffer & J.E. Jones (Eds.), *The 1978 annual handbook for group facilitators.* La Jolla, Calif.: University Associates, 1978.

Cantor, N. *The dynamics of learning.* Buffalo, N.Y.: Foster & Stewart, 1946.

Cantor, N. *The teaching-learning process.* New York: Holt, Rinehart & Winston, 1953.

Carkhuff, R.R. *Helping and human relations: A primer for lay and professional helpers.* New York: Holt, Rinehart & Winston, 1969.

Carkhuff, R.R., & Berenson, B.G. *Beyond counseling and therapy.* New York: Holt, Rinehart & Winston, 1967.

Carson, W.W. Development of a student under the case method. In M.P. McNair & A.C. Hersum (Eds.), *The case method at the Harvard Business School.* New York: McGraw-Hill, 1954, 82–86.

Cartwright, D. The nature of group cohesiveness. In D. Cartwright & A. Zander (Eds.). *Group dynamics.* New York: Harper & Row, 1968, 91–109.

Cartwright, D., & Zander, A. (Eds.). *Group dynamics.* New York: Harper & Row, 1968.

Cautela, J.R. Covert sensitization. *Psychological Reports,* 1967, **20**, 459–468.

Cautela, J.R. *Covert modeling.* Paper presented to the Association for the Advancement of Behavior Therapy, Washington, D.C., 1971.

Chesler, M., & Fox, R. *Role-playing methods in the classroom.* Chicago: Science Research Associates, 1966.

Coch, L., & French, J.R.P., Jr. Overcoming resistance to change. *Human Relations,* 1948, **1**, 512–532.

Coe, W.E., & Buckner, L.G. Expectation, hypnosis and suggestion methods. In F.H. Kanfer & A.P. Goldstein (Eds.), *Helping people change.* New York: Pergamon, 1975, 393–431.

Cohen, P. *The gospel according to the Harvard Business School.* New York: Penguin, 1973.

Cohn, R.C. From couch to circle to community: Beginnings of the theme-centered interactional method. In H.M. Ruuitenbeek (Ed.), *Group therapy today.* New York: Atherton, 1969.

Cohn, R.C. Style and spirit of the theme-centered interactional method. In C.J. Sager & H.S. Kaplan (Eds.), *Progress in group and family therapy.* New York: Brunner/Mazel, 1972.

Collier, R.M. A biologically derived basic value as an initial context for behavioral science. *Journal of Humanistic Psychology,* 1968, **1**, 1–15.

Cook, S.D. Coercion and social change. In R.J. Pennock & J.R. Chapman (Eds.), *Coercion.* Chicago: Aldine, 1972, 107–143.

Cook, W.D. *Adult literacy education in the United States.* Newark, Del.: International Reading Association, 1977.

Cooper, C.L., & Alderfer, C. (Eds.). *Advances in experiential social processes, Vol. 1.* New York: Wiley, 1978.

Cooper, C.L., & Mangham, I.L. (Eds.). *T-groups: A survey of research.* London: Wiley-Interscience, 1971.

Corey, G., & Corey, M.S. *Groups: Process & practice.* Monterey, Calif.: Brooks/Cole, 1977.

Coser, L.A. *Greedy institutions.* New York: Free Press, 1974.

Corsini, R.J., Shaw, M.E., & Blake, R.R. *Roleplaying in business and industry.* New York: Free Press, 1961.

Craik, F.I.M., & Lockhart, R.S. Levels of processing: A framework for memory research. *Journal of Verbal Learning and Verbal Behavior,* 1972, **12,** 599–607.

Craik, F.I.M., & Tulving, E. Depth of processing and the retention of words in episodic memory. *Journal of Experimental Psychology: General,* 1975, **104,** 268–294.

Cronbach, L.J., & Snow, R.E. *Aptitudes and instructional methods.* New York: Irvington Publishers, 1977.

CSC/Pacific, Inc. *The affective domain.* Washington, D.C.: Gryphon House, 1972a.

CSC/Pacific, Inc. *The cognitive domain.* Washington, D.C.: Gryphon House, 1972b.

CSC/Pacific, Inc. *The psychomotor domain.* Washington, D.C.: Gryphon House, 1972c.

Culbert, S.A. The interpersonal process of self-disclosure: It takes two to see one. In R.T. Golembiewski & A. Blumberg. *Sensitivity training and the laboratory approach.* Itasca, Ill.: Peacock, 1970, 73–79.

Cummings, L.L., & Schwab, D.P. *Performance in organizations: Determinants and appraisal.* Glenview, Ill.: Scott, Foresman, 1973.

Cummings, L.L., & Scott, W.E. *Organizational behavior and human performance.* Homewood, Ill.: Irwin, 1969.

Dalton, G.W., Lawrence, P.R., & Greiner, L.E. (Eds.). *Organizational change and development.* Homewood, Ill.: Irwin, 1970.

Danet, B.N. Self-confrontation in psychotherapy reviewed. *American Journal of Psychotherapy,* 1968, **22,** 245–247.

Davis, J.R. *Teaching strategies for the college classroom.* Boulder, Colo.: Westview Press, 1976.

Davis, L.N., & McCallon, E. *Planning, conducting and evaluating workshops.* Austin: Learning Concepts, 1974.

Davison, G.C., Tsujimoto, R.N., & Glaros, A.G. Attribution and the maintenance of behavior change in falling asleep. *Journal of Abnormal Psychology,* 1973, **82,** 124–133.

Davison, G.C., & Valins, S. Maintenance of self-attributed and drug-attributed behavior change. *Journal of Personality and Social Psychology,* 1969, **11,** 25–33.

Delbecq, A.L., Van de Ven, A.H., & Gustafson, D.H. *Group techniques for program planning.* Glenview, Ill.: Scott, Foresman, 1975.

Dewey, J. *Experience and education.* New York: Collier Books, 1938.

Dewing, A.S. An introduction to the use of cases. In M.P. McNair & A.C. Hersum (Eds.), *The case method at Harvard Business School.* New York: McGraw-Hill, 1954, 1–5.

Diedrich, R.C., & Dye, H.A. (Eds.). *Group procedures: Purposes, processes, and outcomes— Selected readings for the counselor.* Boston: Houghton Mifflin, 1972.

Dinoff, M., & Rickard, H.C. Learning that privileges entail responsibilities. In J.D. Krumboltz & C.E. Thoresen (Eds.), *Behavioral counseling: Cases and techniques.* New York: Holt, Rinehart & Winston, 1969, 124–129.

Ditchburn, R.W. Eye-movement in relation to retinal action. *Optica Acta,* 1955, 1, 171–176.

Ditchburn, R.W., & Fender, D.H. The stabilized retinal image. *Optica Acta,* 1955, 12, 128–133.

Donelson, E. *Personality: A scientific approach.* New York: Appleton-Century-Crofts, 1973.

Dooley, A.R., & Wickham, S. Casing the case method. *Academy of Management Review,* 1977, 2(2), 277–289.

Drever, J.A. *Dictionary of psychology.* Middlesex: Penguin, 1964.

Duke, R.D. *Gaming: The future's language.* Beverly Hills, Calif: Sage Publications, 1974.

Duley, J. (Ed.). Implementing field experience education. *New directions for higher education.* San Francisco: Jossey-Bass, 1974.

Duncan, C.J. A survey of audio-visual equipment and methods. In D. Unwin (Ed.), *Media and methods.* London: McGraw-Hill, 1969.

Egan, G. *Encounter: Group processes for interpersonal growth.* Belmont, Calif.: Brooks/-Cole, 1970.

Egan, G. *Encounter groups: Basic readings.* Belmont, Calif.: Brooks/Cole, 1971.

Egan, G. *The skilled helper: A model for systematic helping and interpersonal relating.* Monterey, Calif.: Brooks/Cole, 1975.

Eliade, M. *Yoga: Immortality and freedom.* Princeton, N.J.: Princeton University Press, 1969.

Ellis, A. *The essence of rational psychotherapy: A comprehensive approach to treatment.* New York: Institute for Rational Living, 1970.

Ellis, A., & Harper, R. *A guide to rational living.* Hollywood, Calif.: Wilshire, 1961.

Elms, A.C. (Ed.). *Role playing, reward, and attitude change.* New York: Van Nostrand-Reinhold, 1969.

Epstein, R. Aggression toward outgroups as a function of authoritarianism and imitation of aggressive models. *Journal of Personality and Social Psychology,* 1966, 3, 574–579.

Erickson, C.W.H., & Curl, D.H. *Fundamentals of teaching with audiovisual technology.* New York: Macmillan, 1972.

Erikson, E. *Childhood and society.* New York: Norton, 1950.

Erikson, M.H. The confusion technique in hypnosis. *American Journal of Clinical Hypnosis,* 1964, 6, 183–207.

Ethical standards of psychologists. *American Psychologist,* 1963, 18, 56–60.

Eysenck, H.J., & Beech H.R. Counter conditioning and related methods. In A. Bergin & S.L. Garfield (Eds.), *Handbook of psychotherapy and behavior change.* New York: Wiley, 1971, 543–611.

Farden, C. (Ed.). *Society today.* Del Mar, Calif.: CRM, 1973.

Feldenkrais, M. *Awareness through movement.* New York: Harper & Row, 1972.

Festinger, L. *A theory of cognitive dissonance.* Stanford, Calif.: Stanford University Press, 1957.

Festinger, L. (Ed.). *Conflict, decision and dissonance.* Stanford, Calif: Stanford University Press, 1964.

Festinger, L., Schachter, S., & Back, K. *Social pressures in informal groups: A study of a housing community.* New York: Harper, 1950.

Festinger, L., Schachter, S., & Back, K. Operation of group standards. In D. Cartwright & A. Zander (Eds.), *Group dynamics.* New York: Harper & Row, 1968, 152–164.

Fink, A. & Kosecoff, J. *An evaluation primer.* Washington, D.C.: Capital Publications, 1978.

Fiske, D.W., & Maddi, S.R. *Functions of varied experience.* Homewood, Ill.: Dorsey, 1961.

Flanagan, J. The critical incident technique. *Psychological Bulletin,* 1954, **51**, 327–358.

Flanagan, J.C. A research approach to improving our quality of life. *American Psychologist,* 1978, **33**(2), 138–147.

Flanders, J.P. A review of research on imitative behavior. *Psychological Bulletin,* 1968, **69**, 316–337.

Flanders, N.A. *Analysing teaching behavior.* Reading, Mass.: Addison-Wesley, 1970.

Foster, S.F. *The Club of Rome report on education: Components for a new learning theory.* Unpublished manuscript, University of British Columbia, 1980.

Frankena, W.K. *Ethics.* Englewood Cliffs, N.J.: Prentice-Hall, 1963.

Frankl, V.E. *The doctor and the soul.* New York: Knopf, 1960.

Frankl, V.E. Logotherapy and existential analysis—A review. *American Journal of Psychotherapy,* 1966, **20**, 252–260.

Frankl, V.E. Existential analysis and dimensional ontology. In V.E. Frankl, *Psychotherapy and existentialism: Selected papers on logotherapy.* New York: Washington Square Press, 1967.

Frankl, V.E. *The will to meaning: Foundations and applications of logotherapy.* New York: World Publishing, 1969.

Freedman, J.L., & Steinbruner, J.D. Perceived choice and resistance to persuasion. *Journal of Abnormal and Social Psychology,* 1964, **68**, 678–681.

Freud, S. *Collected papers.* London: Institute for Psychoanalysis and Hogarth Press, 1925.

Freud, S. *The ego and the id.* London: Institute for Psychoanalysis and Hogarth Press, 1927.

Freud, S. *Civilization and its discontents.* New York: Norton, 1930.

Freud, S. *New introductory lectures to psychoanalysis,* W.J.H. Sprott, trans. New York: Norton, 1933.

Freud, S. *The interpretation of dreams,* Standard Edition, Vols. 4 and 5. London: Hogarth Press, 1962.

Freud S. In G. Gordon. *Persuasion. The theory and practice of manipulative communication.* New York: Hastings House, 1971, 365.

Friedlander, F. The primacy of trust as a facilitator of further group accomplishment. In C.L. Cooper & I.L. Mangham (Eds.), *T-groups: A survey of research.* London: Wiley-Interscience, 1971, 193–204.

Fromm, E. *Escape from freedom.* New York: Rinehart, 1941.

Fromm, E. *Man for himself.* New York: Holt, Rinehart & Winston, 1947.

Fromm, E. *The sane society.* New York: Holt, Rinehart & Winston, 1955.

Fromm, E. *The art of loving.* New York: Harper, 1956.

Gadon, H. Teaching cases experientially. *Exchange: The Organizational Behavior Teaching Journal,* 1977, **2**(1), 20–24.

Gage, N.L. (Ed.). *The handbook of research on teaching.* Chicago: Rand McNally, 1963.

Gage, N.L. (Ed.). *The psychology of teaching methods.* Chicago: National Society for the Study of Education, 1976.

Gage, N.L., & Berliner, D.C. *Educational psychology.* Chicago: Rand McNally, 1975.

Gagne, R.M. The acquisition of knowledge. *Psychological Review,* 1962, **69**, 355–365.

Gagne, R.M. Context, isolation and interference effects on the retention of fact. *Journal of Educational Psychology,* 1968, **60**, 408–414.

Gagne, R.M. *The conditions of learning, 2nd ed.* New York: Holt, Rinehart & Winston, 1970.

Gagne, R.M. *Essentials of learning for instruction.* Hinsdale, Ill.: Dryden Press, 1975.

Gagne, R.M., & Briggs, L.J. *Principles of instructional design.* New York: Holt, Rinehart & Winston, 1974.

Gall, M.D., & Gall, J.P. The discussion method. In N.L. Gage (Ed.), *The psychology of teaching methods.* Chicago: University of Chicago Press, 1976, 166–216.

Gambrill, E.D. *Behavior modification handbook of assessment, intervention, and evaluation.* San Francisco: Jossey-Bass, 1977.

Garfield, S.L., & Bergin, A.E. (Eds.). *Handbook of psychotherapy and behavior change: An empirical analysis, 2nd ed.* New York: Wiley, 1978.

Garfinkel, H. *Studies in ethno-methodoloy.* Englewood Cliffs, N.J.: Prentice-Hall, 1967.

Gazda, G.M., Asbury, F.R., Balzer, F.J., Childers, W.C., & Walters, R.P. *Human relations development: A manual for educators.* Boston: Allyn & Bacon, 1977.

Geertsman, R.H., & Reivich, R.S. Repetitive self-observation by videotape playback. *Journal of Nervous and Mental Diseases,* 1965, **141,** 29–41.

Gelfand, D.M. The influence of self-esteem on rate of verbal conditioning and social matching behavior. *Journal of Abnormal and Social Psychology,* 1962, **65,** 259–265.

Gerard, H.B. Basic features of commitment. In R.P. Abelson, E. Aronson, W.J. McGuire, T.M. Newcomb, M.J. Rosenberg, & P.H. Tannenbaum (Eds.), *Theories of cognitive consistency: A sourcebook.* Chicago: Rand McNally, 1968, 456–463.

Gerard, H.B., & Mathewson, G.C. The effects of severity of initiation on liking for a group: A replication. *Journal of Experimental Social Psychology,* 1966, **2,** 278–287.

Gerlach, V.S., & Ely, D.P. *Teaching and media: A systematic approach.* Englewood Cliffs, N.J.: Prentice-Hall, 1971.

Getzels, J.W., & Jackson, P.W. The teacher's personality and characteristics. In N.L. Gage (Ed.), *The handbook of research on teaching.* Chicago: Rand McNally, 1963, 506 –582.

Gibb, J.R. Defensive communications. *The Journal of Communication,* 1961, **11,** 141–148.

Gibb, J.R. TORI theory and practice. In J.W. Pfeiffer & J.E. Jones (Eds.), *The 1972 annual handbook for group facilitators.* Iowa City: University Associates, 1972, 157–162.

Gibbs, G.I. (Ed.). *Handbook of games and simulation exercises.* Beverly Hills, Calif.: Sage Publications, 1974.

Gilmore, A.R. *The bio-physical environment and the incidence of aggression.* Ottawa: The Ministry of State for Urban Affairs, 1974.

Ginsberg, H., & Koslowski, B. Cognitive development. *Annual Review of Psychology,* 1976, **27,** 29–61.

Goffman, E., *Asylums.* Garden City, N.Y.: Anchor Books, 1961.

Goldfried, M.R. Systematic desensitization as training in self-control. *Journal of Consulting and Clinical Psychology,* 1971, **37,** 228–234.

Goldfried, M.R. Reduction of generalized anxiety through a variant of systematic desensitization. In M.R. Goldfried & M. Merbaum (Eds.), *Behavior change through self-control.* New York: Holt, Rinehart & Winston, 1973, 297–304.

Goldfried, M.R., DeCenteceo, E.T., & Weinberg, L. Systematic rational restructuring as a self-control technique. *Behavior Therapy,* 1974, **5,** 247–254.

Goldfried, M.R., & Goldfried, A.P. Cognitive change methods. In F.H. Kanfer & A.P. Goldstein (Eds.), *Helping people change.* New York: Pergamon, 1975, 89–116.

Goldfried, M.R., & Merbaum, M. (Eds.). *Behavior change through self-control.* New York: Holt, Rinehart & Winston, 1973.

Goldstein, A.P. *Psychotherapy and the psychology of behavior change.* New York: Wiley, 1966.

Golembiewski, R.T. *The small group: An analysis of research concepts and operations.* Chicago: University of Chicago Press, 1962.

Golembiewski, R.T., & Blumberg, A. *Sensitivity training and the laboratory approach.* Itasca, Ill.: Peacock, 1970.

Goodall, J. Chimpanzees of the Gombe Stream Reserve. In I. DeVore (Ed.), *Primate behavior: Field studies of monkey and apes.* New York: Holt, Rinehart & Winston, 1965, 425–481.

Gordon, A.K. *Games for growth.* Palo Alto, Calif.: Science Research Associates, 1970.

Gordon, G.N. *Persuasion: The theory and practice of manipulative communication.* New York: Hastings House, 1971.

Gordon, T. *Group-centered leadership.* Boston: Houghton Mifflin, 1955.

Goulding, R. New directions in transactional analysis. In C. Sayer & H. Kaplan (Eds.), *Progress in group and family therapy.* New York: Brunner/Mazel, 1972.

Gouldner, A.W. Cosmopolitans and locals. *Administration Science Quarterly,* 1957, **2,** 281–306.

Gragg, C.I. Because wisdomcan't be told. In M.P. McNair & A.C. Hersum (Eds.), *The case method at the Harvard Business School.* New York: McGraw-Hill, 1954.

Green, S.G. & Taber, T.D. Structuring experiential learning through experimentation. *Academy of Management Review,* 1978, 3(4), 889–895.

Greenfield, L.B. Comments on evaluation in engineering education. *Engineering Education,* 1978, **68**(5), 401–404.

Gregory, T.B. *Encounters with teaching.* Englewood Cliffs, N.J.: Prentice-Hall, 1972.

Griffin, K. The contribution of studies of source credibility to a theory of interpersonal trust in the communication process. *Psychological Bulletin,* 1967, **68,** 104–120.

Grusec, J.E., & Mischel, W. The model's characteristics as determinants of social learning. *Journal of Personality and Social Psychology,* 1966, **4,** 211–215.

Guthrie, E.R. *The psychology of learning.* New York: Harper, 1935.

Hagen, E.E. *On the theory of social change.* Homewood, Ill.: Dorsey, 1962.

Haley, J. (Ed.). *Advanced techniques of hypnosis and therapy: Selected papers of Milton H. Erickson, M.D.* New York: Grune & Stratton, 1967.

Hammer, M. The directed daydream technique. *Psychotherapy, Theory, Research and Practice,* 1967, 4(4), 173–181.

Hanson, P.G. Giving feedback: An interpersonal skill. In J.W. Pfeiffer and J.E. Jones (Eds.), *The 1975 annual handbook for group facilitators.* Iowa City: University Associates, 1975, 147–154.

Hare, A.P. *Handbook of small group research.* New York: Free Press, 1962.

Harlow, H.F. Love in infant monkeys. *Frontiers of psychological research: Readings from Scientific American,* San Francisco: W.H. Freeman, 1966.

Harvey, J.B. Critique of thought reform: East vs. west. *Training in Business and Industry,* 1971, 8(11), 33–35.

Heider, F. *The psychology of interpersonal relations.* New York: Wiley, 1958.

Hendricks, G., & Wills, R. *The centering book.* Englewood Cliffs, N.J.: Prentice-Hall, 1975.

Hicks, D.J. Imitation and retention of film-mediated aggressive peer and adult models. *Journal of Personality and Social Psychology,* 1965, **2,** 97–100.

Hitler, A. *Mein Kampf.* New York: Reynal & Hitchcock, 1941.

Hochbaum, G.M. The relation between group members' self confidence and their reactions to group pressures to uniformity. *American Social Review,* 1954, **79,** 678–687.

Hoffer, E. *The ordeal of change.* New York: Harper & Row, 1964.

Hoffman, L.R. Group problem solving. In Berkowitz, L. (Ed.), *Advances in experimental social psychology, Vol. 2.* New York: Academic, 1965, 99–132.

Hogan, P., & Alger, I. The impact of videotape recording on insight in group psychotherapy. *International Journal of Group Psychotherapy,* 1969, **19,** 158–64.

Holloway, M.M., & Holloway, W.H. The contract setting process. *Holloway Monograph Series, Midwest Institute for Human Understanding,* monograph vii, 1973.

Homans, G. *The human group.* New York: Harcourt Brace, 1950.

Homme, L.E. Perspectives in psychology: XXIV. Control of coverants, the operants of the mind. *Psychological Record,* 1965, **15,** 501–511.

Homme, L.E., Csanyi, A., Gonzales, M., & Rechs, J. *How to use contingency contracting in the classroom.* Champaign, Ill.: Research Press, 1969.

Honig, W.K., & Staddon, J.E.R. (Eds.). *Handbook of operant behavior.* Englewood Cliffs, N.J.: Prentice-Hall, 1977.

Horney, K. *The neurotic personality of our time.* New York: Norton, 1937.

Horney, K. *Neurosis and human growth.* New York: Norton, 1950.

Hornstein, H.A., Bunker, B.B., Burke, W.W., Gindes, M., & Lewicki, R.J. (Eds.). *Social intervention: A behavioral science approach.* New York: Free Press, 1971.

Houle, C.O. *The design of education.* San Francisco: Jossey-Bass, 1972.

House, R.J. Experiential learning: A sad passing fad? *Exchange: Organizational Behavior Teaching Journal,* 1979, **4**(3), 8–12.

Hovland, C.I., Campbell, E.H., & Brock, T.C. The effects of commitment on opinion change following communication. In C.I. Hovland (Ed.), *The order of presentation in persuasion.* New Haven, Conn.: Yale University Press, 1957, 23–32.

Hovland, C.I., & Janis, I.L. (Eds.). *Personality and persuasibility.* New Haven, Conn.: Yale University Press, 1959.

Hovland, C.I., Janis, I.L., & Kelley, H.H. *Communication and persuasion.* New Haven, Conn.: Yale University Press, 1953.

Hull, C.L. *Principles of behavior.* New York: Appleton-Century-Crofts, 1943.

Huntington, S.P. Reform and political change. In G. Zaltman, P. Kotler, & I. Kaufman (Eds.), *Creating social change.* New York: Holt, Rinehart & Winston, 1972, 274–284.

Husband, R. A statistical comparison of the efficiency of large lecture versus small recitation sections upon achievement in general psychology. *American Psychologist,* 1949, **4**(7), 216.

Hyman, R.T. *Ways of teaching.* Philadelphia: Lippincott, 1974.

Ittelson, W.H., Proshansky, H.M., Rivlin, L.G., & Winkel, G.H. *An introduction to environmental psychology.* New York: Holt, Rinehart & Winston, 1974.

Jackson, D.D. (Ed.). *Communication, family, and marriage: Human communication, Vol. 1.* Palo Alto, Calif.: Science & Behavior Books, 1968a.

Jackson, D.D. (Ed.). *Therapy, communication, and change: Human communication, Vol. 2.* Palo Alto, Calif.: Science & Behavior Books, 1968b.

Jakubczak, L.F., & Walters, R.H. Suggestibility as dependency behavior. *Journal of Abnormal and Social Psychology,* 1959, **59,** 102–107.

James, W. *The principles of psychology.* New York: Holt, 1890.

James, W. *The will to believe.* New York: Longmans Green, 1912.

James, W. The varieties of religious experience. New York: Modern Library, 1929.

Janis, I.L. Group identification under conditions of external danger. In D. Cartwright & A. Zander (Eds.), *Group dynamics.* New York: Harper & Row, 1968, 80–90.

Jenkins, D.H. *Laboratory for trainers.* Seattle, Wash.: Pacific Northwest Laboratory, 1960.

Jennings, F.G. *This is reading.* New York: Teachers College, Columbia University, 1965.

Johns, J.L. (Ed.). *Literacy for diverse learners: Promoting reading growth at all levels.* Newark, Del.: International Reading Association, 1974.

Jones, G.N. Strategies and tactics of planned organizational change: Case examples in the modernization process of traditional societies. In G. Zaltman, P. Kotler, & I. Kaufman (Eds.), *Creating social change.* New York: Holt, Rinehart & Winston, 1972, 254–265.

Jones, J.E., & Jones, J.J. *Dyadic encounter: A program for getting acquainted in depth.* La Jolla, Calif.: University Associates Publishers, 1974.

Jones, J.E., & Pfeiffer, J.W. (Eds.). *The annual handbook for group facilitators* (3 vols.). Iowa City: University Associates, 1973, 1975, 1977.

Jones, R.M. *The new psychology of dreaming.* New York: Grune & Stratton, 1970.

Joyce, B., & Weil, M. *Models of teaching.* Englewood Cliffs, N.J.: Prentice-Hall, 1972.

Jung, C.G. The psychology of the unconscious. In *The collected works of C.G. Jung, Vol. 7,* R.F.C. Hull, trans. New York: Pantheon, 1953.

Jung, C.G. The structure and dynamics of the psyche. In *The collected works of C.G. Jung, Vol. 8,* R.F.C. Hull, trans. New York: Pantheon, 1960.

Jung, C.G. *Memories, dreams, reflections.* New York: Random House, 1961.

Jung, J. *Understanding human motivation: A cognitive approach.* Long Beach, Calif.: Collier-Macmillan, 1978.

Kagan, N., Krathwohl, D.R., Goldberg, A.D., Campbell, R.J., Schauble, P.G., Greenberg, B.S., Danish, S.J., Resnikoff, A., Bowes, J., & Bondy, S.B. *Studies in human interaction.* East Lansing: Education Publication Services, Michigan State University, 1967.

Kagan, N., Krathwohl, D.R., & Miller, R. Stimulated recall in therapy using videotape: A case study. *Journal of Counseling Psychology,* 1963, **10**, (3) 237–243.

Kahn, R., Wolfe, D., Quinn, R., & Snoek, J. *Organizational stress.* New York: Wiley, 1964.

Kanfer, F.H. Self-management: Strategies and tactics. In A.P. Goldstein & F.H. Kanfer (Eds.), *Maximizing treatment gains: Transfer-enhancement in psychotherapy.* New York: Academic, 1979, 185–224.

Kanfer, F.H. Self-regulation and self-control. In H. Zeier (Ed.), *The Psychology of the 20th Century. Vol. 4: From classical conditioning to behavioral therapy.* Zurich: Kindler Verlag, 1977.

Kanfer, F.H. Self-management methods. In F.H. Kanfer & A.P. Goldstein (Eds.), *Helping people change.* New York: Pergamon, 1975, 309–355.

Kanfer, F.H., & Goldstein, A.P. (Eds.). *Helping people change.* New York: Pergamon, 1975.

Kanfer, F.H., & Karoly, P. Self control: A behavioristic excursion into the lions' den. *Behavior Therapy,* 1972, **3**, 398–416.

Kanfer, F.H., Karoly, P., & Newman, A. Reduction of children's fear of the dark by competence-related and situational threat-related verbal cues. *Journal of Consulting and Clinical Psychology,* 1975, **43**, 251–258.

Karlin, M.S., & Berger, R. *Experiential learning: An effective program for elementary schools.* West Nyack, N.Y.: Parker, 1971.

Karlins, M., & Abelson, H.I. *Persuasion: How opinions and attitudes are changed.* New York: Springer, 1970.

Karoly, P. Operant methods. In F.H. Kanfer & A.P. Goldstein (Eds.), *Helping people change.* New York: Pergamon, 1975, 195–228.

Katz, D., & Kahn, R.L. *The social psychology of organizations.* New York: Wiley, 1966.

Kazantzakes, N. *Zorba the Greek.* London: Faber & Faber, 1972.

Kazdin, A.E. Covert modeling and the reduction of avoidance behavior. *Journal of Abnormal Psychology,* 1973, **81**, 87–95.

Keeton, M.T., & associates. *Experiential learning.* San Francisco: Jossey-Bass, 1976.

Kelley, H.H. Two functions of reference groups. In G.E. Swanson, T.M. Newcomb, & E.L. Hartley (Eds.), *Readings in social psychology, 2nd ed.* New York: Holt, Rinehart & Winston, 1952.

Kelley, H.H. Attribution theory in social psychology. In D. Levine (Ed.), *Nebraska Symposium on Motivation*. Lincoln: University of Nebraska Press, 1967, 192–240.

Kelly, G.A. *The psychology of personal constructs, Vol. 1*. New York: Norton, 1955.

Kelman, H.C. Compliance, identification and internalization: Three processes of attitude change. *Journal of Conflict Resolution*, 1958, **12**, 51–60.

Kelman, H.C. Manipulation of human behavior: An ethical dilemma for the social scientist. *Journal of Social Issues*, 1965, **21**(2), 31–46.

Kelman, H.C., & Warwick, D.P. The ethics of social intervention: Goals, means and consequences. In G. Bermant, H.C. Kelman, & D.P. Warwick, *The ethics of social intervention*. Washington, D.C.: Hemisphere, 1978, 3–33.

Kemp, C.G. (Ed.). *Perspectives on the group process—A foundation for counseling with groups*. Boston: Houghton Mifflin, 1964.

Kemp, J.E. *Planning and producing audiovisual materials*. New York: Crowell, 1975.

Kepner, C.H., & Tregoe, B.B. *The rational manager*. New York: McGraw-Hill, 1965.

Kesner, R. A neural system analysis of memory storage and retrieval. *Psychological Bulletin*, 1973, **80**(3), 177–203.

Kiesler, C.A. *The psychology of commitment: Experiments linking behavior to belief*. New York: Academic, 1971.

Kiesler, C.A., Collins, B., & Miller, N. *Attitude change: A critical analysis of theoretical approaches*. New York: Wiley, 1969.

Kiesler, C.A., & Kiesler, S.B. *Conformity*. Reading, Mass.: Addison-Wesley, 1969.

Kiesler, C.A., Mathog, R., Pool, P., & Howenstine, R. Commitment and the boomerang effect: A field study. In C.A. Kiesler, *The psychology of commitment: Experiments linking behavior to belief*. New York: Academic, 1971.

Kiesler, C.A., & Sakumura, J.A. Test of a model for commitment. *Journal of Personality and Social Psychology*, 1966, **3**, 349–353.

Kiesler, D.J. *The process of psychotherapy—Empirical foundations and systems of analysis*. Chicago: Aldine, 1973.

Kim, J.S., & Hamner W.C. Effect of performance feedback and goal setting on productivity and satisfaction in an organizational setting. *Journal of Applied Psychology*, 1976, **61**, 48–57.

Kinder, J.S. *Using audio-visual materials in education*. New York: American Book, 1965.

King, M., Payne, D.C., & McIntire, W.G. The impact of marathon and prolonged sensitivity training on self-acceptance. *Small Group Behavior*, 1973, **4**(4), 414–423.

Kirkpatrick, D.L. (Ed.). *Evaluating training programs*. Madison, Wisc.: American Society for Training and Development, 1975.

Kirkpatrick, D.L. Evaluation of training. In R.L. Craig (Ed.), *Training and development handbook, 2nd ed.* New York: McGraw-Hill, 1976, 18.1–18.27.

Klahr, D., & Wallace, J.G. *Cognitive development: An information processing view*. Hillsdale, N.J.: Erlbaum, 1976.

Kline, G.F., & Tichenor, P.J. (Eds.). *Current perspectives in mass communication research*. Beverly Hills, Calif.: Sage Publications, 1972.

Knowles, M.S. *The modern practice of adult education: Andragogy versus pedagogy*. New York: Association Press, 1970.

Knowles, M.S. *Self-directed learning*. New York: Association Press, 1975.

Kohlberg, L. Stage and sequence: The cognitive-developmental approach to socialization. In D.A. Goslin (Ed.), *Handbook of socialization theory and research*. Chicago: Rand McNally, 1969, 347–480.

Krasner, L. The operant approach in behavior therapy. In A.E. Bergin & S.L. Garfield (Eds.), *Handbook of psychotherapy and behavior change.* New York: Wiley, 1971, 612–652.

Krathwohl, D.R., Bloom, B.S., & Masia, B.B. *Taxonomy of educational objectives: The classification of educational goals. Handbook II: Affective domain.* New York: McKay, 1964.

Krumboltz, J.D., & Thoresen, C.E. (Eds.). *Behavioral counseling—Cases and techniques.* New York: Holt, Rinehart & Winston, 1969.

Krumboltz, J.D. & Thoresen, C.E. (Eds.). *Counseling methods.* New York: Holt, Rinehart & Winston, 1976.

Kuhn, T.S. *The structure of scientific revolutions.* Chicago: University of Chicago Press, 1962.

Kulka, A. Attributional determinants of achievement-related behavior. *Journal of Personality and Social Psychology,* 1972, **21,** 166–174.

Lakin, M. Some ethical issues in sensitivity training. *American Psychologist,* 1969, **24**(10), 923–928.

Lakin, M. *Interpersonal encounter theory and practice in sensitivity training.* New York: McGraw-Hill, 1972.

Lapp, D., Bender, H., Ellenwood, S., & John, M. *Teaching and learning philosophical, curricular application.* New York: Macmillan, 1975.

Lawler, E.E. *Pay and organizational effectiveness: A psychological view.* New York: McGraw-Hill, 1971.

Lawrence, D.H. The nature of a stimulus: Some relationships between learning and perception. In S. Koch (Ed.), *Psychology: A study of a science, Vol. 5.* New York: McGraw-Hill, 1963, 179–212.

Lazarus, A.A. *Behavior therapy and beyond.* New York: McGraw-Hill, 1971.

Lefkowitz, M.M., Blake, R.R., & Mouton, J.S. Status factors in pedestrian violation of traffic signals. *Journal of Abnormal and Social Psychology,* 1955, **51,** 704–706.

Leifer, A.D. Teaching with television and film. In N.L. Gage (Ed.), *The psychology of teaching methods.* Chicago: University of Chicago Press, 1976, 302–334.

Lenski, G. *Power and privilege: The theory of social stratification.* New York: McGraw-Hill, 1966.

Levinson, D.J., Darrow, C.N., Klein, E.B., Levinson, M.H. & McKee, B. *The seasons of a man's life.* New York: Knopf, 1978.

Levitt, E.E., & Hershman, S. The clinical practice of hypnosis in the United States: A preliminary survey. *International Journal of Clinical and Experimental Hypnosis,* 1963, **11,** 55–65.

Levy, L.H. *Conceptions of personality.* New York: Random House, 1970.

Lewin, K. *A dynamic theory of personality.* New York: McGraw-Hill, 1935.

Lewin, K. Group decision and social change. In T.M. Newcomb & E.L. Hartley (Eds.), *Readings in social psychology.* New York: Holt, Rinehart & Winston, 1947.

Lewin, K. *Resolving social conflicts.* New York: Harper, 1948.

Lewin, K. *Field theory in social science.* New York: Harper & Row, 1951.

Lewin K. Group decision and social change. In G.E. Swanson, T.M. Newcomb, & E.L. Hartley (Eds.), *Readings in social psychology,* rev. ed. New York: Holt, Rinehart & Winston, 1952, 459–473.

Lewis, D.R., Wentworth, D., Reinke, R., & Becker, W.E., Jr. *Educational games and simulations in economics.* New York: Joint Council on Economic Education, 1974.

Lieberman, M.A., Yalom, I.D., & Miles, M.B. The impact of encounter groups on participants: Some preliminary findings. *Journal of Applied Behavioral Science,* 1972, **8**(1), 29–50.

Lieberman, M.A., Yalom, I.D., & Miles, M.B. *Encounter groups: First facts.* New York: Basic Books, 1973.

Liebert, R.M., Neale, J.M., & Davidson, E.S. *The early window: Effects of television on children and youth.* Toronto: Pergamon, 1973.

Likert, R. *New patterns of management.* New York: McGraw-Hill, 1961.

Likert, R. *The human organization.* New York: McGraw-Hill, 1967.

Livingston, S.A. *How to design a simulation game.* Baltimore, Md.: Academic Games Associates, 1972.

Livingston, S.A., & Stoll, C.S. *Simulation games: An introduction for the social studies teacher.* New York: Free Press, 1973.

Lorenz, K.Z. *King Solomon's ring, new light on animal ways.* New York: Crowell, 1952.

Lorenz, K.Z. *On aggression.* New York: Harcourt Brace and World, 1966.

Lorenz, K.Z. *Studies in animal and human behavior, Vol. 1*, R. Martin, trans. Cambridge: Harvard University Press, 1970.

Lorenz, K.Z. *Studies in animal and human behavior, Vol. 2*, R. Martin, trans. Cambridge: Harvard University Press, 1971.

Lowen, A. *The language of the body.* London: Collier-Macmillan, 1958.

Lowen, A. *The betrayal of the body.* London: Collier-Macmillan, 1967.

Luft, J. *Group process: An introduction to group dynamics.* Palo Alto, Calif.: National Press Books, 1963.

Luft, J. *Group processes: An introduction to group dynamics, 2nd ed.* Palo Alto, Calif.: National Press Books, 1970.

Lundberg, C., & Lundberg, J. Encounter co-training. *Training and Development Journal,* October 1974, 20–26.

Luthans, F., & Kreitner, R. *Organizational behaviour modification.* Glenview, Ill.: Scott, Foresman, 1975.

Maccoby, E.E., & Wilson, W.C. Identification and observational learning from films. *Journal of Abnormal and Social Psychology,* 1957, **55**, 76–87.

MacCrimmon, K.R., & Taylor, R.N. Decision making and problem solving. In M.D. Dunnette (Ed.), *Handbook of industrial and organizational psychology.* Chicago: Rand McNally, 1976, 1397–1453.

McClelland, D.C. *Personality.* New York: Dryden Press, 1951.

McClelland, D.C., Atkinson, J.W., Clark, R.A., & Lowell, E.L. *The achievement motive.* New York: Appleton-Century-Crofts, 1953.

McGeer, E. Personal communication, 1977.

McGrath, J.E., & Altman, I. *Small group research: A synthesis and critique of the field.* New York: Holt, Rinehart & Winston, 1966.

McGuire, W.J. Inducing resistance to persuasion. *Advances in Experimental Social Psychology,* 1964, **1**, 191–229.

McGuire, W.J. Personality and susceptibility to social influence. In E.F. Borgatta & W.W. Lambert (Eds.), *Handbook of personality theory and research.* Chicago: Rand McNally, 1967.

McGuire, W.J. Theory of the structure of human thought. In R.P. Abelson, E. Aronson, W.J. McGuire, T.M. Newcomb, M.J. Rosenberg, & P.H. Tannenbaum (Eds.), *Theories of cognitive consistency: A sourcebook.* Chicago: Rand McNally, 1968, 140–162.

McGuire, W.J., & Papageorgis, D. The relative efficacy of various types of prior belief defense in producing immunity to persuasion. *Journal of Abnormal and Social Psychology,* 1961, **62**, 327–337.

McKeachie, W.J. *Teaching tips: A guidebook for the beginning college teacher.* Lexington, Mass.: Health, 1969.

McKeachie, W.J. The decline and fall of the laws of learning. *Educational Researcher*, 1974, 3(3), 7–11.

McLeish, J. *The lecture method.* Cambridge: Heffers, 1968.

McLeish, J. The lecture method. In N.L. Gage (Ed.), *The psychology of teaching methods.* Chicago: University of Chicago Press, 1976, 252–301.

McLuhan, M. *The mechanical bride.* Boston: Beacon Press, 1951.

McLuhan, M. *Understanding media.* New York: McGraw-Hill, 1964.

McNair, M.P., & Hersum, A.C. (Eds.). *The case method at the Harvard Business School.* New York: McGraw-Hill, 1954.

Mack, A.H. Contracting: An organization development process adapted to classroom teaching. *Exchange: The Organizational Behavior Teaching Journal*, 1979, 4(4), 43–45.

Maddi, S.R. The existential neurosis. *Journal of Abnormal Psychology*, 1967, 72, 311–325.

Maddi, S.R. *Personality theories: A comparative analysis.* Homewood, Ill.: Dorsey, 1976.

Mahoney, M.J. The self-management of covert behavior: A case study. *Behavior Therapy*, 1971, 2, 575–578.

Mahoney, M.J. *Cognitive and behavior modification.* Cambridge, Mass.: Ballinger, 1974.

Mahoney, M.J., Thoresen, C.E., & Danaher, B.G. Covert behavior modification: An experimental analogue. *Journal of Behavior Therapy and Experimental Psychiatry*, 1972, 3, 7–14.

Maier, N.R., Solem, A.R., & Maier, A.A. *Supervisory and executive development: A manual for role playing.* New York: Wiley, 1957.

Maier, N.R., Solem, A.R., & Maier, A.A. *The role-play technique: A handbook for management and leadership practice.* La Jolla, Calif.: University Associates, 1975.

Maltz, M. *Psycho-cybernetics.* Englewood Cliffs, N.J.: Prentice-Hall, 1960.

Manley, R.S. Are t-groups brainwashing sessions? *Training in Business and Industry*, 1971, 8(11), 29–36.

Mann, J. *Changing human behavior.* New York: Scribner's, 1965.

Mann, R.D. *Interpersonal styles and group development.* New York: Wiley, 1967.

Marlatt, G.A., & Perry, M.A. Modeling methods. In F.H. Kanfer, & A.P. Goldstein (Eds.), *Helping people change.* New York: Pergamon, 1975.

Marks, S.E., & Davis, W.L. The experiential learning process and its application to large groups. In J.E. Jones & J.W. Pfeiffer (Eds.), *The 1975 annual handbook for group facilitators.* La Jolla, Calif.: University Associates, 1975, 161–166.

Maslow, A.H. *Motivation and personality.* New York: Harper & Row, 1954.

Maslow, A.H. Deficiency motivation and growth motivation. In M.R. Jones (Ed.), *Nebraska symposium on motivation.* Lincoln: University of Nebraska Press, 1955.

Maslow, A.H. Some basic propositions of a growth and self-actualization psychology. In *Perceiving, behaving, becoming: A new focus for education.* Washington, D.C.: Yearbook of the Association for Supervision and Curriculum Development, 1962.

Maslow, A.H. A theory of metamotivation: The biological rooting of the value-life. *Journal of Humanistic Psychology*, 1967, 7, 93–127.

Maslow, A.H. A theory of metamotivation: The biological rooting of the value-life. *Humanities*, 1969, 4, 301–343.

Mausner, B. Studies in social interaction: III. Effect of variation in one partner's prestige on the interaction of observer pairs. *Journal of Applied Psychology*, 1953, 37, 391–393.

Mausner, B. The effect of prior reinforcement on the interaction of observer pairs. *Journal of Abnormal and Social Psychology*, 1954a, 49, 65–68.

Mausner, B. The effect of one partner's success in a relevant task on the interaction of observer pairs. *Journal of Abnormal and Social Psychology,* 1954b, **49,** 557–560.

Mausner, B., & Bloch, B.L. A study of the additivity of variables affecting social interaction. *Journal of Abnormal and Social Psychology,* 1957, **54,** 250–256.

May, R. *Love and will.* New York: Norton, 1969.

May, R., Angel, E., & Ellenberger, H.F. (Eds.). *Existence: A new dimension in psychology.* New York: Basic Books, 1958.

May, R., Binswanger, L., & Ellenberger, H.F. Existential psychotherapy and dasein analysis. In W.S. Sahakian (Ed.), *Psychotherapy and counseling: Studies in technique.* Chicago: Rand McNally, 1969.

Mead, G.H. *Mind, self and society.* C.W. Morris (Ed.). Chicago: University of Chicago Press, 1943.

Mehrabian, A., & Ksionsky, S. Models for affiliative and conformity behavior. *Psychological Bulletin,* 1970, **74,** 110–126.

Mehrabian, A., & Ksionsky, S. *A theory of affiliation.* Lexington, Mass.: Heath, 1974.

Mehrabian, A., & Russell, J.A. A measure of arousal seeking tendency. *Environmental Behavior,* 1973, **5,** 315–333.

Meichenbaum, D. Cognitive factors in behavior modification: Modifying what clients say to themselves. In C. Franks & T. Wilson (Eds.), *Annual review of behavior therapy: Theory & practice.* New York: Brunner/Mazel, 1973.

Meichenbaum, D. *Cognitive behavior modification.* Morristown, N.J.: General Learning Press, 1974.

Meichenbaum, D. Self instructional methods. In F.H. Kanfer & A.P. Goldstein (Eds.), *Helping people change.* New York: Pergamon, 1975, 357–391.

Meichenbaum, D., & Cameron, R. Training schizophrenics to talk to themselves: A means to developing attentional controls. *Behavior Therapy,* 1973a, **4,** 515–534.

Meichenbaum, D., & Cameron, R. *Stress innoculation: A skills training approach to anxiety management.* Unpublished manuscript, University of Waterloo, 1973b.

Merrill, M.D. *Instructional design: Readings.* Englewood Cliffs, N.J.: Prentice-Hall, 1971.

Merton, R.K. Rate-set: Problems in sociological theory. *The British Journal of Sociology,* 1957, **8,** 106–120.

Miles, M.B., Hornstein, H.A., Calder, P.H., Callahan, D.M., & Schiavo, R.S. Data feedback: A rationale. In H.A. Hornstein, B.B. Bunker, W.W. Burke, M. Gindes, & R.J. Lewicki (Eds.), *Social intervention: A behavioral science approach.* New York: Free Press, 1971, 310–315.

Milgram, S. Behavioral study of obedience. *Journal of Abnormal and Social Psychology,* 1963, **67,** 371–378.

Milgram, S. Some conditions of obedience and disobedience to authority. In I.D. Steiner & M. Fishbein (Eds.), *Current studies in social psychology.* New York: Holt, Rinehart & Winston, 1965, 243–262.

Miller, G.A., Galanter, E., & Pribram, K.H. *Plans and the structure of behavior.* New York: Holt, Rinehart & Winston, 1960.

Miller, J.G. The nature of living systems. In F. Baker, (Ed.), *Organizational systems: General systems approaches to complex organizations.* Homewood, Ill.: Irwin, 1973.

Miller, N.B., & Miller W.H. Siblings as behavior-change agents. In J.D. Krumboltz & C.E. Thoresen (Eds.), *Counseling methods.* New York: Holt, Rinehart & Winston, 1976, 426–434.

Miller, N.E. *The influence of past experience upon the transfer of subsequent training.* Unpublished doctoral dissertation. Yale University, 1935.

Miller, N.E., & Dollard, J. *Social learning and imitation.* New Haven, Conn.: Yale University Press, 1941.

Mills, T.M. *The sociology of small groups.* Englewood Cliffs, N.J.: Prentice-Hall, 1967.

Miner, F.C. An approach to increasing participation in case discussions. *Exchange: The Organizational Behavior Teaching Journal,* 1978, 3(3), 41–42.

Minuchin, S. Conflict-resolution family therapy. *Psychiatry,* 1965, **28**, 278–286.

Minuchin, S., & Montalvo, B. Techniques for working and disorganized low socioeconomic families. *American Journal of Orthopsychiatry,* 1967, **37**, 885.

Mischel, W., & Grusec, J. Determinants of the rehearsal and transmission of neutral and aversive behaviors. *Journal of Personality and Social Psychology,* 1966, **3**, 197–205.

Mitchell, K.M., Bozarth, J.D., & Krauft, C.C. A reappraisal of the therapeutic effectiveness of accurate empathy, non-possessive warmth and genuineness. In A.S. Gurman & A.M. Razin (Eds.), *Effective psychotherapy: A handbook of research.* New York: Pergamon, 1977, 482–502.

Moreno, J.L. *Psychodrama, Vol. 1.* New York: Beacon House, 1946.

Moreno, J.L. *Who shall survive?* New York: Beacon House, 1953.

Moreno, J.L. *Psychodrama, Vol. 1, rev. ed.* New York: Beacon House, 1964.

Morris, D. *The naked ape.* New York: McGraw-Hill, 1967.

Morris, L.L., & Fitz-Gibbon, C.T. *Evaluators handbook.* Beverly Hills, Calif.: Sage Publications, 1978.

Morris, R.J. Fear reduction methods. In F.H. Kanfer & A.P. Goldstein (Eds.), *Helping people change.* New York: Pergamon, 1975, 229–271.

Murray, H.A. *Explorations in personality: A clinical and experimental study of fifty men of college age.* New York: Oxford, 1938.

Nelson, J.G., & Foster, S.F. Needs and means assessment for university teaching improvement: Surveys II and III. *Proceedings of the Sixth International Conference on Improving University Teaching, Vol. I.* Lausanne, Switzerland, July 1980, 235–243.

Newcomb, T.M. *The acquaintance process.* New York: Holt, Rinehart & Winston, 1961.

Newell, A.H., & Simon, H.A. Overview: Memory and process in concept formation. In B. Kleinmuntz (Ed.), *Concepts and structure of memory.* New York: Wiley, 1967, 241–262.

Newell, A.H., & Simon, H.A. *Human problem solving.* Englewood Cliffs, N.J.: Prentice-Hall, 1972.

Nielsen, D.M., & Hjelm, H.F. *Reading and career education.* Newark, Del.: International Reading Association, 1975.

Nizer, L. *My life in court.* New York: Pyramid, 1961.

Odiorne, G.S. The trouble with sensitivity training. In R.T. Golembiewski & A. Blumberg (Eds.), *Sensitivity training and the laboratory approach.* Itasca, Ill.: Peacock, 1970, 273–287.

Odiorne, G.S. The role of the lecture in teaching organizational behavior. *Exchange: The Organizational Behavior Teaching Journal,* 1977, 2(3), 7–14.

Odum, E.P. *Fundamentals of ecology.* Philadelphia: Saunders, 1971.

Ofshe, R.J. (Ed.). *Interpersonal behavior in small groups.* Englewood Cliffs, N.J.: Prentice-Hall, 1973.

Ofstad, N.S. *The transmission of self-reinforcement patterns through imitation of sex-role appropriate behavior.* Unpublished doctoral dissertation, University of Utah, 1967.

Oldenquist, A. *Readings in moral philosophy.* Boston: Houghton Mifflin, 1965.

Olsen, L.C. Ethical standards for group leaders. *Personnel & Guidance Journal,* 1971, **50**(4), 288.

Olton, R.M., & Crutchfield, R.S. Developing the skills of productive thinking. In P. Mussen, J. Langer, & M.V. Covington (Eds.), *Trends and issues in developmental psychology.* New York: Holt, Rinehart & Winston, 1969, 68–91.

Osborn, A.F. *Applied imagination, 3rd ed.* New York: Scribner's, 1963.

Parloff, M.B., Waskow, I.E., & Wolfe, B.E. Research on therapist variables in relations to process and outcome. In S.L. Garfield & A.E. Bergin (Eds.), *Handbook of psychotherapy and behavior change.* New York: Wiley, 1978, 233–282.

Parnes, S.J. *Creative behavior guidebook.* New York: Scribner's, 1967.

Parsons, T. *The social system.* New York: Free Press, 1951.

Patka, T.J. After the classroom: A module on re-entry. *Exchange: The Organizational Behavior Teaching Journal,* 1977, 2(4), 39–40.

Patterson, G.R. Behavioral intervention procedures in the classroom and in the home. In A.E. Bergin & S.L. Garfield (Eds.), *Handbook of psychotherapy and behavior change: An empirical analysis.* New York: Wiley, 1971.

Pavlov, I.P. *Conditioned reflexes,* G.V. Anrep, trans. London: Oxford University Press, 1927.

Pearson, C., & Marfuggi, J. *Creating and using learning games.* Palo Alto, Calif.: Education Today Company, 1975.

Peirce, C.S. How to make our ideas clear. In J. Buchler (Ed.), *The philosophy of Peirce.* London: Routledge, 1940. (originally published 1878)

Pelz, D.C., & Andrews, F.W. *Scientists in organizations.* New York: Wiley, 1966.

Pennock, R.J., & Chapman, J.W. (Eds.). *Coercion.* Chicago: Aldine, 1972.

Perls, F. *Ego, hunger and aggression.* New York: Random House, 1969a.

Perls, F. *Gestalt therapy verbatim.* Lafayette, Calif.: Real People Press, 1969b.

Perls, F. *In and out the garbage pail.* Lafayette, Calif.: Real People Press, 1969c.

Perrow, C. *Organization analysis: A sociological view.* Belmont, Calif.: Wadsworth, 1965.

Pervin, L.A. *Personality: Theory assessment and research.* New York: Wiley, 1970.

Peterson, L.R. Verbal learning and memory. *Annual Review of Psychology,* 1977, **28**, 393–415.

Pfeffer, J., & Salancik, G.R. *The external control of organizations.* San Francisco: Harper & Row, 1978.

Pfeiffer, J.W., & Heslin R. *Instrumentation in human relations training.* Iowa City: University Associates, 1973.

Pfeiffer, J.W., & Jones, J.E. What to look for in groups: An observation guide. In J.W. Pfeiffer & J.E. Jones (Eds.), *The 1972 annual handbook for group facilitators,* Iowa City: University Associates, 1972, 19–24.

Pfeiffer, J.W., & Jones, J.E. (Eds.). *The annual handbook for group facilitators,* 4 vols. Iowa City: University Associates, 1972, 1974, 1976, 1978.

Pfeiffer, J.W., & Jones, J.E. *Reference guide to handbooks and annuals.* La Jolla, Calif.: University Associates, 1975.

Pfeiffer, J.W. & Jones, J.E. (Eds.). *A handbook of structural experiences for human relations training,* 6 vols. La Jolla, Calif.: University Associates, 1969, 1970, 1971, 1973, 1975, 1977.

Phillips, E. *Psychotherapy: A modern theory and practice.* Englewood Cliffs, N.J.: Prentice-Hall, 1956.

Phillips, E., & Wiener, D. *Short-term psychotherapy and structured behavior change.* New York: McGraw-Hill, 1966.

Pirsig, R.M. *Zen and the art of motorcycle maintenance: An inquiry into values.* New York: Morrow, 1974.

Pinder, C.C. Concerning the application of human motivation theories in organizational settings. *Academy of Management Review,* 1977, **2**, 384–397.

Platt, J.R. Beauty: Pattern and change. In D.W. Fiske & S.R. Maddi, *Functions of varied experience.* Homewood, Ill.: Dorsey, 1961, 402–430.

Porter, L.W. *Leadership and organizational commitment in the 1970's: The pep talk and the dodo bird.* Position paper for conference on leadership, U.S. Military Academy, June 1969.

Porter, L.W., Lawler, E.E., & Hackman, R.J. *Behavior in organizations.* New York: McGraw-Hill, 1975.

Porter, L.W., & Smith, F.J. *The etiology of organizational commitments: A longitudinal study of initial stages of employee-organization relationships.* Unpublished manuscript, 1970.

Postman, L. Verbal learning and memory. *Annual Review of Psychology,* 1975, **26**, 291–335.

Postman, N., & Weingartner, C. *Teaching as a subversive activity.* New York: Dell, 1969.

Premack, D. Reinforcement theory. In D. Levine (Ed.), *Nebraska symposium on motivation.* Lincoln: University of Nebraska Press, 1965, 123–180.

Proctor, S., & Malloy, T.E. Cognitive control of conditioned emotional responses: An extension of behavior therapy to include the experimental psychology of cognition. *Behavior Therapy,* 1971, **2**, 294–306.

Proshansky, H.M., Ittelson, W.H., & Rivlin, L.G. (Eds.). *Environmental psychology: Man and his physical setting.* New York: Holt, Rinehart & Winston, 1970.

Quinn, M.E., & Sellars, L. Role of the student. In J. Duley (Ed.), *Implementing field experience education.* San Francisco: Jossey-Bass, 1974.

Rank, O. *The trauma of birth.* New York: Harcourt Brace, 1929.

Rank, O. *Will therapy and truth and reality.* New York: Knopf, 1945.

Rank, O. *Will therapy and truth and reality.* New York: Knopf, 1947.

Rapaport, D. The theory of ego autonomy: A generalization. *Bulletin of Menninger Clinic, 1958,* **22**, 13–25.

Raphael, B. *The thinking computer: Mind inside matter.* San Francisco: Freeman, 1976.

Redl, F. Group emotion and leadership. *Psychiatry,* 1942, **5**, 573–596.

Reich, W., *Character analysis, 3rd ed.* New York: Orgone Institute Press, 1949.

Rescorla, R.A. Informational variables in Pavlovian conditioning. In G.H. Bower (Ed.), *The psychology of learning and motivation, Vol. 6.* New York: Academic, 1972.

Resnik, H., Davidson, W., Schuyler, P., & Christopher, P. Video tape confrontation after attempted suicide. *American Journal of Psychiatry,* 1973, **130**, 460–63.

Reubenhausen, O.M., & Brim, O.G. Privacy and behavioral research. *American Psychologist,* 1966, **21**, 423–437.

Reynolds, J.I. Cases which meet the students' needs. *Academy of Management Proceedings,* 1976, 28–52.

Reynolds, J.I. There's method in cases. *Academy of Management Review,* 1978, 3(1), 129–133.

Richardson, E. The physical setting and its influence on learning. In H.M. Proshansky, W.H. Ittelson, & L.G. Rivlin (Eds.), *Environmental psychology: Man and his physical setting.* New York: Holt, Rinehart & Winston, 1970, 386–397.

Richardson, F.C., & Suinn, R.M. A comparison of traditional systematic desensitization, accelerated massed desensitization, and anxiety management training in the treatment of mathematics anxiety. *Behavior Therapy,* 1973, **4**, 212–218.

Riesen, A.H. Stimulation as a requirement for growth and function in behavioral development. In D.W. Fiske & S.R. Maddi, *Functions of varied experience.* Homewood, Ill.: Dorsey, 1961, 57–80.

Riggs, L.A., Armington, J.C., & Ratliff, F. Motions of the retinal image during fixation. *Journal of the Optical Society of America*, 1954, **44**, 315–321.

Rimm, D., & Masters, J., *Behavior therapy: Techniques and empirical findings.* New York: Academic, 1974.

Ring, K., & Kelley, H.H. A comparison of augmentation and reduction as modes of influence. In D. Cartwright & A. Zander (Eds.), *Group dynamics.* New York: Harper & Row, 1968, 270–277.

Ringness, T.A. *The affective domain in education.* Boston: Little, Brown, 1975.

Roche Scientific Service. *Neurophysiological and pharmacological aspects of mental illness.* Montreal: Hoffmann-LaRoche, 1965.

Rogers, C.R. *Counseling and psychotherapy.* Boston: Houghton Mifflin, 1942.

Rogers, C.R. *Client centered therapy.* Boston: Houghton Mifflin, 1951.

Rogers, C.R. Some issues concerning the control of human behavior. *Science*, 1956, **124**, 1057–1066.

Rogers, C.R. The necessary and sufficient conditions of therapeutic personality change. *Journal of Counseling Psychology*, 1957, **121**(2), 95–103.

Rogers, C.R. A Theory of therapy, personality, and interpersonal relationships, as developed in the client centered framework. In S. Koch (Ed.), *Psychology: A study of a science, Vol. III. Formulations of the person in a social context.* New York: McGraw-Hill, 1959, 184–256.

Rogers, C.R. *On becoming a person.* Boston: Houghton Mifflin, 1961.

Rogers, C.R. The Actualizing tendency in relation to "motives" and to consciousness. In M. Jones (Ed.), *Nebraska symposium on motivation, 1963.* Lincoln: University of Nebraska Press, 1963, 1–24.

Rogers, C.R. *The interpersonal relationship in the facilitation of learning.* Columbus, Ohio: Merrill, 1968.

Rogers, C.R. *Freedom to learn.* Columbus, Ohio: Merrill, 1969.

Rogers, C.R. *On encounter groups.* New York: Harper & Row, 1970.

Rogers, C.R., Gendlin, E.T., Kiesler, D.J., & Truax, C.B. (Eds.). *The therapeutic relationship and its impact: A study of psychotherapy with schizophrenics.* Madison: University of Wisconsin Press, 1967.

Rogers, C.R., & Truax, C.B. The therapeutic conditions antecedent to change: A theoretical view. In C.R. Rogers, E.T. Gendlin, D.J. Kiesler, & C.B. Truax (Eds.), *The therapeutic relationship and its impact. A study of psychotherapy with schizophrenics.* Madison: University of Wisconsin Press, 1967.

Rokeach, M. *The open and closed mind.* New York: Basic Books, 1960.

Rosenbaum, M.E., & Tucker, I.F. The competence of the model and the learning of imitation and nonimitation. *Journal of Experimental Psychology*, 1962, **63**, 183–190.

Rosenberg, M. *Society and the adolescent self-image.* Princeton, N.J.: Princeton University Press, 1965.

Rosenblith, J.F. Learning by imitation in kindergarten children. *Child Development*, 1959, **30**, 69–80.

Rosenblith, J.F. Imitative color choices in kindergarten children. *Child Development*, 1961, **32**, 211–223.

Rosenblueth, A., Wiener, N., & Bigelow, J. Behavior, purpose, and teleology. In W. Buckley (Ed.), *Modern systems research for the behavioral scientist.* Chicago: Aldine, 1968, 227.

Rosnow, R.L., & Robinson, E.J. (Eds.). *Experiments in persuasion.* New York: Academic, 1967.

Roszak, T. *The making of a counter culture.* New York: Doubleday, 1969.

Rothkopf, E.Z. Writing to teach and reading to learn: A perspective on the psychology of written instruction. In N.L. Gage (Ed.), *The psychology of teaching methods.* Chicago: University of Chicago Press, 1976, 91–129.

Rotter, J.B. *Social learning and clinical psychology.* New York: Prentice-Hall, 1954.

Rotter, J.B. Generalized expectancies for internal versus external control of reinforcement. *Psychological Monographs,* 1966, **80** (1, Whole No. 609).

Rowe, M.R., Curb, D., Frye, H.R., Kemp, J., & Vecnendaal, W. *The message is you—Guidelines for preparing presentations.* Washington, D.C.: Association for Educational Communications and Technology, 1971.

Rubin, I. Reduction of prejudice through laboratory training. *Journal of Applied Behavioral Science,* 1967, 3(1), 29–50.

Rubin J.Z., & Brown, B.R. *The social psychology of bargaining and negotiation.* New York: Academic, 1975.

Russell, B. *Freedom versus organization.* New York: Norton, 1962.

Ryan, F.L., & Ellis, A.K. *Instructional implications of inquiry.* Englewood Cliffs, N.J.: Prentice-Hall, 1974.

Sahakian, W.S. (Ed.). *Psychotherapy and counseling: Studies in technique.* Chicago: Rand McNally, 1969.

Sarason, I.G. *Personality: An objective approach, 2nd ed.* New York: Wiley, 1972.

Sarason, I.G., & Ganzer, V.J. Modeling: An approach to the rehabilitation of juvenile offenders. *Final report to the Social and Rehabilitation Service of the Department of Health, Education and Welfare,* June 1971.

Sarason, I.G., & Ganzer, V.J. Modeling and group discussion in the rehabilitation of juvenile delinquents. *Journal of Counseling Psychology,* 1973, **120,** 442–449.

Sarason, I.G., & Sarason, B.R. *Constructive classroom behavior.* New York: Behavioral Publications, 1974.

Schachter, S. Deviation, rejection, and communication. In D. Cartwright & A. Zander (Eds.), *Group dynamics.* New York: Harper & Row, 1968, 165–181.

Schachter, S., & Singer, J.E. Cognitive, social and physiological determinants of emotional state. *Psychological Review,* 1962, **69,** 379–399.

Schaller, L.E. *The change agent.* Nashville: Abingdon Press, 1972.

Schein, E.H. The Chinese indoctrination program for prisoners of war. *Psychiatry,* 1956, **50,** 149–172.

Schein, E.H., & Bennis, W.G. *Personal and organizational change through group methods.* New York: Wiley, 1965.

Schmidt, R.A. Proprioception and the timing of motor responses. *Psychological Bulletin,* 1971, **76,** 383–393.

Schoen, D.R., & Sprague, P.A. What is the case method? In M.P. McNair & A.C. Hersum (Eds.), *The case method at the Harvard Business School.* New York: McGraw-Hill, 1954, 76–81.

Schramm, W., & Roberts, D.F. (Eds.). *The process and effects of mass communication.* Urbana: University of Illinois Press, 1971.

Schutz, W.C. *Joy—Expanding human awareness.* New York: Grove, 1967.

Schutz, W.C. *Here comes everybody: Bodymind and encounter culture.* New York: Harper & Row, 1971.

Schutz, W.C. *Elements of encounter.* Big Sur, Calif.: Joy Press, 1973.

Schwitzgebel, R.K., & Kolb, D.A. *Changing human behavior.* New York: McGraw-Hill, 1974.

Scott, W.A. *Values and organizations.* Chicago: Rand McNally, 1965.

Scott, W.E., Jr. Activation theory and task design. *Organizational Behavior and Human Performance,* 1966, **1**(1), 3–30.

Scott, W.E., Jr., & Erskine, J.A. *The effects of variations in task design and monetary reinforcers on task behavior.* Unpublished manuscript, 1977.

Scott, W.G., & Mitchell, T.R. *Organizational theory: A structural and behavioral analysis.* Homewood, Ill.: Irwin, 1976.

Scott, W.R. *Social structures and social processes.* New York: Holt, Rinehart & Winston, 1970.

Scriven, M. The methodology of evaluation. *AERA Monograph Series on Curriculum Evaluation,* 1967, **1**, 39–83.

Seidner, C.J. Teaching with simulations and games. In N.L. Gage (Ed.), *The psychology of teaching methods.* Chicago: University of Chicago Press, 1976, 217–251.

Shaffer, J.B.P., & Galinsky, M.D. *Models of group therapy and sensitivity training.* Englewood Cliffs, N.J.: Prentice-Hall, 1974.

Shaw, M.E. *Group dynamics: The psychology of small group behavior.* New York: McGraw-Hill, 1971.

Sherif, C.W., Sherif, M., & Nebergall, R.E. *Attitude and attitude change.* Philadelphia: Saunders, 1965.

Sherif, M. Experiments on group conflict and cooperation. In H.J. Leavitt & L.R. Pondy (Eds.), *Readings in managerial psychology.* Chicago: University of Chicago Press, 1964, 408–421.

Sherif, M. Superordinate goals in the reduction of intergroup conflict. In B.L. Hinton & J.H. Reitz (Eds.), *Groups and organizations.* Belmont, Calif.: Wadsworth, 1971, 394–401.

Sherif, M., & Cantril, H. *The psychology of ego involvements.* New York: Wiley, 1947.

Sherif, M., & Hovland, C. *Social judgment.* New Haven: Yale University Press, 1961.

Sherif, M., & Sherif, C.W. *Groups in harmony and tension.* New York: Harper & Brothers, 1953.

Sherif, M., Taub D., & Hovland, C.I. Assimilation and contrast effects of anchoring stimuli on judgments. *Journal of Experimental Psychology,* 1958, **55**, 150–155.

Shostrom, E.L. *Actualizing therapy.* San Diego, Calif.: Edits Publishers, 1976.

Simon, H.A. *Administrative behavior.* New York: Free Press, 1945.

Simon, H.A. *Models of man: Social and rational.* New York: Wiley, 1957.

Simon, H.A. Human problem solving. *American Psychologist,* 1970, **26**(2), 145–159.

Simpson, E.J. The classification of education objectives in the psychomotor domain. In CSC/Pacific (Ed.), *The psychomotor domain.* Washington, D.C.: Gryphon House, 1972c, 43–56.

Singer, B.D. *Feedback and society: A study of the uses of mass channels for coping.* Lexington, Mass.: Heath, 1973.

Skinner, B.F. *The behavior of organisms: An experimental analysis.* New York: Appleton-Century-Crofts, 1938.

Skinner, B.F. *Science and human behavior.* New York: Macmillan, 1953.

Skinner, B.F. *Contingencies of reinforcement: A theoretical analysis.* New York: Appleton-Century-Crofts, 1969.

Skinner, B.F. *Beyond freedom and dignity.* New York: Knopf, 1971.

Smith, H.C. *Personality development.* New York: McGraw-Hill, 1974.

Smith, H.R., & Nagel, T.S. *Instructional media in the learning process.* Columbus, Ohio: Merrill, 1972.

Smith, K.U., & Smith, M.F. *Cybernetic principles of learning and educational design.* New York: Holt, Rinehart & Winston, 1966.

Smith, R.M., Neisworth, J.T., & Greer, J.G. *Evaluating educational environments.* Columbus, Ohio: Merrill, 1978.

South, O.P. Observation guide: On seeing, hearing, and feeling. In R.C. Diedrich & H.A. Dye (Eds.), *Group procedures: Purposes, processes, and outcomes—Selected readings for the counselor.* Boston: Houghton Mifflin, 1972, 127–143.

Staw, B.M., & Ross, J. Commitment to a policy decision: A multitheoretic perspective. *Administrative Science Quarterly,* 1978, 23(1).

Steele, F. *Physical settings and organizational development.* Reading, Mass.: Addison-Wesley, 1973.

Steele, S.M. *Contemporary approaches to program evaluation and their implications for evaluating programs for disadvantaged adults.* Syracuse, N.Y.: ERIC Clearinghouse on Adult Education, 1973.

Steers, R.M. Antecedents and outcomes of organizational commitment. *Administrative Science Quarterly,* 1977, 22(1).

Steiner, C.M. *Scripts people live.* Beverly Hills, Calif.: Grove, 1974.

Stevens, J.O. *Awareness.* New York: Bantam, 1971.

Stewart, D. *Instruction as a humanizing science, Vol. 1. The changing role of the educator: The instructioneer.* Fountain Valley, Calif.: Slate Services, 1975a.

Stewart, D. *Instruction as a humanizing science, Vol. 2. A behavioral learning systems approach to instruction: Analysis and synthesis.* Fountain Valley, Calif.: Slate Services, 1975b.

Stewart, K. Dream theory in Malaya. In C.T. Tart (Ed.), *Altered states of consciousness.* New York: Wiley, 1969, 159–167.

Stiles, L.J. (Ed.). *Theories for teaching.* New York: Dodd, Mead, 1974.

Stoller, F.H. Focused feedback with videotape: Extending the groups' functions. In G.M. Gazda (Ed.), *Innovations in group psychotherapy.* Springfield, Ill.: Thomas, 1968.

Stouffer, S.A., & Toby, J. Role conflict and personality. *American Journal of Sociology,* 1951, 56, 395–406.

Suedfeld, P. The clinical relevance of reduced sensory stimulation. *Canadian Psychologial Review,* April 1975, 16(2), 88–103.

Suinn, R.M., & Richardson, F. Anxiety management training: A nonspecific behavior therapy program for anxiety control. *Behavior Therapy,* 1971, 2, 498–510.

Sullivan, H.S. *Conceptions of modern psychiatry.* New York: Norton, 1947.

Sullivan, H.S. *The interpersonal theory of psychiatry.* New York: Norton, 1953.

Sutherland, E.H., & Cressey, D.R. *Criminology, 8th ed.* Philadelphia: Lippincott, 1970.

Tannenbaum, R., Weschler, I., & Massarik, F. *Leadership and organization: A behavioral science approach.* New York: McGraw-Hill, 1961.

Tanner, D. *Using behavioral objectives in the classroom.* New York: Macmillan, 1972.

Tansey, P.J., & Unwin, D. *Simulation and gaming in education.* London: Methuen Educational Ltd., 1969.

Tart, C.T. (Ed.). *Altered states of consciousness.* New York: Wiley, 1969.

Terborg, J.R., Castore, C., & DeNinno, J.A. A longitudinal field investigation of the impact of group composition on group performance and cohesion. *Journal of Personality and Social Psychology,* 1976, 34(5), 782–790.

Thibaut, J.W., & Kelley, H.H. *The social psychology of groups.* New York: Wiley, 1959.

Thomas, D.H., & Friedman, C.P. Evaluation: Myths, principles and strategies. *Engineering Education,* 1978, 68(5), 405–409, 440.

Thomas, E.J. *Marital communication and decision making.* New York: Free Press, 1976.

Thomas, E.J., Carter, R., & Gambrill, E.D. Some possibilities of behavioral modification with marital problems using sam (signal system for the assessment and modification of behavior). In R.H. Rubin, H. Fensterhein, A.A. Lazarus, & E.M. Franks (Eds.), *Advances in behavior therapy*. New York: Academic, 1971.

Thomas, E.J., O'Flaherty, K., & Borkin, J. Coaching marital partners in family decision making. In J.D. Krumboltz & C.E. Thoresen (Eds.), *Counseling methods*. New York: Holt, Rinehart & Winston, 1976.

Thompson, J.J. *Instructional communication*. New York: American Book, 1969.

Thoresen, C.E., & Mahoney, M.J. *Behavioral self-control*. New York: Holt, Rinehart & Winston, 1974.

Thorndike, E.L. Animal intelligence. An experimental study of the associative processes in animals. *Psychological Monographs*, 1898, 2(8).

Thorndike, E.L. *Animal intelligence*. New York: Macmillan, 1911.

Tiger, L., & Fox, R. *The imperial animal*. Holt, Rinehart & Winston, 1971.

Tillich, P. *The courage to be*. New Haven, Conn.: Yale University Press, 1952.

Tinbergen, N. *The study of instinct*. London: Oxford University Press, 1951.

Tinbergen, N. On war and peace in animals and man. *Science*, 1968, **160**, 1411–1418.

Tinbergen, N. *The animal in its world, Vol. 1*. London: Allen & Unwin Ltd., 1972.

Tinbergen, N. *The animal in its world, Vol. 2*. London: Allen & Unwin Ltd., 1973.

Toffler, A. *Future shock*. New York: Bantam, 1971.

Tolman, E.C. *Behavior and psychological man: Essays in motivation and learning*. Berkeley: University of California Press, 1958.

Torbert, W.R. *Learning from experience: Toward consciousness*. New York: Columbia University Press, 1972.

Torrey, E.F. *The mind game: Witchdoctors and psychiatrists*. New York: Emerson Hall, 1972.

Towl, A.R. *To study administration by cases*. Boston: Harvard University Graduate School of Business Administration, 1969.

Trigg, R. *Reason and commitment*. Cambridge, Mass.: Cambridge University Press, 1973.

Truax, C.B., & Mitchell, K.M. Research on certain therapist interpersonal skills in relation to process and outcome. In A.E. Bergin & S.L. Garfield (Eds.), *Handbook of psychotherapy and behavior change*. New York: Wiley, 1971, 299–344.

Tubbs, S.L. *A systems approach to small group interaction*. Reading, Mass.: Addison-Wesley, 1978.

Tuckman, B.W. *Evaluating instructional programs*. Boston: Allyn & Bacon, 1979.

Turner, R.H., & Shosid, N. Ambiguity and interchangeability in role attribution: The effects of Alter's response. *American Sociological Review*, 1976, **41**, 993–1005.

Twelker, P.A. (Ed.). *Instructional simulation systems*. Corvallis, Ore.: Continuing Education Publications, 1969.

Twelker, P.A., & Layden, K. *Education/simulation/gaming*. Stanford: ERIC Clearinghouse on Media and Technology, 1972.

Unwin, D. (Ed.). *Media and methods: Instructional technology in higher education*. London: McGraw-Hill, 1969.

Varney, G.H. Training organization development practitioners: A need for clarity of direction. *Exchange: The Organizational Behavior Teaching Journal*, 1978, 3(4), 3–7.

Wallen, J.R. *Basic skills for discussing interpersonal relations*. Portland, Ore.: Unpublished material, undated.

Wallen, J.R. *Constructive openness*. Portland, Ore.: Unpublished material, undated.

Walter, G.A. *Augmentation of task group performance through video tape feedback and social learning*. Berkeley: Unpublished manuscript, University of California, 1971.

Walter, G.A. Effects of videotape feedback and modeling on the behaviors of task group members. *Human Relations,* 1975a, **28,** 121–138.

Walter, G.A. Effects of videotape training inputs on group performance. *Journal of Applied Psychology,* 1975b, **60**(3), 308–312.

Walter, G.A. Acted versus natural models for performance oriented behavior change in task groups. *Journal of Applied Psychology,* 1975c, **60**(3), 303–307.

Walter, G.A. Experiencing video tape. In C.L. Cooper & C. Alderfer (Eds.), *Advances in experiential social processes.* New York: Wiley, 1978, 67–88.

Walter, G.A., Austin, D., Beattie, T., & Helfin, B. *Public speaking manual.* Faculty of Commerce and Business Administration, University of British Columbia, 1978.

Walter, G.A., & McDowell, M.T. A transactional analysis of leadership factors and styles. *Interpersonal Development,* 1975/1976, **6,** 153–168.

Walter, G.A., & Miles, R.E. Change self acceptance: Task groups and video tape or sensitivity training? *Small Group Behavior,* 1974, **5**(3), 356–364.

Walton, R.E., & McKersie, R.B. *A behavioral theory of labor negotiations: An analysis of a social interaction systems.* New York: McGraw-Hill, 1965.

Walton, R.E., & Warwick, D.P. The ethics of organization development. *Journal of Applied Behavioral Science,* 1973, **9**(6), 681–698.

Watson, G. What do we know about learning? *NEA Journal,* March 1963, 20–22.

Watson, J.B. *Behaviorism.* Chicago: University of Chicago Press, 1924.

Watts, G.O. *Dynamic neuroscience.* Hagerstown, Md.: Harper & Row, 1975.

Watzlawick, P. A review of the double bind theory. In D.D. Jackson (Ed.), *Communication, family, and marriage—Human communication, Vol. 1.* Palo Alto, Calif.: Science & Behavior Books, 1968, 63–86.

Watzlawick, P., Beavin, J.H., & Jackson, D.D. *Pragmatics of human communication.* New York: Norton, 1967.

Watzlawick, P., Weakland, J.H., & Fisch, R. *Change—Principles of problem formation and problem resolution.* New York: Norton, 1974.

Weathers, L., & Liberman, R.P. Contingency contracting with families of delinquent adolescents. *Behavior Therapy,* 1975a, **6,** 356–366.

Weathers, L., & Liberman, R.P. The family contracting exercise. *Journal of Behavior Therapy and Experimental Psychiatry,* 1975b, **6,** 208–214.

Weber, R.J. *The effects of videotape feedback on interaction behavior and role perception in small decision making groups.* Unpublished Manuscript, University of California, Berkeley, 1969.

Weiner, B. *Theories of motivation: From mechanism to cognition.* Chicago: Rand McNally, 1972.

Weir, J. The personal growth laboratory. In K.D. Benne, L.P. Bradford, J.R. Gibb, & R.C. Lippitt, *The laboratory method of changing learning.* Palo Alto: Science & Behavior Books, 1975.

Wertheimer, M. (Ed.). *Productive thinking, enlarged ed.* New York: Harper & Brothers, 1959.

West, C.K., & Foster, S.F. *The psychology of human learning and instruction in education.* Belmont, Calif.: Wadsworth, 1976.

White, R., & Lippitt, R. Leader behavior and member reaction in three social climates. In D. Cartwright & A. Zander (Eds.), *Group dynamics, 3rd ed.* New York: Harper & Row, 1968.

White, R.W. Motivation reconsidered: The concept of competence. *Psychological Review,* 1959, **66,** 297–333.

White, R.W. Competence and the psychosexual stages of development. In M.R. Jones (Ed.), *Nebraska symposium on motivation.* Lincoln: University of Nebraska Press, 1960.

White, R.W. Ego and reality in psycho-analytic theory. *Psychological Issues,* 1963, 3, 1–210.

Whyte, W.F. *Street corner society.* Chicago: University of Chicago Press, 1943.

Whyte, W.F. *Organizational behavior.* Homewood, Ill.: Dorsey, 1969.

Whyte, W.H., Jr. *The organization man.* Garden City, N.Y.: Doubleday, 1956.

Wicaprio, N.S. *Personality theories: Guides to living.* Philadelphia: Saunders, 1974.

Wiggins, J.S., Renner, E.K., Clore, G.L., & Rose, R.J. *Principles of personality.* Reading, Mass.: Addison-Wesley, 1976.

Wilensky, H.L. The professionalization of everyone? *The American Journal of Sociology,* 1964, **70**, 137–158.

Wilensky, H.L. *Organizational intelligence: Knowledge and policy in government and industry.* New York: Basic Books, 1967.

Wilensky, H.L., & Lebeaux, C.N. *Industrial society and social welfare.* New York: Free Press, 1965.

Williams, R.T. (Ed.). *Insights into why and how to read.* Newark, Del.: International Reading Association, 1976.

Willings, D.R. *How to use the case study in training for decision making.* London: Business Publications, 1968.

Wilson, E.O. *Sociobiology: The new synthesis.* Cambridge, Mass.: The Belknap Press of Harvard University Press, 1975.

Winch, R.F., & Gordon, M.T. *Familial structure and function as influence.* Lexington, Mass.: Heath, 1974.

Witkin, H.A. Psychological differentiation and forms of pathology. *Journal of Abnormal Psychology,* 1965, **70**, 317–336.

Wittgenstein, L. *Philosophical investigations, 2nd ed.*, G.E.M. Anscombe, trans. Oxford: Blackwell, 1958.

Wittgenstein, L. *Lectures and conversations on aesthetics, psychology and religious belief.* C. Barrett (Ed.), Berkeley: University of California Press, 1966.

Wittgenstein, L. *On certainty.* G.E.M. Anscombe & G.H. Von Wright (Eds.); D. Paul & G.E.M. Anscombe, trans. Oxford: Blackwell, 1969.

Wittich, W.A., & Schuller, C.F. *Instructional technology: Its nature and use.* New York: Harper & Row, 1973.

Wolpe, J. *Psychotherapy by reciprocal inhibition.* Stanford: Stanford University Press, 1958.

Wolpe, J. *The practice of behavior therapy.* New York: Pergamon, 1969.

Wolpe, J. *The practice of behavior therapy, 2nd ed.* New York: Pergamon, 1973.

Wolpe, J. Conditioning is the basis of all psychotherapeutic change. In A. Burton (Ed.), *What makes behavior change possible?* New York: Brunner/Mazel, 1976, 58–72.

Woodward, J. *Industrial organization: Theory and practice.* London: Oxford University Press, 1965.

Wyrwicka, W. *The mechanisms of conditioned behavior.* Springfield, Ill.: Thomas, 1972.

Yalom, I.D., & Lieberman, M.A. A study of encounter group casualties. *Archives of General Psychiatry,* 1971, **25**, 16–30.

Young, P.T. *Motivation and emotion.* New York: Wiley, 1961.

Zaltman, G., Kotler, P., & Kaufman, I. (Eds.). *Creating social change.* New York: Holt, Rinehart & Winston, 1972.

Zimbardo, P.G. The effect of effort and improvisation on self-persuasion produced by role-playing. *Journal of Experimental Social Psychology,* 1965, **1,** 103–120.

Zimbardo, P.G., & Ebbesen, E.B. *Influencing attitudes and changing behavior.* Reading, Mass.: Addison-Wesley, 1969.

Zuckerman, D.W., & Horn, R.E. *The guide to simulations/games for education and training.* Lexington, Mass.: Information Resources, 1973.

Author Index

Subject Index